IT'S a b
RUGGE
MATE!

'Big Al' Lester was born in Nelson, the second youngest of four children. As a young man, he played rugby, golf, softball and basketball, all at representative level. Despite these achievements, Al got most pleasure from time spent in the mountains and valleys hunting deer and other wild game.

Starting out in the banking industry, Al later joined the New Zealand Police. Being a solid 6'4" tall, perhaps he was better suited to the latter role. After doing the hard yards, Al was promoted to his current rank of Detective Sergeant.

At 54, Al is still an avid hunter with a love of the mountains and a liking for a beer or two. He lives in Christchurch.

He is the author of seven previous hunting titles: *Hunting in the Raw* (2003), *A Bum in the Bush* (2004), *A Hard Shot in the Hills* (2006), *Off the Track* (2008) *Arse-up Creek* (2010), *Sting in the Tale* (2011) and *Mad Men of the Mountains* (2013).

OTHER YARNS BY 'BIG AL' LESTER

IT'S a bit RUGGED, MATE

The best yarns by

'Big Al' Lester

RAUPO

A RAUPO BOOK
Published by the Penguin Group
Penguin Group (NZ), 67 Apollo Drive, Rosedale,
Auckland 0632, New Zealand (a division of Penguin New Zealand Pty Ltd)
Penguin Group (USA) Inc., 375 Hudson Street,
New York, New York 10014, USA
Penguin Group (Canada), 90 Eglinton Avenue East, Suite 700, Toronto,
Ontario, M4P 2Y3, Canada (a division of Penguin Canada Books Inc.)
Penguin Books Ltd, 80 Strand, London, WC2R 0RL, England
Penguin Ireland, 25 St Stephen's Green,
Dublin 2, Ireland (a division of Penguin Books Ltd)
Penguin Group (Australia), 707 Collins Street, Melbourne,
Victoria 3008, Australia (a division of Penguin Australia Pty Ltd)
Penguin Books India Pvt Ltd, 11, Community Centre,
Panchsheel Park, New Delhi – 110 017, India
Penguin Books (South Africa) (Pty) Ltd, Block D, Rosebank Office Park,
181 Jan Smuts Avenue, Parktown North, Gauteng 2193, South Africa
Penguin (Beijing) Ltd, 7F, Tower B, Jiaming Center, 27 East Third Ring Road North,
Chaoyang District, Beijing 100020, China

Penguin Books Ltd, Registered Offices: 80 Strand, London, WC2R 0RL, England

This collection first published by Penguin Group (NZ), 2014
1 3 5 7 9 10 8 6 4 2

Copyright © text – Al Lester, 2003, 2004, 2006
Copyright © cover illustration – Clint McInnes, 2014
Copyright © cartoons – Gary Tibbotts, 2003, 2004, 2006

The right of Al Lester to be identified as the author of this work in terms of
section 96 of the Copyright Act 1994 is hereby asserted.

Designed and typeset by Claire Gibb, © Penguin Group (NZ)
Prepress by Image Centre Group
Printed and bound in Australia by Griffin Press,
an Accredited ISO AS/NZS 14001 Environmental Management Systems Printer

ISBN 978-0-14357-200-8

A catalogue record for this book is available
from the National Library of New Zealand.

www.penguin.co.nz

FSC
www.fsc.org

MIX
Paper from
responsible sources
FSC® C009448

Contents

Introduction   7

From *Hunting in the Raw*

In the Beginning   15
A Bushman's Breakfast   28
Surrounded by Hard Shots   44
Lost in the Snow   48
A Shot in the Dark   58
Winged Warriors   66
A Gorge-us Hunt   74
Up Slippery Creek   85
Spotted Mullet   94
Of Mountain Men and Deserts   101

From *A Bum in the Bush*

The Mighty Landsborough   121
The Great Round-up   138
Fiordland Found   151
Stewart Island   167
Pukataraki   176
The Moose   186
A Most Unusual Trophy   200

The Hitching Post 211
Big Man, Small Boat 221
Poison Bay 233
West Coast Hospitality 246
Pin the Tail on a Honky 254

From *A Hard Shot in the Hills*

Noah's Ark 263
Neil's Story – the Bay 280
The Silly Season 298
Beating the Baldy 316
The Old Man's Yarn 331
A Hunter's Demise 345
A Head-on Collision 354
Captain Bligh 367
Port Pegasus 379
The Bullshitters' Ball 394

Glossary 415

Introduction

I'm often asked what inspired me to take up writing yarns about the adventures, mishaps and mayhem that I and others have endured while venturing into the New Zealand wild outdoors.

As a youngster, I collected every hunting book ever written (well, almost) and found that they all contained pretty much the same content. The authors were the world's most skilled hunters, the greatest shots, the most outstanding bushmen, and almost all had survived every atrocity that the weather gods could hurl at them. These hunting wonderboys almost never stuffed anything up, always got magnificent trophies and plenty of meat for the freezer. In my youth, I had dreamed of reaching their dizzy heights and securing the same status as the likes of Daniel Boone, Davy Crockett or Wyatt Earp. Sadly, this was never going to be.

In truth, I was then and remain now an average to poor hunter who has had more hunting cock-ups than the rest of the country combined. For every deer I've successfully shot, dozens have escaped only to hide in the bush peering back at me, clearly laughing at my stupidity. I have always managed to see the funny side of the situation and had a good old laugh at myself. I began to wonder if my stuff-ups, with a bit of humour and mayhem thrown in, might just make for good reading. I suspected there was a possible opening there somewhere for a bloke of my ilk to write a book on the oddball, unusual, humorous, weird and fun side of hunting. And so I gave this writing thing a go.

I must have got something right. As soon my first book *Hunting in the Raw* hit the shelves, I was inundated with people keen to tell me all about their own cock-ups and mountain mayhem. It seems that, contrary to my belief at the time, very few people are in fact great hunters. I may not have been quite as useless at hunting as I'd thought (but then again I may have been). Regardless, I seemed to have struck a chord with those possessing a sense of humour and a liking for the bush. Seven books later, I'm still at it.

This book is a catch-up for those who missed out on my earlier books, which are mostly out of print now. The stories hereafter are the majority of the yarns from my first three books: *Hunting in the Raw*, *A Bum in the Bush* and *A Hard Shot in the Hills*. They'll give you a pretty good idea of where I come from and what my mates and I are all about. You'll see that very few deer, tahr, pigs or other animals get shot, due to us being pretty bloody useless hunters who are simply out there having a great time and enjoying the mountains.

Now that we've sorted out how I became a writer, I'll try to give you a handle on what it is about the outdoors that makes me tick. Hopefully this will give you an insight into the contents of this book. But first, a story.

As you may have guessed from the photos in this book, I'm a big bastard, at 6'4" tall and weighing in at 137kg. It's been a while since I had sand kicked in my face and I don't anticipate it'll happen again in the near future. Needless to say, brutes like me were keenly sought after in rugby circles and I managed to get myself into the starting line-up for a few local rugby teams. On top of this, I had a crack at golf, cricket, basketball, softball and just about every other sport known to mankind.

My old man was immensely proud of the fact that my brother and I both made it into various representative rugby sides. There was only ever one story, however, that came to the fore whenever anyone was prepared to listen. It goes something like this.

My brother had been selected to play for Nelson Bays in an Under-18s South Island tournament that was played in Ashburton. He was a hooker, and there were two hookers in the squad. During one particular game, the other hooker was on the paddock and their team's scrum was getting annihilated. This was to the detriment of the scoreboard, which had Nelson Bays well behind with 30 minutes or so left on the clock. It seemed the problem was that the others team's hooker was as hard as hobnail boots and causing havoc in the front row. The coach gave my brother the nod, telling him to get on the paddock and 'sort that bloody scrum out'. Onto the field he ran and when the very next scrum went down there was one hell of a ruckus. When the dust settled, the opposition hooker was semi-conscious, lying on the ground. He was carried off and the game swung in Nelson Bays' favour – they went on to win by six points. According to my brother's coach, the win was due to the 'best bloody punch of the tournament'. My old man brimmed with pride at that vote of confidence in my brother's skills and was disappointed when he left the country and gave the sport away.

I played number eight at the back of the scrum, so these opportunities to 'shine' weren't as frequent as in the front row.

The old man was around in the halcyon days of hunting when he could drive his old Model T to the pub, shoot six deer on the way there, sell them and have a great night out before coming home with a profit in his pocket. Wild deer, pigs and goats were everywhere. Additionally, the rivers ran so thick with whitebait and trout that my old man would often cross by standing on their backs and walking across without getting his feet wet.

It was from listening to my father's hunting yarns that I first got inspired to head into the outdoors to take a look for myself.

Needless to say, my trips there had to be fitted around rugby games and other sporting activities. My old man retired from hunting the day I took it up so I got no tutoring at all, which may explain why I am so hopeless at it. I managed to blunder my way around the bush and learn the basics of bush navigation – water runs downhill to the sea, the sun rises in the east and sets in the west, that kind of thing. I only got myself hopelessly disorientated (read: lost) once and soon learnt that a night in the scrub without home comforts wouldn't kill me. The deer were pretty safe around me then too – for the first couple of years I managed to avoid actually seeing any.

In time, I learned that I loved being in the bush more than being on the rugby paddock and headed there as often as I could. My mates weren't interested in coming for a walk with me as they'd discovered grog and girls. Given this, I spent most of my early years of hunting alone.

One day at a pub, I bumped into a chap called Horse. I'll leave it to your imagination to establish how he got his nickname. Anyway, like me, Horse was a keen hunter so we teamed up. Horse sure had a grand sense of humour. Every time I fell arse over kite, he'd crack up laughing. One day I nearly drowned in a river and he nearly died laughing (a bit of help wouldn't have gone astray). On another occasion, we were packing into a distant hut on a wickedly hot day. I was moaning about how heavy my pack was when Horse told me to harden up and get on with it. On arrival at our destination, he offered me a beer, which I quickly accepted, then he promptly pulled five large bottles of it out of *my* pack. The bastard had put them there when I wasn't looking. He thought that was bloody funny too.

Over the years, I have found that the vast majority of people who venture into the outdoors have a grand sense of humour and a real love of life. I have chanced upon numerous eccentric, weird, humorous, hermit-like or just plain interesting characters. Each had a story to tell and many were so strange that they had to be true. These were the yarns that I found the most interesting and are the source of many of the tales in my books.

Through circumstance, I have spent the greater part of my life living in cities and wishing that I wasn't. The call of the bush is strong and part of my make-up has dictated a need for me to head to the tranquillity of the hills as often as I can. There I find solace and a quiet that can only be provided by the vast expanses of bush or mountains. To look in every direction and see no one is assuring. To shut my eyes and hear only the wind whispering through tussock, the trickle of a creek, the singing of crickets or birdsong is soothing. To fall asleep while lying snuggled within tussock high up a mountain face with the afternoon sun warming my body is a pleasure that words cannot truly bring to life. To watch deer or other wild animals at play brings me immense pleasure. These are the things that draw me back to the mountains time and time again. They are simple things that put the world back into perspective and which clean away the hustle and bustle that is relentless in everyday life.

In the mountains, things seem to be in balance. Often I am overwhelmed by a sense of being at peace. Merely being there seems to cleanse my soul.

Add to the above the great company of other like-minded comedians and hard-cases and I reckon you'll probably understand why the mountains are a magnet to me.

I have had many wonderful experiences there and look forward to many more. After all I'm not much past 50 so should have a few more years and yarns left in me yet.

From time to time, a deer or pig is silly enough to wander in front of me and land itself in my freezer. These by-products of my journeys into the bush taste great and keep my household budget under control. I take what I need and nothing more and make no apology for that.

In my books, I try to capture hunting adventures that are a bit

different from the norm. I hope I've achieved that goal but will of course let you be the judge. In the meantime, it would be a good idea for you to pull your boots on and to venture into the mountains yourself. Who knows – you may even meet one or two of the characters mentioned in this book.

Happy hunting,
Big Al

HUNTING IN THE RAW

In the Beginning

My old man was tougher and meaner than any human being before or after. He had three fingers missing off one hand and two off the other. I reckon he never even blinked when they got cut off. What's more, my old man was probably the best cricket and rugby player New Zealand has ever seen. My childhood memories are filled with stories of wickets taken and tries scored. Strangely enough, my old man's cricket- and rugby-playing skills were missed by the New Zealand selectors of the time, but they were much admired by me.

My old man was a tough bugger. He was positive, strong, took no shit and called a spade a spade. And if he didn't it was probably the result of a few too many years sliding under his belt and the fading of his memory. My youthful memories are filled with tales of his sporting exploits and of better days before everything got modernised. Hell, with what relish he told stories of the great days of hunting in New Zealand. Days when you could crank up the old Model T and shoot a few deer on your way to the pub. In those days deer were worth a few bob and a man could have a big night out on the proceeds from the sale of a deer or two. Given that a big night out ended when the pubs closed at six o'clock, I've recently come to wonder about a few things – but not too many.

The story of deer in New Zealand has been told many times before so I'll try to fill in the gaps as briefly as I can. Deer were introduced into the country in about 1871. The first was released in Nelson, and was last seen trotting off into the bush behind the city. Well, my old man was raised in Murchison, which is about 80 miles from Nelson, so I reckon he was in a good spot to get a look at that deer (or more likely its progeny) as it headed southward.

Murchison isn't a big place. Fact is, it's bloomin' small, and getting into the local cricket or rugby side when my old man was young was as easy as putting your hand up. The best tales Dad told were not about rugby or cricket; they were about hunting. Deer, pigs, rabbits, goats, eels – he'd shot them all. Most from a great distance, and nearly all with one clean shot. Mind you, he often said that accuracy wasn't all it was cracked up to be. 'Anywhere in the eye will drop 'em,' he'd tell me; 'there's no need to get too fussy.'

When Dad told his hunting yarns he was back there living the hunt over again, every movement revisited step by cautious step. I relived every tale with him. I held my breath as the mighty stag strode into the small bush clearing and Dad steadied for the shot. I felt the joy of a hit and the sadness as he stood over the kill. When he told of the mountains he'd climbed you'd see the sweat dripping into his eyes and his shirt sticking to his back. The stories were so vivid I could hear the mountain streams trickling through the rocks, the song of the bellbird, the call of the morepork, the whoosh of the wood pigeon's wings and the wind singing in the treetops. I could feel the rain lash my face during a storm and smell the musty damp forest as the sun strove to dry it. Smoky campfires and warm huts filled my dreams.

I'm certain my old man never took any licence in the telling of his hunting yarns. No way, my old man told it like it was. Me, I was about five when I was first struck by his greatness. He was my hero then and he still is now.

I spent my early years playing sport. Before I was old enough to play rugby I played soccer. You had to be nine to play rugby, and even though I was big for my age at seven, the rules were for everyone. One day, when the time was right, I was taken to rugby training. There wasn't any discussion about that; it just happened.

Needless to say, I followed in my old man's footsteps; I couldn't help it. I had his genes and it was inevitable that I'd play great rugby. Dad told me so, and I'm grateful for that. It doesn't hurt to get a shove along in life, provided it's in the right direction. There were a few years of representative rugby (just like Dad) and a push toward cricket where I fell flat on my face. I'll blame Mum's genes for that.

I'd had a shot at just about every sport by the time I left school at 16 – golf, tennis, basketball, soccer, cricket, softball, small-bore shooting and more. Some successfully and some not. Nonetheless, I enjoyed them all. Mum reckoned I was never home. Dad said the only time he saw me was when I was hungry. Still, you don't get into much trouble playing sport, do you?

But this hunting caper sounded pretty good to me too, so it seemed likely I'd give it a go when I got the chance. Maybe I could be the old man's apprentice. I'd admired Dad's .303 rifle for years. It was safely tucked up in his wardrobe, but often when no one was about I'd sneak in and hold that rifle. In my mind's eye I'd shot hundreds of deer, and just about everything else, without leaving that room.

The first time I fired that mighty rifle was one Christmas holiday. I was about nine and my brother seven. We were on holiday on the Delabosca farm up the Matukituki Valley. My brother and I were allowed one shot each, standing on a terrace and aiming at a pond below. Aim for the middle, we were told. Well, my shot landed somewhere down there, no doubt about it. My brother's shot was smack in the middle of the pond.

'You're the better shot, lad – a natural,' Dad says to my brother. I was gutted. After all my bedroom practice, how could this happen?!

My resolve strengthened. I'd show them. When I got stuck into the deer I'd show them a thing or two about shooting.

My first kill happened on that same farm several years later. Dad and I were hunting a riverflat for rabbits. There on a sandy riverbank was a mob of wild goats. They couldn't move fast in the soft sand and Dad suggested we tackle a couple by hand. I wasn't too sure about this lark, but I waded in with him anyway. Crikey, I hoped they wouldn't bite. Dad got one and it struggled and bleated until he let it go. The old rugby skills were still there, that was for sure, and Dad was pretty delighted with his capture.

We didn't shoot any, but I'd be dishonest if I didn't own up to missing a couple of easy shots at rabbits soon after that. Further along we found a backwash in the river that had partly dried up, cutting off a trout. Dad again employed his rugby skills and tried to tackle the trout in midstream. Trout one, Dad nil. Still, I had a good laugh watching his antics and we had a great bit of fun together.

By now twilight was upon us. The air was cooling quickly and we knew it was time to head home. 'Around the next corner is your last chance for a rabbit,' said Dad.

It wasn't looking good for the great white hunters. Imagine coming home from a hunt with nothing. This never happened, not in my old man's stories anyway.

'There, Dad, in that sandy patch – a rabbit.'

'No, mate, it's only a log. Still, have a shot if you like.'

I fired and the log did a somersault before landing mortally wounded. Stand aside, Davy Crockett, old son. I was now a real hunter, having pulled off a near-impossible shot with an open-sighted .22 calibre rifle. It was the biggest hare I'd ever seen (at that time anyway) and I was the proudest kid alive.

What bloody deer?

Following their release in numerous parts of the country deer were protected for some time. The gentlemen who colonised New Zealand wanted their fine sport to be undertaken in the backblocks of this land. Great thinking at the time, but then things got a bit out of hand. There are no deer that are native to New Zealand. Those that were introduced found the tucker to their liking and rapidly bred, spreading throughout the backcountry. By the 1920s it was not uncommon on backcountry stations to see more wild deer grazing than farm stock. Some measures were taken to bring deer numbers back under control, but the two world wars put paid to those efforts.

During the wars deer numbers reached plague proportions, and by the late 1940s men were employed full time to seek and destroy the deer menace. Most people today would find it hard to believe that deer numbers reached such epidemic proportions. How the reduction in deer numbers was achieved is a great story in itself, but it is one that has been well recorded by others so I'll leave it alone.

By 1976, when I turned 16, the deer had been thrashed into submission and numbers were very low. They had been shot by foot hunters and from helicopters, and captured live by every means imaginable to satisfy the new deer-farming industry. In some areas they had even been poisoned (along with birds and any other life forms that happened to get in the way) and still are today. By the late '70s the once-detested deer were highly prized and valuable animals. Access to farms for hunting was denied to most, and farmers jealously guarded any wild deer on their properties. A deer in the wild had become a very rare commodity indeed.

My old man was hunting during the 1950s when deer numbers were high. His tales of shooting deer from the roadside were true of the time, but not any longer. I was about to get a sharp lesson on the current state of affairs.

As soon as I was old enough I sat for my firearms licence. The government issued me with my first lifetime licence – years later, and at great cost, I had to renew my lifetime licence, so I guess I'm due a couple of lifetimes of hunting, which suited me fine.

Ringing in my ears were Dad's stories of mobs of wild deer just waiting to be shot. He had personally accounted for thousands of them, and it seemed there were more out there just waiting for my arrival. I could hardly wait.

At 16 I'd left school and landed a job with the National Bank in Nelson. My first pay bought a sleeping bag, the second, boots and a pack, the third, a rifle and ammo. At last I was ready to hook into the deer.

Now I had a problem – no transport, nowhere to hunt, and no bloody idea what I was doing. Dad declined to take me on as his apprentice, saying he had officially retired from the hunting game. How could he retire? We hadn't even kicked off together yet! I was sure there was life left in the old hunter, but he managed to prove me wrong. It is true that the hills grow higher and steeper as a man gets older. Still, I had listened to his tales for years and I had absorbed a good deal of his wisdom. I'd tackle the deer on my own. This hunting game must be pretty easy. After all, there were thousands of deer waiting to be shot, my old man never missed, and no doubt I had inherited his natural instinct for hunting and bushcraft. Just like I'd inherited his rugby skills, eh?

Did I hear someone say something about cricket?

The transport problem was solved when I got the nod from Mum to borrow her Morris Minor for a day. She'd seen me bubbling at the gills to get into the mountains and was doing her bit to get me started. Thanks, Mum. Despite my enthusiasm there was no way I could get my mates away from the beers, girls, cars and lying in bed all weekend, so my first trip into the hills would be done solo.

Now something I've learned about hunters over the years is that they have a great knack for distorting the truth. In particular, the truth as it relates to good hunting spots, which are protected by every means imaginable. To go hunting you needed to get permission from someone, so I figured government land was my best bet. After visiting the local office of the Department of Conservation (that's DoC to you and me), and being issued with advice on where the greatest numbers of deer could be found, I was off, armed with a permit for the Hackett and Roebuck blocks behind Nelson.

Now I'll let you into a wee secret about hunting on DoC land. With every permit issued you get a 'kill report' to complete and return after your hunt. From these returns DoC compile their excellent advice on where the highest deer numbers are. Must be right – the returns say so. I've filled in my share over the years and I tell you, mate, they're bulldust. Can't say I've ever met a hunter who's told the truth on one of those forms. But, armed with the current advice based on these 'kill reports', I was now off to the best hunting ground DoC could offer.

Over the years I've had little success hunting on DoC land while armed with a permit. As a result I've come up with the theory that every time a hunter requests a permit from DoC they ring up the deer in that particular hotspot and tell them to bugger off quick. This theory is based on years of intense research on my part, and I can say with some authority that I do best when DoC, or the farmer, don't know I'm having a stroll on their land. I hear you laughing but this is dinkum, mate. No two ways about it, you should get permission before going on anyone's land, but to me it was a sure formula for disaster. Come to think of it, this whole book is filled with them. Disasters, that is.

Anyway, the morning of my first deer hunt finally arrived. The alarm clock hammered away until walloped mercilessly into submission, and I was off quicker than a raincoat in a heatwave.

After heading out in the Morrie Minor, I parked the car at the designated spot, crossed the river and followed the track. Like most hunting areas in New Zealand the direction was generally vertical, or at least it seemed that way. So upward I went into the hills for my first adventure. The pitch black night didn't bother me, but it sure made spotting a deer hard. I'd walked for about half an hour before it got light enough to see much.

I had done a bit of tramping so I knew how to shove one foot in front of the other all right. The initial walk was through pine forest, and the smell of the pines pervades my senses as I write this. Then it was into relatively open country as I followed a stream ever upward. One side was low scrub and the other native bush. I stopped and scoped every bit of open ground I saw. I was starting to wonder where those deer had gotten to and my shirt was sticking to my back just as Dad had described. It was summer and the day was getting pretty warm.

I got to where I was going after a three-hour walk. At about that point I started thinking about how when I nailed a deer I'd have to carry it back. My old man had carried deer further and over steeper country than this, so I got on with it.

Well, that day taught me a couple of things. One was that old deer shit is hard, light brown and crumbly. The other was that the deer population in that area was about as thin as rice paper. I hadn't seen anything resembling a deer.

Still, then as now, there is no such thing as a bad day in the bush. I'd seen some new country, had a look at wild deer territory, got myself bluffed and lived to tell the tale. I managed a sleep by the stream on my way out, and the feel of the sun on my back and the sound of the mountain stream bubbling along was every bit as relaxing as my old man had said.

When I got back to the car some kind bugger – no doubt a city slicker – had helped himself to my petrol. I guess his need was greater than mine and I avoided a long walk by conserving the remaining gas on the downhill bits. I coasted into the nearest garage just as the last drop of petrol evaporated and the motor coughed to a stop.

It wasn't long after this first trip that I met up with Horse. I still couldn't get any of my regular mates to venture into the bush with me but Horse was another story. He was born to hunt. He'd even shot a deer or two in the area I've just described. He had to be good to do that, since by my reckoning there weren't any bloomin' deer there.

Horse and I became great mates. We drank a fair bit and we hunted together a lot. Our biggest bond, in hindsight, was that neither of us was getting any deer.

One night we were downing a pint or two in the Ocean Lodge Hotel, a local Nelson watering hole (let's not get into the issue of age here). I put up the idea of a hunt, and since there seemed no time like the present Horse and I downed our beers, purchased some torch batteries, grabbed our packs and threw in some grub.

Although we tried, we couldn't get anyone else interested in a hunt at 11.30 at night. So off we went, one torch between the two of us.

It didn't take long to figure out why Horse had offered to carry the torch. We staggered into Browning Hut at about 2.30 a.m. A few hours' kip and we were off again, well before first light. Today was the day, I could feel it in my water.

We had chosen to hunt the same spot I'd gone to on my first-ever deer hunt. For the record, DoC had told me the area abounded in both red and fallow deer. The torch gave out just as we reached our highest point. Thank goodness for that – I was knackered. Could it have been that last pint?

Horse set the rules for the hunt. We would sneak along, him in front and me bringing up the rear. I was assured that deer were clever blighters and that they'd try to outflank us, so I was to keep my eyes peeled, with regular checks of our flanks and the rear. I was armed with my old man's years of experience, and was confident this bush-stalking game should be pretty easy. The old timers reckon that 'a deer an hour' bush was considered good. Well, my average was to hell and gone, but I figured things were about to change.

The bush we were in was predominantly beech forest with a small assortment of other deer tucker. Well it was summer, and beech trees tend to lose a lot of leaves. Add to this hot weather and a lot of high winds that brought down numerous branches, and you have one very noisy patch to hunt.

There were a lot of birds flitting about and branches swaying in the wind. Every movement was closely scrutinised by rifle scope, in the hope that it was a deer sneaking away or feeding unsuspectingly. Horse told me often that I was making too much noise. The night's grog was affecting my balance, I thought.

By smoko time – about ten o'clock – we were pretty bushed. The day had got hot and we'd been concentrating for hours. Horse announced that it was time for a break. We sat down and munched on some dry biscuits and cheese we'd managed to throw in my daypack. There were birds everywhere. I must have scoped dozens of them. Between the birds and the wind I'd investigated a lot of potential venison, all to no avail.

'Horse,' I said finally, 'don't you think you'd better shoot that deer down there?'

I'd sighted yet another bird in a dense patch of greenery below. In his leisurely way Horse lifted his rifle and spent a long time investigating the bird I'd set him on to. Look at him – the tease, he's pretending to line up a shot.

Whoompha! He fired. 'God almighty, what'd ya do that for?'

'I got it. I got it. I know I got it.' He was winding me up, that was for sure – wasn't it? There was no deer down there. Mind you, Horse was getting pretty excited for a leg-pull. He even went to investigate, leaving me with strict instructions not to move in case he lost the spot or something. He returned empty-handed about ten minutes later, confirming my leg-pull theory. Then he took another sighting and was off again downhill. He was taking this thing a bit too far. It was time to get cracking; assuming Horse hadn't spooked every animal in the valley with his silly antics.

Then I heard him shout. 'I've found some blood. Come on down.'

My heart missed a few beats. Surely not? No way. I couldn't be so dumb as to put my mate on to the only deer I've ever encountered.

Sure enough, there it was – blood. There was still a bit of deer hair and skin attached to prove it. Shit, bugger, stuff it, and a lot of other internal bashing went on – among, of course, my joy at Horse's finding an elusive venison on the hoof.

'Well, where's the deer?' I asked.

A good scout around found nothing. A very good scout around

found more of the same. We were both really gutted. No way. The gods wouldn't be that unkind.

About twenty minutes later and some distance away Horse found one more spot of blood. We had a direction. Blood spots were hard to find in all those fallen beech leaves. But we worked hard, and eventually we found the deer. It was still alive but clearly on its last legs. It was a fallow hind. The moment Horse saw it he sent a hurried shot in its general direction. Both that shot and the next one missed the deer altogether.

'Hang on, mate, you'll scare it to death at this rate. Take your time and put it out of its misery.'

The third shot was fired from about three metres away, finishing the job started some 30 minutes earlier. Boy, were we elated! We danced, shouted and patted each other on the back as our success sank in.

An examination of the carcass revealed that Horse had shot it diagonally through the rump. This was without doubt a cruel shot that had caused the animal a great deal of suffering. It would have taken a long time to die from the wound, a thought that made me feel very uncomfortable.

Once the deer was gutted it was a long carry back to the hut. I may not have pulled the trigger but there was no doubt about it, I'd found the deer and was due half the credit at least. Horse agreed, and allowed me to carry it half the way back to prove it.

At this time neither of us knew a great deal about butchery so we hacked away in what we thought was the right fashion. All the venison made it out to our freezers, even if a lot of it was turned prematurely into casserole meat.

Once again, there were a couple of things to learn from this.

1. Never point out a deer to your mate until you've shot one yourself.
2. My old man was right. If Horse had shot the deer in the eye, like he should have, we wouldn't have had so much trouble

finding it. You know what? I think my old man had a few clues in this respect.

This hunting business had a bit to teach me yet. There were some harsh lessons to come.

Now I'm an expert

By the time we returned to the pub our tale was so stretched that even I was struggling to get my head around it. Still, never let the truth get in the way of a good story, so, with slight embellishments, we told our tale and sank a beer or two. We even managed to gain the attention of my previously uninterested mates. I later established that they had an ulterior motive in that they fancied venison at our next barbecue.

It's about now that I need to introduce Phil. Now Phil is best described as a good bloke. He is a bushman in every sense. Phil works in the bush felling, hauling and trimming pine trees. He has a beaut sense of humour. It is also true that he has a fairly good idea of what to do with a pint or two of grog. When Phil heard of our success in the deer-hunting game he wanted in. Now getting an experienced guide like myself doesn't come cheap, and I was milking this to the maximum. Finally I relented, for the princely sum of two pints – the next weekend I was taking a guided expedition into the wilderness. As the resident expert I was hoping Phil would cut the mustard and be fit enough to keep up.

So there I was, full of confidence and trotting into the scrub on my first guided hunt. Phil, as it turned out, was, and still is, extremely fit. My legs were pumping ten to the dozen just trying to keep up with him. Hell, I was supposed to be in charge! It soon became clear that we'd better take to the scrub for some bush-stalking. If we didn't, I was going to need search and rescue to find him, he was so far ahead of me.

Well, my call to hit the bush was a good one. Like all great guides I put Phil on to game pretty much straight away. We had only got about halfway to our intended destination. The Hackett River had forked into the Browning Stream and just past the junction we hit the bush on the true right side. The native bush rose quickly, but the lower slopes were pretty much open and easy hunting. There was a mixture of everything deer love to eat, combined with fairly easy travel.

Old muggins (me) decided to take the high road and leave Phil in the open stuff where mugs hunt. Well, I landed myself in all sorts of shit. The scrub was so thick you needed a strong desire for self-mutilation to toil your way through it. I reckon my old man could have heard me back in Nelson, some 20 miles away. It was best described as dog country, and it still is today.

To add to my displeasure, it wasn't long before I heard a shot from Phil's direction. Sure enough, when we met up I'd put him on to a fallow deer and he'd managed a quick shot at it without success. If nothing else, I was consistent. I can find deer for anyone but me. Phil thought I was a great fellow. Imagine giving him the best spot and hunting the crap just to increase his chances of a deer.

I was beginning to wonder about myself. So too, I suspect, was my old man.

A Bushman's Breakfast

It was soon after this that I discovered my propensity for self-destruction. I wasn't earning enough dough working in a bank, and I found myself working evenings in an apple packhouse on Nayland Road, Nelson. I managed to land myself an easy job working for what was then MAF (the Ministry of Agriculture and Fisheries) inspecting apples that were destined for export overseas. It was my job to cart one carton in 50 to MAF so they could pronounce the apples fit for export. Given that a huge number of apples went through that packhouse each night, I found myself kept pretty busy.

Now where is all this leading? I'll tell you. The bloke I worked with, Glen, was as mad as a mad thing. Turns out he was real keen on this skydiving lark. Stuff that, I thought, jump out of a perfectly good plane? You must be stupid, mate!

Anyway, despite his tendency to vacate fully operational planes, Glen wasn't a bad sort of chap. He told a good story and knew how to sink a pint or two, so after some fancy talking on his part I found myself at the Nelson parachute club watching a skydiving movie or two. Now even though these blokes were clearly mad they sure seemed to have a handle on life. They laughed, told stories, drank beer and told lies as good as any I'd ever heard. Maybe there was something in this skydiving lark after all. By all accounts, jumping out of planes was considered normal behaviour by this crowd. Glen sure seemed to fit in without too much trouble. Was I the odd one out?

By the time I'd had a few beers I'd been trapped into having a go. A bloke called Paul Kroupa was given the right to train me, and before I knew it a plane took off and threw me out over Nelson airport. Now things look a bit different from upstairs, and I had a bit of difficulty getting my bearings for the downward trip. Gravity took care of the downward bit, but I needed some orientation for the steering side of things. Luckily Nelson Golf Club was right next door to the airport and I'd spent many a year shunting a ball around the course. I finally got myself orientated and headed in the right direction.

Amazingly, my parachute had opened and I floated to the ground without the great splatter I'd anticipated. A minor problem occurred when I landed on the runway and an Air New Zealand flight had to be diverted to avoid landing on me. It turned out later that the skydiving club got into a bit of trouble over this, but they

chose not to tell me initially for fear of scaring me off. According to Air New Zealand, for every minute a plane is in the air there's a huge cost to the airline. They wanted the skydiving club to pay the extra cost of the diverted flight! Naturally the club declined, reasoning that the passengers at least got better value for their money. As I said, good people, those skydiving blokes.

For a short time after this I lost my direction a bit. The thrill of skydiving is indescribable. Even today I say it is better than sex. I'm told I'm not doing it right and I'm wrong (about the sex thing). Or am I?

I met a lot of great chaps and girls through skydiving. In fact, it changed my life. I saw things differently after that. Of course, unless you've looked death in the eye you'll find it hard to get a grip on what I'm saying. I'd developed a real love for doing things, and a bit of danger didn't get in the road much from then on either.

I've gotten away from hunting somehow – sorry. My skydiving days are a story in themselves so I'll leave it at that. There may be a book in it yet.

Anyway, I met Marcus and Anthony (Cabbage) through the skydiving club. Marcus had originally come from Te Anau, and he had spent a considerable amount of time chasing the formidable wapiti stags. His sister was, without question, absolutely gorgeous. But enough of that. Marcus had the most easy-going nature of anyone I've ever met. He laughed a lot, and he had a smile that was particularly attractive to the ladies.

Marcus was a carpenter by trade but he'd abandoned that and spent most of his time thinking up and having a crack at moneymaking schemes. He was never short of ideas. One of them was bringing the first tandem parachute into New Zealand. He soon chucked away that idea and moved on to the next one. Today tandem skydiving is a huge tourist business – too bad about that one, eh Marcus? There were many other schemes, most of them legal, some of them debatable. Over time he had a firewood supply business, a portable sawmill, a spec building scheme, and numerous others. There was never a dull moment with Marcus and that's why we're still mates today.

Cabbage and Marcus were mates from way back. Cabbage was trouble. Not in the real sense of the word, but generally speaking he invited trouble wherever he went. Cabbage was short, solid, had bright orange curly hair and a mass of freckles. Everyone's first impression of him was 'Here's trouble'. We once stayed at the AA motor camp in Blenheim – we were doing a skydiving display at the Omaka airbase for some show or other. As we booked into the motorcamp the owner lined Cabbage up and said, 'Any trouble out of you and you're all out. Is that clear?' Poor Cabbage, he hadn't even opened his mouth to say anything. So you get my drift about him. Putting this aside he was wonderful fun and was always full of mischief. No challenge was too hard or too much effort. His boundless energy, sense of humour and enthusiasm for life made him the best of company.

But back to hunting. One day Marcus invited Cabbage and me on a hunting trip to the Tablelands. I'd never been there before and the thought of hunting new ground was inviting. The Tablelands is a great tract of land that is designated a Recreational Hunting Area (RHA). According to the rules this meant that only foot hunters were allowed to hunt there and only stags could be shot. The idea was that hinds would be left alone to breed and create extra deer for us foot hunters to shoot. Good theory! Over the years I saw more helicopters in that RHA than anywhere else I hunted.

Now Marcus knew how to enjoy his hunting. He taught me a thing or two about how it was done right and with comforts. First he told me that all we needed was a dozen of beer, a box of matches, some breakfast stuff, a cup and a sleeping bag each. 'Don't worry about the tucker,' he said. 'I've got it sorted.' Marcus, Cabbage and I were on this trip and I was very much the learner. I wondered if my dad could learn a thing or two from Marcus, but thought I'd wait and see. It seemed a bit strange that Marcus, a mere 19-year-old, could know so much about this hunting caper.

We drove to the Flora Saddle carpark in Marcus's old Holden ute. Now that in itself was an interesting experience. The hill was steep and the ute light in the back end. Near the top the incline reached near-vertical proportions. The shingle was loose and traction was a bit hard to get. We spent a fair bit of time getting up this bit with the back end slewing from side to side trying, with limited success, to gain traction. We finally made it, and then we walked in to Salisbury Hut. On the way we passed the Flora Huts, and the first solar heating shower unit I'd seen. This bush shower was impressive. Water was diverted from a stream into a long black polythene pipe that was curled up on a bank. The sun acted as a natural heating unit and warmed the water before it came out of the pipe and cleansed the person underneath it. You had to be quick, though, and scrub up before the hot water ran out and cold took over again.

On the way in I searched for deer behind every bush, twig and branch, and up every creek we passed. We certainly never saw any deer sign on or by the track, which didn't bode well.

'Marcus, this beer's getting a bit heavy. What d'ya reckon we have a thirst quencher?'

'Nah, mate. Not a good idea that drinking and walking. We've got two nights ahead so save it for the hut.'

I had a long drink of mountain water instead. There's something special about clear mountain water. It's cold, refreshing and has a special flavour all its own. It even smells pure. Strangely enough, some bright spark caught on to the idea and now city folk are paying good money to buy the stuff – mountain water sold as 'Bubbling Spring Mineral Water'. Marcus must be kicking himself at missing that one.

We finally arrived at Salisbury Hut at about 9.30 a.m., having started before first light. Now Salisbury Hut deserves a special mention. Firstly, it is not a hut. No way! The Salisbury is a small modern timber house. It's positioned on the side of a beautiful valley and has a view that takes a lot of digesting. There is a plate glass window that covers the entire front of the building, and from it can be seen Gordon's Pyramid (a triangular mountain), the floor of the valley and the surrounding forest. Boy, did it shatter my image of tough mountain men and rugged huts filled with wood smoke. There was even a coal range to cook on.

Well, since they'd taken the trouble to build it, I was going to take the trouble to use it. Unfortunately, one small oversight was that there was no coal for the range. This of course made cooking on it a bit tricky. It was midwinter and the wood from around the area was either already burnt or soaking wet. No one had seen fit to put some wood under the hut to dry out for the next party to use.

Yeah, I hear you. You've got no food to cook anyway, so what's the problem? And you're right. I had, however, snuck in some coffee and sugar – a small comfort to help beat the cold. I couldn't help but notice that there was no food in the hut pantry, and I was really beginning to wonder about Marcus's ability to solve the food situation as promised.

One of his favourite sayings about the bush came to mind: 'Nothing like a bushman's breakfast to kick the day off, eh?'

'A bushman's breakfast?' I'd venture. 'What's that?'

'A breath of fresh air and a good look around, mate.'

The answer was always the same, and it's an expression that still gets used today. Well, a breath of fresh air wasn't going to keep me going, I'll tell you that.

It was a typical Nelson high country mountain day – a hard frost followed by a warm, sunny, crystal-clear day. Mind you, as soon as the sun ducks for cover the temperature sinks instantly – back to bloody cold.

We filled in some time with a walk to Balloon Hut, a return trip along open tussock tops of about three hours. Now there was a great hut. It was everything I'd ever imagined – old, full of atmosphere, with tattered beds, candlewax on every shelf and windowsill, mouse droppings, names engraved in the woodwork and old books tossed into a corner. Even the hut book looked tattered and torn despite being less than a year old.

A search of the hut for food to satisfy my growing hunger revealed one rusty tin of something. There was no label on it, and judging by its rusty state it had clearly been there for many years. I had no idea what was in the can but I slipped it into my pocket anyway. My faith in Marcus's ability to feed the multitudes was fast diminishing.

We saw some goats on the return trip, but after eyeballing them for a while we decided they weren't for us. Nup, we were after venison and didn't want to stuff up a chance at the deer that was surely waiting around the next bend. Okay, you guessed it – we didn't see any deer here either. Over the years I have learned that getting off the tracks for a look is a great start to finding and recovering venison.

Back at the Salisbury some trampers had arrived and were trying to cook tea on the coal range. There was so much smoke in the hut that gulping down air proved difficult.

'You guys can use the oven when we've finished,' one of the trampers offered.

'Thanks, mate, but we won't be needing it. We're having fish and chips,' Marcus replied. This caused great mirth among the trampers – after all, we were a bloody long way from a takeaway shop.

The way I looked at it, Marcus was at least half right. We sure wouldn't be needing the range. We were going to starve.

No matter how much I hounded him, Marcus remained adamant that he had tea under control. To avoid choking to death on the smoke we retired outside to soak up the last of the day's sun. The temperature was dropping quickly. Marcus lay back in the tussock with a self-satisfied grin on his face. He was starting to piss me off, and my gut was reminding me all over again that it was time to throw some tucker inside.

As we lay there, the sound of a plane grew louder. It could be heard down the valley. It must be pretty low, I thought, given that it sounded so close but it wasn't visible in the sky anywhere.

The next moment the plane burst into view and did a tight bank turn over the hut. The pilot was none other than Glen, my apple packhouse workmate and skydiving buddy. Next to him were three other skydivers, all furiously giving us offensive hand signals. The plane disappeared from view further up the valley, only to return moments later banked to one side with a row of the whitest, muddiest-looking backsides I'd ever seen pressed up against the windows. Cabbage stood up and threw a rock in the direction of the plane.

The second pass produced another row of bums on the other side of the plane. The third pass was a prizewinner. The plane slowed to near-stalling speed and glided low past us. A large package was thrown from the window, landing dangerously close to where we stood. A wag of the wings and the plane was gone. The package was not.

Inside it were steaming hot fish and chips – lots of them. There was other tucker as well, all wrapped in heaps of newspaper and held together with masking tape. Hot fish and chips! Just as Marcus

had said! You couldn't get the self-satisfied grin off his face, I tell you. The trampers hadn't bothered to come out to see the plane and had no idea what had occurred. We walked into the hut and quietly sat down on a bunk to eat our tea. Nothing was said, but we sure got some strange looks sent in our direction.

The same procedure was followed the next evening. But this night we had oysters as well. As planned, we washed it all down with the beers we had taken considerable trouble to carry in. Wouldn't want to shake up the beer by throwing it out a plane window, would we?

Our second day was spent hunting off the tracks. Marcus stumbled on to a huge sinkhole with a cave attached. He went down a bit then came back for his torch so he could have a better look. Cabbage and I tracked along with him for a gander. Despite it being after lunch the ground was still hard with frost, which crunched under our feet as we walked. No self-respecting deer would be out at this time of day so we made no secret of our travels and yakked as we walked, Marcus in front, followed by me, then Cabbage. Barely out of sight of the hut we rounded a bush patch and walked through a small clearing. Cabbage prodded me in the back and asked if I was going to shoot that deer. Marcus was already out of the clearing and in the bush ahead.

'What deer?' I asked at full volume.

With a nod of his head Cabbage indicated a fallow hind standing smack in the middle of the clearing, less than 30 metres away. It was just standing there, quietly watching us wander through its playground.

My heart went into overdrive. A bloody deer. On the hoof and right there in front of me. Dad's old .303 seemed suddenly to get very heavy.

What had my dad told me? Yeah, that's right. Take it easy – no sudden movements. As if the deer hadn't seen me I quietly lifted the rifle and eased a bullet into the chamber. As I turned the rifle towards the deer it sensed trouble and walked calmly towards the bush, stopping at the edge for a look back. I was busy being quiet, slow, steady, nervous and everything else when it walked out of sight forever. Shit! I hadn't even pulled the trigger. An easy, close shot, side on, and I forgot to pull the trigger! What a balls-up. Well, not actually a balls-up, more a nothing at all situation that I wouldn't be allowed to live down for a long time to come.

Cabbage got a lot of mileage out of that one, I can tell you. The great white hunter was brought down a peg or two over that. Marcus, who had walked right past the deer, was strangely left out of dispatches when the insults were dished out.

So why did I just watch that deer disappear into the scrub? It had presented one of the easiest shots I was likely to get in a lifetime of hunting and I'd just watched it walk off. I was having a bit of trouble getting my head around what had occurred and, despite having searched my brain files, still couldn't come up with a reasonable explanation. I've since discovered that many other hunters, on encountering their first wild deer, have, like me, simply watched it, forgetting that their objective was to shoot it. My son did the same thing years later, but that's another story. Maybe it's a hereditary thing, though I doubt my old man ever fell into this trap – he never mentioned it if he did.

We went on to have a look at the sinkhole, and some distance down the cave found a gold-mining sluice-box. Later we found out that there was gold throughout the area, and that many years ago miners had unsuccessfully tried to scrape a living from it.

Later that afternoon Cabbage announced that there was a DoC hut hidden somewhere close by. He ventured the thought that there might be coal there, and that in all likelihood DoC would be keen to lend some to us poor cold hunters and trampers so we could warm ourselves up. Marcus decided to go hunting and set off on his own in the general direction of the sinkhole. Cabbage and I went off to find the DoC hut, and sure enough, after a bit of looking, there it was. The door was padlocked but we could see in through the window, and sure enough, there were some bags of coal.

Well, reasoned Cabbage, DoC is funded by the taxpayer and he was a taxpayer. This being the case he had a vested interest in the coal in the DoC hut. Having established that he owned the coal, the door hinges were removed and a half-bag of coal was relocated to Salisbury Hut. With the hinges restored to their rightful position no one was any the wiser. Or so we hoped.

As we were returning to the Salisbury with the coal we heard a shot coming from the general direction in which Marcus had gone. You beaut, mate, I thought, venison! Three seconds later, another shot. Three more seconds and a third was heard. Well, those of you who, like me, know a thing or two about mountain safety will understand that it was suddenly very bloody clear that Marcus was in trouble. Three shots spaced at three-second intervals is the universally recognised distress signal. It means 'I need help – save me quick.' Well, straight away I let off a shot to tell Marcus that we'd received his message and were on our way. There was no reply.

Cabbage and I ran as quickly as we could to Salisbury Hut, dumped the coal and headed off towards the sinkhole. We didn't have a torch so we armed ourselves with candles to fight off the darkness that was fast taking over. We cut holes in the sides of some empty cans and put the candles inside, hoping this would stop the wind blowing them out. We were wrong – it didn't. The cold wind, which by now had become quite strong, blew out the candles as quickly as we relit them.

I had fired off a number of shots to let Marcus know we were on the way but not a single shot was heard in reply. It wasn't long before pitch dark overtook us and it became obvious that we couldn't go any further. Dejectedly, Cabbage and I turned back towards the hut. It was a difficult and slow trip in the darkness, with the driving rain and sleet that had now taken over making things even worse.

Things didn't look good for Marcus, and our minds were conjuring up all sorts of visions – he'd broken a leg, he'd fallen down a sinkhole and couldn't get out – maybe he was unconscious and dying. The latter seemed quite likely since he hadn't replied to any of the shots I'd fired to tell him we were on the way.

Cabbage and I were the only ones in the hut that night and we were feeling pretty miserable. We knew Marcus didn't have much in the way of warm clothing with him, as most of his gear was still lying on his bunk where he'd left it. There was nothing we could do until the next day. We formulated a plan that first thing in the morning we'd race to the sinkhole and see if we could find him quickly. If we had no luck, one of us would run out and get help. It was comforting to have a plan in place.

About an hour and a half after we'd got back to the hut we heard a thump on the porch outside. A possum? Next thing the door was thrown open and in walked Marcus as calm as you like. There was blood all over his arms and face.

'Shit, mate! You all right? What happened?'

As we swamped him with questions the poor blighter couldn't get a word in.

'What are you two on about?' Marcus enquired, calm as. 'Jeez, I need a beer.'

As I've already explained, Marcus was a hard shot by anyone's standards. His story went like this. He'd left the hut and gone to the sinkhole as planned. As he approached it he saw a deer feeding on the grass rim. Marcus was about three hundred yards away and he decided to get closer to make the shot easier. He snuck into the bush and eased himself a couple of hundred yards nearer. When he next poked his head out there were five deer feeding in the sinkhole. Now Marcus, being the seasoned hunter he is, knew there would be a stag nearby, so he waited for it to show itself. After a short wait the stag sauntered into sight at the bush edge behind the sinkhole. Now's my chance, thought Marcus, and he promptly sent a shot into the wilderness. Having missed the stag he turned his attention to the hinds, which were milling about uncertain what to do. He let off a shot at a hind but again missed. His third and final shot connected and down went a hind. Marcus one, deer five.

Now here's the fun bit. Marcus heard my shots and wondered what I was up to. He even thought I was on to venison myself. He never clicked to the fact that he had fired three shots spaced out at three-second intervals in the manner of a distress signal. Nope mate, it never occurred to him. What's more, even if it had, he couldn't have replied anyway. He only had three bullets with him for the whole trip, and he had run out of ammo.

Then Marcus discovered that he didn't have a knife with him to gut the deer. Using his initiative, he dragged the deer under some bushes for cover and tried to pull the skin off it. He tried tearing it, starting at the bullet hole, but that idea wasn't a goer. He succeeded in creating a hell of a mess and covering himself in a lot of blood but not much else. By then it was getting dark and he realised he'd have a problem getting back to the hut. After a lot of arsing up, knee and elbow skinning, and walking into trees he finally made it back. Cabbage and I were so pleased to see him that it took a fair bit of self-control to pretend that we hadn't really been worried, and in fact had hardly even noticed he was missing.

As it turned out, we still had a problem. None of us had thought to bring a hunting knife along. Perhaps we were too used to getting nothing but lost. I had a steel-bladed butter knife in my pack, but it was so blunt you'd have trouble cutting toast with it. We spent some hours that night grinding an edge onto the knife, placing ash from the fire on the top of the coal range and then wetting it. The paste acted like a grindstone on top of the worn metal surface, and we managed to get a good sharp edge on that knife. The last of the beers were finished as the sharpening took place. The cold sure doesn't dampen your thirst.

The next morning we returned to the deer and set about butchering it. True to his word, Marcus hadn't prepared it very well. But to our surprise and pleasure the knife held its edge well and we managed to skin and butcher the animal with it. The rain never stopped as we performed this operation and the roaring southerly wind blew sleet into the bush, making proceedings very unpleasant. By the time we had finished we were frozen.

We shared out the meat between the three of us and made our way out that morning. By the time we reached the ute the weather had cleared up and it had gotten hot. That's the South Island mountains for you.

Did I mention that I was 17 years old at the time of this trip? Further, I'd seen my first deer in the wild but failed to shoot it. This hunting game was taking a bit of sorting out. Maybe I needed to have another talk with my old man.

Big Red

Marcus and I returned to the Tablelands on a number of occasions. Every trip brought new adventures and experiences, but none as memorable as that first one.

On one trip we met an interesting bloke at Salisbury Hut. He was tall and lean, and he didn't say much. He gave the impression that you needed to take care not to say anything to upset him or he might take some remedial action to modify your behaviour. He was a real hard bush type, and he didn't seem too tolerant of us youngsters in the hills. He had penetrating eyes that seemed to see right through you, and a mass of red whiskers that'd need an axe to remove them. His boots were well worn and tattered, and his Swannie was falling to bits. In my mind at least, this all added up to the picture of a real hard-case hunter.

When we returned to the hut on the first night of the trip this bloke had a large, very dead, red hind hanging up in a tree. I couldn't help but notice that it had been head-shot just as my old man reckoned they should be. The bloke had rigged up a muslin cloth to keep the blowflies off the carcass. It was so cold that I didn't think this was really necessary, but I decided to keep my mouth shut.

The bloke defrosted a bit when we supplied him with a couple of the precious beers we'd carried in, and he answered my many questions. It seemed he was unemployed and spent most of his time in the bush hunting to supplement his benefit. He clearly loved the mountains and the freedom they offered – you could tell by the way he talked about his experiences and the look in his eyes as he told his tale. It was the same look I'd seen in my old man's eyes when he talked of the hills and hunting trips long past.

He never offered his name, nor a handshake, nor much else for that matter. Nonetheless, he was the sort of bloke that was hard to forget. I took to calling him 'Big Red', although not to his face, of course. I guessed that Big Red wasn't much inclined towards taking on a normal job, as at that time work wasn't hard to get.

Big Red had hunting in the Tablelands well and truly sorted out. There is a good road from the Flora Saddle carpark to well past the Flora Huts, but it's blocked by a padlocked metal gate. Most people walk along this road for about an hour until the start of the track is reached. In all honesty this road walk used to piss us off. Big Red had sorted the problem out by taking a pushbike with him. He would ride his bike from the Flora Saddle carpark, down past the Flora Huts and on past the road end. He'd then hide the bike in the bush when the going got too tough. He claimed that when he got a deer he'd carry it to his bike then wheel it to his waiting car.

Big Red was clearly no slug at this hunting caper. He reckoned that DoC locked the gate so that only they had access to the easy hunting offered by driving in. He maintained that DoC wanted to discourage hunters, and that locking the gate was their way of doing it. I don't know if he was right or not, but at the time it sure sounded reasonable.

Now I'm mentioning Big Red because he gave me some really sound advice on hunting and I reckon it needs sharing. As we talked I asked about finding deer. I mentioned that I was an expert at finding them for everyone else but struggled when looking for myself.

He replied, 'Son, you young fellows wouldn't recognise a deer unless it was side on, in full view, and had a big fluorescent sign hung around its neck.'

I thought that was a bit tough but I encouraged him to go on.

'You're in too much of a hurry. Slow down. Take the time to have a real look. Not just for a deer, but for parts of the deer. A nod of its head, a leg under a bush, a branch let go as a deer feeds from it. A bum poking out of a bush. A flick of an ear as one lies in the tussock. Take the time to look and you will see. Yep, no doubt about it. Slowing down's the answer.'

Well, I'll tell you this. That was the best advice I'd been given to date and it's still the best advice today. That bit of advice changed not only my way of thinking about hunting but also how I hunted. I slowed down after that, and since then I've slowed down even more, but the results keep getting better. Funny that, I slowed down but the hunting game sped up – the results of my efforts, that is.

The last I saw of Big Red was as he walked off down the track with the deer safely tucked up in a wheelbarrow! Yep, like everything else he even had that side of things sorted.

You know what's strange? I don't recall my old man mentioning this 'slow down' thing, so I reckon I'd been under a handicap up to this point. Maybe he did mention it, but being young I'd failed to take it in properly. Look out from now on, mate.

Surrounded by Hard Shots

About now I was having a go at small-bore, indoor shooting. Some old schoolmates and I had found a local club and got ourselves invited along for a shot. We met all sorts there, but one I remember more than the others was tall, thin, female and drop-dead gorgeous. I thought I'd better add the female bit in case you got the wrong idea. Things are a bit liberal these days so I don't want your mind travelling a path that's not right.

Anyway, I found that I wasn't particularly suited to the discipline of target shooting but I enjoyed the nights out. One chap I met through the range was Paul, who told tales of wild pigs, deer and possums. Now Paul had access to a bach at Okiwi Bay in the Marlborough Sounds. Given our common interest, it wasn't long before I let him invite me there for a weekend's hunting.

We arrived at the bach after dark on a Friday. The bach more than met my expectations. A man could go so far as to call it a three-bedroom house, but for an ongoing desire to fit the mould of a rugged hunter type. There was hot water, an electric oven and all the other mod cons – great stuff.

The plan for the weekend was simple. Stay up all night

spotlighting for possums along the roadsides; come first light we would take to a firebreak in the scrub where deer and pigs abounded, round up a couple, carry them back to camp and rest up before going fishing for blue cod. Sounded easy and Paul reckoned he'd done it plenty of times before. I was told that it was far too early for spotlighting when we arrived, so we'd better have some of the beer we'd brought in with us. Now I do not advocate mixing alcohol and guns in any way, so you'll have to forgive me for being young and foolish at that stage.

We had several beers each and left the bach about 11 p.m. Paul drove his old Cortina and I aimed the spotlight up every tree, bush and telephone pole we drove past. At regular intervals a possum was spotted. The routine never changed. Paul would slam the brakes on far too hard and we would come to a long sliding stop. Most times we'd stop on the roadway but on a couple of occasions we ended up in the ditch at the side of the road. It had something to do with Paul being more interested in watching the possum than the road. Add to this the fact that the roads we were travelling on were gravel ones. We took turns at holding the light and shooting the possum. Usually the possum would climb the nearest tree or pole and sit there looking down at us. The .22 rifle we were using was armed with a scope that had been well sighted in, and most of the possums were killed with a clean shot to the head. We didn't bother picking up the carcasses as at that time there was a downturn in the demand for skins and they just weren't worth the effort.

By 4 a.m. we had travelled a lot of miles and thinned out the possum menace considerably. A fair bit of ammo had been sent from the barrel, and we had both had our fill of shooting possums. It was time for a quick bite to eat before getting stuck into those pigs and deer.

It got light about 5 a.m., by which time we were well up a firebreak looking for wild game. For a long time we walked uphill, and for an equally long time down the other side. We were about to give up when a goat walked out a few yards ahead of us. It gave a child-like bleat and just stood there looking at us. Total confusion reigned as neither Paul nor I wanted to shoot it. We argued back and forth, trying to encourage each other to cleanse the country of this feral menace. It was no good. Neither of us was interested in goats so we simply told it to bugger off in clear and specific terms. After a couple more bleats to get itself going the animal quietly wandered off back into the gorse from which it had emerged.

The disappointment wasn't that great. A pig would have been nice, and a deer even better, but we both knew how far it was back up the hill we'd just descended and the thought of carrying an animal back up it was bordering on sickening.

We trudged back to the vehicle and drove back to Okiwi Bay. We were both stuffed. The long night out followed by the fruitless walk had taken its toll and I was about ready to pack it in.

'No way, mate,' said Paul. 'We've got breakfast to catch.'

Now I had an instant vision of trundling off to catch a feed of blue cod, but alas no.

'I think a feed of whitebait would be just the story,' Paul said.

Well, a man only had to take a butcher's out the window to see that the tide was nearly out and quickly heading further out. Any fool knows that you only catch whitebait on an incoming tide – get on the planet, man. Paul insisted that he knew what he was about so we headed off to the beach with an old, rusty, box section whitebait net in hand.

Now if you're inclined towards totally legal practices I'd ask you to cover your eyes when you read the next bit. Open them when you get to the next chapter.

For people who don't know about whitebait, they are tiny, transparent fish that are caught during a short season when fishing for them is legal. There are strict rules on how and when they can be caught. Us city kids were completely ignorant of all this, of course, so we acted in a totally innocent fashion.

Paul promptly walked to a creek at one end of the bay. Just above the tide mark he placed the net in the water, with its opening facing upstream. Now I was sure he had gone mad from lack of sleep. The net goes the other way to catch the whitebait as they travel upstream.

The creek was about six feet wide and very shallow. Paul placed some rocks and sticks on either side of the net, forming a large V that ended inside the net. Next he walked upstream a fair way, and armed with a large stick he raked the stream bottom from side to side as he walked back towards the net. He kept this up until he reached the net, then he quickly lifted it out of the water and there wriggling furiously in the bottom of it were great fistfuls of whitebait. I thought this was bloody marvellous, especially considering my previously unsuccessful whitebaiting efforts. The same procedure was repeated at another stream at the other end of the bay, and with the same result.

Two very happy fishermen returned to the bach and cooked up a huge feed of whitebait for breakfast. I remember that we made 27 whitebait patties with our catch. Given that each patty was a small frying pan full, that was a darn good catch.

After that we slept until mid-afternoon, when Paul's dad woke us up. The tide was right.

'Are you guys coming fishing?' Too right we were.

The boat was launched from the beach not far from the front of the bach. We sped off into the open sea to a spot that was known only to Paul's family. I was sworn to secrecy, and in all the years since I have never disclosed the location to anyone. Mind you, it has helped that I had absolutely no idea where we went or how to get back there. I'm no great seaman, as you'll see in a later chapter, so I was more concerned with holding down my breakfast than mapping my location for later reference. The fishing was great and we managed to catch a good number of large blue cod.

The weekend was a great success and I thoroughly enjoyed myself. If you get to read this, Paul, thanks again, mate. Still, I couldn't help but ponder the fact that yet again I'd failed to bring home the venison. I must be doing something wrong.

Lost in the Snow

Horse reckoned there was no need to take a compass into the hills when he went hunting. It's not possible to get lost, he stated with total conviction. How could you get lost in a country that's only a hundred miles across at the widest point? Being a mountainous country, reasoned Horse, you only had to follow any stream and it would lead you back to civilisation and safety. I was being taught by a master, I thought, so it was only natural that I would follow his fine example and do without this frivolous navigational aid myself.

It was never long after a hunt before the yearn to return to the mountains took over. Once again Horse and I were in Browning Hut. It was late November. We had walked in after work on a Friday evening and hoped for an early start in the morning. The weather turned nasty overnight, and we woke to high winds and torrential rain. We did the only sensible thing to do in this situation – rolled over and went back to sleep. My sleeping bag was warm inside and the situation outside wasn't. By lunchtime the weather had picked up a bit, but not enough to encourage us outside.

At about 2.30 things picked up a lot. The wind still howled but the rain had abated to an occasional shower. Horse and I had both seen enough of the hut walls and we elected to risk a hunt in the rain. Now I'm not a great one for taking the comforts of home into the bush with me, so I had only my Swanndri, a woollen singlet and a pair of torn shorts for protection against the weather. The modern lightweight raincoats hadn't been invented yet, and I didn't own a raincoat at that time anyway.

The hunting below the hut wasn't to our liking and the wind didn't suit a hunt to the north.

'I reckon we should bolt into the Roebuck,' said Horse. 'The wind is all wrong for it but if we race along the top ridge for a ways then have a good break before dropping over the sides and hunting back into the wind, the deer shouldn't smell us.' Sounded good to me.

The area we were to hunt is to the north of Browning Hut. The wind was blowing really hard from the south. It normally takes some time for a southerly to blow over so it was unlikely there would be a change of wind direction that afternoon. After leaving the hut we followed the track uphill until, after a 20-minute climb, we reached the Browning Saddle. At this point the track continues over the top and down into the valley below, after a few hours reaching Roebuck Hut. I have never been to this hut. A lot more walking brings you out near Canvastown on the Marlborough side of the Richmond Range. At the saddle we veered left, climbed to the ridgetop and followed it for about an hour. In those days there wasn't a track along the ridge, and apart from some red tape and toilet paper hanging from trees here and there the route was unmarked. During our walk along the ridge the weather deteriorated a bit, with more rain squalls coming through. All in all it wasn't very pleasant travelling and I was grateful that the rain was at my back. We finally came to a stop and Horse asked which side I would prefer to hunt. The plan was to drop down over the side and traverse back into the saddle, after which we would return via the track to the hut, a nice hot feed and a warm sleeping bag.

I elected to take the western face as I hadn't hunted there previously, and duly dropped over the side. Straight away I was on to a fair bit of fresh deer sign, with numerous hoofprints and droppings. Despite being wet and cold I got focused really quickly. I was a bit sheltered from the wind so the travel wasn't unpleasant, though the odd rain squall still came through just to remind me who was in charge. I sidled along slowly, taking great care to examine any sheltered spot or likely feed area. As I travelled I crossed many small ridges that branched off the main ridge we had travelled along. I wandered up and down as I bush-stalked, taking the path of least resistance as I went.

After about two hours of slow bush-stalking my ability to concentrate was starting to diminish. I reasoned that I was about 15 minutes of quick walking from Roebuck Saddle, and I knew that as soon as I hit the track my hunt would effectively be over. Despite the cold, I was enjoying the outing, and I decided to drop to the bottom of the face I was hunting on and follow the creek, reasoning that it would take me back to Browning Hut. By doing this I would be able to hunt right to the hut door and thus increase my chances of bagging an animal. Down I went, stalking all the way. The bush was wet and travelling quietly wasn't hard. Each time I accidentally knocked a branch I was drenched with rainwater, and not long after I headed downhill the fog started to come in. Small puffs of it at first, then it got progressively heavier until I could see only about 20 feet in front. No matter, I thought, I would soon hit the creek and that would lead me straight back to the hut.

Soon enough I struck the creek and made off downstream at a fair pace. It had turned a lot colder and the fog had got really thick. I expected to reach the hut in about 15, maybe 20 minutes, allowing for the bush-bashing required. About three-quarters of an hour later I was starting to ponder my whereabouts. Nah mate, no worries, the hut must be close now, just box on and you'll soon get there. Well, soon didn't arrive, and after another half-hour's travel I reasoned that I must be well past the hut by now. I had already crossed the creek so I should have walked right past the door.

About this point I started to get a bit panicky. My heart was racing and my brain was trying hard to keep up. What in the world had gone wrong? As I stood by the creek the heavy mist was noticeably wet. Not yet as wet as I was, given my travels through the dripping bush, but nonetheless wet. I had got really hot while I was walking hard trying to reach the hut, but as soon as my heat-generating activity ceased my body temperature started to drop quickly. I knew I had to think my way through this predicament or I was going to be in real trouble. All my clothing was soaking wet, not that I had much on anyway, and I certainly didn't have any means of keeping warm should I get bushed for the night. The total sum of my safety kit was a few matches I had in my top pocket. They were stored inside an empty film canister along with a piece of striker to get them going. I had no food with me.

After a bit of thinking I reasoned that if I wasn't where I thought I was I must be somewhere else. Pretty clear so far. Maybe I had dropped down into the creek too early and got caught up in another valley that would also lead towards Nelson. If so, I should be heading southwest. Was I? Hell, how would I know? The fog prevented me getting a look at the lay of the surrounding hills, I didn't have a compass, and I'd noticed a distinct lack of signposts. If I could get a bearing on north or south I would be able to get out okay.

I had heard that moss grows on the south side of the trees in these parts, given the direction that the sun travels each day. Seemingly the southern side of tree trunks doesn't see the sun, so moss grows on that side only. I can tell you that I looked at plenty of trees and there was definitely no moss on any of them anywhere. Putting the thinking cap back on I pondered a few other options, like yelling for help, going like a mad thing in one direction and crossing my fingers that it was the right one, and praying for a miracle. None of them seemed likely to solve my situation.

I finally decided to fire three well-spaced shots into the air and see if Horse heard and responded. I climbed up the creek bank and onto a small open slip face. I fired three times and waited . . . nothing. A quick count of my remaining bullets revealed that I had four shots left. Well, I reasoned, I have enough for one more try at the three-shot thing and then one for myself. The one for myself was of course to put me out of my misery should I end up starving or freezing to death.

Get a grip on yourself, man. Action is better than inaction. I decided to return along the path I had come. That was the way I'd got lost, so that was the direction to go to fix the problem. If I struck the right ridge I might find the red tape or toilet paper that I knew was hanging in the tree branches there.

Off I went. I frequently saw my own footprints in the creek bed, and for some reason I found this comforting. When they stopped appearing I reasoned that it was time to go upward, and I took off in that direction. Trouble struck not long after. The fog was still as thick as ever but the much-needed daylight was fading really fast. This posed a dilemma. To box onward would leave me in the dark, wet and without shelter. Even if I found the correct ridge it was unlikely that I could make my way out in the pitch dark. There wasn't any chance of navigating by starlight; the fog had taken care of that. God Almighty. If only I could get a look at the stars I could establish north and south from the Southern Cross.

Decision time had arrived again. This time it was easy. I needed shelter, preferably dry, and I needed it fast. The hardest part was actually making the decision that I was bushed and was going to spend the night out in the scrub. After that my initial panic soon disappeared. Once I had made the decision and was taking steps to carry it out, a real sense of calmness overtook me. It was a really uncanny feeling that I can't put into words. Well, plenty of hunters had slept out before me and survived, and so would I. I found a large tree that had been blown over. The roots of the tree had lifted a large ball of dirt with them, leaving a shallow cavity underneath. The base of the cavity was dry and sheltered from the prevailing wind. I quickly gathered up some branches and foliage and lay them against the upturned tree roots. The shelter created was minimal, but it was better than nothing. I managed to scavenge up a small quantity of dry twigs and some semi-dry branches. If I could get a fire going in the cavity I would be a lot happier.

Darkness arrived about the same time as the torrential rain. My efforts to light a fire had proceeded well until the rain doused it and wet my remaining matches. That was it. I was about to spend the night curled up in a wet, soon to be muddy, hole, in my shorts and very wet Swanndri, with only the torrential rain for company. I was wrong about the torrential rain bit though. After an hour or more the rain stopped, only to be replaced by a steady fall of snow.

You must be bloody joking, mate, I thought. It hadn't snowed in this part of the country for a hundred years or more. I tried to look on the bright side of things but there wasn't one. As I lay there in total misery Horse's words went through my mind over and over again: 'It's not possible to get lost in New Zealand, mate.'

Well, I was in the process of showing him a thing or two about getting lost. When I stop to think about it though, I wasn't really lost, was I? I knew I was in the Richmond State Forest, which was somewhere to the east of Nelson. There ya go. I wasn't lost after all.

The night was long and cold. Actually, very long and very, very cold. I fell asleep at one point, which I knew wasn't a good idea. When a man is as wet and cold as I was there is always the chance that he won't wake up. Hypothermia is the state a person's body goes into when his system starts to close down all the extremities in order to keep the vital organs going. If things get too bad you never wake up as the body closes down altogether and you die. Staying awake tends to stop this happening. Anyway, I woke feeling frozen. The rain had stopped and when I looked out of my inadequate accommodation I saw stars lighting up the sky. Words cannot describe how I felt. A fine day was sure to follow as the wind had also stopped. The sun always rises in the east and sets in the west. I'd get my directions sorted out from this and find my way out no trouble at all.

The quiet of the forest was nearly deafening. I didn't care, I was going to be out of there as soon as the sun poked its head up. It was only about 1.40 a.m. by then and sunrise was a long way off. I didn't sleep again, but I felt strangely elevated at the certainty of getting out to a feed and a hot drink. I spent the remainder of the night resting my forehead against a tree, walking on the spot and trying to slap some life into my arms, legs and upper body. One saving grace was that I was wearing a good woollen hat that kept my head warm throughout.

As dawn approached I got a handle on the required direction and continued on uphill. About two hundred metres from my temporary home I hit the top. I came out smack on a spot I had been to on a number of previous occasions. It was a large clearing at the upper end of the ridge Horse and I had travelled together the previous day and was real close to where we had split up. I found myself having a good look over the clearing. I was there at dawn and it was too good an opportunity to let go. Much to my disappointment there was nothing about in the open.

It was fairly easy going along the ridgetop. I walked along quietly, keeping a sharp lookout for deer as I went. It was very early and I was right in the heart of venison country. There were fresh deer droppings at regular intervals, which only served to heighten my expectations.

As I brushed through a patch of dense beech tree regrowth a large red hind crashed out of the bush and dashed over the side to my left. I was caught totally by surprise and never even raised my rifle before she was gone. A quick pace forward to get a look at the deer's departing backside sent another deer crashing after the first. Again, the regrowth didn't allow me more than a quick look at the departing animal. Well, it was clearly time to take stock of the situation. Deer two, hunter nil. This seemed to be a recurring theme in my hunting efforts. I crouched down and tried to see through the tangled mess of thin tree trunks ahead of me. At best I might be able to identify some deer legs if there were any more hiding here. Well, I waited and looked for some time before deciding that I had spooked the only two deer in the area. I stood up, gathered my wits and made off towards Browning Hut. Ten paces further along three more deer burst from the undergrowth. This time they took off to my right. I got a real fright, as they had stood perfectly still for about ten minutes following the hasty departure of their mates. Needless to say, my shooting skills weren't up to speed and not a shot was fired. Words cannot describe my disappointment at seeing five deer and not even getting a shot at one. I waited a long time in the general area, reasoning that the deer would try to mob up again and would need to cross over the ridgetop to do so. Well, if they did it wasn't while I was watching. Deer five, hunter nil.

Soon after all this I heard a shot from the direction of Browning Hut where I knew Horse would be worrying himself sick. I returned a shot to let him know I was on my way, and jogged back to the hut. I'd had enough disappointments for one day.

As I got within sight of the hut I saw Horse backing out of it with his pack on his back. He was pulling the door shut behind him. 'Where do ya think you're going then?' I yelled.

Horse nearly fell over with fright. He let loose a long string of choice swear words, which I interpreted as an enquiry as to whether I had enjoyed my night out. I informed him that while it had been a little damp I was most disappointed that he hadn't joined me.

It turned out that Horse was about to head back to town to raise the alarm. I was struck by his concern. While I had heard his shot, he had not heard mine, and he had decided that I was well and truly in the brown sticky stuff and that help was required. Had I arrived at the hut a minute or two later he would have been gone.

Horse mentioned that he felt I was a bit selfish staying out overnight and leaving him to play cards in the nice warm hut on his own. He reckoned that he now preferred playing solitaire as he'd had so much practice in my absence.

Anyway, it wasn't long before Horse gathered his wits, and having established that I intended to have a feed, a hot drink and then a sleep, he decided that a hunt was in order. Down went the pack and Horse was away. He didn't waste much time on conversation, did Horse.

When I tried to eat I found that I couldn't swallow and my throat hurt. I gave up on the eating idea and eventually fell asleep. I felt a bit better on waking. As I lay in my sleeping bag I couldn't help but wonder how I'd got myself misplaced (read: lost). It didn't take long to figure out.

I've already described the area Horse and I were hunting. The main ridge sloped uphill to the point where Horse and I separated. Conversely, I had to hunt and sidle back downhill to reach Browning Saddle and my route back to the hut. The main ridge has a lot of smaller spurs leading off it. Well, when I dropped over the side and started sidling back towards the saddle, I passed over a number of ridges leading off the main one. At some point I had crossed over the main ridge, thinking it was just another spur. I hadn't seen any toilet paper hanging in trees to indicate that I was crossing the main ridge, so I carried on thinking I was heading in the right direction. I'll blame the fog for that. At the point of crossing over the main ridge I had completed a 180-degree turn and was heading in completely the wrong direction. Had I continued following the creek I ended up in I would have reached safety for sure, about ten hours later and somewhere near Marlborough. The good news was that the extra bullet I'd saved for myself wasn't needed.

Horse returned late in the afternoon, having sighted a fallow stag in the bush behind the hut. The stag was in full flight when he saw it and he never even raised his rifle. That's how it often turns out when you're bush-stalking fallow deer. It is for me, anyway. We walked out that night with the aid of torches. All in all, the trip had been a large learning curve for me.

Now there must be a lesson or two in this lot, wouldn't you say? Firstly, Horse was right. You cannot get lost in New Zealand but you sure as hell can get bushed. Getting bushed is a bit different to being lost. Getting bushed means you know roughly where you are but are temporarily misplaced. A bit of thinking should solve the matter, even if it takes a day or two. Lost is when you have no idea at all where you are.

Secondly, as Horse stated, it might be frivolous taking a compass into the bush but me, I'd be taking one from now on. Thirdly, in future I was going to take a daypack with me. It was going to contain a raincoat, warm gear, a first-aid kit, a guaranteed means of starting a fire even in the wet, and some tucker. Who knows, it might even come in useful for carrying meat out should I get lucky.

I made a mental note to ask my old man if he ever got lost. He never mentioned it if he did.

A Shot in the Dark

The Marlborough Sounds, at the top end of the South Island, are surrounded by very steep hills that fall sharply to the water's edge. When Captain Cook, an early explorer, released a number of goats and pigs there he hoped they would breed and be a source of food for fellow sailors in future years. How right he was. Both animals took a liking to their new home and their populations exploded into something matching that of the Indian subcontinent. In later years deer were released, and they also found the grub and the lay of the land to their liking.

As a result of all this the Sounds became a popular hunting ground, and in 1979 it was the scene for a hunting trip I made with Horse. By this time Horse had come to an arrangement with his dad and between them they had purchased a fibreglass boat that was powered by a large Evinrude motor. We towed this water-borne venison, pork and goat recovery boat to Elaine Bay one Friday night, and eagerly awaited the morning to see what hunting offered.

I'd better let you know who 'we' were. Obviously there was Horse and me, but we were also accompanied on this trip by Phil, who you've already met, Warwick and Smailey.

Warwick's the sort of bloke that comes to mind when you think of a tough New Zealand bushman. He's of average height, strong build, has short-cropped blond hair, and always has a roll-your-own cigarette in his mouth. If there wasn't a smoke in his mouth it was because he was busy rolling one.

Warwick never had much to say about anything. He preferred action to talking, and no sooner had someone suggested we go to the local pub for a beer than he'd be seated in the car waiting. Warwick wasn't too keen on backing out of a fight either, should one land itself in front of him. On the other hand, he did back out of one situation that he found himself tied into. A few years after this hunting trip he got himself engaged. The big day arrived and the bride fronted up, but where was the groom? Several years later Warwick returned after a wee visit to Australia, wondering where the bridal party was. A woman can be more frightening than a wild boar if she's not handled right, and Warwick had figured he wasn't ready to tackle that one yet.

Smailey, on the other hand, was a happy-go-lucky mate who found the good side of everyone. He'd go out of his way to help anyone, and he didn't have much trouble working up a laugh. He was the first to arrive at a party and the last to leave, but while he enjoyed a drink or two he never seemed to fall much under the influence of it. I've always been meaning to ask him how he managed this, but somehow never got around to it.

Anyway, to get back to Elaine Bay. Our arrival was celebrated in the usual fashion, and morning found us great hunters wrapped in our warm sleeping bags, having forgotten about our planned early start.

Horse eventually roused everyone out of bed and announced a revised plan to spend the day fishing for blue cod. Now that idea had a great deal of merit, and was soon agreed to by all. The boat was duly backed down the concrete launching ramp into the sea, where it drifted off the trailer and was promptly rowed to shore by Horse to enable the rest of us to climb on board.

Once we were all on board the boat had to be pushed off from the shore, which meant the unfortunate soul who drew the job had to get wet up to his knees or higher. Warwick was far too cunning to get caught with this job, and was securely seated up the front with me crushed up beside him. Horse and Phil were already on board, which left Smailey to do the honours. Well the boat was a bit stuck to the shore due to the weight of the four males already on board, so Smailey had to put in a bit of extra effort to get us water-borne. After a lot of pushing and shoving he'd failed to make any headway at all, so Warwick nodded his head in Smailey's general direction to indicate that perhaps I should give him a hand. As I stood up, Smailey gave one almighty push forward, the boat lurched seaward and so did Smailey and I. I fell forward into Horse's waiting arms, nearly making Horse fall out of the boat, and Smailey stumbled, tripped and fell full-length into the sea.

Naturally the dry occupants of the boat erupted with laughter, which only served to goad some unusually strong language from Smailey. Meanwhile he was compared to a wrung-out wet cat, soggy spuds, damp socks and numerous other indignities before being hauled aboard.

It would be fair to say that our nautical careers did not get off to a good start. The only one of us who knew anything about boating was Horse, whose total experience was one water-skiing trip with his father. But being young and fearless we set off into the open seas. With a lot of luck and not much skill we fluked a terrific spot for fishing and cod, which to my mind is the best-tasting fish there is.

Having caught all we needed we were off back to shore. At this point the shore didn't look too far off, and Horse enthusiastically pulled on the starter cord. The motor refused to start. This went on for some time before Horse announced the obvious – that the motor wouldn't start and we would have to row back.

Now the prospect of this wasn't good. We had come approximately eight miles from Elaine Bay and rowing back would take hours. The situation became even more complicated when we discovered that we hadn't put the oars in. There we were bobbing about in the Tasman Sea at the peril of the gods. At this point the gods decided that we had had it too good, and without any warning a strong offshore wind took up and we found ourselves rapidly advancing on Australia and leaving behind the shores of New Zealand.

Horse took the cover off the motor and started tinkering with its internal workings, which was comforting to those of us who had a fondness for dry land and a preference for New Zealand soil. As we all crowded around Horse, pretending we knew something about motors when in reality we didn't, someone accidentally knocked a small piece of the motor's workings overboard and we watched it disappear into the big blue sea. This didn't improve our situation any.

By now I wasn't feeling too flash. The shore was drifting further away, the sea that had been so calm when we started was getting decidedly choppy, and the effects of seasickness were sneaking up on me. Smailey had dried out a fair bit but he mentioned a couple of times that he wasn't suffering from heat stroke either. Warwick was busy rolling another cigarette. He hadn't said much up to this point but managed a 'Reckon it's a bit far to swim'. That was it. He didn't seem too worried, as he had taken the trouble to bait his fishing hook and lower his line over the side. Not much worried Warwick. Phil was strangely quiet.

Horse was still busy tinkering with the motor. He had a bit of sandpaper working at one point and at another was busy with a length of fine wire. Suddenly, out of nowhere, Horse gave a pull on the starter cord and the motor burst into life. I felt my seasickness subsiding, and even Smailey looked decidedly more cheerful. Horse was busy holding onto something in the motor, and after it had kept going for a few minutes he instructed Warwick to hold onto it for him. This done, we turned and headed for the shore at a slow but steady pace. I never did find out what was wrong with that motor, but ever since that day I have felt happier when any boat I am in is real close to the shore.

Horse spent the remainder of the day making permanent repairs to the outboard motor, and about teatime announced that it was fixed and ready for some night hunting by spotlight.

Now the land around Elaine Bay was steep and bush covered. The bush went right to the water's edge, but there were many clearings and areas where the bush had slipped away during heavy rain. The exposed areas were often covered in grass and other succulent food much enjoyed by deer, pigs and goats. Warwick reckoned he knew the area well and that we stood a good chance of shooting a deer on one of those clearings.

Now here was an interesting proposition. I had never been spotlighting for deer from a boat before and it sounded like a good idea to me. I'd heard my old man talk about shooting deer by spotlight so I was really looking forward to having a go myself.

The night was calm and the water almost as flat as a mirror. We had tested Warwick's spotlight and all our rifles had been sighted in to ensure they were accurate. We had five rifles on board – a .22 and four heavier calibres – and a fair amount of ammunition. There was no moon but the sky was clear and there were enough stars to give some visibility. We eased our way around the coastline, with Warwick shining the spotlight towards the hill faces as we went.

'What do we do if we spot a deer?' I enquired.

'Shoot it,' came the collective reply. Well, that sounded simple enough.

'How will we recognise the deer?' I asked.

'You can't mistake a deer's eyes when the spotlight hits them,' Horse stated confidently. 'They glow green and stand out like a naked nun in the spotlight.'

We spotted a number of possums and shot a few with the .22 as we travelled around the coastline. Each slip face was carefully examined, but we weren't having much luck. After several hours the novelty was starting to wear off and the night had turned cold. I was thinking of suggesting that we return home when the hill face above us lit up with four sets of bright orange eyes.

'Deer,' ventured Horse.

'Bloody oath,' exclaimed Warwick. I had no idea what was attached to the eyes but these blokes knew what they were doing, so deer it was. There was a general uncoordinated shuffling and reaching for rifles, which caused the boat to start rocking violently from side to side.

Warwick held the spotlight on the eyes, which seemed to be a long way off, and two rifles were aimed up the hill in their general direction. We couldn't see the bodies that were attached to the eyes and the boat was still rocking fairly violently, making it near impossible to take proper aim. I certainly couldn't hold my scope steady on any of the sets of eyes, and found them appearing and disappearing from my view as the boat rocked back and forth.

'I don't think those are deer eyes,' Phil said suddenly.

'Of course they bloody are,' hissed Warwick. 'We're miles from anywhere. They can't be anything but deer eyes.' Smailey chipped in to agree.

'They are deer,' said Horse. 'Now shut up and let me have a crack.'

Phil continued trying to convince everyone that we were not looking at deer eyes.

Suddenly Horse's rifle boomed, breaking the silence of the night. The boat rocked even more violently than before. In the quiet that followed Horse's shot there was a bleating of sheep as the mob above us made for cover.

'Bloody hell! You were right,' exclaimed Warwick. 'We'd better get the hell out of here before a farmer gets interested in what we're doing. You didn't hit the thing, did ya? Horse?'

'Hell, how would I know,' came the reply.

A bit of listening with the motor off revealed there was no more bleating coming from up the hill. This told us one of two things: one, that Horse had clean missed, which in this case was good, or two, that Horse had pulled off a fantastic uphill shot from a moving boat, which was bad. Either way it was time to make a fast exit from the general area.

We had travelled a long way as we searched the hillsides, and when you concentrate on an activity you tend to forget about keeping track of your location. We had travelled across a number of bays as well as the main sound. By this time it was pitch black and cloud cover had come over, preventing us seeing the surrounding hills. Getting a bearing on where we were was just about impossible. We motored along for a long time, frequently shining the light on the surrounding hills in an effort to establish our location and work out the direction of travel for home.

At one point we travelled across the main sound with the spotlight turned off. When Warwick turned it back on we found ourselves just metres away from a collision with the shore. In mild panic we made a quick turn before heading off again in what we hoped was the right direction. The spotlight remained turned on from that time onward.

Through good luck, and not through good navigation, we stumbled into a bay that had a light showing at the head of it. We decided to call in to the bay and visit the occupier of the bach, with the intention of getting directions for home. It turned out that the bay we were in was the one we were looking for – Horse reckoned that he had known all along and was just having us on. Yeah, right!

I learnt a couple of things from this nautical experience that you might find handy to remember. Firstly, sheep do not have green eyes, they are short and woolly, and they have a higher cholesterol content than venison. Secondly, shooting from a boat is, generally speaking, a bad idea, and one I never tried again.

The only time my old man mentioned venison and water in the same story was when he told me how he had floated a deer or two down the Buller River tied to truck tyres as it was easier than carrying them on his back. He certainly didn't mention trying to shoot deer from the floating tyres. I think he was a bit too cunning to fall into that trap.

Winged Warriors

Marcus and Cabbage were great mates and spent a lot of time planning unusual activities together. One evening at the parachute club they announced that they were going to walk the Heaphy Track. So what, we all thought. Half the world has walked the Heaphy Track.

'No, mate,' interjected Cabbage. 'You're not hearing us right. Marcus and me are going to walk along the coast from Karamea to the Farewell Spit lighthouse. Not exactly the Heaphy Track but parallel to it all the way.'

For those of you who are unfamiliar with the Heaphy Track, I'll put you in the picture. At the top of the South Island of New Zealand, in the northwest corner, is a wilderness park named Kahurangi National Park. The park covers 452,000 hectares of bush-clad mountain country and crystal-clear rivers. There are no roads, and foot access is the only approved means of travelling within the park. Kahurangi is a Maori word that translates to 'treasured possession'. The western side of the park is bordered by the Tasman Sea and a very rugged coastline. There is no track along it. The Heaphy Track is situated within the park and is an inland track from near Collingwood, at the top of the South Island, to Karamea, on the West Coast.

Now the mental state of both Cabbage and Marcus had, at times, been a bit questionable, and this idea had some of their mates a bit worried. I was familiar with the coastline they intended to travel and I knew the going would be really tough. The coast was littered with steep cliff faces and pounding seas that would make walking along the beachfronts impossible in many places. The tide was obviously going to be a factor, and they would also have to avoid colonies of sea-lions and seals. I mentioned that I thought they were headcases for even contemplating such a venture.

Marcus's enthusiasm couldn't be dampened no matter what was said to discourage him.

'I reckon we'll see plenty of deer,' he told me. 'Do you want to come?'

'No bloody way, mate. Deer or no deer, as far as travelling that coast goes, it's dog country and I'm staying put,' I said.

It was early summer when Cabbage and Marcus took off on their adventure. They had been gone a few days when one morning at the skydiving club Paddy piped up and suggested that we go visit them. Paddy reasoned that if they were walking the coastline we should be able to find them by flying along it until we bumped into them. No one was too keen on going until Paddy announced that he would pay for the hire of the plane. About this point there was an all-in fight for the remaining three seats in the aircraft.

The fight duly sorted itself out and four of us, Paddy included, climbed on board a Cessna 207 aircraft. The victors were Junior Hoon, Doug and me.

Now Paddy is the original hard man. If it could be done he'd done it. If it couldn't be done he was on the verge of doing it. In short, Paddy was irrepressible, full on, and a great deal of fun to be around. Paddy had a real thing about anything to do with flight. I first met him on my second trip to the parachute club.

There was Paddy with his parachute laid out on the floor. He had a large pair of scissors and he was happily chopping great lengths off the support lines. I was a bit dubious when I later saw him with a simple needle and thread sewing the shortened lines back onto his chute. The parachute itself was a square one – one of the first to come into New Zealand. If it flew Paddy was into it first, or as near to first as he could be.

Paddy worked in the venison recovery business as a bulldogger, someone whose job was to jump out of airborne helicopters onto fleeing wild deer. He would then wrestle the deer to the ground and hog-tie its feet before cramming it into the chopper and taking off after another deer. In later years net guns were developed, which made bulldoggers obsolete, so Paddy advanced to net-gun shooter. Paddy and his mate were a great team and both made extremely good money while the venison farming industry was screaming out for stock from the wild. At the peak of the wild venison recovery period hinds were selling for over $3000 each. Some days Paddy and his pilot were bulldogging up to nine deer.

Paddy later went on to be a goldminer, possum trapper, builder, oilrig worker and expert on almost everything. There is no doubting that Paddy has brains, and lots of them. He reads science magazines prolifically and has a bent towards anything electronic. Paddy was to become a lifelong friend of mine – he is a hunting man, so I guess it was inevitable.

Junior Hoon is another real character. He's short, of medium build, game to try anything, and cheeky as they come. Most people take a liking to him before he opens his mouth. He has an infectious smile and boundless enthusiasm for life. Junior Hoon lived life in the fast lane – large motorbikes, hot-rod cars, skydiving, and anything else that was exciting. A bit of mischief wasn't too uncommon when he was around. Nothing scared Junior Hoon, and taking risks was just part of his nature. Mind you, he wasn't keen on spiders.

Doug was Junior Hoon's best mate and handbrake. Doug had

a few clues about him and spent a lot of his time keeping Junior Hoon from killing himself. Doug was an easy-going, relaxed sort of guy who was destined to succeed in life.

As we all piled into the Cessna Paddy buckled himself into the pilot's seat, completed the pre-flight checks, and soon we were flying across Tasman Bay towards our destination.

'Let's go and have a look for a deer,' Paddy suggested as the plane veered towards the mountains. That decided, he then told us he'd take us for a flight through some of the mountain country he hunted by helicopter. Even though it was now mid-morning he reckoned we could see a deer or two if we got lucky.

We entered the mountains by flying over the Tablelands and past Salisbury Hut, then flew onward over the Karamea Bend and past the Roaring Lion. After that we flew further south towards the Murchison ranges and other mountain areas I don't know the names of. All the way Paddy was hugging the mountainsides as we flew above the bushline, up and down valleys, past hanging valleys high up mountain faces, and wove through the many mountain peaks.

The scenery was incredible. If you can imagine the Rocky Mountains of America covered in snow and basking in sunshine, then you've got the picture about right. The mountains stretched into the distance as far as the eye could see. Not that I noticed the scenery much at the time as my eyes were peeled looking for deer.

We flew along one mountain face well above the bushline. The tops were covered in snow, with tussock grass poking up through it at regular intervals. I was seated up front with Paddy on my right. As I looked out my window I saw a small mountain lake below us. A large stag and a hind were running through the shallow water, sending masses of spray in their wakes.

'Two deer,' I said, pointing excitedly. Paddy couldn't see the deer from his seat so he leaned across me in an effort to get a better view, but only succeeded in throwing the plane about wildly as he forgot the 'plane needs a pilot' bit.

Having regained control, but now forgetting that we were not in a helicopter, Paddy threw the plane into a sharp wingtip turn away from the mountain towards the valley centre. The tight turn continued until we had completed a manoeuvre that resembled a loop-the-loop. At its completion we were flying straight back at the hill face. Paddy was totally absorbed in looking for the fleeing deer, which were still plainly visible to me but strangely not to him. As the mountain loomed up with terrifying speed an oblivious Paddy exalted, 'There they are . . . I see them, I see them.'

'For !!#!!**!# sake, Paddy, we're going to crash!' Doug yelled from the back of the plane, furiously pulling at Paddy's shirt to try to bring him back to the reality of our impending doom.

Paddy's action was immediate. His face told the story, and absolute horror describes it well. He pulled hard on the control stick and again veered to the right. I held my breath, eyes flared wide and my butt puckering flat out. I was sure a crash was unavoidable and readied myself for the impact. Junior Hoon in the back was uncharacteristically quiet.

The ground welled up fast as Paddy continued to fight with the controls. I swear our wheels touched down momentarily and dew was sprayed over the plane's front windscreen as the prop cut through tussock.

Incredibly, the inevitable crash didn't happen. We found ourselves once again flying over great open spaces, hugely relieved to be alive. Paddy, irrepressible as always, stated that he'd planned it that way and enquired what the fuss was about. Doug answered by vomiting into a pullover he'd brought with him. The smell, in the confined plane, was not pleasant but we suffered it in silence. We were all lost in thoughts of our recent near-death experience.

Paddy continued to maintain that we were never in any danger as he had it 'worked out' to the last millimetre. I noticed, however, that from then on we didn't fly close to the mountain any more.

Turning towards the West Coast, we began our search for Marcus and Cabbage. Having located the township of Karamea, their intended starting point, we flew north along the coast looking for them.

The coast was exactly as I remembered it – very rugged and impenetrable, with waves pounding the shore at regular intervals. As we searched we saw seals, sea-lions and a vast variety of birdlife. From above, the coastal bush looked very thick and wind-lashed.

'There they are!' exclaimed Junior Hoon, pointing at two figures running along a small shingle beach. What a sight lay below us. Cabbage and Marcus were literally running for their lives. A large sea-lion was lumbering after them and seemed to be gaining ground. I held my breath, fearing they would not make it to safety. It was a close thing but both managed to scramble up onto a large protruding rock, just avoiding being crushed to death by the sea-lion. I couldn't help but wonder if the sea-lion thought Marcus and Cabbage were also bull sea-lions and that they were after his females. After all, both had pot bellies and might bear a resemblance to bull sea-lions with their kit off.

Paddy couldn't resist a bit of showing off, so he did a fly-by at very low altitude. This provoked a non-flattering hand signal in response from Marcus. Cabbage was busy checking that he was still in one piece, but soon regained his composure.

Not satisfied with one fly-by, Paddy proceeded to do another two or three, each time barely missing them with the plane's wheels. When the humour of this had definitely passed, Cabbage armed himself with a rock and had us fair in his sights ready for the next pass. Fortunately Paddy spotted the potential danger and veered off to one side well out of Cabbage's throwing range. We were close enough to see that Cabbage meant business.

Well, the challenge had been made. 'What ammo's on board?' Paddy asked.

A quick search revealed Doug's spew-filled garment and a first-aid kit. Everyone agreed that Doug's garment would be the first to go, followed by anything else that wasn't tied down. The next fly-by was made just out of Cabbage's range. A few civil aviation rules were bent and out went the spew-filled garment. It fluttered down well wide of the mark, which in hindsight was a good thing. I suspect their sense of humour might not have stretched to getting clobbered by a spew-filled missile. Still, since we missed, I'll never know.

Next went some rolls of bandage from the first-aid kit. These harmless, but well-aimed, missiles caused Cabbage and Marcus to duck to one side, which wasn't easy as they were still finely balanced on their safety rock with the sea-lion eagerly waiting for them below.

Next came disinfectant and a tube of Savlon antiseptic cream. After this we ran out of ammo so Paddy, bored with this game, took off out to sea. A few kilometres offshore he did a tight turn and barrelled back towards the shore. He was only a few feet above the sea, and the plane was aimed straight at Marcus and Cabbage. As we got closer that glazed look came over Paddy again. He had a target in his sights and nothing was going to stop him. We charged towards the coast. Did I mention the cliff face directly behind our intended target? Again my heart missed a beat as certain death loomed up on us.

'Paddy, you ##***#**##* idiot!' roared Doug, who had had about enough of Paddy's flying for one day. Having received the message Paddy pulled the plane into a near-vertical climb before doing a wing over and peeling off to one side. This time he got a real flea in his ear from both Doug and Junior Hoon. I was busy trying to hold my breakfast down so I didn't contribute much to proceedings at that point.

A wing waggle to say goodbye and we were off. Needless to say, a few bums were bared in the final fly-by. Hey, it's a tradition. Didn't the same thing occur at Salisbury Hut with our fish and chips?

We continued up the coast to the Farewell Spit lighthouse before turning east and taking a straight, over sea, route home. In about 20 minutes we had travelled the route Marcus and Cabbage would take five days to walk. The return flight to Nelson airport was uneventful, with Paddy pulling off a perfect landing on our arrival. The plane belonged to Paddy's boss, and I suspect an oversight might have occurred when it came to paying the rental.

Paddy learnt a lesson or two from this flight:

1. A fixed-wing plane does not fly like a helicopter.
2. There is no airstrip to land on where we touched down in the mountains.

I haven't been up in a plane with Paddy since that day. I would if he asked me, but fortunately he hasn't.

My old man told me a lot of stories about hunting for deer but he never mentioned any excursions from the air.

A Gorge-us Hunt

Word got around Hokitika quicker than crabs get around a brothel – Graham, a local, had bagged five deer. Some semi-serious interrogation had established the general area of his success, although no one believed him when he said he had shot the deer at the back of Lake Kaniere. No way was this true. Graham was a self-respecting hunter type and the exact whereabouts of his hunting hotspot would need a more cunning method of extraction.

At a local watering hole a group of keen hunters, myself included, listened intently as Graham told the story of his successful hunt. The tale of the difficult stalk through tangled supplejack, bush lawyer and dense bush had us all on tenterhooks.

The deer twigged to Graham's approach before he could reach an ideal position for shooting, and realising that the lead hind was about to thump her leg down to give warning to the others, Graham had opened up while still semi-entangled in bush lawyer. His first shot dropped her on the spot, causing the others to mill around too long for their own good. Graham managed to bag all five before any made it back into the bush from the slip face they were feeding on.

As we listened we were merrily feeding beer after beer into Graham in an effort to relax his guard and establish the true location of his success. A small fortune had crossed the bar without a single slip of the tongue being made by Graham, who remained intent on hanging on to his secret while consuming as much free beer as he could.

I took it upon myself to slip from the bar and frisk his vehicle, which was parked outside begging to be searched. You never know your luck, I thought, Graham just might have been silly enough to leave his hunting permit in his ute. If he had, I would at least know which hunting block he had been on.

I was leaning through the door of the ute with my bum up and head down, making a hasty search of Graham's glovebox, when I was caught in the beam of a very strong torch.

'What do you think you're up to, lad?'

Bloody hell! It was the law. A bit of quick thinking was called for.

'Gidday, officer. My mate Graham's inside boasting about the five deer he shot. He's trying to convince everyone he shot them up the Styx River behind Lake Kaniere. He told me the permit that'll prove it is in this glovebox. I'm having a look for it now.'

'I reckon he's having you on all right, young fellow,' the policeman replied. 'Graham surely wasn't there, nor were the deer he shot.'

'How do you know that?' I asked.

'Because he was hunting behind my mate's place. I was there when he rang and asked permission to cross his land.'

Now I was on to something. It took a bit more weaselling but I finally got the location out of my new friend. It probably helped that I played rugby with his son-in-law.

Armed with my new knowledge, I returned to the hotel feeling very smug indeed. A hunting excursion into new territory was brewing in my mind already. I watched and listened as the others kept plying Graham with drinks but made no headway on their mission. Strangely enough, I was no longer buying Graham drinks, but I enjoyed the excessive hospitality supplied by the others. My lips were also sealed.

Later I consulted with my mate Paddy and we planned an overnight hunting trip into the said area for the next fine weekend. We weren't sure when that would be, since the Coast had been experiencing a spell of very wet weather. I duly arranged a permit covering the next month, and including an adjacent hunting block to the one I wanted to hunt. A man can't be too careful in a small town. The man from the DoC office might well let others know where I was hunting, and I didn't want that, did I?

Paddy and I were headed to Doctors Creek, which is really more of a small river than a creek, and runs parallel to and south of the Hokitika River. I purchased a map of the area and spent hours studying it. Strangely, I have continued this practice over the years despite the fact that a map shows only where the clearings are and the contours of the land. A map never shows how dense the bush is, how much bush lawyer it has or if you can actually traverse the ridgetops. I've also noticed that they do not indicate the whereabouts of any deer that may reside in the locality. Those you have to find yourself.

A fine Saturday eventually came our way, and after a quick phone call to the farmer to get permission to cross his land we were off. Paddy drove us to the Hokitika Gorge where we parked the ute and shouldered our packs. We stopped on the swing bridge that spans the river and watched two trout as they lazily cruised the milky glacier-fed waters. Then we walked onward, travelling around the foot of the hill through farm paddocks for another half-hour until we happened upon the farmer. He was a very pleasant chap who was happy to stop and talk. He told us how in his younger days he used to herd cattle through the Doctors Creek gorge and summer them on the flats above it. He made a point of telling us to travel the true left side of the creek when we got to the gorge itself. If we didn't, he warned, we would get ourselves bluffed above the gorge. Now this was advice that a couple of keen men needed. After this we duly said our goodbyes and walked onward.

We soon left the easy going of the farm paddocks and ventured upriver. At times it was quicker to walk in the river itself. The water was very clear but the bottom was a slimy, slippery brown. All the rocks and stones were as slippery as eels and extra care was needed to save ourselves from a very wet experience. Dense bush fell to the river edge most of the way. We came upon the occasional small sandy beach, and each was covered with deer hoofprints. On a larger clearing we found the remnants of a recently used camp. Being the cunning hunter I was I felt sure that it was the remnants of Graham's camp, and given the amount of fresh sign on the beaches it was fairly obvious that there were a few deer about.

Paddy and I were headed to the three large clearings above the gorge. The map showed that we had about five kilometres of bush to travel but, as I said, maps don't tell you how difficult the walk will be. We had no idea how long it would take us to get there and unfortunately had forgotten to ask the farmer when we had the chance. We also had to climb over the gorge and didn't know how long that would take.

Prior to leaving, Paddy and I had performed a joint packing exercise. We had divided out the weight in equal quantities to ensure that neither of us suffered more than the other. My suggestion that we put a can or two of beer in our packs was flatly rejected by Paddy. 'You don't need grog in the hills,' he had stated. I was armed with a small tent that we would share, and Paddy carried a cooking billy and the small quantity of food we needed. Add to this a sleeping bag, rifle, bullets and toothbrush each and that was about it.

As we slipped and slid along, the sides got steeper and more claustrophobic as we got further upriver until finally our way was stopped by the sheer walls of the gorge itself. While the river had only been a foot or so deep up to this point, it was considerably deeper through the gorge. We peered upriver, contemplating our next move.

'I wonder if we could sidle through it without needing to climb up and over?' Paddy pondered out loud.

'Hell, why not give it a go, eh?' was my reply as I tore on upriver. Before long I found myself hanging off shrubs and rocky outcrops as I endeavoured to climb along the near-vertical rock walls. I was finely balanced with one arm at full stretch above my head and holding on to a small shrub as I pondered a long jump onto the next rock that protruded from the river. Having made the decision that the manoeuvre was on I let go of the shrub at about the same time as it let go of the rock wall. I made a heroic lunge for safety and my boot reached the safety of the rock but my momentum caused it to slip over the side and onto the brown slippery surface just beneath the water. All hell broke loose as I desperately scrambled to recover from this predicament. Arms flailing, I went arse over kite and fell backward full length into the river. My desperate and unsuccessful efforts to keep my rifle out of the water only served to add to Paddy's amusement as he looked on. Several acres of skin had been removed from my elbows and hands by the rock face, and blood flowed freely into the river as I recovered my composure and carefully regained my feet. Paddy was reeling with laughter as I stood there up to my chest in water. All I could think of at that moment was, 'Thank God there are no sharks in New Zealand rivers.'

Having abandoned all thoughts of travelling through the gorge we duly set about climbing above it. It was about 7.30 p.m. by this time and we still had about two hours of daylight left before dark. Since the farmer had told us the easiest route through the gorge was to travel above it on the true left of the river, a very wet me set off up the side of the hill. 'Where the hell are you going?' asked Paddy.

'The true left of the river. That's what the farmer said, didn't he?'

'Yeah, but that's not the true left. You're going up the wrong side,' Paddy replied.

At that point we had a lengthy discussion on the matter of which side was or was not the 'true left' of the river. Paddy reckoned the true left of a river was the left-hand side as you faced upriver. I thought it was the left-hand side as you faced downriver. When boiled down, neither of us was really certain which was correct, so in the end we decided to toss a coin and be guided by luck. We had a 50/50 chance of getting it right so it was as good a method of sorting out our dispute as any.

Up we went on the left-hand side as we faced upriver. The going was very steep and tiring. We climbed hand over hand in most places, and it soon became apparent that we should have started the climb well before reaching the gorge itself. Sweat dripped into my eyes, twigs and dirt fell down the top of my shirt, and I soon wished I wasn't hanging so precariously to the cliff face. Things weren't helped any by Paddy constantly prodding me from below with the barrel of his rifle and telling me to hurry up. Progress was very, very slow. On more than one occasion the bush I was hauling myself up on gave way under my weight and I came close to taking Paddy and me on a long plunge to a rocky demise below. At another point Paddy mentioned in rather strong terms that if I didn't take my foot off his head he would propel me up the cliff face by means of a bullet up my butt. What more encouragement does a man need to become an efficient mountaineer?

Two hours soon disappeared and so did the daylight. A dilemma confronted us. We were still hanging somewhat precariously on the face we were climbing, could not possibly make our destination by nightfall, and we were feeling very tired. We jointly decided to camp up at the first suitable site we could find. The light had all but faded to darkness when we came upon a narrow, bush-covered ledge. A bit of clearing soon created enough room for our tent, which we hastily erected. There wasn't much space for anything else.

Our next dilemma soon surfaced. We had no water. Paddy decided that he would take a quick sidle around the face we were on to see if there was a stream nearby. He didn't get far in the darkness before getting into difficulty and soon returned to the safety of the tent. It doesn't take a brain surgeon to figure out that dehydrated food isn't much use without water. Add to that the fact that both Paddy and I were as dry as buffalo chips in the Sahara.

'Now don't you wish you hadn't told me to leave the beers behind?' I asked Paddy in a condescending sort of way. All I got in reply was a grumpy look.

'Wouldn't a beer go down well now?' I persisted. Still no reply. 'Didn't you hear me?' I pressed.

'Don't give me this shit,' Paddy finally replied. 'It won't do you any harm to go without. Look at the gut on ya.'

I think his sense of humour had reached its limit. We were getting personal. Without any further ado I reached into Paddy's pack and pulled out two not-so-cold bottles of beer. Unbeknown to Paddy I had slipped them into the pack back at his caravan when he went to the men's room and after he'd said we weren't taking any.

Strangely enough Paddy wasn't upset at all by this turn of events and promptly joined me in consuming the beverages. We dispensed with an evening meal and used the beer to wash down a packet of biscuits we had with us. Very tasty.

The uncomfortable night soon passed. While I didn't think I'd slept a wink, Paddy complained bitterly about my snoring in his ear. I told him that if he'd kept his ear a bit further away

I wouldn't have been able to snore in it. Both our senses of humour were a bit stretched that morning.

It didn't take long to pack, and we soon continued our upward climb. We had decided to press on to the Doctors Creek flats. The going soon became easier as we crested the worst of the gorge walls, then we found ourselves climbing through areas of crown fern, semi-open bush, bush lawyer and dense supplejack. We were forever untangling ourselves from the rope-like supplejack vine and the going was again very slow. I was leading as we crested a rise, and before us was a small area that was flat and covered in crown fern. Standing peering at us, side on and in the middle of it, was a large hind. She was happy to just stare at us and made no effort to run. It took me only a millisecond to raise my rifle, centre the crosshair on her front shoulder and let loose a shot. The deer was only 30 metres away and a kill was a certainty. The smoke hadn't even cleared before the hind leapt over a fallen log and bolted away through the tangled undergrowth. She gave no indication of being hit. I immediately gave chase and took a bearing on her direction as she disappeared over the brow of a small rise. Only a few seconds had elapsed from the time I sighted the deer until it disappeared from view.

'You bloody missed,' roared Paddy. 'Don't bother chasing it. It'll be miles away by now.'

There was no doubt about it, she was hit all right, I told Paddy with complete certainty. No one misses from that close. Hell, the barrel was nearly touching it.

Paddy was having a field day taking the mickey out of me, directing his most colourful and descriptive language at me and my poor shooting ability. Well, I wasn't going to accept that I had missed, and I set out to find the deer, which was sure to be dead by now. I searched for over an hour without success. I found the deep tracks of the fleeing deer and followed them for some distance. At no time did I find any blood that would have supported my theory that I had hit it. Paddy was so sure I had missed that he never even helped with the search. He simply followed me as I searched, constantly thinking up new lines of derision about my shooting powers.

I guess I deserved all I got, given what I had dished out to him when he had failed to see the hind at Lake Kaniere some months earlier. Finally, in disgust, I admitted defeat and gave up the search. Paddy had also had enough of fighting with the supplejack and we decided to return home. That feeling of being absolutely gutted came over me yet again. Another deer had escaped. I was beginning to have grave doubts about my future in the hunting game.

When we finally made it down to the river I set up a target on the bank with a view to testing my rifle. The target was about 40 metres away. I fired three shots across the river, all of which missed the target altogether. The shots fell all over the place, with no two landing in the same area. A quick examination of my scope revealed that the crosshair inside was also falling about all over the place. Clearly the scope had suffered some major damage when I had fallen the previous evening while playing mountaineer in the gorge. Some rather obvious dents and scratches gave support to this theory.

As we walked back to the ute through the farmer's paddocks I noticed some deer fencing that was nearly hidden behind a large pile of fallen trees. Further investigation revealed a deer trap that was protruding from the foot of a small ridge that led onto the farmer's property. Most of the trap was hidden in the native bush but the bottom end, which had first attracted my attention, threaded through the fallen trees. Clearly the trap required further investigation. I crept up on the enclosure and discovered two hinds had been caught in it. They were busily pacing the fenceline looking for a means of escape. There was none. Paddy and I watched them for a while then I investigated further. The trap had been cleverly placed at the foot of the ridge. Above it was a well-worn deer track that had previously led to the open paddocks below. The farmer (presumably) had erected the large, high-fenced enclosure at the ideal location to catch the wild deer as they came off the ridge and onto his paddocks for a feed of lush green grass. Above the trap at either side of the entrance was a single strand of number eight fencing wire that was pulled taut at about waist height across the entire ridge. This wire steered the deer towards the open entrance to the trap. Once inside, the deer walked into a concealed wire. This wire was attached to a possum trap that was sprung and pulled a pin out, releasing the hinged gate. The gate was suspended like an open cat-door and fell downward, closing the entrance and trapping the deer inside. Given that the whole trap would have cost no more than three or four hundred dollars to erect, and that each wild deer caught at that time was fetching up to three thousand dollars, it was a very profitable enterprise.

Paddy got a bit excited about those deer, and I nearly had to confiscate his rifle to stop him releasing them from their tortured existence by means of a quick execution and fast trip to his freezer. He reasoned that deer were still listed by the government as noxious pests and the trap was on government land for which we had a permit. By his reasoning our permit allowed us to take deer from our authorised hunting block. That trap was on our authorised hunting area and therefore the deer were ours. The effort of stopping him fell just short of applying a restraining hold and carrying him out on my back.

As I pondered the events of this trip a number of things came to light:

1. I was not going to take up mountaineering.
2. Paddy knew more swear words than I did.
3. You work out the 'true left' and 'true right' of a river by facing downstream and knowing which is your left hand.
4. If your rifle takes a big knock during a hunt take the time to fire a couple of test shots through it to check the sights have not been affected. You may scare off a deer or two by doing this but at least you won't miss one later on if you get the chance.

I decided to give my old man a call to see if he'd ever had trouble with his rifle when he was hunting. They never had scopes in his hunting days so in all likelihood he hadn't. He never mentioned it if he did.

Up Slippery Creek

Back in town I managed to keep quiet about the deer I missed up Slippery Creek. Slippery Creek was my code name for Doctors Creek, since I didn't want to destroy the secret status bestowed upon it by Graham. Unfortunately Paddy didn't see things the same way as I did and told everyone he met of my misfortune. Perhaps I was being a bit sensitive – on the other hand, given the number of people who had suddenly taken to calling me Davy Crockett, perhaps I wasn't.

My sorrows were drowned at the Red Lion Hotel where Jim gave me a fair hearing and shouted me a beer or two to help me forget. By the time I'd bought a few of my own I was ready to get right back on the horse and get me a deer or two. I'd noticed that while the Red Lion Hotel had a large open fire, around which many a beer was consumed, it did not have the required huge stag's head that should be prominently displayed above it. I raised the matter with Jim, who fully agreed that this was an unfortunate omission and appointed me 'hunter of the head', dispatching me back into the hills to resolve the problem.

One small difficulty occurred to me when I sobered up. To date

I hadn't even shot a stag, let alone a huge, world-class trophy one. Oops, must've been the beer talking. I decided this was the sort of mission best tackled alone, away from any source of ridicule or distraction, and during the roar that was fast approaching. Now all hunters know that the roar is the only time of the year that the red stags are vocal. They give their lion-like moans in their endeavours to attract wanton hinds and to warn off promiscuous juvenile stags. This occurs over a two- to three-week period in April and it is the time when the stag has his best set of antlers on. I planned my attack for this period, although I was well aware that most hunters on the Coast also hunt the roar. I didn't want to be in the hills surrounded by trigger-happy once-a-year hunters so I planned to take some annual leave and make my foray into the bush in the middle of the week, knowing that most hunters attach their hunting trip to a weekend.

I decided on Slippery Creek for my roar hunt. I'd viewed the area with Paddy and had noted the many ridges and creeks that fed into the main river. I figured that I would select a creek and follow it up until I found a good campsite for a base. After that, getting a trophy stag would be a mere formality.

So, one Tuesday in early April I left work early and drove to the Hokitika Gorge carpark. Mike had been very understanding about my desire to shoot a stag and had let me knock off early and on full pay. Great bloke Mike. It was a typical autumn day. The skies were clear, the sun was weak and it soon gave way to the chill of early evening. I walked quickly past the farm paddocks and made my way up Slippery Creek, then headed up the last side creek on the 'true right' before the gorge started. The going was slippery and obstructed by the many trees and logs that jammed the creek at regular intervals. The creek bed was cold and damp, and while it might have been appealing to a deer it left me feeling somewhat uninspired.

A solid 40 minutes' climbing and a lot of sweat later brought me to a modest slip that was covered in grass and had fresh deer droppings liberally dispersed over it. Clearly this was a spot visited by the local deer population when seeking a break from the cover of the oppressive bush. I reasoned that the chill of night would condense the air and create a cool downhill breeze by morning, therefore I needed to erect my tent somewhere below the slip to ensure that my scent was not carried to the unsuspecting stag I sought.

I traversed away and downhill from the creek. About five hundred metres away I found a small depression in the bush and set up camp there. My tent filled the entire space but it met my requirements for a night out. After quickly setting up my base I returned to the slip and secreted myself in the bush where I had a clear view of it. Nothing appeared so after a while I returned to the tent by torchlight. As usual, I had difficulty getting used to my own company. I was fine while I was busy doing things but when all was quiet and I was lying in my sleeping bag with nothing but my thoughts for company I was overcome with that lonely, isolated feeling I described earlier. It usually takes a day or two on my own for me to get over these feelings.

It was a long and uncomfortable night. I hadn't taken a bedroll or any other form of mattress and slept directly on the tent floor. The ground underneath the tent was cold and damp, and it didn't warm up even with me lying there all night. Add to this the numerous tree roots that criss-crossed beneath me and you get the overall picture.

I crawled out of my tent as the day turned from pitch black to that hazy first light. Mist hung heavily in the air, giving a damp start to the day. As I had expected, there was a steady downhill breeze, which allowed me an into-the-wind approach to the clearing. I stood for a while beside the tent letting the blood circulate through my stiff and sore body. The bush was deathly quiet and the misty fog that hung in the air only served to heighten the mystique of the forest.

I quietly made my way through the bush towards the slip. The forest was damp underfoot and even stepping on small fallen branches failed to create any noise. A man had to wonder why deer would choose this wet area to live in but the sign proved they had.

The quietness of the bush also helped the deer avoid detection. I would have to keep a vigilant eye out for movement.

I eased towards the slip and squatted down in a spot that gave me a good view of it. There was nothing out when I arrived but I elected to wait a while to see if daylight encouraged any movement. The mist wasn't showing any sign of letting up, which probably wasn't helping the situation any. I waited for about an hour before my patience ran out. Since it was the start of the roar I decided it was about time to offer the local stags some encouragement.

In preparation for the trip I had visited a local deer farm and spent some time listening to the stags roaring in their paddocks. I in turn gave them my own version of a lovesick stag. They didn't seem too upset by my efforts, and some even joined in to create a symphony with me.

I stood up, cleared my lungs, took a deep breath and gave my best shot at pretending to be a stag roaring. It wasn't long before my throat became hoarse and dry, and I ended the effort with a long coughing fit. If that didn't wind things up nothing would. I strained my ears, waiting for the sound of stags crashing through the bush towards me, intent on tackling this new threat to their harems. Alas, not a sound was heard in reply. Several more attempts ended with the same result, and I decided my efforts must have scared them off. Having established this I set off on a slow climb uphill into the wind. I had soon climbed onto a nearby ridge and was surprised at the openness of the bush there. I had a clear view at times of up to several hundred metres. Most of the time I could see at least 50 metres in one direction or the other. I gave frequent roars as I went, hoping to provoke a reply. The higher I climbed the more open the bush became, in total contrast to the dense, almost impenetrable bush in the valleys and creek beds below. At one point I came upon several hectares of a fine, light-green-coloured fern. It was a magical spot that reminded me of a misty scene in Sherwood Forest from the movie *Robin Hood*. I sat and watched this area for a long time before escaping its magic.

I had no trouble imagining a stag walking proudly through the fern with his impressive head held high.

By about 10.30 I had become bored with bush-stalking and decided to return to the tent to get my book, which I had forgotten to take with me when I left first thing in the morning. It was my habit to take a book with me when I bush-stalked, and when I found myself getting tired or bored I would find a spot with a good view and sit down for a read. Each time I turned the page I'd cast my eyes around, without making any bodily movements, to see if a deer had entered my area of vision. When suitably rested I'd resume hunting again. Try it some time. I have bagged a number of deer over the years while sitting quietly reading a book.

I returned down the same open ridge that I'd climbed. I still gave the occasional roar but by that time my throat had become very hoarse and sore. I approached the slip with caution. I'm not sure why, as the wind was still coming downhill behind me and would surely be carrying my scent to anything below me. Still, you never know, do you?

As soon as the slip came into view I stopped and watched. Moments later a movement below caught my eye. Directly below me, about 50 metres away, I saw a bush shaking and swaying vigorously. There was no way the birds could be causing such a commotion so further investigation was needed. I sidled across a short distance in an attempt to take my scent away from the direction of the bush and quietly moved downward.

Suddenly, from behind the bush walked a huge stag. He had his head down and was intent on beating up the bush. Clearly he had no idea that I was about. I raised my rifle and eased a round into the breech. As I looked through the scope I saw that the stag had a very, very impressive set of antlers and I started shaking uncontrollably. Buck fever? I'd read about it and here I was experiencing the whole gambit. I lowered my rifle and took a few very deep breaths. I knew the stag wasn't in a hurry by the way he was giving the bush a solid working over so all I had to do was get my shit together and he was mine. A few more deep breaths and I had myself under control. By this time the stag was standing side on to me and presented an easy target at a distance of about 40 metres. I raised the rifle and centred the crosshairs on the middle of his front shoulder. Another deep breath and a word of caution to myself to squeeze the trigger and not jerk it. The loud boom of the shot shattered the silence and I watched overjoyed as the stag cartwheeled downhill at the impact of the bullet. It came to rest about 30 metres below the point where it was standing when I shot it.

I ran down the hill towards the stag, only to see it stagger unsteadily to its feet. It stood watching me, unable to walk off. It was hit hard for sure so I stopped and watched. It made to walk off and fell over, again rolling down the hill. I felt there was no point in putting another shot into it as the stag was clearly about to drop dead of its own accord. I couldn't believe it when the stag again got to its feet and made to stagger off. I wasn't worried as it staggered from tree to bush, bouncing off them as it went. I walked quietly along behind it, keeping back a fair distance so as not to spook it any further. As I crested a small rise I found the stag standing with its legs splayed. It strained its neck to look back and watch my approach, clearly on its last legs. It made no effort to get away. Feeling sorry for the animal I decided to put it out of its misery with a shot to the base of the neck. I loaded another bullet into the chamber of my rifle and slowly raised it. As I did so I accidentally touched the hair trigger and a shot fired into the ground in front of me. This gave the stag a new lease of life and it took off in full flight into the scrub ahead. I could have wept. How could I be so stupid? How could this be happening?

I can tell you that at that point I was very near to crying. I was in the bush miles from anywhere, and who was going to know but me? I was feeling pretty upset by this turn of events, but I managed to gather my wits again and set off to find the stag – after all, it was dead on its feet anyway. I tried to follow its tracks and for a short distance I was successful, but I lost the trail above a very deep old creek bed. I found a way down into it but couldn't find any sign of the stag anywhere. I finally found some deer tracks and set off after them, some time later realising that they couldn't belong to my stag. There was no blood and my stag was well hit. Very well hit, so I should have found blood at some point well before then.

I returned to the point of origin and started my search again but try as I did I could not find that deer nor any sign of him. I fell into a state of depression and eventually gave up looking. The stag bogeyman had struck for the second time.

I had no way of knowing exactly how many points the stag had as I didn't stop to count them before getting my first and only ever dose of buck fever. I clearly remember the head being a very wide bowl shape with many points on the tops. I'm too scared to even venture a guess at the number of points it had, but suffice to say that it came from the Rakaia herd, which is famous for its huge trophy heads. How can I say this? Well, Slippery Creek runs parallel to the Hokitika River. The Whitcombe River runs into the Hokitika River and the Rakaia herd entered the West Coast via Whitcombe Pass. So there you have it – a huge Rakaia trophy stag gone to waste.

I packed up and returned home a very despondent fellow. I went over and over events thousands of times in my head as I walked out. How could it be that I had not been able to find that stag?

That night I sat in the Red Lion Hotel staring blankly at the wall where Jimmy had promised to hang my trophy head. So far so good, but the head was still missing. Jimmy's promise of unlimited beers should I donate such a stag to his pub was inspiration enough for any young fellow. The more I drank the more I knew I could find that stag. It was there in the bush dead as a dodo and waiting for me to come and get it. Come and get it I would. That decided, I swallowed a couple more beers, arranged to borrow a motorbike in the morning and went home to sleep off my efforts at drowning my misery.

The next morning found me mounted on the motorbike screaming through the countryside on my way to recover the stag. It was as good as found. The motorbike would shorten the trip by about an hour as I could ride it across the Hokitika Gorge swing bridge and through the farm paddocks to the mouth of Slippery Creek.

I made the long walk back up to the slip determined to locate the stag and return triumphant. With sweat dripping into my eyes I arrived back at the point where I had accidentally discharged the bullet and set off to find my stag. I walked directly to the point where the stag had disappeared into the creek and jumped straight in. I continued onward and to my total amazement almost immediately found a very large pool of frothy dark red blood on and beside a large ponga trunk where the stag had stopped to rest. The blood was full of large air bubbles, a sure sign that the stag had been lung shot. How in the world I had missed finding this the day before had me completely stumped.

Now, where was the stag? He hadn't travelled far from the point where I'd accidentally fired the shot into the ground to the point where he had rested against this trunk. Given this it was unlikely that he would have moved far from the spot where I was standing. I searched for tracks and soon found some heading uphill. I couldn't believe what I saw. Surely the stag was so badly injured it wouldn't be heading uphill. I soon found a few spots of what I believed was blood to confirm that I was wrong, then the trail petered out in a mass of crown fern. Was I beaten again? Surely not. I searched and searched and searched some more. I never found that stag, and eventually I returned home once again empty-handed. The walk out seemed even longer than the day before. I was feeling absolutely gutted by this turn of events, and declared that if I ever met the stag bogeyman in person I was going to choke him out.

Today, many years after these events, I still have a recurring nightmare about that stag. I wake up each time filled with the same feeling of despair that I felt at the time of my failure. Who says the past can't haunt you?

Now there is a lesson or two in this lot. I didn't learn them at the time, but I can apply them to this situation now.

1. When a wounded red deer takes off it will usually travel in a relatively straight line, taking the route of least resistance as it goes. Had I taken off after the stag and maintained the same course I had seen it take, I would have caught up with it the morning I shot it.
2. I now believe that the tracks I saw heading uphill from where I found the frothy blood did not belong to the stag. I also believe that I did not find small spots of blood as I thought. The stag was dead on its feet and would have lunged downhill to its final resting place. I allowed myself to believe that the stag had gone uphill and didn't do the obvious of searching downhill. An animal losing that much blood couldn't have gone uphill and left so little evidence.
3. I should have stopped at one of the many deer farms I rode past and asked to borrow one of their farm dogs. It would have found the stag in an instant. Me being young and foolish probably didn't help.

I think my old man located every stag he ever shot at. When you shoot them in the eye they don't go far, do they? He never mentioned losing any if he did.

Spotted Mullet

Gary and I sat in the Red Lion Hotel looking through the large windows and watching his father, Ralph, extract a dinghy from the Hokitika River. Protruding over the bow of the boat was a set net that he had just collected from the river mouth. The dinghy was a small lightweight aluminium one so we didn't feel the need to offer him any assistance.

'Does your old man catch many fish?' I asked Gary.

'Never seems to go hungry,' was his noncommittal answer.

'What type of fish does he catch?' I continued, not wanting to let the topic go.

'I dunno. Let's go and ask him.'

With that we finished our beers and walked across the road to where Ralph was busy tying the dinghy to a small trailer. The work was done by now so we felt safe making an approach.

'Had any luck?' Gary asked.

'A bit,' Ralph replied as he carried on securing the boat.

'What'd you catch?'

A small nod of his head in the general direction of the floor of the boat was all the reply he could muster. Gary and I peered in and saw a mixed collection of predominantly smallish silver fish about a foot in length. There were a couple of larger fish. I had no idea what they were.

'What're they?' I asked.

'Small ones are herring. Bigger ones are spotted mullet,' replied Ralph.

'They good eating?' I enquired.

'Herring's all right. Spotted mullet's good. It's my favourite. Cooked in tinfoil with a bit of butter, lemon juice and some herbs . . .' Ralph's eyes glazed over and he licked his lips as he thought of the tasty treat he was describing. 'Nothing better.'

There were no two ways about it. Gary and I were about to have a crack at this fishing lark. After a fair bit of weaselling and a lot more fast-talking, interspersed with promises that we would take great care of his net and boat, Ralph finally and reluctantly agreed to lend us his equipment. Plans were made and the following day we were to launch our assault on the local fish population.

Gary picked me up as arranged. He had the boat in tow and we soon arrived at the launch ramp across the road from the Red Lion. We lifted the dinghy from the trailer and soon had it floating at the river's edge. Gary tossed me his car keys and told me to park the car across the road in the hotel carpark. He was going to attend to the motor-starting side of things while I was away.

The car duly parked, I returned to the river where Gary was drifting not so quietly downstream about five metres from the

shore. He was semi-kneeling on the floor of the boat, paddling furiously with only one oar as he tried to return to the riverbank. He reminded me of those native Indians of South America as they paddle their dug-out canoes on the Amazon River, but minus the relaxed environment. The outboard motor sat unattended on the riverbank where the boat should also have been.

'What the hell are you doing?' I enquired as I watched him drift further from the shore and steadily downriver.

'I'm trying to get back in. What does it bloody look like I'm doing?' came the indignant reply.

'Wouldn't it have been easier if you'd attached the motor before launching the boat?' I asked.

'Don't be a smart-arse,' replied Gary, who was fast losing the battle to return to shore. 'Give me a hand.'

'Oh yeah,' I said. 'I suppose you want me to jump in and tow you to shore?'

I was walking along beside him as he drifted merrily downriver while we exchanged pleasantries.

'Whatever it takes, but don't take all day about it,' came the terse reply as Gary increased his rowing efforts and drifted further from the shore.

I was thinking of Ralph's instructions as I watched Gary heading downriver. The time to launch the boat, he'd said, was when the tide goes slack between going out and starting to come in again. We were a bit early and hadn't quite got to the slack tide part when we put the boat in the water.

'All going well, and if you're lucky,' I yelled, 'you'll come back in when the tide changes.'

Gary failed to find any humour in this and just about ruptured his boiler while abusing me for my lack of loving care.

'Isn't there a rope in the boat?' I asked. There was. 'Don't waste your energy rowing against the river, try to angle towards that small point up ahead.'

Gary renewed his efforts, this time using the current to assist him. He soon came within easy distance of the shore and threw me the rope. Fortunately it was still tied to the bow of the dinghy.

With the rescue mission completed we towed the dinghy back to our starting point and got under way again, this time armed with a motor, life-jackets and two oars. We followed Ralph's detailed instructions and duly set the net across a portion of the river. There was nothing to do now but wait. There was little point in sitting idly on the river watching our lives slip by so we took the only real option left open to us. We promptly returned to the shore, crossed the road and joined the 'Sunday School' session at the Red Lion.

If my memory serves me right I had a shocking day on the pool table. Gary and I played for beers and he didn't appear to buy many that day. He had a great fondness for winning, and was very reluctant to leave many hours later when the time for retrieving the set net arrived. I duly ushered him across the road and together we relaunched the dinghy.

Everything went according to plan and we soon arrived at the marker buoy from which one end of the net was suspended. The dinghy was very unsteady as we pulled the net onto it. After coming close to falling into the river on more than one occasion we soon discovered that the retrieval process was far easier if done from the sitting position. At regular intervals we stopped to remove a herring or a spotted mullet from the net. In total we caught nine herring and four spotted mullet.

During the net retrieval process I had noticed the arrival of a new-looking red four-wheel-drive utility truck on the riverbank. The sole occupant watched us recover the net and our catch. With the net and the catch safely stowed at the front of the dinghy we quietly motored up and down the river investigating a few interesting possies to set it on our next fishing expedition. Then, having seen all there was to offer, we set sail for the shore. As we neared the shore Gary noticed the red ute for the first time. The driver had pulled up at the top of the ramp.

'How many fish did we catch today?' Gary asked me.

'Nine herring and four spotted mullet,' I replied.

'Right. Well, don't forget that,' Gary said.

'Ahoy, Gary,' the occupant of the ute called out as we drew near.

'Gidday, Bruce,' Gary replied.

'Get a few, did you?' asked the man.

'Yep. We done all right,' Gary said as he eased the nose of the boat onto the shore.

I jumped out holding the rope and dragged the dinghy further up the bank. The man helped us carry the dinghy to the waiting trailer and at the same time had a look at our catch. As the boat was placed on the trailer the man reached into the dinghy and took out a spotted mullet.

'What's this then?' he asked Gary, holding the fish out towards him.

Gary reached out, calmly took the fish from the man's hand, said, 'Spotted mullet', and threw it back into the dinghy.

The man retrieved the fish, held it out towards Gary again, and said, 'No, it's not. It's a trout.'

Gary again took the fish from the man's hand, calmly re-examined it, and casually tossed it back into the dinghy.

'No, mate, you're mistaken. That's a spotted mullet. No doubt about it.'

It was a statement that left no room for negotiation on the matter.

'Hang on a minute,' the bloke gasped as he yet again retrieved the fish from the floor of the dinghy. 'That's not a mullet. That's a trout. Look at the fin structure.'

'I thought you of all people would know your fish,' Gary replied. 'It's a spotted mullet, not a mullet as you call it. Take a look at the spots.' He pointed to the markings on the side of the fish.

Quite a lengthy debate followed on the subject of what sort of fish we had caught. I was none the wiser, not being a fisherman myself, but I couldn't help but wonder at the ignorance of the man. I casually glanced back into the boat and by chance noticed a small identification tag attached to a fin of one of the other 'spotted

mullets'. Now why, I wondered, would someone go to the trouble of tagging an ordinary spotted mullet? Mullet were as common as mud, weren't they? Feeling a bit concerned by this discovery I casually shuffled a few items in the boat and covered the tagged fish. Just in case, you understand.

Although the debate between Gary and the man never got heated it was certainly intense. Gary was adamant that the fish was a spotted mullet and the man was equally adamant that it was a trout. In the end the man – who coincidentally was a fish ranger who had the power to confiscate boats, cars, nets and all other equipment used to unlawfully catch the licensed and protected trout species – decided that Gary and I had made an honest error and let us off with a warning. He was even kind enough to let us keep the four offending fish, as well as the tag that he never saw.

Later on Gary continued to protest his ignorance of the trout identification issue to me, as did his father, Ralph. Ralph proclaimed that the tinfoil, butter, lemon juice and herbs formula would work just as well on trout as it did on spotted mullet.

What's this got to do with hunting? The answer is nothing at all. I've related this incident as it goes to show you the creative and interesting types that live on the West Coast and whom I had the pleasure of mixing with during my short time living there.

Before heading off into another hunting tale I just want to say that it is a very, very bad idea mixing boating and alcohol. We did and we got away with it. We were young, stupid and very lucky (in more ways than one).

Of Mountain Men and Deserts

One morning Mike summoned me to his office and told me that I'd accomplished all I could in Hokitika and it was time to move on. Hold on, mate, I argued, there are a lot of hunting spots I haven't had a look at yet. No need to rush away, is there?

Unfortunately Mike didn't share my point of view. It seemed that I was destined for greater things and the bank had decided I needed a bit more rounding off. I'd had a few beers during my time in Hokitika and argued that I was already round enough. Further, any more rounding was going to have a detrimental effect on my rugby-playing ability.

'Look at the move as a chance to hunt a bit of different country,' Mike retorted. 'There are tahr and chamois around the Mt Cook region. You'll be able to have a crack at them.'

So, I lost that argument and was duly transferred to Twizel. Hell, I'd never even heard of the place, let alone had any idea where it was. But Mike was right about one thing: Twizel was close to Mt Cook. The town is perched right in the middle of the arid MacKenzie Basin, which is on the eastern side of the mountains of the Main Divide. I was to be moved from the rainforests of the

West Coast to a high country desert in the east.

The village of Twizel was originally built to service the staff working on a major hydro development scheme that was under way at that time. It was a man's town, with most of the population of about 6800 mainly transient workers being males. In total there were no more than a dozen single women over the age of 16. Take out the less than appealing ones and you had only two or three potential girlie friends left. As you can gather, this was not a great prospect for a virile young man in the best years of his life.

So it was with a great deal of anxiety that I pulled into town. The lucky bastard who was leaving and whose job I was to fill met me and gave me a run-down on the place. I was to live in a single men's hostel, in which there were 92 occupants, one of them a woman. I had to wonder how she qualified for a room in a single men's hostel. I was to learn that she was a very popular young lady indeed.

Living in the hostel was compulsory. There was no other accommodation available as all the houses were allocated to project workers who were married. To compensate for this inconvenience my employer kindly subsidised my accommodation and meals. My living expenses plummeted.

On my first evening I was taken on a tour of the hydro development project. No two ways about it, it was a very impressive undertaking. Four new power stations were being built along 39 kilometres of man-made water canals. The canals diverted water from lakes Tekapo, Pukaki and Ohau through four additional power-generating stations before it spilled back into Lake Benmore. At the time of my arrival the project was well under way and was due for completion three years later.

My host for the tour, Alan, was a keen trout fisherman and he pointed out numerous spots that he reckoned were hot. We stopped to fish several of them, and sure enough he landed a trout each time. Now as I've already explained, I'm no fisherman, but a man's always got to keep his mind open to new experiences and opportunities. After all, I was now stuck in the desert with no women to chase so I was definitely on the look-out for activities to amuse me.

As we explored the area I was struck by the huge number of rabbits that dotted the landscape. Nearly every bend in the road revealed dozens more, in what appeared to be a never-ending mass of hunting opportunities. It didn't take a genius to figure out that the rabbits were a major problem that needed sorting out. The landscape was already a very barren one without rabbits denuding it further.

The tour finished, I was returned to barracks and unceremoniously dumped. When you don't know a single person in a town it is very easy to feel isolated and alone – a bit like staying in a hut on your own. I resorted to the tried and true method of getting to meet people and went to the local pub. There was a mixed bag of men there, most of them hard-looking characters, and the only female present was the bar lady.

Armed with a jug of beer I parked up in a corner. By chance I was sitting next to a table of middle-aged men who were talking about an upcoming rabbit drive. I eavesdropped with great interest until I finally managed to edge in on the conversation. They turned out to be members of the local deerstalkers' association, and talk soon turned to tahr, chamois, deer, Canadian geese and other local game animals. These guys made it sound like getting either a chamois or a tahr was a near-impossible task. A casual glance at their midriffs suggested that none of them would be able to venture too far up a mountain these days, and if they had in the past it must have been many pints ago. Still, they were a great bunch and I was soon armed with an invitation to join the rabbit drive, which was to take place the next morning. Shotguns were apparently the order of the day, and since I owned only two firearms – a .270 and a .22 calibre rifle – someone offered to lend me one.

The next morning I was picked up by Howie in his new 500 cc Suzuki 4 x 4. It was bright yellow, and was the subject of much derision on the part of his hunting mates during the day. We drove about ten kilometres north of town and met the others on Pukaki Downs Station. Like all the farms in the area it was dry, dusty, barren and showed little sign of what kept the resident population of sheep alive.

Up till this point I had never fired a shotgun. I was given the appropriate instructions and fired a test shot to get the idea of 'shot spread'. I was used to sending one very small and well-aimed projectile at my targets. This shotgun business seemed a bit easy given that over a distance of 15 metres the 'shot spread' covered an area larger than the size of most rabbits.

The idea was simple. We were to form a straight line, after which we were to walk slowly forward shooting any rabbit that jumped up in front of us. There was an assortment of 'the best rabbit dogs in the country', which flushed the rabbits from their hiding places. I was under strict instructions to only shoot forward, never to the side. Shoot a dog and I would be next – there wasn't much to misunderstand about that.

So it was that I came to be quietly walking the line surrounded by members of the Twizel deerstalkers' club and other assorted hangers-on. In total there were 14 of us, and every few seconds a shot was fired at a fleeing rabbit, which was left where it fell. The rabbits were certainly numerous, and the farmer whose land we were on was delighted to have us there lowering his rabbit population.

After 15 minutes I hadn't even fired a shot. Plenty of rabbits had sprung up in front of me but I'd failed to get a bead on them before the hunter on either side of me fired and killed it. They were very quick and had obviously had a lot of practice.

The line gradually became less straight as we travelled a dry creek bed that was liberally dotted with matagouri bushes. Matagouri is a large, dense, rounded shrub that has large numbers of strong, needle-shaped thorns protruding from it. A stab from one of the thorns often leads to infection, or at least a very sore wound, and over time everyone became very focused on avoiding the thorns and less focused on the rabbits.

As I eased myself from between two bushes a movement to the left caught my eye. Being keen to shoot my first rabbit, and having been beaten to the draw too often already, I heaved the barrel in the general direction of the movement and touched the trigger. In the same instant I saw a dog giving chase only a foot behind the rabbit and gaining quickly. I couldn't stop and the shotgun boomed. In slow motion I saw the dog cartwheel over several times before quickly regaining its feet and scampering back to its master. There were spots of blood on one of its hindquarters and it displayed a slight limp. Strangely, the rabbit I'd hoped to hit lay dead beside the spot where the dog had fallen. Tensely I waited, poised for the next shot which, according to the briefing, would be aimed at me. I felt terrible and knew I'd stuffed up badly.

'Ya ##@%#@ mongrel!' yelled a huge man just along from me. I was really in the shit here. 'How many ##%*@© times have I told you about that? You slow-learning bastard, wait till I get my hands on you.'

I was tempted to turn and start running but I didn't really give myself a chance, having seen how good a shot the bloke was. Everyone else turned around to see what had happened. Christ, that was all I needed. I was going to have to explain myself to everyone. Welcome to Twizel, you idiot.

I was about to stammer a weak excuse when the dog sidled up to the man and was promptly given a solid kick in the ribs.

Shit, if that's what he does to the victim what's he gonna do to me? I thought.

A long string of abuse followed, but it seemed it was all aimed at the dog.

Hang on, I thought. I'm missing something here.

It turned out that the man had been trying for quite some time to train the young dog to flush out rabbits. The dog was very quick, and was never more than a pace or two behind the rabbits, which meant its owner got very few safe opportunities to shoot the rabbits and not his dog. He had fired at exactly the same moment as I had, and he thought he had shot his own dog. I wasn't about to enlighten him. In fact, I decided that I had just bagged my first rabbit by shotgun and struggled to contain a self-satisfied smirk. The dog's injuries were subsequently examined and found to be only superficial. I noted, however, that they were not exactly where they should have been if the shot had been fired by the dog's owner, but were rather more on my side of its body.

Nothing more was said about the incident, and I was duly invited to join the local deerstalkers' club. The door was opening to many new adventures.

As a point of interest, 148 rabbits were shot that morning. Many more got away. I have used a shotgun to hunt rabbits on only two occasions and this was one of them. I find rifles more to my liking, preferring their long-distance accuracy.

The following weekend there was a trap shoot at the deerstalkers' club, which I attended even though I wasn't a shotgun man. I met a few more people but found that generally speaking the keen hunters were the initial group I had stumbled upon. For most of the day I watched the competition and tried to drag information on the area's hunting prospects out of the locals. They were a tight-lipped bunch and I didn't make much headway in that department.

With the main event over I was singled out for a bit of training in the use of shotguns. I was given numerous instructions on the 'right' way to go about trap shooting, and tips such as 'Lead the target' and 'Follow through with the shot' were given with relish. With the whole club watching I was pressured into having a go. I stood behind the dug-out and gave the command 'Pull', as I'd seen occur throughout the day. The target came flying out at a fearsome rate. Holy hell, I thought, I can't hit that. I waited until it had reached the top of its upward climb and started to quietly drop from the sky. At this point I had managed to get a good sight on the target and squeezed the trigger. As the target exploded and fell to the ground an encouraging cheer went up. I heard Slim, who was my main tutor, mutter 'Fluke', then he suggested that I try again. I followed the same procedure and duly shattered the second target.

'That's not how you do it,' Slim stated flatly. 'You shoot the target on the rise. Not on the fall.'

'I can't see the problem, Slim,' I retorted. 'I'm hitting them, aren't I?'

This didn't meet with his approval at all. He took his shotgun from me and announced that he had made a mistake. The shotgun was on full choke, which limited the spread of the shot and made hitting the target more difficult (at least according to Slim it did). He proceeded to remove the offending 'full choke' and sent me up for another shot. By this time I was feeling supremely confident as I'd hit two out of two. The game was easy.

'Pull,' I instructed. The target sailed away and I followed my established procedure of waiting for it to reach its peak and start to fall before firing. This time the target continued on its way and fell to the ground intact. I couldn't figure it out. I was very confident of the shot. Subsequent shots, with the full choke removed, produced one miss after the other. Slim duly announced that I had a long way to go before getting up to speed, and retired from lesson one a satisfied man. Me, I'd decided that I was a rifle man.

Tahr-zan

Several months after my arrival I was in the cafe eating tea when a tall, skinny bloke sat down beside me and introduced himself as Richard. He went on to say that he had just spent the weekend hunting tahr on his own near Mt Cook. Like me, he was relatively new to Twizel, and he asked if I'd be interested in going on a tahr hunt with him the following weekend. Now I was definitely a starter, but I wasn't too sure how we were to go about hunting this new animal. Richard said he had seen a few on his last trip but had not been able to get close enough to take a shot at one. He wanted to return to the same area for another go.

I couldn't help but warm to Richard. He was clearly a very fit man as there wasn't a scrap of fat on him. Further, he possessed a wicked sense of humour and had a naughty look in his eye, the sort the ladies find so appealing.

That week I did a bit of research on tahr. I even spoke to the local DoC ranger to get his opinion on things. Everything I read said that tahr lived high up on the mountaintops, surrounded by dangerous icefields and unclimbable terrain. They were extremely wary, possessed terrific eyesight and were very difficult to stalk. In addition, should a man be lucky enough to shoot one he would be unlikely to be able to retrieve it because when they were shot they often fell down vertical cliff faces and smashed themselves up on the rocks below. Yep, getting a tahr was going to be a challenge all right.

I asked the ranger what type of crampons I should purchase for my intended hunt. His reply took me by surprise: 'If you need crampons, boy,' he said, 'you're hunting too high.'

I grilled him about this and his reply was simple and seemed to make sense.

'Tahr, like any other animal, need to eat. There's not much sustenance in rock so while they might prefer to live at the highest altitude possible they still have to find vegetation to eat. There's nothing much up there so they have to come down to feed. Winter's the best time as most of the tucker they like is covered by deep snow, so they are forced to come down a lot lower to eat.'

Nothing too complicated about that. I'd just saved myself a small fortune by dispensing with the need for crampons, ice pick and a whole assortment of superfluous equipment. I decided to dispense with the rope idea as well.

Richard and I settled on an overnight trip. It was early May and we had already had a few falls of snow in the township. We left in darkness one Friday evening, our destination the Whale Stream hut, which we planned to walk in to by torchlight. After a 40-minute drive from Twizel along the Mt Cook Highway we reached the new Ferintosh Station homestead, which had recently been built beside Whale Stream. The farmer was very friendly and helpful, and he gave us a few tips on the likely areas to find tahr and others to steer clear of. We also delivered a few items he had asked us to pick up for him when we rang to get permission to hunt his property.

The track up Whale Stream proved to be a narrow, stony farm road for all but the last quarter hour's walk. It was a beautiful clear, starlit night with a partial moon and the ground was covered with snow that reflected the moonlight, giving us ample visibility without our torches. That walk will always sit in my memory as one of those magic moments in the mountains. The air was cold but crisp and very clear. The mountain walls that towered above us presented in a way that I have never witnessed again despite 20 subsequent visits to this valley. They seemed to glow, and were like the guarding fortresses of a great uneven castle.

Having crunched our way through the frozen snow for an hour and a quarter we arrived to find a small, very cold, hut perched on the edge of Whale Stream. The bank of the stream was quickly eroding away and would undermine the hut if it were not moved soon.

The hut itself was very plain, and had two beds, a bench, a window and a small fireplace. There was no fuel for the fire and nothing burnable lay in the surrounding wet scrub. We resolved to bring in our own coal on any future trips and to drive in if the farmer would let us.

Richard and I discussed the morning's hunt as we cooked our tea on the small gas stoves we each carried. Richard was adamant that we should hunt together, and in the same area he had seen the tahr the previous week. That agreed, we proceeded to shake and shiver through the night in our poor-quality sleeping bags. Although there were a number of very high-quality sleeping bags on the market, neither Richard nor I could afford them and we made do with our low-level bags. A considerable portion of the night was spent awake watching large plumes of frosted breath escaping from our mouths.

Two very cold men broke the surface before dawn. Staying in bed didn't appear to be a great option given the numbness of our toes. As I was getting ready to venture forth I asked Richard how much ammo I should take with me. Like an experienced old tahr hunter, he replied, 'Just grab a handful.'

Putting complete faith in his infinite wisdom I duly reached into my pack and removed exactly a handful of bullets for the day's hunt. We set off up Whale Stream, which incidentally was frozen solid, then after a short distance we turned left and headed up a small side creek. Snow lay thick on the low vegetation and we often fell through the crusted layer of ice that covered the snow and everything beneath it. Before long my shins were badly grazed and sore from the cuts I received as I fell through the ice layer. Richard didn't suffer this problem as much as I did, being considerably lighter.

Above us was an impressive series of near-vertical bluffs, which I was later to name 'The Castle Faces'. We stopped often and glassed the bluffs but saw nothing, so we decided to traverse to the right and take a look in the next gully. After a lot of slipping and sliding through ice and snow we finally eased ourselves up to the crest of the small ridge and got a clear view into the gully. I took the first look and couldn't believe my eyes when I immediately saw a herd of about nine tahr feeding at the base of the bluffs there. I beckoned Richard to join me and it took him a while to focus on the spot where the animals were quietly feeding. After a hasty retreat we discussed our options. We decided we were too far off for a shot, and elected to sneak closer by staying hidden behind the ridge and continuing upward.

After a stiff climb I again snuck over the ridgetop for a look. The tahr were still feeding quietly and had no idea we were there. We couldn't climb any higher owing to the ominous rockface that stood in our way, so it was now or never. We commando-crawled over the ridgetop, taking care not to skyline ourselves in the process. The shots we had to take were still two hundred or more metres uphill. Getting comfortable was near on impossible and neither of us could find a useful rifle rest despite having all the time in the world to do so. I could see a number of nannies but I wasn't able to locate the bull tahr. Richard confirmed that he couldn't see a bull either.

Time ticked away slowly, both of us itching to let loose but hoping to sight a bull tahr before we did so. Eventually a large beast emerged from a previously unseen nook in the rocks and headed down towards the feeding nannies. I frantically whispered to Richard that a bull was coming our way but he couldn't see it and I couldn't exactly stand up and point it out to him.

'He's right out in the open,' I whispered. 'I'm going to have a go.'

'Right you are, mate,' came his seafaring reply. 'I still can't see him but I'll take a nanny for food anyway. Give the three count when you're ready.'

'Three, two, one, fire.'

All hell broke loose. I clean missed the bull but I could see where the bullet had struck rock between his legs. Richard also missed. Both of us hastily reloaded and fired again, and again and again. My rifle took only four bullets so I soon found myself reloading before opening up again on the quickly fleeing animals. I was amazed at how quickly they could move over the steep, rocky ground. Having emptied my second magazine of bullets I thumbed the remaining two rounds I had into the magazine. Neither of us had had any joy so far.

The bull I'd been chasing uphill disappeared from view. I was gutted. Eight shots and not a single hit. Then, for reasons I still cannot fathom, the bull walked back into full view and silhouetted himself on the skyline above me. I aimed well above him and fired again. The bull stood there unmoving and I again thought that I had missed. Then, after a short time, he buckled at the knees and fell to the ground dead. I had finally worked out the range and was aiming about a foot over the top of the bull's back when I shot him. I was ecstatic and yelled out loud to celebrate. As I did this a huge bull came into full view about 30 metres above the one I'd just shot. Compared to my bull this one was massive – perhaps a third bigger in bodyweight and carrying a much longer and darker mane on his chest. I could not assess the length of his horns, as the distance was too great.

I struggled to control myself. There was the ultimate – my dream bull. I had no idea whether Richard had seen the animal or not, but I soon steadied my sights several feet above his chest, which was front on to me. I was very unsteady and not at all confident of the shot. I fired and saw the bullet kick up rock dust between his legs. He turned but failed to run off. I quickly worked the bolt action and steadied myself for the next shot. I was really comfortable with the shot and felt that I knew exactly how much fall I had to allow for to bag this animal. I squeezed the trigger in expectation of hearing the boom and seeing the bull fall to the ground. Nothing.

No boom, nothing more than an insignificant click as the firing pin landed on an empty chamber. I had run out of bullets.

Words cannot describe how I felt. There, standing on a rock high above me, was a great trophy bull tahr and I had run out of bullets.

In the hut far below I had another 20 or more spares that I had taken the trouble to carry up the valley but failed to bring up to where it counted. How stupid could I be?

Meanwhile Richard was still busy firing at the quickly vanishing animals, until he also ran out of bullets. I thought of his reply to my earlier question about how much ammo I would need, but there was no need to rub it in. Richard was feeling somewhat embarrassed and it showed.

We struggled up to where my bull lay. A quick examination soon revealed that I hadn't bagged a world record or anything near to it, but nonetheless I had a bull tahr and was a very happy man. Richard, while disappointed at not bagging a tahr for himself, was as delighted by our success as I was. A large number of photographs were taken as we shared what was for me at least a very special hunting moment. This was the first of many hunts we were to make together.

I skinned and butchered the animal on the hill, amazed at how tough the pelt was to remove. It had a layer of fat over its chest that was at least an inch thick. On later hunts I often saw tahr standing on exposed ridges facing into strong, freezing cold winds trying to cool themselves, and it is no wonder that they have such a thick layer of fat.

The return trip to the hut was a nightmare. The additional weight I carried meant that I crashed through the top layer of ice with every step. I was a very tired hunter when I finally staggered into that hut.

The head and all the meat made their way back to the hostel freezer. Although the head was no trophy I had it mounted, and today when I look at it the memories of that first-ever tahr hunt return.

Tahr meat tastes as good or better than any venison I've ever eaten. I once had some sausages made up from 10kg of venison, 10kg of tahr and 10kg of mutton (for the fat content, as the two other meats are both lean). I added to this some tomato puree and green onions. Those were the tastiest sausages I have ever eaten, a fact agreed to by the many others who test-drove them with me.

As far as I know Richard never shot a tahr, as he was moved to another location to complete his training as an electrical technician. But both before and after he left we had many hunting adventures together.

Finders keepers

I returned to Whale Stream on 21 separate occasions, and I soon came to realise that it was a breeding ground and didn't hold many bull tahr. I saw tahr on 19 of my trips, which gives you an idea of how many were there at that time, and I have no doubt that similar numbers or more still roam there today.

I soon learned the tahr's habits and would often head to Whale Stream after lunch on a Sunday to shoot a nanny for meat. It was a simple matter of climbing to a certain area I'd identified, then waiting. Like clockwork, the tahr would turn up and travel through a small saddle to their feeding grounds. There wasn't anything difficult or scientific about it, all it took was a bit of energy, and there was always the chance of running into a bull tahr while I was at it.

On one trip I took two new chums, Steve and Gary, for a day's hunting. Again we drove to Whale Stream at night and with the permission of the farmer drove up his track as far as we could go. The track had washed out about 15 minutes' walk from the hut.

Knowing how cold the hut was we armed ourselves with a half-sack of coal and some dry wood to get the fire going. I told my mates that it was an hour and a quarter's walk from the road, neglecting to state that the road I referred to was the main Mt Cook Highway and not the farm track we had just driven up. My new mate Gary kindly offered to take the first spell at carrying the coal. Needless to say his offer was accepted with relish and it was duly agreed that we would take turns at carrying the heavy load. We also agreed that we would change over carrying duties every 15 minutes.

As we neared the last corner before the hut came into view I generously offered to take over carrying the coal. Gary, having checked his watch, refused to relinquish his load, saying that he had a further five minutes of carrying to complete. I kindly let him finish the chore and allowed him to take the coal all the way to the hut door, where Steve and I thanked him for his mammoth efforts in taking care of our heating problem single-handedly. It is fair to say that we also copped a bit of flak for our wee deception.

We spent a warmish night in the hut and took off at first light to explore the Castle Faces above. Constant glassing of the skyline would often produce a view of a tahr cooling him or herself in the cold winds that tormented the mountains.

After a while we decided to split up and meet at a given point some distance away. I elected to hunt on my own and quietly made my way along the base of the Castle bluffs. I carefully glassed the gullies above and below as I went. Cool low cloud drifted across the mountaintops and at times limited visibility to a hundred metres or so.

I wasn't alone during my hunt. A kea deemed my presence interesting enough to visit me and hop from boulder to boulder, just out of my reach, as he followed my progress. Like all kea he was a fearless and inquisitive bird. I stopped and chatted with him briefly, at the same time tossing him an apple core. He quickly cottoned on to the fact that it was edible and perched himself on a nearby rock to eat it. While balancing on one leg he fed the apple core into his beak with the other. When he had had enough of my company he glided effortlessly from his perch, caught a strong updraught and was soon soaring high overhead. I could hear his loud caw for quite some time after. I have a soft spot for kea and despite their reputation for killing lambs I am always pleased to see them when I venture into their mountain realm.

At one point I decided to climb higher and a steep gravel chute offered me the opportunity to do so. Steep, solid rock faces bordered either side and underfoot the scree gave way under my eager steps. The chute was narrow – only about five metres wide at its mouth. I had climbed only a short distance up it when something protruding from the gravel caught my eye. Closer inspection revealed the barrel of a rifle poking out from the loose shingle. I soon extracted the rifle from the gravel's grip and found myself holding a Brno .270 calibre rifle mounted with a Kahles scope. This was truly the world's greatest rifle/scope combination – a type and quality that I could never hope to own myself.

There I was, three-quarters of the way up the Ben Ohau mountain range with a clear view of the Tasman Glacier below, and the gods had delivered a very expensive piece of hunting equipment to me. What a dilemma I faced. I wanted that rifle more than I can describe, but I was also torn by an honest bent that told me to hand it in to the local police station. How had the rifle ended up where it was? Who owned it? Should I just shut up and keep it?

A close inspection of the rifle and scope revealed a few small scratches and a bit of surface rust on the barrel but little other damage. I shouldered the rifle and proceeded to our prearranged meeting point. Steve was the first to spot the rifle and duly questioned me about it. He was very impressed by my find, and felt that under the new gun law I should keep it. The law he was referring to was a stupid piece of legislation that the government had recently put through, which required a person to be licensed to own firearms but failed to record what or how many firearms they actually had. Under these rules I could retain possession of the rifle and no one would know where I had got it or even that I had it. This did not solve my dilemma, however, since I could not forget that the rifle belonged to someone else who was entitled to have it back.

Back at the hut I inspected the rifle more thoroughly and deemed it safe to fire a few shots from it. It was the same calibre as mine so I had the correct ammunition for the test. As expected, the rifle was very well balanced and a pleasure to fire. The recoil was minimal compared with the terrible beast I owned, and the scope remained accurate despite the obvious scratches on its side. It was very tempting to keep this beauty.

As we made our way back to Twizel we continued to debate the pros and cons of handing the rifle to the police or keeping it. In the end the decision was mine alone and I deemed that honesty was the best policy. The following day after work I took the rifle and scope to the local police station where I handed it to Constable Harris. He was most surprised to see it, and was able to fill in the gaps and tell me how the rifle and scope came to be lost up Whale Stream.

The story went something like this. During the winter three men were hunting tahr together in Whale Stream, above the spot where I later found the rifle. Everything was covered in ice and snow, making travel slow and dangerous. The men found their progress halted by a small snow and ice field that had to be crossed to avoid a very long detour. The first man had chanced a quick sprint across the face and made it safely to the other side. The second had crossed by chipping out footsteps with the toe of his boot and taking cautious steps until he reached safety some 20 metres away. The third man had tried to cross using the same footholds as the second but the snow, which was sitting on solid ice underneath, gave way, causing him to slide downward and into the rock chute below. The man was unable to arrest his fall and quickly gathered speed. He bounced mercilessly against the sheer rock walls of the chute and suffered fatal injuries. As his two friends rushed to his aid one of them also slipped on the ice, causing him to drop his rifle as he struggled to stop his fall. The rifle disappeared down the chute and was lost in the snow and debris. The body of the deceased and his rifle were later located, but not the rifle I subsequently found buried in the shingle of that chute.

I sleep well at night knowing that I was honest and did what I believed was the right thing. There was, however, a sequel to this. When I next met up with Constable Harris he informed me that the gentleman whose rifle and scope I had found was extremely pissed off with me. It seems that he had ordered a brand new Brno .270 calibre rifle and Kahles scope, but when I found the missing rifle the insurance company cancelled his claim. It seems that I was thought of as a proverbial bastard.

Now I think there must be a lesson or two hidden away in this lot, don't you?

1. Give me a rifle – I am not a shotgun man.
2. Full choke on a shotgun is only for experts at long shots (like me).
3. I am lucky that dogs can't talk.
4. You don't need to hunt high to get tahr. You need to hunt cunning.
5. A handful of bullets is not enough.
6. Honesty pays?

My old man never hunted tahr so he had to take me at my word on this one.

A BUM
IN THE
BUSH

The Mighty Landsborough

As a kid I listened to the many tales my old man told of his deer-stalking days, 'when he was younger'. No two ways about it, in his day deer were at plague proportions and vast mobs of them could be found ranging the open places at any time of the day or night. The menace needed sorting out and my old man accounted for a fair percentage of them, no question about it. Most were shot in the eye, as he told me they should be, and none got away once his rifle's foresight came to rest on their pupils. Armed with a natural instinct for hunting, passed to me through his genes, and the knowledge imparted to me by his many hunting yarns, I was sent forth into the mountains and forested hills to continue the family tradition of deer eradication.

Boy, did I get a shock. My early years of stumbling about the mountains uncovered a few grim facts on the current state of the deer menace. Firstly, they were no longer a menace. On the other hand, the helicopters that were hunting for the few remaining animals were. From the late 1960s through to the turn of the century wild deer were hounded mercilessly by helicopters, ground hunters and just about every man and his dog, as high prices were paid for venison meat destined for the insatiable German and American markets. Deer were caught live to stock the fledgling New Zealand deer farming industry, which thrives today, and the constant hunting pressure reduced the wild deer population from plague proportions to that of an endangered species.

A young man in the mountains at that time had to work real hard to find a deer, let alone be lucky enough to shoot one. I suffered a few setbacks and made plenty of hunting foul-ups during those early years.

Fortunately I met a bunch of good bastards whose company and sense of humour made my many trips into the hills memorable and a lot of fun. I didn't bag many animals as a beginner, but I did serve a sort of 'hunting apprenticeship' under the guidance of my old man and a few mates who were more 'in tune' with the environment. By the time I was in my early twenties I was ready to recommence my assault on the current deer population. After all, they are still classified as noxious pests, aren't they?

I couldn't help but wonder about the stag bogeyman that kept getting in my way whenever I happened on a stag. Although unseen, the bogeyman was there as sure as they turn tomatoes into sauce. I hadn't stumbled upon many stags, that was for sure, but every time I had, the stag bogeyman stepped in and made sure that something went wrong and they never graced the wall above my fireplace. I was left with nothing but troubled memories of what might have been, 'if only things had gone a bit differently'. The one prize I sought more than any other was a trophy stag. I hadn't shot one yet, and I was beginning to wonder if I ever would. I was determined to achieve my goal, but somehow I knew there were a good few lessons to learn in this hunting game yet. I had developed an uncanny knack of finding hinds, but those stags were proving to be a different story. Maybe it was time to consider a change of tactics.

By the time I turned 24 I had been employed by the National Bank for seven years. I had been transferred three times and was then based in Twizel. One day my boss, Murray, called me into his office and told me the bank had decided to round off my training a bit more, and that I was to be transferred to Kurow. Now, for the uninitiated, Kurow is a one-horse town with two pubs and a general store, situated below Lake Aviemore in the Waitaki Valley in the South Island. There was absolutely nothing about Kurow that would inspire a young, single man into a state of rapture.

'You must be bloody joking,' I stammered when the proposition was put to me, but alas he was not. Fact was, Murray was pretty determined that I would go whether I liked it or not. Right then and there I raised the white flag and threw in the towel. I'd had a bellyful of sharpening pencils, shuffling numbers and being transferred around the country at the whim of my employer. It was time to investigate new career options.

I packed my bags and trundled off to the nearest city, Timaru. I landed a job doing shift work, and as a result found myself lumbered with almost eight weeks of holidays to dispose of each year. A man could fit in a few hunting trips with that amount of leave.

Before I knew it I'd got myself tangled up with a couple of keen local hunters. One of them, Wayne, was the keenest tahr hunter in the whole world. Most weekends he was off into the mountains chasing them. On the odd occasion he would chase a deer or two, but tahr were his greatest obsession. I met Wayne while I was having a beer at a local watering hole, where he proudly boasted of the many trophy tahr he had bagged. I was a little sceptical and made the mistake of saying so. Before I knew it I was in his weathered 4 x 4 Landcruiser being whisked off to his home. Sure enough, his walls were covered with mounted tahr heads. Six or so had horns over 13 inches in length. Wayne also had two whole tahr mounted and on display in his lounge. They too were impressive, but they went some way to explaining why Wayne was still a single man at 27 years of age.

For each of his trophies Wayne had a tale to recount, and I was left in no doubt at all that he was a very experienced tahr hunter who had the evidence to prove it. I was impressed, and after a bit of weaselling managed to get myself invited on a hunt or two.

Now Wayne was a diminutive, skeletal man of about 5'7". His thin features were crowned by a prematurely balding head and he had a prominent moustache. He was humorous and very quick-witted. A man had to be careful what he said, as Wayne had the knack of twisting things at the most inappropriate times and causing considerable embarrassment. His small frame also disguised the fact that he was superbly fit, and tough as they come. In fact, when most people were ready to quit he was just warming up.

The telephone rang one day not long after I had met Wayne.

'I've booked a deerstalking trip in the Landsborough. There's a spot there for you if you want it.'

Too bloody right I did. Hell, every hunter worth his salt had ventured into the mighty Landsborough, and I had read many articles and books about their adventures there. An opportunity like this wasn't to be missed.

On the designated day Wayne picked me up and we were off up-country. We stopped at the township of Fairlie to pick up Mickles, the third member of our party, who I had not met before. Up till this point I had thought Wayne was pretty diminutive, but Mickles was smaller again. He stood about 5'3" in height, and was perhaps a bit fuller-bodied than Wayne. He had a dense stock of dark hair, and immensely strong hands. By trade Mickles was a blade shearer (a person who shears sheep with hand-operated cutters), and he was a tough and hardy individual. Having experienced the rough living of shearing gangs, he knew a good few swear words and his speech was habitually inflicted with them. He had a broad smile that never left his face, and he turned out to be great company in the mountains.

Our transport into the Landsborough was by way of a helicopter flight that was originally planned to leave from Glentanner Station near Mt Cook. This would take us straight up over the Ben Ohau

Range, then west until we dropped down into the Landsborough Valley. The flight would take about 15 or 20 minutes.

The night before our departure the pilot had phoned and offered to fly us from the Tekapo airfield, at no extra cost, if we got there by 9 a.m. This would save us 40 minutes' driving time, and give us a free helicopter trip over some new country to boot. Apparently, the helicopter was flown each night from Glentanner Station to the Tekapo airfield, where it was secured in a hangar, then each morning it returned to Glentanner where it was used to ferry tourists up, over and around Mt Cook. As the helicopter was making the trip from Tekapo to Glentanner anyway, there was no additional cost to the helicopter company in taking us from Tekapo instead of Glentanner Station. You can bet your boots we were at the airfield with plenty of time to spare.

The helicopter was a Squirrel, and therefore had a large cargo capacity. We took with us every luxury known to mankind, including large tents, camp stretchers, chairs, tarpaulins, gas cookers, camp ovens, a large axe, several Tilley lamps and plenty of booze. We may have got a bit carried away with the luxuries, actually, as when it came time to board the helicopter we had trouble fitting ourselves in.

This was my first helicopter flight, and I was rapt when I was given the prime seat up front beside the pilot. The ground swept away literally just under my feet as we took off and veered west. I had an unobstructed view through the front Perspex bubble, and soaked up the surroundings as we flew over the nearby army camp and training grounds. At one point we saw a number of troops making their way on foot over the rolling, tussock-covered country, and further on we sighted several tanks and some armoured personnel carriers. We shuddered past these and continued over Lake Pukaki before making a brief stop at Glentanner Station to drop off some equipment. A short time later we took off again, destined for the Landsborough Valley and our campsite. We eased upwards as we headed towards Mt Cook along the side of the Ben

Ohau mountain range, with the pilot hunting for updraughts to help us climb over the range. What a strange sensation it was when we crested the top and the walls of the mountains disappeared from beneath us. Suddenly we found ourselves flying thousands of feet up, with nothing but air for a long distance below. A look down past my feet gave me an unobstructed view of the wide, flat floor of the Dobson Valley below. Then we crossed the next mountain range and got our first view of the Landsborough. We were near the head of the valley, and vast areas of broken grey rock stretched north for miles before merging into a series of jagged, snow-covered peaks. To the south the grey rock gave way to vast rolling tussock tops and stunted mountain scrub. I was taken aback by the sheer size of the tussock tops, which seemed to roll on forever. My previous experience of this type of country was of significantly smaller ranges.

The helicopter made a rapid descent over broken alpine scrub and stunted beech forest before touching down on Kiwi Flat, the uppermost flat of the Landsborough Valley. In the aviation game time is money, so we were quickly unloaded and the helicopter was gone.

The quietness of the place soon took over. The valley was about half a kilometre wide, and the flat we were on was edged with native beech trees and bordered by the Landsborough River itself. The river was clear and running low after an extended period of fine weather. The helicopter pilot had warned us that if we crossed the Landsborough River to hunt we should return at the first sign of rain, as it can come up very quickly and we might find ourselves stuck on the wrong side. I had once come close to drowning in a flooded river, so I already possessed a healthy respect for them and took note of his advice.

We erected our tents and set up the camp. Wayne had been there before and knew how he wanted things. I put up a small tent some distance away from the others, as I had had reports previously that I snore rather loudly and I was trying to be considerate to my new hunting mates. We created a large, dry shelter by suspending several huge tarpaulins over a number of branches Wayne had left there on an earlier trip. By early afternoon it was time to take off for a hunt. I elected to hunt across the river since it was so low. The crossing presented no great difficulty, but as always the river was just deep enough to ensure that my family jewels received their customary unwanted dunking in the cold, snow-fed water.

The bush I hunted was relatively open and quiet to stalk. I made my way up the hill face with the intention of reaching the open tussock tops by mid-afternoon. It never happened. The skies darkened and it soon started to rain. The pilot's warning about not getting stuck on the wrong side of the river should it rain was ringing in my ears so, reluctantly, as I was near the tussock tops, I made a hasty retreat. The rain remained steady for several hours but stopped almost as soon as I got back to camp.

About half an hour before dark a blue Hughes 500 helicopter flew across the tussock tops I had headed to earlier. I watched it swoop into the head of the gully I had recently vacated, then it disappeared from view for several minutes. When it reappeared

there were two deer hanging on the hook underneath it. Because of the constant hunting pressure placed on the wild deer herds by helicopters, deer were as rare as rocking horse shit, and to have been so close to some only to be robbed by the rain and a helicopter left me feeling really pissed off. In my mind those deer were mine, and they had been stolen from under my nose. That I would have located and shot them was as certain as God made little green apples (in my dreams). I note here that for every deer sighted during my early years of hunting I saw about 50 helicopters. Needless to say, hunting helicopters would have been more productive.

It was early April and the temperature dropped quickly as soon as the weak sun ducked for cover. Our liquor supply consisted of a considerable quantity of port and beer, and it is fair to say that we were unlikely to run out during the trip. Port has a wonderful warming effect, and it proved to be very popular indeed. Each night we lit a large fire that not only warmed us but created a homely feel to the camp. Even today I don't feel that a camp is complete until there is a fire burning.

The next day we were all away well before first light for a hunt. The day was cold and misty and had a brooding, morose feel to it. By mid-morning the weather had deteriorated to steady rain and I returned to camp without sighting any game. Wayne and Mickles were already back in camp when I arrived.

By late afternoon Mickles had had enough of sitting about, and set off on an evening hunt along the flats above our camp. Conditions were miserable, and the only real certainty was that he was going to get a very wet arse. Wayne and I elected to stay put and enjoy the relative warmth of the fire and the port.

Mickles dripped back into camp about half an hour after dark. He was as wet as he could get which, given the now torrential rain, didn't surprise us. We couldn't help but notice a spring in his step, however, and this, added to the huge grin that swallowed most of his face, aroused our interest.

'Any luck?' Wayne enquired.

'Some,' replied Mickles as he shucked off his raincoat.

'Well?' asked Wayne.

'Well what?' came back Mickles.

'Well, did ya get a bloody deer or not?' Wayne urged, with a 'this is like pulling teeth' expression on his face.

'Might have,' replied Mickles. He was clearly enjoying teasing Wayne and was milking the moment for all it was worth. He wandered off and got himself a towel and a beer.

'Well, are ya gonna tell us about it or not?' Wayne demanded.

'Might,' Mickles replied as he dried himself off.

This little exchange was as funny as a play. These two knew each other well, and each knew how to wind the other up. Mickles was enjoying every second. Wayne, continuing to get unsatisfactory answers to his enquiries, started a play fight with Mickles and told him that if he didn't cough up the required hunting report this bloody instant, he was going to be thrown back out into the rain until he got his act together.

'Right-oh. Right-oh, you win,' said Mickles, raising his hands in mock surrender. 'I bagged a bloody big stag, but it's only a nine-pointer.'

'Well, where is it then?' I asked.

At this point Mickles decided to come clean and tell his tale, which went something like this. After leaving camp he had stalked just inside the bush edge to the top of the flats. By the time he got there he was absolutely soaked, and was giving strong consideration to chucking it in and returning to camp. It was only his concern about the ridicule he was sure to get from Wayne and me that inspired him to go on. He bush-stalked above the flats for a time, then stumbled upon a large clearing that was completely surrounded by beech forest. A long look over it revealed nothing, so he continued on upriver until he struck the next major side creek. It had taken on huge proportions, with large volumes of water roaring down it, so he wasn't game to attempt a crossing. After climbing up the side of the creek for some distance, Mickles had finally had enough and decided to return to camp. The day was drawing on and he knew it would be close to dark by the time he made it back.

As he was motoring homeward the previously mentioned clearing came to mind. He made a detour back, and as soon as he relocated the clearing he saw two stags standing smack in the middle. One was a spiker (a one-year-old stag), the other a large-bodied animal that carried antlers bearing nine points. With water running into his eyes Mickles took a standing shot at the nine-pointer, only to see it bolt off into the nearby bush. The second stag departed far too quickly for him to get a shot at it. Being uncertain that his shot was good, Mickles entered the bush at the same point as the stag, and made a thorough search for it. He found it lying dead as a dodo about 30 metres inside the bush edge. The stag had a massive body and Mickles, knowing full well that he would never be able to carry it on his own, gutted it, dragged it to a sheltered spot, and left it to be butchered and recovered the following day. Mickles one, helicopter two.

Getting a wet arse clearly has some rewards, and served to prove the old adage that you don't find deer warming themselves by your campfire.

Needless to say, with fresh meat for the camp taken care of, we helped Mickles celebrate his success. One or two too many were had by us all. Come morning, I was away at first light for a hunt downriver, while Mickles and Wayne went to recover the meat. The day started out wet but soon cleared to become fine and sunny. Crossing the river was not on, so we were all restricted to hunting, for that day at least, on the camp side of it.

The next four days saw us hunting in fine weather, but although we all put in long days only one more deer was sighted. This was seen by Wayne, who had climbed a steep scrub-covered hillside only to come face to face with a hind that was looking down over the edge at him. There was nothing Wayne could do. He was hanging onto the face with both hands and had his rifle slung across his back. Letting go wasn't an option. Once the introductions were sorted out the hind made off at a great rate and without fear of a pursuing bullet.

Each day we were out before daylight and back after dark. Sometimes we would return to camp for lunch or to gather firewood, but we always went back out for an evening hunt. The flat we were camped below had an airstrip for fixed wing aircraft. I suspected that it hadn't been used for a long time, as the tussock was almost thigh height and would have been a pilot's nightmare to land on. There were also the remnants of a frequently used campsite at the top end of the flat. I found out later that this was the launching point for a company that takes clients on rafting trips down the Landsborough River.

As could be expected on the West Coast, the weather didn't hold fine for long. We woke one morning to torrential rain and lashing winds. For two days it never let up and we all elected to stay in camp and wait it out. On the second night the wind abated just before dark but the rain still pounded down. The noise of it thundering down on our tarpaulins was deafening. At one point during the evening Wayne departed to the privacy of the bush for a leak, and when he returned he asked if we could hear someone yelling. By this time we had all consumed large rations of port and our senses were somewhat diminished. Mickles and I told Wayne not to be so blooming stupid. Obviously, given the two days of torrential rain and strong winds, no one in their right mind would be out and about. How could they have got into the Landsborough in such atrocious conditions anyway?

Wayne was adamant that he had heard someone yelling, and dragged me away from the noise of camp and into the rain to listen with him. Nothing. A very wet and loud nothing!

'There you go,' Wayne said. 'Did you hear that?'

'Hear what?' I asked.

'I heard someone yelling again,' he replied.

'Mate, you've had too much port. You're hearing things,' I stated, having strained my ears but heard nothing. Furthermore, we had a fire raging and two Tilley lamps shedding bright light over a large area. If there was anyone out there they couldn't possibly fail to see our camp. Maybe it was time Wayne returned to civilisation before he went completely stark raving mad.

'Let's get out of the rain before we drown,' I suggested. 'Your imagination's playing tricks on you.'

'I'm sure I heard someone calling,' Wayne insisted as I dragged him back to camp.

After some serious lowering of our supplies and singing ourselves hoarse we finally turned in for the night. By then the rain had eased from torrential to steady, and the prospect of an early morning hunt had improved from 'not a happening thing' to 'marginal'.

As the dying embers of the fire ebbed, the volume of our snoring grew. If there had been anyone out there who was silly enough to miss our well-lit camp, he or she would surely have been guided to it by the resonant tones of three drunks snoring.

Morning came. We all missed hearing the alarm clock (possibly because we didn't have one). Three very miserable, hungover hunters crawled from their scratchers at the belated hour of 7.30 a.m. Seemingly a few hours' sleep wasn't enough for these hardy mountain men.

Ever the optimists, Wayne and I decided to dispense with breakfast and take a quick trot along the flats to bag the 'sure to be there' animals that would by now be gracing them. This seemed a certainty as, against all odds, the day had dawned fine and clear. After two days of torrential rain and strong winds it seemed obvious that the deer would be seeking comfort in the open places free of dripping forest and lashing branches.

We had only travelled a few hundred metres from camp when we bumped into a very bedraggled and wet-looking bloke. He was carrying the biggest backpack I have ever laid eyes on. It was huge, and I had to look hard to find the tramper hidden beneath it. The man was middle-aged and sported a few days' growth of untidy whiskers that in time would turn into a dense beard. Strangely, in his hand he carried a large, brightly coloured golf umbrella that was folded away and being used as a walking stick. The chap was so skinny I was in awe that he could lift the pack he carried, never mind make the soggy progress he was making, and with relative ease too.

'Gidday mate,' Wayne greeted him. 'Where the hell did you come from?'

'Been looking for the hut that's supposed to be on this flat somewhere,' the man answered. 'Can't find the bloody thing anywhere.'

'What hut?' countered Wayne.

'The bloody hut that's supposed to be on this blimmin' flat, that's what bloody hut,' replied the clearly pissed-off man.

'There isn't a hut on this flat, mate,' Wayne said emphatically. 'As far as I know there never has been.'

'According to this there is,' said the man, holding out an old, weathered map of the area. 'Look for yourself.'

We both took a gander at the map and sure enough, marked at the top of the flat we were standing on, was a hut, just as the man had said.

'Well, I'll be a monkey's arse,' exclaimed Wayne. 'You're right. Well it sure isn't there any more.'

'You're dead right there, mate,' the man agreed flatly.

After the introductions were made we invited the man, whose name I don't remember, back to camp for a yarn, a hot brew and a feed. Now this chap's story went something like this. He was travelling alone, and had started his journey at Mt Cook village. He had climbed the Sealy Range and intended to make a lengthy mountain traverse over a ten-day period. He had traversed the mountaintops in deteriorating weather until he reached the head of the Landsborough. At that point he decided, due to the atrocious weather, to make a dash for the safety of the Landsborough Hut as marked on his map. He had made a difficult descent into the valley in appalling conditions. He did not have a tent with him, and his only wet-weather protection was his umbrella, and the jacket and over-trousers he wore. He had a bivvy bag that fitted his sleeping bag with little room to spare. This was intended for fair weather use only, and was not a substitute for a tent. Given the absence of a hut, he had been forced to sleep under a very wet bush in torrential rain, with little protection. Needless to say he had managed to get himself, his sleeping bag and all his possessions thoroughly soaked.

In strange conjunction with Wayne's touch of temporary insanity, the man claimed to have yelled his lungs out the previous night, hoping that someone might hear him and give him directions to the sanctuary of the said hut. After a bit of needling from Wayne, I was forced to acknowledge that perhaps he wasn't as drunk as I had suggested, and that just maybe he had heard the man's calls the previous night. Neither Wayne nor I could fathom how he had failed to see our well-illuminated camp or hear our singing and snoring. After all, the man had slept under a bush within three hundred metres of our camp and claimed to have walked the length of the flat three or four times before giving up his search.

Now a wee point of interest here is that DoC, in their infinite wisdom, had recently declared the Landsborough and its surrounds a 'Wilderness Area'. These areas, although liberally dotted with nice warm, user-friendly huts, were set aside as special areas that were to be returned to their pristine, original and untouched state. To achieve this, all the huts and other intrusive man-made things were removed. Maintenance of the tracks was stopped, and all was allowed to return to its natural wilderness state. Lovely. The 'greenies' must have been in raptures. Trouble was, there are hundreds if not thousands of maps out there that show that huts exist where they now don't, and some people (take our new-found mate as an example) get caught short. People can die of exposure when caught out in lousy conditions, and all for the sake of a 'Wilderness Area' whose huts have been removed by well-meaning persons who probably haven't left the grounds of Parliament for years. Strangely, the people who most often visit this remote area are hunters who come in on foot and by helicopter. A nice warm hut would improve the area in their eyes, I can tell you that. A man has to ask why they would remove existing huts from such a remote area in the first place. Anyway, enough said.

Our guest must have thought he'd walked into the Parkroyal Hotel. We served him a huge feed of baked beans, sausages, bacon and eggs, followed by a can of peaches, all washed down by many cups of hot coffee. He declined our offer of a can of beer to finish the meal. The fire was nudged up to a roaring furnace, and his gear was hung up to dry while the meal was digested.

While I enjoyed talking with this man I found some aspects of his adventure strange and unnerving. Firstly, he claimed that he hadn't told anyone of his intended route, or in fact that he was in the mountains at all. The only food he had was porridge and sugar, yet he was in there for ten days on his own. Attached to his pack were items of climbing equipment such as ropes and crampons, which seemingly were more important than food or items of comfort such as a tent. He went on to tell us that he intended to travel down the Landsborough some distance and then to forge a route west over the range and into the next watershed. He hoped to encounter a bit of rock climbing on the way, and eventually to return to Mt Cook village via the Copland Pass and the Hooker Valley. He was supremely confident of his ability, and argued that porridge contained all the fuel he needed to complete his journey. I felt tired just hearing him talk about the distance he intended to travel.

Several hours later he had repacked and was on his way. My last view of him was as he emerged from the swollen river several hundred metres below camp. He had picked a calm part of the river to cross, which conversely adds up to being a deep part. As a result, he was up to his chest in floodwater at the deepest part and most of our efforts to dry his gear were rendered wasted. I kept a close eye on the newspaper on my return to civilisation but never read any reports of a missing climber. Mind you, since he claimed no one knew he was in the hills, maybe he was reported missing from somewhere else and I never heard about it.

We were due out that afternoon and set about dismantling our camp. The day was gloriously fine, without a single cloud in the sky. The meat that was hung in a nearby tree had got wet and gone off, so Mickles salvaged what he could and the rest was buried in the bush.

When the helicopter hadn't arrived to pick us up by dark we hastily re-erected our camp and pondered our situation. We didn't have a mountain radio, so we couldn't call up and find out what was wrong. We discussed all sorts of possibilities, the worst being that the helicopter had crashed and no one knew we were in there. Actually, we had told our workmates where we were, but they wouldn't kick in with any action for a day or two yet. Starving wasn't going to be a problem, though, and if it became necessary we could always walk out. Our route would take us over the Brodrick Pass, down the Huxley Valley, into the Hopkins and on to the Ohau ski lodge, where we could place a call and put all those worried people out of their misery.

We spent a comfortable but subdued night in camp. Come morning we again packed up and waited and waited and waited. By mid-afternoon we had all but given up hope, when suddenly we heard the unmistakable sound of an approaching helicopter. Moments later the pilot touched down and dismounted. He quickly informed us that despite it being a fine day on our side of the ranges there had been a thick fog on his, making our earlier extraction from the Landsborough impossible. That's the way it is when you are reliant on air transport in the mountains, and this was not to be the last time weather hindered my hunting plans.

The flight out was every bit as thrilling as the inward journey. As soon as we crested the top of the valley we saw proof that the pilot was not telling us porkies. Dense layers of billowing cloud that were not visible from our valley home greeted us. The pilot made his way carefully through the cloud and descended into what seemed to me to be total white-out conditions. I was a bit nervous and expected to hit the mountainside at any time. Fortunately this didn't happen, and we soon broke through the cloud over the waters of Lake Pukaki. After a stopover of several hours at Glentanner Station while the helicopter made several tourist flights, we were bundled up and flown back to the Tekapo airfield, where our trip into the mighty Landsborough came to an end.

The Great Round-up

Many a great scheme has been hatched over a beer or two, but when Wayne told me of his plan for the following weekend I knew he had finally gone mad. Maybe some of that rainwater from the Landsborough had infiltrated his thinking parts and affected his brain.

'You've got two shows of pulling that one off, and both of them add up to none at all,' I told him confidently.

'Don't be such a negative bugger,' he retorted. 'In fact, you'd better come too. The more hands on deck the better our prospects.'

Now I've tried a few shady tricks from time to time, and occasionally risked doing something that was outright dangerous, but this scheme was leaning towards the bloody ridiculous. Accepting this, it sounded like a bit of fun, so without hesitation I was in, and accepted Wayne's offer. The following Friday we climbed into my Bedford van and made for Tekapo.

Once again we spent the evening at the Tekapo Hotel, where I was introduced to a group of Wayne's up-country mates. I had played rugby against a few of them in my earlier Twizel days, and got on well with them all. Believing them to be part of the said 'scheme', I went to extremes to ensure that I fitted in and was accepted as one of the bunch. I consumed large quantities of beer and told grubby jokes as well as any of them – the end result being that we had a huge night out and an early start just wasn't going to happen.

I awoke to a throbbing headache and bright sunlight warming my face through the curtainless window. Why do we do these things to our bodies? Wayne was nowhere to be found. I searched the bach from one end to the other and back again – nothing. In truth, I couldn't remember him coming home with me, and I recalled that he was getting on particularly well with one of the locals at one point in the evening. The way I felt, it was a blessing that he wasn't there. He may well have been keen to get on with his silly plan and I, regrettably, wasn't up to it at that point.

Snow lay thinly on the ground outside and it was pretty chilly. The log fire needed to be prodded into life to warm the bach, but as was to be expected, there was no wood inside to stoke it with. I was still fully clothed, having been too tired to get undressed the previous night, so I slipped on my shoes and staggered outside to the woodpile beside the weathered wooden garage. Parked beside the woodpile was Wayne's old 4 x 4 Land-Rover. I noticed that the windows were completely fogged up and that it was impossible to see inside. A pull on the unlocked door and a quick look inside soon revealed Wayne's whereabouts. There, snoring contentedly in the rear with a sleeping bag draped over him, was the great white hunter himself. Why he had chosen to sleep there when there were a number of perfectly comfortable, soft beds inside is anyone's guess. A couple of loud thumps on the roof of the vehicle above Sleeping Beauty soon had him swearing and cursing and back in the land of the living. Wayne didn't look too flash at the best of times, and this wasn't one of those.

'Come on, ya lazy bastard, your mates will be waiting to get going,' I urged.

'What mates?' Wayne asked.

'That crowd we were guzzling with last night. They're coming with us, aren't they?' I enquired.

'Coming where?' asked Wayne.

'With us on our hunt,' I replied, thinking that last night's grog must have really got to him.

'Nope. What made you think that?' he asked.

'Dunno. I just assumed they're the blokes we're giving a hand to.'

'You must be joking,' Wayne laughed. 'Those useless buggers wouldn't climb a hill even if there was a pub giving out free grog on the top of it. We're giving Serge a hand. You'll meet him later today. Now bugger off – I'm going back to sleep.'

Well, I'd certainly made a few new acquaintances the previous night, but seemingly I had been a bit presumptuous in assuming they were to be our hunting buddies. Maybe that explained why there wasn't any talk of hunting during the evening.

By late afternoon Wayne and I had both recovered from our efforts, and we wandered a few doors down the road to meet up with Serge. Now, Serge was a full-time professional hunting guide. He stood about 6'0" tall, was lean and fit, and had a handshake that nearly tore your arm off. He had a broad German accent and his complexion resembled that of well-tanned leather. Serge had a way of making a bloke feel comfortable in his presence, and I took a liking to him straight away.

Serge offered tahr, chamois and red deer hunts. Possums and rabbits were a sideline that was thrown in for free to keep the clients happy when the weather wasn't co-operating. He only offered fair game hunts, where the stalking was done on foot. If the client wasn't fit enough to get to the hunting grounds, shoot a trophy and then get back to civilisation, bad luck for them as they paid for his services anyway. Obviously his business was reliant on foreign hunters who were happy to pay the huge (by my standards anyway) fee for a guided hunt. Sending clients home with stories of successful hunts, and trophies to prove it, was the best advertising he could get and he worked hard to ensure they stood a good chance of success. Serge didn't like failing his clients, and he spent a lot of time in the mountains locating tahr and chamois for them to hunt later.

We managed to get ourselves invited to tea, and Serge's wife prepared a magnificent dish of wild rabbit saddles casseroled in red wine, with many secret herbs and spices. Dining with us that night was Serge's Austrian client, whose hunt we were assisting with the following day. Wayne and I were promoted to the rank of assistant guides. We had a great night, swapping many stories of hunting in New Zealand and Austria. We felt very privileged to be residents of New Zealand when we were told of the huge cost of obtaining a hunting licence in Austria. These licences only gave the purchaser the right to hunt, and did not guarantee that they would see, let alone shoot, an animal. Our client had not shot a chamois even though they are a native animal of his country. Despite this, his target for the following day was tahr. Arrangements were finalised for the morning and we set off home knowing that we would be up in a few short hours' time. I was already wishing I hadn't drunk as much red wine as I had.

Well before dawn we travelled the gravel road on the east side of Lake Tekapo that eventually leads into the Godley Valley. Our destination was the 'Round Hill' skifield, which at that time had been abandoned. As we parked the two vehicles in the carpark the starlit sky faded from the blackness of night to the half-light that signals the start of a new day. The snow underfoot was frozen solid and we knew we were in for a fine day's hunting.

A slightly subdued group of four trudged up the gut to the right of the skifield as we made our way to a low saddle several hundred metres above. Each time we exhaled, our breaths formed into great clouds of frosted air in front of us. When we reached the saddle we sat and glassed the steep rock and scree faces across the wide valley that had opened up to us. I was glad of the rest, as my lungs were heaving and my head thumped from the effects of the previous night's indulgences. Both Wayne and Serge had high-powered spotting scopes that made both Serge's client and me feel inadequately equipped with our low-power binoculars. A look back to where we had come from revealed why the skifield was called Round Hill. The name describes it exactly. The field was a very large, gently sloping dome that would be grand for learners and those who just sought a relaxing day's skiing.

After declaring that there were no animals on the opposite face, Serge gave us a briefing on his expectations for the day. 'From here we cut up the ridge behind us. Always stay below the skyline, as I know there are two chamois somewhere on the face we have just glassed and if we don't get a tahr we will try for one of them on our return.'

'So far so good,' I said. 'But when does our main plan kick in?'

'We have some climbing to do first,' Serge replied with a knowing grin.

Up we went. Vegetation was sparse on the bare face we climbed, with only a few clumps of tussock and the occasional Spaniard grass poking through the snow. Progress was slow and much of the climbing was up scree slopes where each step gained was fought for against the loose, shifting gravel that constantly tried to return our feet back to their starting point.

I was nearly knackered when Serge called for the next stop just below the summit of the ridge we were on. The client was struggling even more than I was, and I was beginning to have grave doubts about his fitness for hunting the steep mountains of New Zealand. As he threw himself to the ground for a rest he muttered in his strained accent, 'I'm foooked.' There could be no doubt what he meant as he lay there heaving in large gobs of crisp mountain air.

Being careful not to reveal themselves against the skyline, Wayne and Serge edged their way around a large rock that sat on the ridge top. After they had glassed the opposite faces briefly, Wayne exclaimed, 'There's one,' and pointed out a lone chamois to Serge and the client. The chamois was standing on a very steep, rocky buttress about a kilometre and a half away. The buttress was surrounded by large scree slopes, and I would not have thought

it would hold an animal of any type, let alone a chamois (I was still young and silly and had a lot to learn). There was a marked absence of any visible food for it to exist on. I did not risk taking a look at the chamois myself in case it spotted the flurry of activity and made a hasty exit.

A council of war was held, and the client was asked if he wanted to stalk the chamois at that point. He did not. We planned and made a lengthy traverse above and past the animal as we made our way to another area where Serge had located a large mob of unmolested tahr that were eagerly awaiting our arrival – the largest bull of the mob being keen to emigrate to Austria and take a look at half the world as it travelled there. After assessing the state of the client, I took over carrying his rifle – it was all part of the service, and as neither Wayne nor I had brought a rifle with us, it was no hardship.

We had been climbing and sidling over some pretty tough country for about five hours by the time the client announced that he was totally buggered and wasn't going any further. Now the poor chap was definitely carrying a spare tyre or two around his gut, but up to this point he had displayed a lot of courage and determination. Serge wasn't having a bar of him quitting, and announced that it was time for a break and a bite to eat. Further, he stated that we were very close to our destination and that we had no more climbing to do.

We enjoyed a lengthy break on a sunny ridge with a view over many miles of pristine, snow-covered mountains. In every direction jagged peaks broke the horizon. The view was similar to what I would expect to see from the top of Mt Everest. It was magnificent, and made the trip well worthwhile whether our hunt was successful or not.

The client made a remarkable recovery after a meal of sandwiches and several cups of hot tea from our flasks, and as we made off towards our final destination I thought for a moment that he would break into a run.

We crested a low brow on the ridge and there, stretching for miles before us, was an unexpected surprise. The grey broken rock that we had climbed over all day gave way to a huge, high valley that ran west for many miles as it sloped gently downward. Snow lay thinly on the ground, with tussock poking its head through at regular intervals. To the east, about a kilometre away at the head of the hanging valley, was a series of large bluffs that looked totally out of place where they were located. The change in landscape was remarkable. Serge hunkered down below the skyline and signalled to the rest of us to do the same.

'We've arrived,' he said blandly, not suppressing the huge smile on his face. 'Time to put our plan into action.'

The scheme that I had thought so bloody ridiculous up to this point didn't look so bad now that I could see the setting. I'd better let you in on the plan about now. If I don't, you'll have trouble keeping up with the proceedings that follow.

It was our intention to round up a mob of tahr that Serge had previously located and which were living on the isolated bluffs situated at the head of the hanging valley that was now before us.

When I was first told that Wayne and Serge intended to round up tahr I, of course, thought the idea stupid to say the least. Hell, all the tahr I'd seen to date were attached to bloody great mountains and were precariously perched above deadly drops that certainly wouldn't allow for them to be 'rounded up'. As I surveyed the hanging valley I began to realise that Serge and Wayne's plan had changed from impossible to darn right likely to work.

Here's the plan. The bluffs we were eyeballing were totally surrounded by tussock country. Therefore, to leave them the tahr would have to travel over open, gently sloping ground. Now it is well known that tahr will, by natural instinct, climb away from danger, usually right up to the top of the mountain where they stand for one last look at you and to show off their superior climbing talent before disappearing over the top and away forever. Wayne and I were to sneak underneath these bluffs and make ourselves clearly visible to the resident tahr. They, spotting us, would quietly make their way to the top of the bluffs and, in all likelihood, stand there unsuspecting as huge stationary targets for the client, who would be waiting in ambush above. Simple, isn't it?

I started to get the feeling that those as yet unseen tahr were as good as in the bag. Wayne and I took a long detour to ensure we weren't spotted by the tahr before we were meant to be. We had been told to make our presence known beneath the bluffs at exactly 2.45. Having waited out of sight until the allocated time we made our way across the open tussock faces below the bluffs. We talked loudly, and managed to make sufficient noise for the tahr to observe our arrival. Despite some serious looking we couldn't see the tahr, but we felt certain they were aware of our presence and would be making their way upward into the ambush.

Before long two figures appeared on the horizon at the top of the bluffs. They were waving their hands frantically as if trying to tell us something but we couldn't figure out what. We watched as they made their way quickly down to us.

'What's all the waving about?' enquired Wayne.

'Didn't you see them? You must have seen them!' exclaimed the very excited client as he pointed down into the valley below.

'Seen what?' I asked.

'The tahr. The tahr. There. Down there,' he stammered, continuing to point down the valley.

We sat down and glassed the distant tussock. Sure enough, well below and now far away was a mob of tahr that were fast disappearing down the open tussock valley.

'What happened?' I asked.

Serge told the story. 'We snuck above the bluffs by staying hidden on the other side of the ridge above them. As soon as we climbed over the ridge top to get a view down to the bluffs below we surprised the mob feeding on the open tussock above them. They saw us straight away and made off down through the bluffs at a great rate.' The client hadn't managed to fire a shot at them.

I could tell by Serge's expression that he was pissed off with the client's efforts but wasn't saying so at that point. We hadn't seen the tahr depart as we had remained hidden from view as instructed until our allocated arrival time, which was by then too late. The fact that Serge had found the mob of tahr in this remote and unlikely place was amazing. I can only speculate that he had stumbled upon them while looking for chamois. The small bluff system was surrounded by tussock and was a long way from what I would consider to be normal tahr habitat.

The client was clearly pretty upset with himself and apologised profusely. He didn't have to. It was his money that had got him there, and it was he who had to live with not getting a tahr despite being placed within 50 metres of a whole herd of them. As always when hunting, he should have been prepared for action at any time. (Hang on a minute, mate. I've fallen into that trap myself many times. Still do occasionally.)

Serge went overboard trying to make the client feel better about the situation. After all, all was not lost. There was always the chamois that we had spotted on our way in, which was just waiting for him to return and shoot it. This cheered the client up somewhat.

We made steady progress back to a spot well above and back from where the chamois was living. The wind was in our favour and things looked good for an easy stalk for our client. He and Serge eased over the edge and made their way as quietly as they could on the loose rock surface down the side of the very steep face. It was agreed that Wayne and I would remain on top and stay put until either we heard a shot or 5 o'clock arrived, whichever came first. At that time we would head back to our vehicles and meet up with the others there. They would sidle across the face after shooting the chamois and on hitting the leading spur would travel down it to the vehicles. Sounded too simple. We knew that we would not get back to our vehicles until well after dark. None of us had taken torches, since we had planned to be back at the vehicles by late afternoon. When would I ever learn to be fully prepared at all times?

Serge and the client had been gone less than half an hour when we heard the loud crack of a rifle shot. We felt elated, certain that we had success at last. There was only the one shot, which served to consolidate our view that a kill had been made. Wayne and I peered over the valley side but we couldn't see the others. Since travel was easier on the ridge top, we didn't go down to check on their success but continued onward towards home as planned. The day had become windy and very cold by the time the other two left for their stalk, and before we got moving again dense cloud started to roll over the tops from behind us. We hadn't travelled very far before we were engulfed in dense fog. Wayne didn't seem too worried by this turn of events but I wasn't that happy. I had spent a cold wet night out once before due to fog and I hadn't been able to feel comfortable in it since. It didn't help that this was the first time either Wayne or I had been on this mountain range.

I followed along behind Wayne for what seemed like ages. The fog smothered the remaining daylight and brought darkness on earlier than normal. 'Shouldn't we be heading down over the side about now?' I asked.

'Not yet, mate,' came Wayne's reply. 'Another ten minutes and we should be able to drop straight down onto the vehicles.'

To my mind we were well past them, but if Wayne was going to get lost and spend a night out in the open I thought I'd better hang around to keep him company. Eventually, and in very poor light, we dropped over the side. The loose running scree made for a rapid descent and in minutes we lost about five hundred metres in altitude. To my surprise, when we broke clear of the fog I discovered that we had not yet travelled far enough to be above the vehicles. We came down near the saddle where we had first rested earlier in the day. A final descent in darkness, down the gully to our waiting vehicles, was made slowly but without difficulty.

Serge and the client were not at the vehicles when we got there, but this didn't surprise us as we knew they would have been delayed butchering the trophy chamois and were likely to arrive soon. We waited and then waited some more. I began to get a bit concerned for them as the cloud cover had added to the total black-out that now surrounded us. Wayne flicked on the lights of his vehicle to give them guidance should they come down the same gut as we had.

A good hour and a half after dark two weary figures emerged from the blackness. No matter how hard I looked I couldn't see an animal attached to either of them. The client was clearly absolutely bushed and was tripping over everything, including his own feet. Their progress was slow and tortuous, even with their destination in sight. When they arrived the client collapsed across the bonnet of Serge's vehicle, gasping for air and clearly exhausted. I wondered if Serge would get his fee if his client dropped dead on him.

We wrapped the client up in a blanket and fed him a warm cup of sweetened tea from the thermos before Wayne enquired, 'And where's the chamois then?'

The client dropped his head and didn't appear too inclined towards telling us. Our eyes searched out Serge, who gave us a 'not now if you don't mind' look.

Wayne wasn't about to be put off, and persisted, 'Well, where is it then?'

'We missed,' Serge mumbled, trying to downplay things.

'Well, what's the story then?' Wayne demanded.

Serge reluctantly told their story. They had eased over the valley side and made good progress down the face. The stalk had been easy as they had struck solid rock not far from the top, which allowed for quiet travel. They sighted the chamois lying half-asleep on a rock bench some two hundred metres below them. It had no idea they were there and Serge had encouraged the client to take the shot then and there but he wouldn't have any part of it, saying he wanted to get closer to make sure of the shot. He was the client, so Serge was left with no option other than to try to get closer and risk the chamois hearing their approach and taking flight.

They made slow but steady progress down the face without warning the chamois of their approach. When they were within 90 metres of it Serge told the client to take the shot as he didn't believe they could get any closer without warning the animal. The client lay down and set himself up for a relatively easy resting and slightly downhill shot.

The chamois, which had a good set of well-curved horns, was still dozing on the rock, and conditions could not have been better for an easy rested shot. After an eternity the client fired, and to Serge's horror he saw rock fly up over the back of the chamois. The chamois took instant flight, making a rapid bounding, zigzag departure. Serge asked the client if he wanted him to shoot it, but was told an emphatic 'No!'

The client wasn't able to get a bead on the fleeing chamois for a second shot so that was it, the hunt was over. The client, who had had a very big day in the New Zealand mountains, was absolutely stuffed and getting him off the hill had proven difficult. His combined tiredness, disappointment and misery at missing two opportunities to secure trophy animals had left him feeling totally gutted. There wasn't anything we could say that would make him feel any better either. He will live the rest of his life thinking of what might have been.

Little did the client know that he may well have been a participant in the world's first tahr round-up.

Fiordland Found

There were no two ways about it, I had had a gutsful of moving from town to town and was ready to plant my butt for a decent spell in one location. Trouble was, Timaru didn't seem to fit the bill, so I packed my bags and headed to the big smoke of Christchurch. The move was a bit like the country boy coming to town.

The hardest thing to get the hang of was the traffic lights that appeared at almost every intersection. Didn't these city drongoes know the road rules? I received a couple of traffic tickets for going through red lights before I got the hang of actually stopping to waste a few minutes while the empty intersection cleared so I could proceed safely to where I was about to safely go.

City revenue gatherers were in the habit of hiding cameras up poles to catch people who, like me, were in too much of a hurry to get on with life and who weren't much concerned with waiting for non-existent traffic at empty intersections. Enough said.

I soon found myself tagged by a lady friend and before I had a chance to realise what was happening I was a father and my hunting got placed on a limited licence. I did manage to meet a few like-minded hunter types, though, and skipped town as often as practical to replenish the meat supply in the freezer.

One day I answered the phone at home, and the conversation went something like this . . .

'Hi, Al. Me here. I've got a bit of a problem and I'm hoping you can help me out.'

Hell! He had a problem. What about me? I didn't even know who I was talking to, but I played along as I tried to figure it out.

'You'd better tell me what the problem is and I'll see if I can help.'

'We've drawn a wapiti block in Fiordland and it's left us in a bit of a fix,' said the unknown voice.

Shit hot, I thought. Someone's pulled out of his party and I'm about to get an invitation to join them. Bloody ripper. I was still kind of curious as to who I was talking to though.

'Who's pulled out?' I asked, searching for a clue.

'What do ya mean?' came his reply.

'You are one short for the wapiti hunt, aren't you?' I enquired.

'No – what made you think that?'

'You said you had a problem,' I countered.

'Yeah, we do.'

'And it's not that you're one short for your wapiti hunt?'

'No, it's not.'

'Well, what's the problem?' I asked, feeling somewhat let down even though I had no reason to be.

'Well, it's just that, thinking we would miss out on the wapiti ballot, we booked an alternative trip to Fiordland anyway.'

'I still don't see your problem,' I responded.

'It's that my son and his mate want to go on our alternative hunt and neither has hunted before. I was wondering if you would take them and show them the ropes.'

Now here was an interesting proposition, if only I could figure out who I was talking to.

'Sounds all right, but why me?' I asked.

'You bring in a bit of venison and tahr to be made into sausages, so I figure you must have some idea of what the game's about,' answered the voice, which I finally identified as that of my local butcher.

Being a thrifty person I was in the habit of scavenging every morsel of meat from every game animal I shot. When I had gathered up a good quantity of scrap meat I'd take the lot to the butcher and have it made into sausages and meat patties. The butcher was a good sort and always found time to stop and have a yarn about hunting and other manly pursuits. He had hunted in Fiordland and mingled with many of the famous helicopter pilots and meat hunters in the days when wild deer outnumbered farm stock. He always got a gleam in his eyes when he talked of his hunting days. It was the same distant look my old man got when he told his hunting tales.

After establishing that his son was 17 and that his mate was 18 and in the army, I agreed. It was under these circumstances that instead of me chasing the meat, the meat man came to be chasing me.

Having met the two prospective hunters, arrangements were made and soon enough I was off into the uncharted waters of Fiordland.

Needless to say, my long-suffering wife required the family car so I found myself crammed into the rear of a teenager's 'hot' Escort car, complete with missing exhaust and fluffy dice hanging from the rear-view mirror.

The vehicle was filled to capacity with three packs, three rifles, bulk food, booze, fuel containers and an outboard motor. Add in me, being a man mountain of 196cm and weighing 119kg, and that left breathing space only as we thundered across the Canterbury Plains, through the Mackenzie Basin, past Queenstown and into Te Anau where we were to spend the night. The trip took eight hours, and by the time we arrived my ears had lost all sense of hearing as a result of a mixture of loud music and no exhaust. To add to my misery, while crammed into the confines of the rear seat I had somehow managed to put my neck out. I was in a fair bit of pain and couldn't move my head in any direction. Needless to say, urgent medical attention was required.

My new hunting mates kindly dropped me off at the doctor's surgery then promptly buggered off to the THC bar (now called The Moose) on the waterfront. Can't say I blamed them, as my preference would have been to be there myself.

By extreme good fortune a physiotherapist was visiting Te Anau that day. A bit of pulling and prodding semi-sorted out my neck problem. By the time I left the surgery I had regained partial movement and was armed with an assortment of relaxant pills. My plan was to sink a few liquid pills to see if that fixed the job, but before I could I had to call in at the Air Fiordland office to meet Russell, the pilot who was flying us in the next morning. Russell wasn't there when I called but the lady on the counter said he would meet me at the THC bar and that I should proceed there to take my medicine. Sound advice.

So, forgetting the ages of my hunting mates (the legal age for drinking then was 20), we settled in for a hearty session at the hotel. The day was sunny, and despite it being early April it was pleasantly warm. We waited and waited for Russell to make himself known. We had no idea where we were to meet the plane in the morning, and catching up with him was crucial.

Half an hour after dark Russell arrived. Despite the bar being near full he walked straight up to me, thrust out his hand, and with a smile that reached from ear to ear said, 'You must be that big bastard the girls in the office are talking about.' After some introductions it turned out that he was right.

Russell was almost the spitting image of my mate Wayne from Timaru. He was a small, lean man of about 45 and stood approximately 5'5" in height. He had a shiny, near-bald pate, some thin bands of hair above his ears, and a healthy moustache. His handshake was firm and his eyes sparkled as do those of all people with a huge enthusiasm for life. I noticed that his fingers were semi-crippled by arthritis. He wore what turned out to be his preferred clothing of a light blue flying shirt, navy trousers and unpolished black shoes. I took a liking to Russell straight away. He joined us for a few beers as he wound down after a busy day of flying. We swapped a good few yarns before calling it quits around midnight.

After spending the night at the local motor camp we were off at dawn. The plan was for us to drive to the Hollyford Valley airstrip where we were to meet Russell at 9 o'clock.

We followed the Te Anau to Milford Sound road for an hour or more before turning right into the Hollyford Valley. The road was spectacular, with native bush growing over the top of it and forming a tunnel of trees in many places. The scenery was every bit as magnificent as I had imagined, with sheer rock faces forming the valley sides and wide tussock flats that eventually gave way to dense bush as we approached the main mountain divide. We passed many small, clear mountain lakes that were littered with fallen and long-dead trees.

We made a quick stop at 'Gun's Camp', a camping ground, store and museum situated near the start of the Hollyford Track. The wiry old man who ran the store was Murray Gunn, the son of a famous folk hero from the area. Murray tried to sell the young chaps some bottles of water 'that had the electricity taken out of it . . . genuine electricity-free water straight from the tailrace below the Manapouri power station'. They almost bought some too.

We drove the remaining three kilometres to the Hollyford airstrip. Well, the sign said 'Hollyford airstrip', and the arrow pointed in that direction, but all we could find was a bend in the road with a gravel pit at the end. It certainly didn't look like an airstrip, but nonetheless it had to be the place where we were supposed to be.

We drove to the end of the short strip of road and parked the car there. The valley was sided by high, sheer rock walls. On the lower slopes there was a thin band of native bush, and running parallel to the road we were parked on was the clear-flowing Hollyford River. As soon as I left the safety of the car sandflies hit me with amazing ferocity. There were millions of them and they attacked in swarms, or at least it seemed that way. There was no respite from them, and despite it being a sunny day I quickly returned to the confines of the car.

Nine o'clock came and went with no sign of Russell. By ten I was starting to get a bit concerned. About then a stag started roaring from within the bush across the river. Needless to say I was galvanised into action, the sandflies instantly forgotten. I quickly grabbed my rifle and shoved some bullets into the magazine. The stag was settling in well and was by this stage roaring at regular intervals. He was not more than four hundred metres away in the band of bush across the river. Having sorted out the direction the wind was coming from I set out to cross the river well below the stag. I was knee deep in the river when I clearly heard the sound of an approaching plane. Bugger.

Russell had told us the previous night that he was going to squeeze our flight in between other tourist flights and that he wanted us ready to go when he arrived. I shot back to the car and was almost there when the plane banked steeply around some tall trees near the road-end. It straightened and dropped quickly into its approach with a noticeable drop in engine revs.

Holy shit! I thought. He's going to land on the car.

From my skydiving days I knew that visibility from the cockpit of the plane would be limited, and I feared the pilot would not see the car parked on the road-end that was clearly going to be his landing strip. At the last instant Russell saw the obstruction, gunned the plane's motor and pulled up again. Realising that we had made a major stuff-up by parking on the road, I yelled to my mates to move the car immediately.

Russell buzzed the strip on his way back down the valley to ensure the offending vehicle had been removed from the airstrip. It had been, and the way was now clear for him to line up for a second attempt at landing. Russell touched down safely after following the same procedure as in his first attempt.

To say that Russell wasn't happy conveniently understates the situation. He gave us an uncensored version of our pedigrees, a telling-off we fully deserved. He also mentioned that pilots only get to die once, and that he would prefer it to be through a mistake he made rather than through the thoughtless actions of some city slickers. Message received.

Russell remained pretty grumpy with us as we flew to Martins Bay. The in-flight commentary was very limited, but his annoyance was justified.

We flew above the Hollyford River as we travelled towards Martins Bay. On either side were steep, weathered, smooth rock walls that oozed water even though it was fine and sunny. The valley proper was covered in dense native forest, with the

Hollyford River meandering through it towards the West Coast. The river was very clear and I amused myself trying to spot trout and deer from the plane.

Near the junction of the Hollyford and Pyke rivers Russell veered left and took a shorter route over a low saddle. Soon we got our first look at Lake McKerrow and could see clear to the coast some 18 kilometres away. The lake was flanked on either side by very steep bush-clad mountains. The tops were a mixture of exposed rock and sparse tussock and were every bit as steep and rugged as I had imagined them to be. The whole way we were spoiled with brilliant scenery, and it was easy to see why tourists by the thousands travel huge distances at great cost to see it.

Towards the bottom end of the lake Russell pointed out the Hokuri Hut, which was to be our home for the next nine days. The hut sat on the lake edge a few kilometres above where the river spills out on its final journey to the sea. A short distance away on the seaward side of the hut, the Hokuri Valley branched off to the north.

Russell veered the plane up the valley and told us that we should concentrate our efforts around that general area. He generously flew us up the valley, showing us a number of clearings, access routes and 'hot spots' that he knew of. At one time Russell had been a professional deer hunter, both by foot and from helicopters, so I took a serious interest in any tips he gave us.

At the coastal end of the lake the valley widens into large forest-covered flats with low hills on each side. At regular intervals we saw private huts dotting the lakeside. The Hollyford River flows approximately nine kilometres from Lake McKerrow to the coast, averaging about a hundred metres in width the whole distance. For the final three or four kilometres the river is flanked on one side by large sand dunes and on the other by low scrub.

Russell made a wide circumnavigation of a semi-cleared piece of land on the northern side of the river where a mown airstrip ran alongside it. As we flew over the coastal end Russell pointed out a colony of seals that were basking on the rocks below.

The trip was planned for us, and all we had to do was front up at the arranged places at the arranged times. Part one was flying into Martins Bay. We were to be met there by Neil Drysdale, who would lend us a dinghy to take our gear up the Hollyford River and across Lake McKerrow to the Hokuri Hut. This was why we had brought an outboard motor and fuel with us. Further, the boat would open up huge tracts of land for us to hunt and offer a means of getting out in an emergency should we need to. It was all too easy.

Russell made a soft landing and taxied the plane towards a small building situated near the middle of the runway. The building turned out to be a meat safe and diesel-powered chiller for hanging the many deer shot by the landowner. Parked beside the building was a three-wheeled motorbike with a trailer attached to it. After the plane came to a stop and the motor died, a man emerged from the meat safe. After we had extricated ourselves from the plane, Russell introduced us to Neil.

Neil was about 50 years old, had a huge chest, solid legs, and was, generally speaking, of a very solid build. Despite this he was

no more than 5'5" tall. He had square facial features and sported three or four days' growth of whiskers. His mop of unruly hair was predominantly and prematurely grey.

Mooching around Neil was a Weimaraner bitch named Penny. I later found out that Penny was the key to Neil's consistent success while hunting. Her finely tuned nose sought out deer and led Neil to them as surely as an alcoholic finds a pub.

While we were being introduced to Neil we were hit by swarms of sandflies. I was wearing long pants but had on a short-sleeved shirt, and in self-defence I constantly swatted the sandflies as they launched a full-on attack upon me. There were millions of the damned things, and any exposed skin was fair game. Neil, on the other hand, was wearing a pair of shorts and a loose-fitting singlet. He must have been on friendly terms with the local sandfly population as they weren't bothering him at all.

'Gidday, lad,' Neil greeted me as he pumped my hand vigorously. From that point on, and for many years to come, Neil referred to me as 'lad' whenever we spoke. Prior to our arrival Neil had been busy in the meat safe preparing three deer carcasses for the flight out to civilisation with Russell. After loading our gear onto the waiting trailer we watched as Neil finished preparing the carcasses.

It was very encouraging to have heard a stag roar at us earlier in the day and then to see three deer hanging in Neil's meat safe. There must be hundreds of them in these parts, I thought. Maybe it was just like the old days my old man used to talk of when deer were in plague proportions and shooting them was as easy as getting out of bed. I was getting a really good feeling about this trip already.

I hadn't shot a stag as yet, and seemed to have a strange knack of finding only hinds. The few stags I stumbled upon had, through varying stuff-ups on my part, all managed to avoid getting shot. I put this down to the 'stag bogeyman' who, although unseen, was always finding new ways to get a laugh out of my misfortune.

By now it was lunchtime, and Neil invited us all to his hut for a brew and a bite. Soon after that Russell was off, with the deer carcasses duly stowed on board. Neil offered to show us the way to the Hokuri Hut and how to survive the traps of river navigation. Most of our gear was stowed in Neil's aluminium boat, and the two young fellows elected to follow Neil and me in the dinghy we were borrowing. We travelled slowly up the river with the dinghy close behind, and Neil pointed out various shallow parts and some submerged logs that needed to be avoided. When we reached the lake proper Neil left the youngsters behind as we powered across it.

As we went Neil gave me a running commentary of the area's history. About two kilometres below the Hokuri Hut we eased into a deep-water bay that formed an ideal harbour. Neil told me that the bay was in fact a surveyed township called Jamestown. Numerous land titles had been surveyed many years ago when Jamestown had been intended to be settled and established as the nearest New Zealand port to Australia. The plan was for gold to be conveyed from the Otago goldfields to Jamestown and then shipped to Australia. The town never came to anything, but many of the surveyed sections remain in private ownership today. At that time there was only one private hunting bach there.

We motored onward and soon arrived at the Hokuri Hut. The others were still a long way behind us as Neil and I unloaded the boat and placed the gear in a large pile on the gravel beach. We then walked the 30 or so metres to the hut, which was in a small clearing surrounded by native bush on all sides. There was a large porch on the lake side, with a healthy stack of firewood piled on it. Inside was a large open fireplace, a dining table and a series of bunks contained in two open-ended rooms. The bloody sandflies were there in their millions, so all the windows had fine wire flyscreen covers in an effort to keep them outside. All in all it was a very comfortable hut.

Before long the others arrived, a brew was had, then Neil set off back to his hut. He told us he'd be back in a day or so to see how we were getting on, and he even offered to take any deer we shot back to his chiller. I had never had it so good.

Neil's parting piece of advice was, 'Don't take the boat out onto the lake when it's blowing from the east. Chops the lake up real bad and chances are you'll drown yourselves.'

It was about 3 o'clock by the time we were settled in properly. We had the hut to ourselves and I was keen to explore the area. I took off to the mouth of the Hokuri River, a walk of 15 minutes along a slippery track covered with roots, rocks and mud. There were plenty of deer tracks on the soft gravel beaches but no fresh deer droppings. I wandered into the bush for the rest of the afternoon but failed to see any deer. I was pleasantly surprised at the openness of the bush. From the air it had looked dense and impenetrable, but in many places it was quite open and easy to hunt. The floor was damp and very quiet to stalk.

I have deliberately avoided describing my two hunting companions. This is partially due to the fact that I didn't know much about them to start with, and also because some of the events that follow might prove embarrassing for them if they were identified and that wouldn't be fair. To get around this problem I have given my companions fictitious names, as they turned out to be good company but in need of some refinement as far as bush etiquette goes.

Brian, at 17 years of age, had just left school. He was about 5'8" tall, of thin build, and missing the hardening characteristics associated with a teenager on the verge of becoming a man. His facial features were fine and the customary whiskers of youth were as yet absent. A dense mop of thick, collar-length hair completed the picture. This being his first hunt, he was fizzing at the gills to bag a deer. He was armed with a new rifle, the calibre of which I don't remember. Brian didn't have any fancy hunting gear but instead had kitted himself out in a pair of jeans, a t-shirt and a green army surplus jersey.

Joe (an alias derived from *G.I. Joe*) was 18 and a volunteer territorial soldier in the army. He was of similar build to Brian but had greater confidence in himself. His light brown hair was cut in the standard army short back and sides, and the shadow of whiskers indicated his transition to manhood. Joe had an air of confidence about him and chatted freely. His quick wit and sharp sense of humour soon became apparent.

That night we indulged in a few beers but retired early as we were all heading out at first light for a hunt. I offered to take one of my companions with me for the day, but both declined, as they preferred to hunt together.

I took off well before dawn and again made for the rivermouth, waiting inside the bush edge there for daylight to arrive. When it finally did there were no deer cavorting about in the open. A quick waltz up the small flat revealed more of the same so I headed into the bush on the true left of the Hokuri River for a stalk. Bush travel was relatively open but most gullies were tangled with supplejack vine and some bush lawyer that at times made the traverse along the lower slopes troublesome. There was a lot of crown fern but little of what I deemed to be good deer tucker available, and little evidence of deer sign. By 9.30 I had not seen or spooked any animals and was beginning to lose concentration, so I stopped for a snack before continuing my sidle up the valley. I hadn't travelled far after my break when I sighted a hind a mere 30 metres away, standing motionless and staring down at me from above. Camp meat featured high on my list of priorities, so without hesitation I raised my rifle and neck shot her. The hind was quite small and her coat was very rough and unkempt. From this I deduced that she was probably a motherless fawn now aged about six months – prime eating.

I arrived back at the hut at around midday. About an hour later my mates, who had elected to hunt above the hut, returned. They too had been successful and were overjoyed. They told their story with great enthusiasm and were justifiably rapt with their efforts. Their story went something like this . . .

Having climbed high they happened upon a big slip and discovered a large hind grazing on it well below them. They decided they would both shoot at it simultaneously to ensure success. Fair enough so far. Both settled themselves for resting downhill shots. On the three count they opened fire. The hind tumbled over and began rolling down the slip. My mates, deeming her to be still alive, fired again and again and again, and I'm not sure how many times over and above this until it finally wasn't moving. Chances are it was only moving due to the continuous impact of the great many bullets and was probably dead after the first volley. Brian and Joe were elated and made their way to the hind. When they reached it they discovered that their efforts had been very effective, and that almost every part of the deer's body was riddled with bullet holes. Never having hunted or killed an animal before, they had no idea how to butcher it (a situation I had also been in many years previously). They managed to hack the deer into submission, taking the front and hind legs and also the portion of back steaks that wasn't damaged beyond use by bullet trauma. The load was divided up between them for the return carry to the hut. They had failed to take a daypack with them so they had struggled back, dragging and carrying the meat as best they could. They were in one hell of a state on their arrival back at the hut, and were covered in blood, mud and vegetation.

Brian and Joe were justifiably thrilled by their success. After all, they had achieved in one day what had taken me several years. I shared their elation and we all celebrated with a few beers. My mates were a bit upset when I showed them how to field butcher the meat, as a large percentage of the meat they had struggled so hard to drag off the hill was damaged beyond use and had to be thrown away. We all went out again that afternoon for another hunt but we sighted nothing more that day, or in fact for the next four days.

It is my habit when in the bush to wash myself every day, whether it be summer or winter. While at the Hokuri Hut I headed to the lake after dark each day and got in fully clothed. It was April and the lake was bloody cold. Armed with a bar of soap I'd give my clothes a good wash, throw them ashore, then give myself a good scrub to finish off. My wet clothing was hung up to dry beside the fire each night, and was clean and dry at the start of each day.

This routine could only be done after dark when the sandflies had disappeared – getting naked before then would have resulted in a great feast for them and an itchy pincushion effect on me. Despite the sandflies going to bed at dark there was no respite from biting insects, though, as the mosquitoes came out to play as soon as the sandflies went away.

While we were at the hut Neil visited us often to see how we were getting on. Most days he would have a deer or two in his boat. These were shot somewhere up the lake and his visits would be made as he returned to his hut. Each evening before dark we would also see helicopters working the guts and gullies across the lake from our hut. Occasionally one would fly overhead and disappear into the mountain range behind the hut. Most days we saw a deer or two hanging beneath the helicopters. Given the high pressure placed on wild deer over a very long period of time, I could only wonder how they managed to avoid becoming extinct.

Stewart Island

The blood of a hunting man wouldn't run red if he hadn't at some time yearned to hunt the elusive white-tailed deer of Stewart Island. When a bunch of Twizel hunters jacked up a trip and put out the call for some extras to make up numbers and reduce costs, I was in quicker than a con man finds a sucker.

White-tailed deer are only found in two locations in New Zealand – at the head of Lake Wakatipu and on Stewart Island. These deer are elusive and very wary. They have a reputation for silently appearing in front of a hunter where moments before there had been nothing. I had read a lot about these 'ghost' deer and was itching to have a crack at them myself.

And so, on an April day, seven hearty blokes assembled at Bluff and spent a night on the juice in the local pub. Needless to say, too many beers crossed my lips, and our departure time arrived far sooner than was comfortable. The day that greeted us was a real bummer. The wind howled, and a look across the harbour revealed a huge, angry swell, despite its sheltered location.

The Wairua, the ferry we were catching on the first leg of the journey to our hunting block, strained against its moorings at the wharf. Still suffering from the excesses of the previous night, I was not looking forward to crossing Foveaux Strait in it.

With our gear safely stowed on the boat, we headed for the warmth of the bar. Fortunately it was shut, and wouldn't open until after the ship set sail. Some of us played cards to take our minds off the surging motion of the boat, others hugged the railing, hoping the fresh air would help settle their queasy stomachs. As soon as the ferry was set free from its moorings it started to heave and shudder. Even while the ship was still inside the harbour we were thrown about, and playing cards became impossible. Plenty of people were delivering their breakfasts over the side to the sea gods, and I admit that I was feeling a bit rugged myself and had to retreat outside to the wind and sea spray in the hope of retaining my breakfast.

Needless to say, the trip across the strait was miserable. At one time I was standing in a corridor that gave open passage from one side of the boat to the other. A number of huge waves broke across the side of the boat and flowed ankle-deep through the passageway, making the phrase 'holding on for grim death' take on a new reality. No one was more pleased than I was to reach the sanctuary of Halfmoon Bay on Stewart Island.

The second leg of our trip was to be by a small fishing boat owned and operated by Herbie Hansen. Herbie met us at the wharf, but said we might have to spend a night there to wait out the storm. He asked us to return a couple of hours later, when he would make a final decision on whether to head to our hunting block that day or wait.

We spent the time exploring Halfmoon Bay, where a highlight was seeing a pet white-tailed deer in a small enclosure beside the only hotel. On our return, Herbie made the call that we were off.

The decision to go had been somewhat forced by an additional passenger who was to travel with us – the local constable, who had received reports of poaching on one of the southern hunting blocks. Apparently hunters from adjoining blocks were on the verge of an all-out war and threats had been made that someone would get shot, all because one party was poaching on the other's block. The situation wasn't helped by additional reports that one of the poachers was hunting with a pistol, a forbidden weapon on the island.

After securing our gear below deck, we again headed to sea. Herbie's fishing boat bobbed and heaved a lot more than the ferry had, and I soon wished that option two – staying put – had been selected. During the voyage I grilled the policeman, and was pretty impressed with his hunting stories. I gained the impression that the people who wrote about the white-tailed deer clearly had bugger-all idea of how it was done, as my new-found friend insisted they were easy meat and that he had personally walloped hundreds of them. I noted that he had his rifle with him, and when I enquired about it, he replied, 'Once I've sorted out the poaching problem I just might bag a deer or two before Herbie comes back to get me.'

He added that although he had the use of a police boat he didn't want to use it in case the poachers saw him arrive and hid the pistol. It was his intention to get dropped off and walk to the offender's camp, pretending to be a tramper. He hoped they would not suspect who he was, and that they would unwittingly disclose the pistol's existence.

About three hours later we arrived at our destination, Pikaroro Point, on the northeast side of the island. As we unloaded the dinghy that was to ferry our gear ashore the constable pointed out a deer as it quietly snuck away through some ponga trees and crown fern. Seeing it really fired me up, and also gave added credibility to the constable's stories.

As our gear was being manhandled from the boat to the dinghy, Herbie made it clear that he was less than impressed by the fact that we had packed much of it in cardboard boxes. When wet, these disintegrate, and common sense suggested that our gear should have been stored in string potato sacks or something similar. Amazing, isn't it, how obvious common sense is when it's pointed out to you. Fortunately we managed to get our excessive amount of gear safely to our campsite without any cartons collapsing. I began to wonder how much hunting was going to be done, given the mountain of beer that was landed. Herbie waved farewell and continued south to drop our constable friend off at his destination.

A Maori tribe owns the Pikaroro Point block and we paid them a fee for the privilege of hunting there. Other parts of Stewart Island are national park, and no fees are required.

Our campsite was situated above a steep embankment, beneath a cluster of stunted, wind-tormented trees. There were a number of new tarpaulins scattered about the campsite, all branded with the New Zealand Railways logo. We turned a blind eye to how they came to be there, due to the excellent shelter they subsequently provided. Ask no questions and you'll be told no lies.

After erecting a large tent for cooking and drying wet gear, and another for sleeping quarters, we all set off for a quick exploration of our block. This was cut short by a lengthy hailstorm. Some of the hailstones were bigger than wine-bottle corks, and cover had to be sought during the heaviest falls to avoid serious injury.

According to the information I had read about white-tailed deer, they prefer to live close to the coastline and often feed on the kelp that washes up on the beaches. Armed with this pearl of wisdom, the next morning I set out with Simon to stalk the foreshore near our camp. Our plan was to hunt in a figure-of-eight pattern. This meant one of us hunted the scrub, sea grass and bush nearest the sea, while the other hunted further inland. Every three hundred metres or so we would cross over and swap hunting spots.

The ground was thickly covered in hailstones when we set off at first light. Hunting the shoreline proved the most difficult. It was steep, and often broken by low cliffs and dense scrub. I drew the first inland beat and, not wanting to get ahead of Simon, I strained to keep an eye on him as he struggled along. After our first position swap, I discovered just how hard the sea beat was.

We had only been on the go for 30 minutes when it was again my turn on the inland beat. Simon disappeared over the side into thick scrub and instantly a white-tailed deer popped out of it some 30 metres ahead of him. It had clearly been spooked by the noise Simon made, and I watched its white tail flash as it bounded off through a dense patch of supplejack. I didn't expect the deer to stop, and despite my best efforts I could not get my scope crosshairs to settle on it. I couldn't believe my luck when the deer stopped and peered back in Simon's direction. Its tail was up, giving a perfect highlighted white target in the dim light of the bush. A shot fair up its jacksy sorted out the camp meat situation, and we were only a short distance from camp too.

That was the only live deer I saw while armed with a gun on this trip, and I was bloody lucky to get it. Needless to say, little credit was given to Simon who was blissfully unaware of how events had unfolded. I hunted hard every day but only succeeded in locating a number of dead and clearly poisoned deer. I inspected every carcass but in each case found no bullet hole. There wasn't supposed to be any poisoning of deer on Maori hunting blocks, and I was very disappointed at finding this to be untrue.

For the uninitiated, I'd better let you in on a few details about the topography of Stewart Island. Firstly, while the island does have a low mountain range at its southern end, it is predominantly low-level rolling country. The highest waterfall is a mere four or so metres in height. The coastline is made up of many bays, which range in size from tiny to massive. A lot of them look alike, and often it is difficult to distinguish one from another. Throughout mainland New Zealand a hunter needs only to follow a creek or river and he will eventually find his way to safety. This is not always the case on Stewart Island. Often a creek will flow inland and dissipate into a swamp, leaving any hunter who thought he was headed towards the coast very frustrated and disoriented. Armed with this knowledge, I had taken the precaution of taking a compass with me to ensure I wouldn't fall into that trap.

Towards the end of our trip, and given the lack of deer sightings along the coast, I decided that an inland hunt was called for. It was early afternoon when I headed out of the camp and walked south across the peninsula we were camped beside and into the next bay. From there I took a compass reading and headed directly inland. The theory was simple enough – head in on one compass bearing and return by heading 180 degrees in the reverse direction. I hunted slowly, checking my bearing occasionally, and was all concentration. I circumnavigated patches of windfall and took the occasional detour around dense patches of bush and areas of supplejack.

Time has a habit of disappearing quickly when you are hunting, and when I next looked at my watch it was about an hour short of dark. I had been on the go for nearly three hours, and although I had been travelling slowly I knew I had covered a fair bit of territory. More importantly, I hadn't sighted a deer or even spooked one to get me excited. I headed for home, not much bothered with being quiet or stalking. After half an hour's steady walking I hadn't reached the coast and decided that, in view of the fading light, I'd better rattle my arse along a bit. I broke into a half-run, and some time later started to doubt the compass and myself. Surely I should have hit the coast by now? I knew I had wandered off my bearing from time to time but not far enough, I thought, to cause me any problems. My heart started racing, but with a bit of effort I managed to convince myself that I was in fact headed in the right direction.

Like a cold drink in the desert, suddenly the coast 'just appeared' in front of me. I broke free of the scrub and stood studying my surroundings from the top of a small bluff. No doubt about it, I had never been in this bay before.

'Christ! How far off my compass bearing have I wandered?' I asked myself.

Darkness was only a quarter of an hour away, and I had to choose a direction to travel to return to camp. Common sense told me I should head to my left, that being the opposite direction to the one I had taken when I left camp. I took off at a fast trot, hoping to get a look into the next bay before dark. I hadn't covered more than two hundred metres when I fell arse over gimlet. I had been foot tripped by the guy ropes of a tent some bastard had pitched smack on the deer trail I was following. Closer inspection revealed the tent to be one of our own. I had come out of the bush a short distance from our camp, and hadn't recognised the bay from where I emerged. Wouldn't it be embarrassing if anyone found out?

If the hunting was not very fruitful the fishing was great, and getting a feed of blue cod was as easy as throwing a fishing line into the water. At low tide we gathered paua ('abalone' to some), and this, added to our supply of venison, meant we dined like kings for the full seven days we were on the block. My only regret was that we didn't have a diver with us to gather crayfish and perhaps oysters to supplement our 'humble' diet.

We suffered gale-force winds, snow and hailstorms during our stay. They all added to the experience, and the weather was

perhaps a blessing in that it kept us in camp long enough to put a hole in our ample supplies of beer.

The sandflies on this block were the hungriest bastards I have ever suffered in New Zealand. Their savagery was comparable to a school of piranha fish at feeding time. Any attempt to wash before dark was foiled by their relentless and vicious attacks. Despite this, the day of our departure arrived too soon. While we waited for Herbie, a final cook-up of paua was had on the beach. Another member of our party prepared and cooked the feed, using my clean frypan, which is part of an enclosed kit, as none of the others was readily accessible. I went fishing and presumed the pan would be cleaned and returned to my pack when the feed was over. I discovered some weeks later, when I next went to use it, how wrong I was. The frypan had green fungus growing all over it and the smell was horrendous. The kind buggers hadn't cleaned it before returning it to my pack and I hadn't checked it on my return.

Herbie told me that our constable friend had recovered the said pistol, and thus prevented all-out war between the offending hunting parties. He had stayed in their camps for several days, making sure things had settled down before he left. Herbie claimed the constable had shot five deer from their blocks while he was there. Apparently this didn't go down too well with the holders of the hunting permits, but given their earlier behaviour they weren't in a position to complain.

When we got back to Bluff I picked up a copy of the local paper, the *Southland Times*. In it was an article about the day we had travelled to Stewart Island. It said that conditions were so bad that day that the ferry master considered turning the boat around and returning to Bluff. The winds were apparently among the strongest ever recorded for the area. In view of this, I felt immensely proud of the fact that I had managed to hold onto my breakfast under testing conditions, and despite a heavy night out prior to our departure.

Pukataraki

Now there are bosses and there are bosses. If you've ever worked for a bastard boss you'll know where I'm coming from. The veritable bastard boss thinks that a worker who spends more than two minutes on the toilet is ripping the business off. On the other hand, the good bastard boss thinks a bit differently. He knows that a bloke who spends a few extra moments on the can is deep in thought and is, generally speaking, thinking up ways of making the business work better and thus generate more profit. Must be right or people wouldn't spend so much time there, would they?

It is fair to say that on the odd occasion while a man's absent from the 'work face' his mind might wander to the mountains, and he might therefore be a bit less productive than he would otherwise have been. But a good boss can be recognised by his character, and his ability to separate work from play. He knows what the score is, and seems to be finely tuned to the way his employee is thinking, and thus gets a fair day's work out of his staff.

It was while I was on the toilet contemplating jacking up another trip into the mountains that a voice lurched over the top of the cubicle next to me.

'I hear you're a hunting man, Al.'

Jeepers, it's the boss, I thought.

I hadn't realised he was beside me, and instantly thought that he was there keeping an eye on me.

'Yep, mate. Sure am,' I replied, hoping he wasn't timing the event.

'I'm heading into the hills to spook up a deer or two with a couple of mates weekend after next. There's a spot for you if you want to tag along.'

Too bloody right I did. The voice belonged to Russ, my immediate supervisor. Now as far as bosses go Russ was a good bastard, although up to this point I hadn't realised that he was a hunting man. I was also relieved to establish that he didn't have the clock on me. If he had, I might have set a record for the longest dump, time-wise I mean.

Russ stands at about 6'0", is of average build, and at that time was showing signs of having outgrown his haircut; the balding patch on the front of his darkly tanned forehead gave testament to that. Russ was a bloke everyone took a liking to. You couldn't do otherwise, as he went out of his way to be helpful, had a great sense of humour, and told numerous yarns without repeating himself. He also had a habit of pulling pranks on folks, and a bloke had to be a bit careful around him else he might find himself on the receiving end, much to the amusement of everyone else.

I was later to find out that Russ suffers from 'Jekyll and Hyde' syndrome and has two distinct personalities. One is a townie who, while humorous and great company, is a bit reserved and doesn't 'bend the rod' too far. The other is his out-of-town persona. Now this out-of-town chap hits his straps about the same time as the 4 x 4 hits the gravel and a pint hits his tonsils. If a man was looking for a few laughs and good company in the hills, he couldn't find better.

Long before daybreak on the designated day, I was picked up from my home and whisked away towards the Canterbury high country. In the flat-deck, single-cab truck was another chap who

I had not previously met. His name was Jock, and he seemed to spend a fair bit of his time winding Russ up, in a light-hearted sort of way.

We stopped and picked up a fourth member of our party, Kevin, as we made our way inland. Clearly I was the odd one out on the trip, as the others all knew each other well. Prior to picking up Kevin the three of us had crammed into the front cab, but getting four in wasn't an option. To solve the problem Russ and I assigned ourselves the prime spots on the rear deck of the ute. Not that they seemed at first glance like the prime spots, until we discovered that the weekend's supply of beer had been stashed there as well. Without any further ado, Russ and I launched into it.

All was going well as we travelled into the Lees Valley in fine but cold winter conditions. We were headed to the Pukataraki hunting block. Russ had somehow weaselled a gate key from the local runholder, the use of which would take three to four hours' walk out of the journey. In compensation for this shortened travelling time we had thrown in a few extra beers to ensure that we really enjoyed our visit.

After leaving the graded road of the Lees Valley we cut across farmland towards our destination. By the time we had passed through the normally locked gate the weather had deteriorated considerably. The weak sun had disappeared, and the temperature dropped from bearable to bloody freezing. Russ and I heaved a tarpaulin over ourselves in an attempt to keep dry, as a heavy fall of sleet cum snow descended upon us. Russ reckoned the answer was to be as cold inside as out, and chucked me another beer. Jock and Kevin, who were as warm as toast in the front cab, were oblivious to our plight.

Our intention was to drive to a hut on the top of the range and to hunt from there in the evening and again at first light. Soon enough we were headed uphill on a rough farm track. None of us had been to the hut before, but it was clearly marked on the map and we had no doubt that we could find it. We struck trouble when we found ourselves sliding sideways on the now very wet and muddy track. The ute had road tyres on it and they were proving very unsuitable for the conditions. We were slipping and sliding all over the place, and several times it looked like we were going to slide clean off the track. By the time we decided to flag the idea of getting to the top of the hill we had suffered half a dozen near-death experiences and several heart attacks each. The return trip to the bottom of the hill was very entertaining and, at times, dangerous. I found that the beers helped to relieve the tension, and was quite satisfied that I could vacate the ute in an instant if we rolled over or slid off the track. Russ didn't seem too concerned either. By this time we were both freezing cold and couldn't have cared one way or the other anyway.

At the bottom a quick consultation of the map revealed that there was another hut a few kilometres up the creek from where we were parked. The rough track that led upstream didn't inspire me much, as it closely resembled a one-lane sheep track. Half a kilometre later we found ourselves stuck in a deep creek that we had been forced to try and cross. The trip into the creek bottom was accomplished without any problems, but we found ourselves stuck firmly when Jock tried to drive out the other side. Our warm heroes from inside the heated cab yelled instructions on how Russ and I could extricate them from the predicament they had got us into, but showed a remarkable reluctance to get out and help.

It soon became obvious that we were going to have to remove more than a few shovelfuls of dirt to free ourselves from the mud trap we were in. Reluctantly Kevin and Jock entered our frozen world, only to discover that their treasured supply of beer had been substantially lowered.

Having already suffered the intense cold of the sleet and snow, I wasn't inclined towards jumping into the deep, snow-fed stream to attach the winch rope that was going to be required to pull us out of our predicament. Even more reluctantly, Kevin found himself wading the creek with water lapping at his private parts. Not long after this we were free of the creek and the call was made to head back. The track we were following was clearly better suited to a four-legged mode of transport than four-wheel-drive. A further scan of the map revealed a hut on a flat not far from our current location but in the opposite direction. Within half an hour we were parked beside it. Now that hut had a really good feel to it. It was very, very old, had a rusted roof, and a good coating of mouse droppings everywhere. A more welcome home couldn't be found anywhere. The gods poked their nose in at the same time as we arrived at the hut by clearing away the sleet and bathing us in brilliant sunshine.

Before long we had a raging fire burning and the world seemed good again. The fifth member of our party, Mr Jack Daniels, soon made his presence known, and all thoughts of hunting were forgotten. Finding ice for the drinks wasn't a problem. The cold snow lying on the ground outside took care of that.

Now if you've ever been on a hunting trip with a bunch of blokes you have not met before, you'd have to agree that the quickest way to find out how they tick is to fill them up with a few beers. Before you know it, a chap's real character comes to the surface. Well, Jock and Kevin also turned out to be really good bastards.

The food and grog had been arranged by Jock and we had all chipped in a few bob to take care of the cost side of things. When the time for our evening meal arrived, Jock produced a full length of fillet steak. He proceeded to roast a large assortment of vegetables in a camp oven and told us to fry our own steaks, which we were to cut from the fillet. I took my lead from Jock and hacked off a piece of steak about three inches thick. The final touch was two bottles of red wine that Jock produced as we sat down to eat.

Now this all seemed very civilised, and about this time I was beginning to think that my new-found companions had this hunting caper sorted. Nonetheless, I decided I shouldn't rush my decision on the matter, and that I'd better wait a bit longer to see. Numerous jokes were told and I learnt a fair bit about each of the characters I was with. I'd be lying if I didn't acknowledge that we all had a few too many drinks, and that the level of intelligent conversation had all but evaporated by the time we retired to bed. It was during this time that I first heard Jock say, 'I don't care who your father is, you're not walking on the bloody water while I'm fishing here.' This was his catch-cry for the trip, which he used whenever he didn't agree with what was going on.

Some time in the middle of the night we were woken by Jock bumbling about the hut causing a huge racket as he tripped and stumbled over a series of pots and pans.

'What the heck are you up to?' slurred Russ.

'I'm hungry,' Jock replied. 'Thought I'd have another cook-up. Want some?'

Before we knew it round two of fillet steak was on the go. This was okay by us, but when Jock decided that a side dish of onions was 'just the story' it brought tears to our eyes. The hut was filled with the aroma of freshly cut, eye-watering onions, and we suffered badly until the door was opened and the cooking stopped. This feed turned out to be even better than the first one.

As Jock sat eating and slipping in a few more glasses of Jack Daniels he commented, 'You know what? A man sure has a lot of fun making himself sick.'

This comment kind of sums Jock up. He has boundless energy, a wry wit, and laughs easily. Don't be fooled, he's a very intelligent man, but he has the knack of relating to people in an easy-going sort of way. He stands at about 5'10" and is deceptively skinny. His slightly stooped shoulders and hawk-like facial features were accentuated by the large, oval glasses he wore. Jock and Russ were great mates. Were then and still are. They had hunted together throughout the Canterbury region for many years, and that night they told many hard-case tales of their adventures. One story stuck in my mind so I'll share it with you.

When Russ and Jock were newly married young men they managed to convince their brides that they were great hunters and providers. According to them they had only to be given approval and they would take off into the mountains and return with great quantities of expensive venison that was normally enjoyed only by lords and kings. This powerful argument in favour of a hunting trip was met with unexpected enthusiasm, and our heroes duly set off into the mountainous Canterbury backcountry. At this time Jock and Russ were both carpenters and met the standard 'hard case bastard' requirement of that job. Two motorbikes were pulled onto a trailer and off they went. At the road-end the bikes were off-loaded and our heroes set about loading their gear into packs and onto the motorbikes. Problem one was encountered when the standard crate of beer that each of them had couldn't be balanced on the said bikes without risk of breakage. This problem was pondered for some time before a decision was made to cram everything into the packs they were to carry on their backs. As you can imagine, getting 12 large bottles of beer into each of their packs, along with tents, clothing, food, cooking equipment and sleeping bags wasn't going to be easy. Clearly there was a problem. Russ eventually announced that he was going to have to leave some of the beer behind. Jock's response to this proposal was, 'Don't be stupid, ya idiot. Throw out the food.' And that's exactly what they did. Faced with the same situation today I reckon their decision wouldn't alter.

Having said that, food was clearly of considerable importance to Jock, and it was some time before we all settled down again to grab some sleep. Well before daylight the next morning I headed off upstream for a hunt. The country was new to me so I thought I'd locate the hut we had headed to the previous day. There had to be a good chance of spotting a deer as I travelled the creek bed, I thought.

After two hours' walking I still hadn't reached the hut. Every time I rounded a bend in the creek I expected to see it, but I didn't. It was now well after daylight and the day had become hot. This was typical of high country weather – snowing one day and a heatwave the next.

I rounded a corner and startled two Canada geese. They stood in the creek and honked at me, but they didn't fly off. I decided that any self-respecting deer would have returned to the bush and settled down for a day's sleep long before now. Given this, the geese were fair game. I lined up on one of them and let rip. The goose dropped dead on the spot. The second one flew off before I could sort it out as well. I wasn't overjoyed by my success, but realised that it was likely to be my only chance of getting something for the pot that day.

By a fortunate fluke I had shot the goose through the lower neck and hadn't ruined any of the meat. I did, however, have a problem. I had never before shot a game bird, and had absolutely no idea how to dress it out. I decided to lug it back to the hut where the 'experts' could give me a lesson, and headed back with the bird in tow. I was the first to get back to the hut, and promptly set about lowering the beer supply. Given the heat of the day it was an easy task. Kevin returned not long after I did, but Jock and Russ were nowhere to be seen.

We had all left the hut at about the same time, just before 5.30. When Jock and Russ hadn't returned by 9 p.m. I started to wonder if they were okay, and went for a walk down the valley to see if I could locate them. I soon spotted them, but they were still miles away and were sauntering towards the hut. I returned to the hut and grabbed three ice-cold beers from the creek before setting off again to meet them. About 15 minutes from the hut I hid in some scrub and ambushed them, firing a round into the air as they walked past my hiding spot. Russ and Jock nearly shit themselves. After informing me of my pedigree and rearranging their underpants they decided, when I produced the cold beers, that I wasn't such a bad sort after all.

It turned out that they had had a huge day in the hills. After walking for hours while glassing the open tussock country, and having sighted no game, they finally entered a patch of scrub near the valley head. They stalked this together for a short time before stumbling onto a large boar that was asleep there. Unfortunately neither Jock nor Russ had noticed the boar before Jock nearly stood on it. All hell broke loose, with the pig taking off into some thick scrub and Jock jumping into the waiting and safe arms of Russ for protection. Once they had sorted themselves out Jock insisted that Russ take off into the scrub after the boar.

Now Russ is no slug when it comes to bringing home the bacon, so without hesitation he launched himself after the fleeing boar. As he tiptoed through the scrub searching intently for the mobile bacon pack, it dawned upon him that our resident hero, Jock, was safely tucked away in an open patch of bush watching proceedings.

'Hold on a minute, mate! How about you get in here and I'll watch how you get on?' Russ proposed.

'Don't be silly. You're into it, so get a move on,' Jock replied in an encouraging tone.

Russ tiptoed around the patch of bush for some time before he decided that Jock had the better end of the deal and called it quits. Pig one, Jock and Russ nil.

Later that evening I got a lesson on how to butcher the Canada goose and had a crack at cooking the breast fillets. I don't know what went wrong but when it came to eating them they were as tough as boot leather.

The fillet steak and onions got another shake-up that night. We also ran out of beer which, given the pressure that had been applied to our stock, wasn't that surprising. As good luck would have it the fifth member of our party, Jack, came to the rescue yet again.

The return trip home was made in brilliant, fine conditions. Maybe this was why Kevin and Jock reckoned it was their turn on the back of the ute.

It would be fair to say that the trip couldn't be regarded as a raging success but, on the other hand, there's no such thing as a bad weekend in the mountains. On the positive side of things I'd met three good bastards and seen a bit of new country to boot. A man can't ask for much more than that from a weekend, can he?

The Moose

When a bloke is onto a good hunting spot he should keep his mouth shut or else others might just try to sneak in on the action. Worse still, word could get to some poaching buzzards who, before you know what's going on, will get in and hammer the spot, thus rendering it busier than Heathrow Airport. While there is no doubt that this is beaut advice and generally speaking should be adhered to, I did find myself boasting about my trips to Fiordland to anyone keen enough to listen. Before I knew it I was headed south again with Russ, Rex and Paul. Our destination was the Hokuri Hut.

We arrived in Te Anau in gloriously fine weather and, having booked into the Luxmore Hotel for one final night of luxury, gathered at the Moose Hotel to make plans over a few beers. We arrived at about 3 p.m. and it would be fair to say that by 9 we had all consumed a fair amount of the proverbial. My mate and pilot Russell Baker had joined us and was also in fine form, telling jokes and yarns of his professional deer-hunting days.

For the sake of clarity you'll have to take note that 'Russ' is my workmate and 'Russell' is the pilot.

That evening the bar was running a promotion on a particular brand of beer. For every glass consumed an entry form was handed to the purchaser, who filled in his or her name and telephone number and returned it to the bar staff. There was to be a raffle-type draw the following day and the winner was to receive an expensive mountain bike as the prize. Needless to say, we had decided that the bike was destined to return to Christchurch with us and thus, to increase our chances of this occurring, we consumed vast quantities of the said product. Each entry form was laboriously filled in and returned to the barman to put into the box that contained the entries. We were certain we would win; it was almost inevitable given the dozens of entries we had submitted. I was, however, mildly concerned when I noticed how few of our entries actually made it into the competition box. I observed that most were neatly folded and placed under the box instead of in it. A man couldn't help but wonder if a local resident was destined to win that bike. I know that we didn't.

I'd better tell you about Rex and Paul so you get a feel for the events that follow. Rex is a tall, sinewy man, who was then aged about 35. His short-cropped brown hair, frown lines and lean face

give him a serious outward appearance – Rex looks every bit the athlete and is a dead keen hunter. While he possesses a wry, dry sense of humour he tends to lean a tad towards the serious side of life until a few beers loosen things up.

Paul is also over 6'0″, and possesses the same athletic build as Rex. A thin, neatly trimmed moustache sits on his top lip and has the effect of making him look like a stern man which, generally speaking, he is not. Mischief is part of his make-up and he has to work hard to take anything seriously. Now, beer affects Paul differently to the rest of us. When Paul drinks he becomes serious and seeks deep, meaningful discussions. The rest of our group, when drunk, just ham it up, tell jokes and laugh a lot.

Gathered around our table was our hunting party of four 6'0″-plus jokers, Russell the pilot, and a small group of local Te Anau people who were also enjoying the jokes and company.

At some point in the evening the hotel door eased open and a large group of diminutive Asians of unknown nationality crept inside. There were about 30 of them all told, with a fair mixture of young and old, females and males. One elderly gentleman was heard to exclaim 'All Blacks' as he pointed excitedly in our direction. The group talked furtively among themselves and there was a lot of excited chatter as they lined up at the bar, in nice neat rows, to purchase drinks. Our group copped a fair bit of attention from the new arrivals.

I noticed Paul sidle away from our table and approach the elderly gentleman who had taken so much interest in our group. A short time later, with a serious look on his face, Paul ushered the Asians across the room and lined them up in front of our table. After getting our attention by loudly clearing his throat, Paul addressed the Asians in a very official voice. 'Ladies and gentlemen,' he said, 'I'd like to introduce you to the "All Black" forward pack.'

Rex nearly choked on his beer and wasn't able to stop himself from spurting a mouthful across the table as he struggled to contain his disbelief. Russell raised his glass and proposed a hearty toast

to the 'All Blacks'. Everyone at our table, entering into the spirit of the occasion, now raised their glasses towards the Asians and loudly proclaimed, 'The All Blacks', before emptying their vessels in one long swill. This gesture of support for our fine All Black team could perhaps have been mistaken as being an acknowledgement of Paul's introduction.

There was a lot of smiling and head nodding in our direction as they bowed and then spontaneously burst into a lengthy round of applause in recognition of our assumed status. Before long we were surrounded and were getting our backs slapped and our hands shaken all over the place. Once we got over the shock of our 'All Black' call-up it became apparent that we could not let this marvellous photo opportunity go unrecorded. Rex and I assumed the positions of front row props and duly suspended Russell between us as the hooker. Since Rex and I are both mountain-sized men at about 6'4" tall and Russell is about 5'3", his feet were left swinging a good foot clear of the floor. The Asians thought this was fantastic, and camera shutters were clicking continuously. Soon the others from our group joined in and we formed a complete scrum in the middle of the hotel. With loud calls of 'Heave' we gave an impromptu lesson on how the 'All Black' scrum worked. On each call of 'Heave' we moved forward, knocking aside tables and chairs as we went. This was a clear demonstration of how nothing could stop the mighty 'All Black' rugby scrum. The show finished with Russell sitting on my shoulders catching empty plastic beer jugs that were being thrown, line-out style, over his head.

Paul then stated in his most authoritative voice, 'This, ladies and gentlemen, is a demonstration of the line-out technique we intend to use on our next tour. You will note the obvious advantage of having one's hooker seated above the tallest player. This is a strategy that we believe will win us more line-out ball and thus allow us to remain the world's greatest rugby team.'

Paul never wavered in his role as manager, and kept up the facade for the remainder of the evening. When things settled down a bit we allowed more photo opportunities, in which the Asians themselves could also be included. Rex, Russell and I stood facing the many cameras as the Asians, two at a time, knelt behind us and took up the lock positions. Their spectacled heads poked out the front as they smiled huge toothy smiles to record this fantastic event. Our guests were so delighted with their impromptu lesson in scrumming, and at meeting the 'All Blacks', that we weren't allowed to pay for any further drinks that night (not that we really needed any more anyway). I would love to have seen the photographs and have heard the stories told about that night in 'The Moose'.

The next morning we fronted up at Te Anau airfield to meet Russell. Normally we would have met him at the Hollyford airstrip, but as the plane was in Te Anau anyway it seemed logical to load up there. Russell announced that there was room on board for one passenger to be flown from there to Martins Bay. The others would have to drive to the Hollyford airstrip and meet him there for the flight in. We drew straws and I was fortunate enough to draw the winner.

Russell flew low up the Eglinton Valley and we searched for deer and pigs as we went. Although we sighted none I enjoyed the flight greatly. As we approached the main mountain divide, cloud formed in front of us and forced Russell lower into the tight valley. While I got a bit concerned, Russell didn't appear to have a care in the world. At one point we entered a solid bank of cloud that obscured all vision, then moments later we broke free and arrived on the West Coast side to a brilliantly fine and clear day. When we arrived at Martins Bay Neil was there to meet us. After exchanging greetings we unloaded the plane and Russell returned to collect the others. After they had arrived, and following the usual round of coffees, Neil duly transported us to the Hokuri Hut.

As always we had a large supply of food and beer. We had even snuck in some port and garlic for marinating the venison that we would surely score. With great enthusiasm we set out each day well before daylight, full of confidence. After all my boasting about Fiordland everyone in our party knew that the deer were out there in their hundreds just waiting to be knocked over.

Rex, Paul and Russ couldn't contain their enthusiasm to get on with the hunting. On the first night they decided to go spotlighting, a method they declared would 'sort out our meat requirements for the week'. After kitting themselves up for a long cold night, and with great fanfare, they headed out the door. I chose to remain and head to bed as I wanted an early start for my morning hunt. Some five minutes later the door burst open and in waltzed the three intrepid hunters. They duly undressed and got into bed.

'What's the story?' I asked.

'There's a full bloody moon, isn't there,' grumbled Rex. 'It's nearly daylight out there, so it's a waste of bloody time spotlighting, isn't it?'

I certainly couldn't argue with that. After five days not one live deer had been sighted by any of us and the troops were getting a bit pissed off. The odd deer had been seen swinging beneath the ever-present helicopters, but those don't count. I suspect my mates might even have entertained thoughts that I had duped them into coming to this useless hunting spot.

On the sixth morning I was up well before daylight and enquired who was heading out for a shot. Rex responded, 'What's the point? There aren't any bloody deer out there anyway.' He then rolled over and went back to sleep. This sentiment seemed to reflect everyone's feelings as no one else got up either.

I decided to head to the Hokuri River, cross it and hunt the area behind Jamestown. There was the remote chance of seeing a deer out on the rivermouth flat. After slipping and sliding along the very wet track, I arrived at the bush edge far too early, and had to stand in the dark for about 20 minutes. Just as it became light enough to make out features, I heard a rattle of stones on the beach. I strained my eyes but couldn't make out the source of the noise. I eased myself along the bush edge until I again heard the rattle of stones, this time a lot closer. Still I could not make out an animal, until finally I spied two stags browsing along just inside the bushline. They were very hard to make out and were no doubt heading back into the scrub. I lined up on the first animal, which was by then only about 40 metres away, and fired. I heard it crash off and turned my attention towards the second animal, which had changed direction and was running off along the shingle beach. Before I could get a bead on it, the stag turned and crashed off into the bush.

I could hear the first stag crashing around in the scrub, so I assumed it was well hit and about to expire. I waited and listened to keep a bearing on it but didn't give chase. I got one heck of a fright when the stag broke out of the bush a few metres from me and made off clumsily down the beach. A well-aimed neck shot finished the matter.

The hut was almost visible along the shore so, leaving the deer behind, I returned and woke the sleeping beauties. After boasting that the deer were back, I invited them to come and see what fresh venison looked like. Truth is I felt some help with carrying the meat wouldn't go amiss either. All of a sudden everyone was keen to go hunting again. Rex, who had earlier declared that there were no deer in Martins Bay, found a new lease of life and volunteered to assist me.

Having taken care of the camp meat situation, I felt that a decent wash was in order. Rex offered me the use of his camp shower. Up to this point I had bathed every day in Lake McKerrow which, for the record, was freezing cold. Rex's shower unit consisted of a large plastic bag with a small plastic shower nozzle attached. Warm water is poured into the bag, which is then suspended from a tree. A tug on the nozzle and voilà, you're having a shower – bloomin' marvellous. I should have been wary of such a kind but unsolicited offer. As soon as I got to scrubbing my privates Rex appeared with a camera and started recording the event for posterity. Does the man have no shame?

About 1 o'clock Paul returned to camp with the hindquarters of a very large stag draped across his back. He looked absolutely buggered, and stated that he unquestionably was.

Paul's story went like this. Having been dragged from his slumber by my noisy morning antics he felt that a renewed effort was justified, and he set off along the lake edge until he reached a large creek that looked to have easy access up it. How wrong he was, and before long he found himself clambering up some pretty rugged rockfaces and small waterfalls. Eventually he reached more open country, and happened upon an area where all the small vegetation had been trashed. Deciding that he had located a stag's rutting pad, Paul took his time and stalked the area slowly and cautiously. After about ten minutes a movement from below caught his eye. Sure enough, there was a stag dealing to a small shrub with its antlers. It had no idea that Paul was there, and a well-placed shot finished the matter. Although pleased to get a stag, Paul was disappointed that although it was very large bodied it carried only six points.

Shortly after Paul's return two trampers arrived at the hut. The woman stated that about an hour's walk towards the lake head she and her partner had discovered a deer lying injured on the track. She was most concerned for the deer, and said that she had given it a drink of water from her bowl. This seemed unbelievable so we questioned her in detail, but she remained adamant that there was a deer and that it was badly injured. She even suggested that it would be humane for one of us hunter types to go and put the animal out of its misery.

Rex and Russ accepted the challenge and returned several hours later carrying the deer that they had mercifully killed. They had carried the whole carcass back, and set about butchering it behind the hut. When the skin was removed it became clear that the animal had thrashed around for a long time before being discovered. The meat was severely bruised and we eventually deemed it unedible. There seemed to be a degree of irony in them having struggled with the heavy carcass for over an hour only to throw it away. At the very least Rex and Russ could console themselves with the knowledge that they had spared the animal from starving to death or dying from dehydration.

We were then left pondering the deer's demise. Fiordland National Park has tens of thousands of acres of bush where an animal could fall, injure itself and eventually die. How was it that the hind had come to rest on a track? It had clearly not fallen there from any great height as the area was not steep and was covered in bush. My amateur postmortem revealed that it had no broken bones, and the only outwardly visible sign of injury was that its neck was twisted to one side and couldn't be straightened. I have not discussed this matter with a vet, but a mate from within the deer recovery industry suggested that the deer might have been suffering from a condition he called 'wry neck'. He said that wry neck sometimes happened to deer he captured, and further claimed that it was always fatal. I'll have to take his word on that.

That afternoon Russ and Rex decided that they would camp

overnight at the Hokuri forks and take a look around the flats in the morning. That evening, as they packed their way to the forks, they saw two deer feeding on a slip above the sagging wire rope bridge that spans the Hokuri River. Russ shot one, and regrettably Rex missed the other.

That day we shot four deer and saw six altogether. They were all in vastly different areas, and I struggled to understand why none of us had sighted any on the previous five days. Little did I know when I stated earlier that morning, 'The deer are back,' how accurate my statement was to prove.

Our mate Neil picked us up early on the afternoon prior to our departure and moved us downriver to his bach. He reckoned we needed to have a few beers with him and Russell, who was flying in that evening ready for an early departure in the morning. Further, Neil had sorted out a local stag that he felt we should be able to nab at first light the following morning, providing of course that we didn't overindulge.

The move downriver went without a hitch. The latter part of the afternoon was spent boning out our deer carcasses in Neil's meat safe, where we were protected from the ever-present sandflies.

The day was gloriously fine and Neil's airstrip turned into something resembling Auckland airport. Many light planes and a helicopter came and went, all filled with good sorts with an inclination to spending time in the great outdoors and enjoying Neil's company over a brew.

At about 4 o'clock we were all standing to the side of the airstrip saying farewell to some visitors when a Cessna 180 circled the airstrip and, after a very shaky approach, made a safe landing. I watched the plane taxi off the runway and make its way to the grass parking area on which we stood. With a roar of the motor the plane's tail was swung vigorously around to bring it to rest, facing back towards the airstrip. At that point the pilot made a serious miscalculation of distance, and while this manoeuvre was being carried out the plane's tail struck the prop of Russell's aircraft, which was also parked there. The impact was brief and appeared insignificant. Russell, who couldn't suppress a sudden flare of anger, took a long look at the prop before declaring that no damage was evident.

The pilot of the offending plane turned out to be a woman who had flown in from the Mackenzie Country and was seeking mountain flying experience. She was very apologetic, and highly relieved when Russell declared his aircraft to be damage-free. Her blonde hair and long legs may have contributed to this hasty declaration.

By nightfall most of the visiting aircraft had departed, leaving about ten of us to enjoy a social evening together. We told stories and swapped jokes until well into the morning. A bottle or two of whisky fell over, and by the time we went to bed most of us were talking 'well thought out' but thoroughly unintelligible gibberish.

No sooner had our heads hit the pillow than Neil was shaking us awake. 'Come on lads. Time to get that stag.'

Now you may notice that I don't feature in the following wee excursion. The reason was simply that when I tried to throw my body out of bed it refused to work. I'll put it down to a lack of sleep. Therefore the following is Russ, Rex and Neil's story, as related to me later.

It's appropriate that I mention here that there are many privately owned 50-acre blocks in Martins Bay, and with the heavy bush cover the boundaries are very difficult to define. Because of this, a person could be forgiven should he accidentally cross a boundary and inadvertently hunt a neighbouring property.

It was pitch black outside as Russ, Rex and Neil eased out of the hut and made their way cautiously to the airstrip. Only Rex and Russ carried rifles. They had agreed that Rex would take the first shot at any animal they saw, as he was the only member of our party who hadn't bagged a deer so far.

Neil flicked the light along the airstrip, but due to the cold air a thin layer of low fog sat over it and not much could be seen. Undeterred, they walked quietly along a well-formed track that headed east towards the bottom of Lake McKerrow. Every now and then Neil would nudge Rex to tell him to be prepared to shoot before flicking on the light to illuminate each small bush clearing. This pattern was repeated often and a fair distance covered before the light gradually started to change from pitch black to growing daylight. A quiet morning breeze stirred and the fog began to gently swirl about.

Neil indicated that they were approaching an area where he had seen a stag several times over the past week. He further mentioned that there was a hut nearby, and that under no circumstances was a shot to be fired in the direction of the river. (Oops – they must have accidentally crossed over the boundary.) The spotlight was no longer required but visibility was at best strained. As they eased towards the edge of a large clearing a hind barked her warning signal and could briefly be seen staring towards them before being lost in a patch of drifting fog. Rex had spotted the hind and was concentrating hard in her general direction, willing the fog to clear. Their advantage had clearly gone after the hind spotted them, and without doubt any animals would be quickly making their way to the safety of the bush.

Russ stood beside Rex and both had their rifles held high, ready for a quick shot should one present. Moments later the fog lifted briefly and in the intense silence Russ saw a stag making its way towards the far bush. He swung his rifle towards it and waited for Rex to take the shot, as agreed. As the stag neared the cover of the bush Russ mentally urged Rex to fire. To his frustration the stag quietly slipped into the forest without a shot being fired. Unfortunately, Rex hadn't seen the stag at all.

Back at camp we scoffed a huge breakfast before loading the plane in readiness for an early departure. Our farewells said, those on the first flight boarded and made ready for take-off. Russell warmed the motor and went through his pre-flight procedures. After a time he shut the motor down and instructed us to leave the plane. Something was wrong. It turned out that the plane's motor could not be throttled back to lower the revs for landing purposes. It seemed that when the visiting aircraft's tail had struck the propeller the previous day it had stretched the throttle cable a fraction, causing the problem. Help was summoned via the aircraft's radio, but unfortunately a mechanic could not be arranged immediately to repair the plane. Russell made other arrangements for us, organising a private pilot to come and return us to civilisation.

The rescue plane arrived at about 1 o'clock. The pilot stated that he was in a hurry, and that he did not have time to make two trips as we had originally planned. We therefore had to fit all our gear onto the plane. Now this was an interesting prospect, given that we had five adults (counting the pilot), four deer and four packs. With a lot of effort everything was crammed in. Fortunately the pilot had had the foresight to remove the seats before his departure, thus creating some extra space. It turned out that, provided a man didn't take large breaths, we could all fit in at a squeeze.

Farewells done, we again taxied to the end of the runway. The motor revved and we were soon charging along the bumpy grass airstrip. As we neared the end of the airstrip the motor suddenly cut back and the brakes were applied heavily. The plane slewed to a halt in the long grass beyond the end of the runway, then struggled to turn before taxiing back to the far end of the runway. The pilot informed us that he had failed to reach a certain groundspeed by a given point and therefore we wouldn't have got airborne before we ran out of runway which, obviously, would lead to a crash. Needless to say, this was something we all wished to avoid.

The second attempt to take off was a repeat of the first and again had to be aborted.

Before the third attempt the plane's tail was backed well into the scrub to generate an extra few feet of runway. All went well, and with the wheels clearing the bush at the end of the runway by millimetres we found ourselves floundering in the sky but nonetheless airborne.

Some two hundred metres from the end of the strip stands a long-dead totara tree. It was directly in our flight path. Screaming in our ears was the stall warning buzzer, which was frantically telling us that we were about to fall from the sky due to a severe lack of airspeed. Now a lack of airspeed in an aircraft equates directly to a lack of control over it. We were headed directly towards certain doom without the ability to steer away from it. With considerable skill the pilot slewed the plane on a clumsy sideways slide that allowed us to slip past the tree without the resounding crash that I was expecting. Eventually we found ourselves floundering over the Hollyford River. We flew up the river at a height well below the treetops beside us. The plane was clearly struggling to stay in the air and, while remaining airborne, was not gaining any height. This state of affairs continued until we were about halfway up Lake McKerrow, when the stall warning buzzer finally stopped screaming in our ears. All went well for the rest of the flight. As we made our final approach to the gravel airstrip at the Hollyford Valley the stall warning buzzer again kicked into life, but despite this a safe landing was made.

Russ (a nervous flier) asked as we drove back towards Te Anau what the buzzer in the plane was for. He became noticeably distressed when told that, for most of the flight out, we were on the balance point between flying and falling from the air.

The only one of us who failed to get a deer on this trip was Rex who, having stated that there were no deer there, probably sealed his own fate.

A Most Unusual Trophy

Over the years I'd written many long-overdue letters, but regularly failed to muster enough energy to put them in an envelope and post them. Being a thoroughly modern man, I purchased a computer pretty early in the piece and got myself up to date. I quickly realised that this email thing was just the trick for getting those letters sent. Hell, you didn't need a stamp or an envelope, and you didn't have to go to the post office to send it! One click of a button and your mail was delivered, and even a receipt supplied if you wanted one – blooming marvellous.

Where's this leading? Good question, so I'll tell you. I opened my email one evening to find a very interesting proposition awaiting my perusal. It was from the organisers of a hunting competition that had taken place in the Nelson Lakes area a few years earlier. A second competition was being organised, this time in the Tararua Range and Haurangi Forest Park. Again, entries were limited to the first 30 paid-up teams of three hunters.

Was I interested? Hell yes! Without worrying about the minor detail of finding two other team members, I emailed an entry. I wrote out a cheque and posted it the next morning to confirm the spot. I put the word out that morning, and, before lunchtime, both slots had been grabbed. Ron, who had entered the earlier competition with me, took one, and Sticky took the other.

The competition was set for May, a bit late for the roar, which we reasoned would be well over by then. The stags should be moving about trying to regain condition after a torrid month of sexual activity. In due course we received confirmation of our entry, and were advised that we had drawn the mid-Waiohine block in the Tararua Range. We were again to be transported to our block by helicopter which, given that travel to most blocks was either by four-wheel-drive or on foot, was a fortunate draw.

On the prescribed day Ron, Sticky and I arrived at Christchurch airport all fired up and raring to go. We struck a bit of trouble at the check-in counter when we declared that we had firearms and gas canisters with us. The guns, we were told, couldn't go on board without permission from the captain. No problem, we said, go ahead and get it. Not so easy, we were told, since at that point they didn't know where the captain was. Would we mind standing aside, because we were holding up the queue. After a long and frustrating wait and a few harsh words our weapons were finally allowed on board. This was after they had found someone who knew something about rifles and had confiscated our rifle bolts. The gas canisters were also confiscated, never to be seen again. Now all this was a bit frustrating, but nonetheless understandable.

At Wellington we recovered our packs and rifles, then uplifted our rifle bolts from the Air New Zealand counter. A quick trip by shuttle bus got us to Wellington railway station, where we again went through the 'You can't take firearms on the train' routine. This was sorted out quick enough when we pointed out that there wasn't a war going on in New Zealand at that moment, and the shooting season for humans was currently closed. Further, if we were going to shoot anyone it would be the attendant, as he was starting to really frustrate us. After a few searching glances up and

down the platform the attendant, seeing that no help was at hand, agreed that we were harmless and allowed us to proceed.

When we arrived at Masterton we were greeted by one of the competition organisers. This kind gentleman took us grocery shopping, arranged to replace the confiscated gas canisters, and jacked up a discount at the local liquor store. Talk about a highly organised event.

By early afternoon we had been dropped off at the Tauherenikau racecourse where, in readiness for an early start the next day, all the competition entrants had rooms booked for the night. That evening a briefing was held in the Tauherenikau Hotel, where a few locals gave us advice on the blocks we were to hunt, access to them, and tips on the best spots to find a deer.

The next morning, those of us who were being flown to our blocks by helicopter were bussed to the pick-up point. Conversation was a bit limited due to excessive intakes of alcohol the previous night. Our team was to be the second to get flown in, but things changed a bit when the first team had their gear weighed and it came in well over the allowed limit. We were then promoted to first in, while the other team sorted out what items were to be left behind.

The country we flew over was new to us, and the pilot gave a running commentary on likely spots for deer and the general history of the area. The flight took less than ten minutes but it was a great experience. I craned my neck to take in all the terrain I could prior to landing. Take it from me, the country we were dropped off in was, and still is, bloody steep.

The mid-Waiohine Hut is situated at the bottom of a gorge above the Waiohine River. On either side of it were very steep, bush-covered faces that led to tussock tops some two to three hours' climb above. The tops themselves were narrow bands of tussock that seemed insignificant compared to the vast openness of the South Island tops I was accustomed to. There were no flats, with only the occasional small clearing beside the river. The hut itself was a standard DoC one. It had several bunks and a table with bench seats. Unlike the orange-painted South Island huts this one was painted green.

There were a number of prizes up for grabs, with the top one being for the best stag shot. There were also prizes for the longest trout, the most animals shot, heaviest hindquarter, heaviest pig, longest tusks and most unusual trophy.

Now Sticky is a hard shot. He is a West Coaster, and that puts him in the hard case bracket straight away. Sticky manages to avoid the sun, or else the sun avoids him, because he's always a pasty white colour regardless of the time of year. This is possibly due to the amount of time he spends out of the sun and in the West Coast hotels drinking beer. Thin, wispy, blond hair tops a balding pate, and a moustache sits somewhat uncomfortably on his top lip where it wipes the froth from his beer and guards his nose from sandflies. Sticky had taken his rifle for a few walks but, generally speaking, was pretty new to the hunting game.

For the first two days we didn't get to test our hunting skills. By mid-afternoon on the first day the weather had turned to custard. Rain squalls lashed the hut, driven by a ferocious wind that didn't abate for several days.

On the third day, as gentle drizzle fell through low, misty fog, Sticky decided he'd had enough. 'I'm out of here,' he declared as he gathered up his rifle and daypack. He reasoned that it could be fine on the mountaintops, which hopefully would be poking out above the cloud. With that he set off.

Ron and I took a side of the valley each and hunted the local area.

Before long I was soaking wet and the rain had regained its earlier intensity. It is fair to say that neither of us saw any fresh deer sign. All in all it was not very encouraging.

Sticky returned to the hut just before dark. Draped over his shoulders were the hindquarters of a large spiker stag. He was dripping sweat and looked absolutely shagged from the long carry he had made from the tops.

Apparently he had taken two and a half hours to climb to the tops through the mist and drizzle. As soon as he arrived there the cloud sank into the valleys below, and for the first time in days he was immersed in brilliant sunshine. He climbed to the top of a high tussock ridge where he had a good view in all directions, and got out his binoculars to glass the general area. As he searched, the cloud lifted and sank a number of times. One time when the cloud cleared he spotted a spiker feeding in a small clearing some distance away. Despite being concerned about the constantly changing conditions and fog, Sticky set off to stalk the animal, leaving his pack to mark the spot where he should re-enter the bush on his return.

The wind was in Sticky's favour and after half an hour he arrived at the point where he had first sighted the spiker. Nothing. The animal was nowhere to be seen. Sticky was very, very disappointed. He was not one to give up easily, though, and he reasoned that the animal had been feeding when he first spotted it and that it had been raining for days. It was therefore likely that the animal would still be out in the open somewhere sunning itself or still feeding. Staying just inside the bush edge, Sticky followed the natural contours along the ridge, keeping a constant lookout. After ten minutes of slow stalking he crested a small spur to find the stag quietly feeding out in the open. It fell to his shot without ever knowing that Sticky was there.

With the arrival of fresh meat we felt inclined to celebrate and allowed Sticky to shout for his success. Fresh back steaks, marinated in garlic and port, provided dinner that night, washed down, needless to say, with a few beers.

The next day was fine but windy. We all hunted hard but didn't sight an animal between us. Clearly they were up high. For our final day we elected to return to the tops where Sticky had had success. We were up and away well before dawn, climbing through the damp bush. Unfortunately the cloud was down and the climb was made in heavy drizzle. I wasn't nearly as fit as Sticky and Ron, and they soon left me behind, saying they would meet me at the top. When I finally arrived I found them hiding just inside the bushline, seeking protection from what was by then torrential rain and gale-force winds. Visibility came and went as clouds were blown across the tussock tops.

Ron declared that he hadn't climbed all that way to sit in the scrub, and led us up onto a high point on the ridge. The wind fair howled, and the furthest we could see at any time was about a hundred metres. Conditions were miserable and cold so we returned to the bushline to wait for an improvement. Two hours later nothing had changed, except that it was getting wetter, colder and windier.

'Stuff this,' stated a very wet Ron. Nothing more needed to be said. We all gathered our things and set off back to the hut. Just before we arrived there the gods had a laugh at us by clearing away the cloud and bathing us in sunshine. The irony did not escape us.

We had a quick lunch, after which Sticky declared that he was going to catch a huge trout. 'I've got to win a prize somehow,' he said.

An hour or so later I decided I'd check up on Sticky. I clambered upriver for a bit before locating him as he fished a great-looking hole in the river.

'Any joy?' I enquired.

'I had one on several holes lower downriver, but it got off,' a rather glum Sticky declared.

No sooner had Sticky made this statement than a trout took his lure and sped off downstream, peeling nylon from his reel as it went. Sticky did his best to slow the fish's progress but it made its way determinedly downstream with Sticky stumbling after it. The fish shot through a series of small rapids with Sticky in close pursuit. He tripped and stumbled over logs and rocks both large and small, and I was certain he was going to arse over into the river, but somehow it didn't happen.

After several more mad dashes the trout circled in a large pool, with Sticky keeping the tip of his rod high and pressure on the fish. Again the trout took off downstream with Sticky in hot pursuit. He finally managed to hold it up in a series of shallow rapids, and after a long time he quietly eased the trout to the shore. With his rod held high he reached down with his free hand to take hold of the fish. It gave one final, desperate flick and the hook fell from its mouth. Sticky, seeing his hard-won prize drifting downriver, threw his rod to one side and launched himself at the trout. He fumbled it a number of times as it quickly regained its strength and determination to escape. Seeing that things had taken a turn for the worse, Sticky now dived full-length into the water and onto the fish. He desperately tried to clamp it against his chest but the fish again managed to wriggle free of his grasp, so in final desperation Sticky, now lying full-length in the river, flicked it from the water and onto the shore. The trout landed on the gravel but before Sticky could finally secure his catch it managed to flick itself back into the river and swim off. Sticky was gutted, and very wet to boot.

While I had witnessed the whole event, I have to acknowledge that I didn't at any time offer Sticky any assistance, a point he discussed with me in clear and specific terms and with the use of large amounts of strong language. To be honest, I was more interested in getting a photograph than helping him. Strangely, he failed to get his fish and I failed to get a decent photograph of the momentous occasion.

I couldn't help but wonder how it was that Sticky had so far grabbed all the highlights of the trip. He'd got a deer and almost got a fish. Ron and I had got wet and that was about all. As I clambered across the now warm, dry rocks on my return to the hut I spotted a large (and no doubt ferocious) spider sunning itself on a rock.

I was fascinated by the sheer size of it. The spider would easily have covered the whole back of my hand if it were sitting on it. Now this led me to wonder about the prize for the most unusual trophy. How could I capture the spider without damaging its frail body, I pondered?

The hunt was on. With great care I removed my camera from its case and commenced my stalk. I was very aware of my shadow, and was careful not to cast it over my prey. Sensing my presence, the spider made off and hid under some driftwood, only to have it lifted by the hunter to re-expose it. Eventually I managed to herd the spider into my camera case and close the zip.

On my return to the hut I fired half a can of fly spray into the camera case. Come morning, I reasoned, the spider would be well dead and I could display it on a piece of visually appealing driftwood. I checked on progress several hours later and found that it was still alive, and tried to crawl from the camera case as I opened it. The second half of the can of fly spray was duly emptied into the case and the zip sealed again.

That evening it was surprisingly hot. After an unsuccessful evening hunt and a late tea we all retired to our bunks to read. Sticky had the bunk behind the door, while Ron and I occupied the bunks further along the same wall. We had left the door open because of the heat, and were all reading quietly when Ron nudged me with his foot. I looked up and he nodded towards the door. There was a large, dark-skinned possum inside the hut, sitting on its hind legs kangaroo-style, watching Sticky read. It was so intent on watching Sticky that you would have thought it was reading the book with him. Sticky was so engrossed in his book that he had failed to notice the arrival of his new mate, who was only half a metre from his head.

A number of small missiles were launched at Sticky before he finally got annoyed enough to look in our direction. Again Ron nodded at the possum. Sticky nearly shit himself, and recoiled towards the wall. The possum also recoiled away from Sticky, and a Mexican stand-off was reached. They both kept their distance, eyeing each other nervously, before Sticky whispered, 'What're we gonna do?'

'Catch it, of course,' declared Ron. 'You might win the most unusual trophy prize by bringing in a live possum.'

There then followed a meaningful conversation between the three of us on how we were going to capture the poor possum. This was held in low whispering tones and the possum had to strain its ears to hear. Finally it got the drift of what was being planned

Neil Drysdale with Penny,
inside the Hokuri Hut.

Jock opted to have his 40th birthday party in the bush.

The proof.

Richard, with whitebait on his mind.

Sticky (left) and Ron freezing their arses off on the tops, above the mid-Waihini Hut.

Batsey.

Neil arriving at the Hokuri Hut.

Richard on the 'Shark Beach' at Stewart Island.

Bob hunting up some tucker, Stewart Island.

Crummy and Kevin drag an easy one from the airstr

Speed limit,
Stewart Island.

Tutaekuri looking
towards the Trent river.

Jerusalem
Creek.

Kaipo Hut.

Kevin, waiting for a deer.

Hollyford airstrip:
(L–R) me, Russell Baker, Crummy and Kevin.

Crummy.

(L–R) me, Jock and Russ in the Kaipo Hu

My first tah

Me inside Hackett Hut, 2002.

and made for the door. Sticky, sensing yet another one was getting away, slammed the door shut at the same time as the possum made its exit. Well, the door shut all right and the possum wasn't inside the hut any more, so we struggled to figure out why there was such a hell of a commotion going on outside.

'What's that?' enquired Sticky.

'You heartless bastard,' Ron replied.

'Ya what?' retorted Sticky, as the commotion continued.

'You've caught the poor bugger's tail in the door,' Ron told him. Sure enough, half the poor possum's tail was trapped inside the hut.

Its claws could be heard going ninety to the dozen on the deck outside as it tried unsuccessfully to run to the safety of the nearby trees.

As soon as Sticky realised that he'd trapped the possum's tail he opened the door and finally allowed it to escape, having lost all thoughts of taking it home with him. Now I am no possum lover, and in normal circumstances believe that the best possum in New Zealand is a dead one, but on this occasion I felt very sorry for it and was pleased when it was set free.

Come morning, when I opened my camera case the spider did not leap from it. It had curled up into a tight ball. Being delicate, it required careful handling to stretch it out again. I carefully mounted the spider onto a piece of driftwood, where its sheer size gave it quite an imposing look.

Just after midday the helicopter buzzed our hut. We went outside to see what was up, as we weren't due to be picked up until 4 o'clock. The pilot advised us that the weather was due to pack it in again, and asked us to be ready for pick-up in half an hour. It was fortunate we were all in camp at the time, or we might have found ourselves stuck on the block for another three days waiting for the storm to pass. As it turned out, by the time we were picked up the wind had again started to howl down the valley and ominous clouds were gathering on the horizon.

After showers all round and a change of clothes at the Tauherenikau racecourse we headed to the hotel to suss out how the other competitors had fared. By all accounts no one at the hotel had had any great success on the hunting front. There were not many tales of success being told.

At about 6.30 everyone left the hotel and headed to the function centre at the racecourse, where we were having a huge do and prizegiving. Those who had been fortunate enough to bag stags had them on display, and an official from the New Zealand Deerstalkers' Association measured the antlers to sort out a winner. As it turned out the official wasn't really needed, as there was an obvious winner. I'd like to tell you about a head with a 40-inch span and a length of nearly 50 inches, but if I did I'd be lying so I'll stick to the truth.

The winning stag was an unimpressive eight-pointer with stunted antlers. Still, the bloke who shot it was rapt with his prize of a .270 calibre rifle.

There was an impressive array of entries for the 'Most Unusual Trophy' prize. There was a live rabbit, a piglet, slightly used toilet paper displayed on a broken rifle stock, a shop mannequin with an arrow through the neck, a dead possum with a cigarette in its paw and a note hung around its neck saying 'Smoking kills', a mouldy old sock festering away in a sealed plastic bag, a series of eels laid out in a circle, each with its tail in the mouth of the next as if they were eating each other, and of course my spider.

For the record, my fearsome spider won the prize.

Tucker that night consisted of crayfish tails, spit-roasted wild pork, venison, paua, kingfish, possum stew, whitebait fritters and just about every vegetable known to mankind. As I said, the competition was a highly organised affair.

The Hitching Post

A man passes a few milestones as he progresses through life. Some are of great importance, like leaving school, getting a gun licence, shooting your first deer, looking old enough to get served in a pub, and losing your virginity (not that important really). Then there are other milestones that a man's not always that keen to reach. The guts of this yarn sorts out one such event.

It all started when I got cornered by my mate Russ in the bar after work.

'You'd better make sure you're not working next weekend,' he said.

'Why's that?' I asked.

'Jock's having his fortieth birthday party and you're invited.'

'So why do I need to take the weekend off then?' I countered.

'He's having it in the scrub. We're off for three days on the grog at the Hope Kiwi Hut up the Hope River.'

'You must be bloody joking,' I said. 'Can you imagine anyone's wife or girlfriend roughing it for three days in the bush? There'd be a revolt.'

'The women aren't coming,' Russ replied. 'Jock wants a men-only affair where he can let his hair down a bit.'

'Let his hair down,' I said. 'He'll get it bloomin' well cut right off when his missus hears about this.'

Russ insisted that all had been cleared by the war offices, and we set about making plans. On the designated day I was picked up by Russ and Jock. The back of the 4 x 4 sat a bit low due to the huge quantities of grog that Jock insisted on shouting his mates. There was just enough space in a corner to shove my sleeping bag, a toothbrush and a change of clothes. There were another two vehicles, and a total of 11 blokes. The three vehicles were to travel independently of each other, and we were to meet up at the hut some time late in the day. Problem number one, which was gaining vehicle access to the Hope Valley, had been taken care of as the owners of an adjoining property had given their permission for us to drive across their land.

As soon as we departed Jock declared that there would be no drinking alcohol in his vehicle until we were off the tarseal, on the gravel, and in four-wheel-drive. That's okay by me, I thought; after all, we had three days of hunting and partying ahead of us. We had only travelled five minutes down the road and were driving past Christchurch airport when Jock suddenly swerved off the road and pulled onto the gravel berm. He then put the vehicle into four-wheel-drive and demanded that he be given a beer right there and then. Who could argue with logic like that? The standard for the trip had been set – beers all round it was.

Before heading up the Hope Valley we stopped at the homestead of the high country station that we were to cross. After a lengthy yarn with Cliff, the owner, we continued onward via a well-formed gravel road on the property. Russ declared that we needed to make a detour to another private hut on the property to uplift a gas cooker that he had stored there. This suited us fine, as a bit of 4 x 4 driving is always great fun and often challenging.

We travelled inland for about 20 minutes, driving past huge numbers of farmed deer contained in well-maintained paddocks.

Reaching high above us were many steep tussock- and scrub-covered hill faces. The tops of them consisted of jagged rock, scree and not much else. Great country for wild and tame deer, chamois and wild pig.

After making a long and extremely steep descent to the Skiddaw Stream we emerged on the far side and made steady progress up the hill face towards our destination, the 'Orange Hut'. Fresh pig rooting could be seen at regular intervals, so we all kept a good lookout for animals.

'There's one,' Russ yelled, pointing aggressively across a large gorge. Sure enough, about three-quarters of a kilometre away a massive black boar was gaily trotting across the hill face. Jock slewed the vehicle to a quick halt and a mad scramble followed as we all sought our rifles, bolts and ammunition, which were buried somewhere in the back. The pig didn't seem to be aware of our presence and kept going at a steady trot. Given the distance between him and us this did not surprise me. A quick calculation convinced me that I had no show whatsoever of shooting the pig at that distance. A plan emerged in my mind to run about five hundred metres downhill, angling towards the pig. Clearly the gorge between us was an impediment that I was not going to cross before having to open fire. I had forgotten all about the others, and set off down the hill at a fair gallop.

I had only run about 40 metres when Russ yelled out, 'Hey Al, you'd better duck, mate, or we might accidentally hit yah.'

A quick glance backward revealed two keen hunters with their rifles poised and ready over the bonnet of the vehicle.

Holy shit, I'm out of here, I thought, and promptly removed myself from the line of fire.

Between us we calculated the distance to be about seven hundred metres. On the count of three we all fired. The first volley had no effect whatsoever, as all our shots fell several metres beneath the target. The pig didn't even notice them nor change his pace.

I aimed about eight inches above the pig for my second attempt but this too fell below it. In total I fired four shots at the pig, but none were too threatening. By the time the pig disappeared into a band of scrub I was aiming a good two feet above its back. This still wasn't enough elevation and didn't even give it a decent hurry up. I don't know how many shots the others fired.

No doubt about it, though, either we were bloody useless shots (this may well be the truth) or that pig was a damn sight further away than we thought.

'It's a bloody good thing we missed,' Jock said philosophically.

'Now why would you say that?' asked Russ. 'A pig this early in the trip would have been just dandy.'

'Yep, but look how far you would have had to carry it,' replied Jock.

'What do you mean me?' Russ asked. 'The job always goes to the most experienced and senior man and that's you, mate.'

'Not on your life,' retorted the birthday boy. 'You young fellows need to take better care of us oldies, you know. You'd better tidy up your thought processes from now on, mate. As of tomorrow I'm officially old. That makes the carrying jobs all yours.'

'But I'm older than you,' Russ replied. 'That makes you the packman!'

The debate raged on for the rest of the trip to the Hope Kiwi Hut. One thing I can tell you is that it was a really huge pig. I have seen a fair few but this was definitely in the granddaddy bracket.

With the gas cooker duly picked up, we set out for our final destination. It was late winter and by the end of the afternoon the ground had begun to thaw out. We slipped and slid our way back to the gravel road, then a short drive later we dropped from the terrace we were on down to the wide river flat below. Pig rooting was evident all over the show so we kept a good eye out for some pork that would require a bit less carrying. The bit less carrying thing had become especially important to me, as it had finally been established that I was the youngest and therefore it would be my job to recover any vehicle-shot pork. Unfortunately no more pigs were sighted. The others had already arrived at the hut by the time we got there, and the party had started without the birthday boy.

Before I go any further I'd like to say that the 'Hope Kiwi Hut' does not exist. It is in fact the 'Hope Kiwi Mansion', and it is a very modern timber home. It has running water and a series of bedrooms containing numerous beds. A man would be hard pressed to describe it as a high country hut. Mind you, it doesn't have a flushing dunny.

Up to this point I hadn't met the other members of the party. I kind of got a feel for things to come when, as a group, they converged on Jock, wrestled him to the ground and forced him to drink a full pint of gin and tonic. 'Just to get things started,' he was told. Jock reckoned there wasn't much tonic in it either.

Unpacking took only moments as we had little (other than booze) to take care of. Not long after our arrival it was dark. This was taken as a sure sign that the party should continue. Jock tried to protest (but not very hard) that his birthday wasn't until the next day, but I don't think anyone other than me heard him.

That night was an absolute ripper. Everyone drank far too much. Many great yarns and jokes were told, and everyone's nose grew an inch or two longer from occasionally distorting the truth. Poor Jock got really sewn up, and I couldn't help but wonder how much his head would hurt in the morning. He had been made to drink pints of beer, gin, rum, some green-coloured stuff and much, much more. I'll concede that I wasn't feeling that flash myself.

Despite this, come morning I was up and away before dawn. Never having hunted the area before, I chose not to get too adventurous and didn't hunt far from the valley floor. The several bass drums and brass bands playing in my head helped me make that decision.

The nearest thing to anything exciting that happened during the hunt was when a Canada goose honked at me unexpectedly. I was up a narrow side creek in a place where I was neither looking for, nor would have expected to find, a goose. I came very close to leaving marks on my undergarments when it let rip at me. Enough said.

I was back at the hut by early afternoon and took great pleasure in having an afternoon sleep. To my surprise Jock and most of the others were still out hunting. My evening hunt proved no more successful than the morning's; in fact, we didn't even see an animal between us that day or the next.

Our second night in the hut was a repeat of the first. Given that it was Jock's birthday, this was only proper. My enthusiasm for drinking had, however, diminished somewhat. The following morning only Jock went for a hunt. We planned to head out late that morning, so everyone else enjoyed a sleep in.

The day was gloriously sunny, and despite the heavy frost on the ground we all gathered in the sun outside the hut to lean on the horse-hitching rails and drink hot coffee. The valley is about a kilometre wide at this point, and the floor proper was covered with tussock. A shallow river ran through the middle of it, and the sides were bordered by steep hill faces that were covered in a patchy mixture of scrub, bush, matagouri and tussock.

As we drank our coffee we watched Jock walking back to the camp along the vehicle track that divides the valley floor. Numerous jibes were yelled at him as he approached, mostly advising him how useless he was as a hunter. Hell, he hadn't shot any more deer than the rest of us, and we hadn't even left the hut to get ours.

'Hey, hunter man,' Dick addressed Jock with his arm outstretched and finger pointing at something. 'I bet you couldn't even hit that magpie (a black-and-white bird, considered by many to be a pest) sitting on the fencepost over there.'

'A piece of piss,' Jock replied. 'Watch and weep.'

He proceeded to take careful aim, his rifle resting on top of the horse-hitching rail. We all gathered around to see the marksman take the shot at the magpie, which was about a 150 metres away.

Boom! The rifle fired, Jock's glasses fell off and the magpie stayed put, having failed to notice that it was being shot at. All very amusing to those present, who gave Jock a good ribbing about his inaccuracy.

'None of you bastards could do any better,' challenged Jock.

At that comment everyone marched inside the hut and returned with their rifles in hand. The magpie still hadn't cottoned on to what was going on and continued to sit happily on the fencepost.

It was decided that we would take turns at shooting at it, and we drew straws to set the order. Four more shots by budding Wild Bill Earps failed to stir the bird from its resting spot.

After the fifth shot was fired, Jock's brother, Les, wandered from the hut. He cast his eyes around and said casually, 'Aren't you jokers going to shoot those deer?'

Needless to say we all thought he was playing silly buggers, as he didn't seem too excited about things. Another shot was fired at the magpie, and again missed. Les casually repeated that he thought we should be shooting at the deer. Someone finally took the trouble to look where he was pointing and exclaimed, 'Holy shit! He's right. Look!'

At that we all took a gander across the valley and sure enough, in plain view, two deer were quietly walking along the lower slopes. There was a combined clatter of rifles being loaded and several were placed across the hitching rail as their optimistic owners prepared to take extremely long shots at the animals.

'For crying out loud,' interrupted Russ. 'None of you can hit a bird at one-fifty – how in hell do you think you'll hit a deer at three or more times that distance?'

He had a good point there.

'Why don't a few of you get in a vehicle and quietly drive a bit closer. The deer don't seem too bothered by the racket and there isn't much cover for them to hide in.'

That agreed, four of the crew quickly departed across the valley. The rest of us watched the action from our hitching post. The deer quietly wandered into a very small patch of low matagouri scrub. We watched intently, some of us through binoculars, and were certain that they never left the patch of scrub. This was going to be easy. All the guys had to do was wander into the scrub, shoot both the deer, and bring home the venison. How easy can it get?

All four left the vehicle, fanned out into a single line and quietly climbed the hillside. They had also seen the deer enter the patch of scrub, and they seemed to have things pretty well under control.

Although we watched our intrepid hunter mates walk through the small patch of bush where the deer were hidden, we didn't hear the anticipated sound of rifle fire. How could they possibly have missed seeing them, I wondered. The group crossed and recrossed the patch without success. The ghost deer had vanished without trace. All 11 of us had watched the deer enter the scrub, and we were all certain they had not left it. I have witnessed similar events a number of times, and I am in awe of the ability of deer to simply disappear. This was clearly a case of deer two, intrepid hunters none.

What surprised me most was that the deer were there at all. It was broad daylight, helicopter hunters had been thrashing the hell out of the area, and there was the added pressure of foot hunters as well.

Now to give you an idea of how much grog was taken in on this trip I'll let you in on the inventory. Jock shouted a dozen of beer for every year he'd spent on the planet. Further, he had purchased a bottle of every spirit that was on display above the bar where he usually drank. At a guess this amounted to about 15 bottles of spirits. This was topped up by the additional grog the rest of us had brought (just in case we ran out).

The problem was that we still had some beer left over. Jock thought it would be a great shame to go home and have to tell our supporters that we weren't up to the challenge and had actually brought grog home with us. 'No way,' said Jock, 'is that acceptable.'

At this point Dick came up with a remedial scheme that seemed to have merit.

'We are ten kilometres from the tarsealed road,' he stated. 'There are eleven of us, less the three who will be driving. That leaves eight serious drinkers. If we drink a can each for every kilometre we travel until we get to the tarseal, and give a dozen to the cocky, we will cut the beer and keep to our rule of no drinking on the tarseal.

'That is,' he continued, 'provided the drivers drink a beer every three kilometres as well.'

That agreed, and with the packing done, we started our homeward journey in convoy. The system worked well. After each kilometre the leading driver stopped and declared a drinks break. The surrounding area was surveyed for pigs and deer while the proverbial was consumed at a leisurely pace, and when we were ready we moved on again.

After our fourth stop I was starting to get a taste for the stuff, and a few more yarns started to surface. Then, having drained our beers, we started off again. We had travelled no more than a hundred metres when the lead vehicle stopped. We all piled out to see what the problem was. Dick, who was driving, sat calmly in the driver's seat and awaited our arrival.

'What's up, mate?' asked Russ.

Dick nonchalantly looked at his wristwatch, said, 'Eleven o'clock, lads. Time for smoko,' and promptly handed out another beer each.

Before we reached the homestead we realised that none of us really wanted to go home. That decided, we deviated to the Orange Hut where we had a late lunch and a barbecue of lamb chops and bacon.

On our way out we stopped and had another yarn with the runholder. We happened to mention the big black boar we had seen three days earlier while on our way to the Orange Hut. The following weekend Jock received a phone call from Cliff. He was told that a local pighunter had caught the boar, which weighed in at a whisker under 250 pounds. This was massive by anyone's standards, and I had to wonder how I managed to miss such a large target. It turned out that the pig had been feeding on a dead cattle beast and had been regularly commuting from heavy cover, to and from the carcass.

As you can see, Jock's birthday was anything but normal, but somehow we managed to survive.

Big Man, Small Boat

Isn't it strange how life takes all sorts of unexpected twists and turns? One moment everything's on track and a man's as happy as a happy thing, then voilà, your car blows up, your house burns down or some other bastard gets the promotion you thought was yours. Occasionally, however, these twists change for the better the direction a bloke takes in life.

I was pondering the above as I stood on the deck of the *Aurora* watching the northern shores of Stewart Island slip by and an albatross glide effortlessly beside the boat. We were heading to Port Pegasus, at the southern end of the island, and I had five new mates on board with me.

It all began when a non-hunting cobber of mine asked if I'd like to go on a hunting trip to Stewart Island. 'It won't cost you much, as the trip's being sponsored,' he declared. 'My mate asked me if I'd like to go but a week in the scrub doesn't do it for me.'

Given my current financial position, the prospect of a cheap hunting trip was indeed music to my ears. I was on the telephone straight away to secure the spot. The man I spoke with, Clint, had a deep, guttural-sounding voice, and I picked immediately that he was a large and probably obese man. Putting this aside, he was keen for me to come along, and we arranged to meet at a local pub later that afternoon.

I arrived early. There were only two people in the bar, one of them being the barman, Jeff, the other a short, thin chap. I joined them while I waited. The topic of conversation was the selection of the All Blacks for the upcoming first World Cup of rugby. As always, we all had strong opinions on the matter. For the life of me I can't figure out why the selectors don't just come down to my local and take advice from us knowledgeable rugby enthusiasts.

We had been yarning for a while and I was beginning to think that this Clint joker wasn't going to front when the wee chap thrust out his hand and said, 'Name's Clint. You must be Al.'

Holy shit! That caught me by surprise, but I did my best to pretend that it didn't. The telephone voice didn't match the man standing before me at all. Come to think of it, I hadn't even noticed the similarity of this bloke's voice as we spoke. I was busy looking for the fat man.

Clint was, as I have said, a shortish, thin man who was in his early forties. He had an easy-going, jovial manner and seemed to have a strong liking for beer. I decided straight away that he was a good sort. By a strange coincidence Clint lived a mere two hundred metres from my home, but I had never clapped eyes on him before.

It turned out that several others had also pulled out of the trip so Clint asked if I knew anyone else who might be interested in coming along. I said I'd see what I could do, and after getting the dates etc. sorted out, we departed. When I got home I told my lady about the trip and, given that the costs were minimal, she was happy for me to go. That night she took off to get her hair cut. While there, she mentioned the trip to her hairdresser who promptly declared that her husband, Mark, would be keen to come along. I received a telephone call from him before my lady returned home. Further, Mark had another mate who was also keen to go, should there be a spot available for him. As I said at the start, life takes some strange twists and turns and has a way of sorting itself out.

The *Aurora* is a twin-hulled aluminium boat with two powerful motors. After about three and a half hours we arrived at our destination at the northern end of Port Pegasus, which is a very large natural harbour. We were dropped off at the concrete wharf that in the past had serviced a now non-existent settlement.

In years gone by small quantities of gold and tin had been discovered in the Port Pegasus area. The discoveries were hyped up well beyond what they should have been, and in the late 1800s a rush of hopeful prospectors arrived in the bay. For some years people tried to scrape a living from the harsh environment. The gold wasn't there in workable quantities, so the miners turned their attention to recovering the tin. This also proved unprofitable and the township was abandoned.

The tide was out when we arrived, and since the wharf was in a shallow bay the *Aurora* couldn't berth beside it. We ferried our gear to the shore in an aluminium dinghy we had hired and a small inflatable owned by Clint. Our camp was soon erected, and we went our separate ways to explore. I took off for a hunt behind the camp while the others went joyriding, fishing and exploring the harbour. The fishermen returned with plenty of blue cod (the tastiest fish in the world) for tea – bloody marvellous. In total there were six of us and up to this point we didn't know much about one another. I'll introduce the others as we go along.

Dave was the oldest in the expedition, being in his mid-forties. He was a hard-case, portly man who wore a wispy, scraggly beard that didn't suit him. Dave wasn't a hunter and he soon got dubbed 'camp mother' as he took on the cooking duties. He had spent a lot of time in and around Fiordland and turned out to be a bit of a hard shot.

After dark we lit a huge bonfire in a 44-gallon drum that some kind person had left there. We were consuming a few of the proverbial and were generally getting acquainted with each other when it was noticed that Mark and his mate A. K. were missing. These two had put up a small two-man tent beside our huge one.

'For a bit of privacy,' they had said.

'Are you two in there?' Clint yelled as he gave their tent a good shake.

'Yep. What do you want?' a voice replied.

'Hadn't you better come on out and have a drink with us?' Clint enquired.

'No thanks. We're having an early night. We'll be away before dawn for a hunt.'

'I think it would be appropriate for you to join us for a few,' continued Clint.

'No, mate. Sorry, I don't drink,' A. K. replied. Now this was a turn-up for us hardy drinking types.

'Well, come and have a Coke or something,' countered Dave.

'No thanks,' responded A. K.

Not satisfied with the response so far, Clint told them that should they fail to front for a few proverbials then he would have to take some form of remedial action. Even this failed to evoke a response.

'Here,' Clint said as he handed me a spotlight. 'Point it at me and when I give the word turn it on.'

'Now, are you getting up or not?' Clint again addressed the tent.

'No,' came the collective response.

'Righto then, you've had your warning,' Clint declared. 'Lights please, Al.'

At this point I turned on the spotlight to discover that Clint had lined himself up between me and the tent. He had his willie out, and both he and it were clearly silhouetted against the tent side.

'No more warnings,' Clint stated. 'Come and join us or I fire.' This was greeted by total silence. Without further ado Clint opened fire. Well, you can be assured that this had the desired effect. Mark was out of the tent before Clint was able to zip himself up. A. K., on the other hand, still refused to budge.

Mark quickly defrosted and joined us for a few drinks. He was really keen to get on with his hunting, and had mistakenly thought that an early night was the key to getting an early start. So that you get a better feel for Mark I can tell you that he was about 25 years old, was fresh-faced, and had legs that were a touch too close to the ground. He was always impeccably dressed and clean shaven. Mark didn't swear much, which was fair enough for a self-employed businessman. He turned out to be a good sort with a grand sense of humour.

Come the next morning, both Mark and A. K. were gone well before light, as promised. Nothing unusual about this, so were we all. That is, with the exception of Jeff and Dave, who weren't hunters.

About lunchtime A. K. and Mark returned to camp. I was lucky to see them, as they were both dressed in full army camouflage outfits. A. K. had even taken the trouble to put on face paint.

About this time I started to have real concerns about A. K. For a start he hadn't joined us the previous night for a yarn and a few laughs, and now here he was covered in make-up, dressed in full camouflage gear and carrying an AK-47 rifle. Yep, you heard me right, a bloody AK-47 automatic assault rifle (guess where his nickname came from). Fortunately for us and any animals on the island the rifle had been restricted to operate as a semi-automatic. The scope was mounted on the bizarre overtop handgrip that comes with these weapons, and I was amazed that it could be set to hit anything, being so far above the barrel. The fact that A. K. didn't drink was fine, but these other things made me wonder a bit.

No deer were sighted that day, but by the end of it we had all been fishing and caught our own tea. We had also found an old wire crayfish pot hidden under some bushes. Knowing that the owners would insist on lending us the pot, we borrowed it, and using a few fish heads for bait set it in a likely spot not too far from camp. Sure enough, the next day we retrieved it and had caught our first crayfish.

Life couldn't get any better, could it? Well, the answer is yes it can and did. After a bit of searching we discovered a scallop bed nearby and also a good supply of juicy rock oysters to add to our menu. We had indeed found paradise.

The third day was gloriously fine and calm, so we elected to collectively explore the harbour. Now fine and dandy you might think, except that we only had the two small boats and there were six of us. Again, no problem, except that we only had one outboard motor and that was a tiny one. The hired boat was supplied with oars only. Not to be beaten, we put Clint's motor on the aluminium dinghy and set out with the rubber ducky in tow.

Five adults crowded into the aluminium dinghy, while A. K. sat in the inflatable nursing the craypot, which we were going to set at another likely spot. We travelled almost the full length of the harbour at an incredibly slow pace, stopping to explore a number of beaches and tidal inlets as we went. Most were covered in deer prints, which encouraged me greatly. By mid-afternoon the sun had disappeared behind a bank of cloud that had snuck in on us and a breeze had taken up. We turned for home. The breeze quickly became a head wind and the sea began to get choppy. Given the lack of freeboard due to the large adults on board and the strain of towing the inflatable, progress was slow and at times scary. At regular intervals we had to bail water from the boat.

Seafaring Clint was having a great time and was clearly in his element. Me, I was a bit concerned at the wind and the ever-increasing distance we had wandered from the shore. My urgings to Clint that we travel a bit closer to land were ignored with relish.

At one point we had the choice of quietly making our way around the shoreline of a large bay or risking a crossing through the open and now very choppy water. Without hesitation Clint took off into the open waters. I went from unhappy to downright worried.

After several near-death experiences and being almost swamped several times we finally made it to the bay where we were camped. Inwardly I breathed a sigh of relief and thanked the hunting gods for looking after me. They must have had a good chuckle when, for reasons known only to Clint, he again headed out to sea. If I hadn't been hanging onto the boat for grim death I would have thumped the bastard.

We struggled across our bay and after an eternity reached the far side, which was sheltered from the now strong wind as it was in the lee of the low hills. By the time we arrived A. K., who had been bobbing about in the inflatable behind us, had changed colour to a light shade of green which almost matched his camouflage outfit.

'Why the hell did you do that?' Mark demanded.

'We need some fish for tea. I thought we'd do some fishing in this sheltered spot,' was Clint's reasoned reply.

How could you argue with that? None of us had died, and Clint was as happy as could be as he lowered his line into the water.

Before dark that night the weather had packed a real sad. Torrential rain, driven by strong winds, lashed our tent. Occasionally a huge wind gust would crash through camp, threatening to carry our big tent away with it. By morning we hadn't had much sleep. In an effort to stop the tent disappearing we had laid our beds along the windward side to prevent the wind getting under it. This worked successfully until just before dawn when a massive wind gust collapsed the front half. It was all hands on deck as we fought to stop the tent flying away.

By mid-morning the rain had ceased, the clouds had parted and the wind had dropped to just below gale force. Running repairs were made to the tent before we settled in for a game or two of cards. Geoff, the sixth member of our party, entertained us for over an hour by relaying the story of a mate's recent divorce. Now I accept that this isn't generally speaking a topic for humour, but this story was a real classic and had me in fits of laughter. If it wasn't for the shortage of space in this book I'd tell you the tale.

Geoff is a great storyteller. Every tiny detail was embellished with enthusiasm, and he laughed constantly as each piece of the saga unfolded. His zest for life was obvious, and in many ways he reminded me of an oversized leprechaun. He was tall and lean, with longish blond hair that was swept backward in an elf-like way from his forehead. He never stopped smiling and had mischief written all over him.

About midday Mark left the tent, only to return seconds later very excited.

'There's a blooming deer on the beach across the bay,' he stammered.

Everyone was suddenly galvanised into action. Rifles were gathered, and the sound of bullets being loaded into them took over. In what seemed like seconds, three avid hunter types were lying on the wharf taking aim at a poor white-tailed hind that was running about and playing on the small sandy beach.

'Don't shoot,' I told them. 'It's about five hundred metres across the bay and this gale makes getting it almost impossible.'

Common sense soon took over and everyone agreed. Mark could head over there later and have a crack at stalking the deer. The only shots taken at that time were by camera.

As I have said, the tides at Pegasus Bay were large. The water rose and fell about three metres between tides, which made it necessary for us to tie the boats to a nearby tree.

By late afternoon the wind had stopped, and Dave, Mark and A. K. took off in the aluminium dinghy. The idea was for Dave to drop Mark and A. K. off at likely looking spots for a hunt, then return before dark to pick them up. They rounded a point and looked into the bay. There, playing on a sandy beach, was a stag. It stopped to look at them before continuing its playful dance.

A. K. got very excited and stood up, causing the boat to rock viciously and nearly capsize. Both Mark and A. K. then prepared to shoot the stag from the rocking boat. Dave managed to talk them out of this, and eased the craft into the shore. The boat bobbed against the rock with repeated loud metallic clunks, but strangely the stag took no notice of the noise. A. K. was the first off the boat. He took the deer with a single shot. This surprised everyone, since we all thought his rifle was totally inappropriate and would probably be useless for deer hunting (my opinion on this hasn't changed).

The hunters returned to camp victorious, with A. K. posing at the front of the dinghy with his chest stuck out and shoulders pinned back. He was absolutely rapt about his success. The boat was tied to the wharf and the stag brought ashore for everyone to look at, while A. K. posed for numerous photographs with it.

The following day saw more rain, so we stayed in the tent relaxing and pondering our options. As the morning progressed, a gentle breeze arrived to push the rain away. Not long after the wind arrived, I heard a regular metallic clanking sound. The others heard it too, so we all went outside to see what was up. There, dangling from the wharf, was the dinghy with the outboard still attached. The tide had gone out and the boat was suspended, fully airborne, from the short rope it was tied to. In all their excitement our heroic hunters had failed to tie the dinghy to the tree as they should have. Geoff, Clint and I had great fun taking the mickey out of the others as they struggled to sort the problem out.

Later that afternoon we put into action the plan we had formulated on the first day. This was to camp overnight on as many beaches as we practically could. Given that every beach had signs of deer having played on them, we felt that we stood the best chance of getting game this way.

Taking pup tents and sleeping bags, we were duly dropped off at likely looking beaches. Clint and A. K. had a bay each, while Mark and I were to camp together since our spot had a series of beaches and we could cover more of them together. After setting up camp Mark and I explored our beaches. Several of them had great spots where we could take cover yet still have a full view of the beach. Mark selected one that suited him and I chose another, and we settled in to wait.

Now I need to make a special mention of the sandflies here. I have hunted large portions of both the South and the North islands, including trips to Fiordland (whose reputation for sandflies is legendary), and I can safely declare that the most vicious, relentless and numerous collection of the little bastards lives on Stewart Island. Great swarms of them attacked as I waited for a deer to walk into my trap. Before long I could stand it no longer and snuck away into the scrub for a bush stalk.

As I wandered past Mark's hide-out I stopped for a yarn. I had only been gone for a few minutes when I heard a shot and returned. Sure enough, a spiker had wandered onto the beach and Mark had taken it. The plan was working.

I left Mark to it and continued bush-stalking. The country was reasonably open, with liberal doses of crown fern, beech forest and a few broadleaf trees. I had no luck, and in failing light was returning to camp when a noise below me caught my attention. I strained my eyes but could not make out the source of it. Every now and again I heard the sound, but for the life of me I couldn't see the cause. I was motionless, and had my rifle loaded and ready, feeling certain that what I heard was a deer. There – I saw a movement, then another. Looking through my rifle scope I strained to make out the deer. By then it was almost dark and it had to appear soon or I wouldn't be able to see it. My eyes focused on the next movement and I was quietly taking up the trigger pressure when a large brown kiwi (a flightless bird) wandered into view. My heart had been pounding in anticipation and I'll admit to being a bit disappointed that it wasn't a deer. The kiwi's beak was constantly probing the ground for food as it wandered along, and it was this sound that I had heard.

To my pleasure the kiwi probed its way towards me. I didn't want to frighten it, so I remained motionless. The bird casually wandered up to me, and without even being aware that I was there prodded my boot with its beak before walking across my foot and continuing on its way. The kiwi was slightly taller than my knee height, and I was surprised at how big it was.

The next day Dave picked us up. We were lucky the weather hadn't closed in, because if it had we would have had to wait out the storm at our campsites. The small dinghy couldn't have handled heavy seas. Mark's deer was the only one seen that night.

On our return to the wharf camp Dave told us that he had nearly shot a deer himself. 'How could you?' A. K. asked. 'You don't have a gun.'

Dave explained that at about 1.30 in the afternoon, after consuming a few beers, he had gone to the end of the wharf to have a slash. Before things got under way, and while he was holding his weapon in his hand, a deer wandered from the bush and walked along the beach beneath him. Having no faith in the power of his weapon or his ability to make a clean kill, Dave held his fire and let the animal carry on undisturbed.

Soon after Dave had sighted the deer, he and Jeff tramped to the top of the Tin Range where they camped out. During the night they were kept awake by the regular, unmistakable booming call of a kakapo. They were thrilled to hear the bird calling as it was believed they had all been caught in an effort to save them from extinction.

The following day we were picked up early for the return trip to Bluff. The day was gloriously fine but for a strong southerly wind. This created absolutely huge waves that helped us along. Our captain allowed the boat to ride up onto the top of each wave as it caught up with us, then proceeded to surf it until the wave finally overtook. This made the return journey a lot more fun and interesting than it might otherwise have been.

By the end of the trip I'd come to grips with everyone in our party, and by and large they were all really good bastards. I'd even grown more accustomed to A. K. and his unique way of seeing things, though I'd be lying if I didn't admit that I hadn't fully made up my mind about him yet.

Thus ended a great week in an isolated part of New Zealand's paradise. Dave subsequently contacted DoC and told them about the kakapo he had heard while camped on the Tin Range. The well-informed but ignorant person he spoke with told him that he was hearing things, and that there were no kakapo on Stewart Island. There couldn't be, Dave was told, as DoC had caught and removed them all. Just between you and me, I'll let you know that I have more faith in Dave than the wally from DoC.

Poison Bay

I couldn't help but notice how excited Scott was when I answered the phone. In his typically enthusiastic manner he was babbling away ninety to the dozen. Trouble was, he was yakking so fast that I couldn't make out what he was trying to get across to me.

'Slow down a bit, mate. I can't understand a word you're saying.'

'I've done it, I've done it,' Scott said, finally managing to speak in English that was clear enough for me to understand.

'It would be bloody helpful if you'd tell me exactly what it is that you've done,' I replied.

'I've just arranged for us to hunt the roar on the best hunting block in Fiordland. That's what.'

'Now which block might that be?' I asked.

'Poison Bay, mate,' Scott answered. 'It's a couple of bays to the south of Milford Sound. There's no doubt about it, mate. It's the hottest hunting spot down there.'

I had hunted in Fiordland at least once a year for the past ten years or so, and thought it a bit strange that I hadn't even heard of Poison Bay.

'How exactly did you get onto this hot spot?' I asked.

'I know a bloke down there who owns a helicopter charter company. I rang him last night and he put me onto it. He reckons he hasn't taken anyone to the spot for several years now and that it should be absolutely teeming with deer. Even better, the block is right by the sea and we can catch fresh fish as well. He told me to make sure we pack our surfcasting gear.'

I am always keen to explore new hunting territory so I gratefully accepted Scott's invitation to join him.

For the benefit of those who haven't met Scott I'll let you know that he isn't a keen hunter at all. The fact is that he is totally fanatical about hunting. Once he went so far as to tell me that he felt totally naked when he didn't have a rifle in his arms. Scott is a very fit and exuberant man who was then aged about 30 years. He stands at close to 6'0" in height, grows whiskers faster than anyone else I've ever met, has far too much energy and possesses a grand sense of humour. Over and above all this the man is afflicted with a good brain and has university degrees coming out of his ears. Strangely he doesn't fit my usual perception of a hard-case hunter type; however, he does knock over quite a few beers without too much prompting.

Before I knew it we were huddled in our vehicle at the Milford airstrip awaiting the arrival of the helicopter pilot. Grant and I had left Christchurch the previous evening at about 8 o'clock, and we had travelled overnight to reach our destination on time, making a brief stop at Waimate to pick up the other two members of the party. Our current problem was that we had allowed a couple of hours extra to cover vehicle breakdowns that hadn't happened. We had arrived very, very early.

The reason we were huddled inside our vehicle was that, despite it being reasonably fine, the moment we left the car we were attacked by squadrons of vicious, man-eating sandflies. They attacked with relentless energy and managed to take home a good few lumps of human flesh before we retreated to the vehicle (I may have exaggerated a bit here, as sandflies suck blood and do not bite).

Given the abundance of these man-eaters, I was a bit apprehensive about our intended seven-night tent-bound adventure.

Eventually the pilot arrived and we were invited into his office for brews all round. He explained away his rather pronounced limp by merrily telling us that he had crashed a helicopter the previous evening while deer hunting. His story went something like this. He had taken out a shooter and together they were searching for deer on the steep faces of a local mountain range. They had spotted two deer and managed to live-capture one of them. It was sedated and bundled into the rear of the helicopter before they took off to see if they could capture another. Without warning the motor simply cut out and stopped. Unfortunately they were high up a mountain face and there was no clear area for them to make a semi-controlled crash landing onto, so the helicopter crashed in some high mountain scrub. Fortunately neither the pilot nor his shooter was seriously hurt, in contrast to the helicopter, which suffered extensive damage. After he had delivered us to our hunting block they were going to recover the helicopter from its unfortunate resting place.

We quickly loaded the helicopter and left. There can be no doubt whatsoever that the scenery throughout Fiordland is among the most breathtaking and beautiful in the world. The Milford Sound, a long, narrow fiord, is bordered on both sides by near-vertical rock- and bush-covered mountain faces. Water oozes from the bare rock walls and the mountaintops above are sharp, glistening slabs of solid rock, ice and snow. Numerous hanging valleys spill their water into the main fiord via high and spectacular waterfalls.

Initially we flew low over the harbour at the head of the fiord before veering left and following a very steep-sided valley to the south. The pilot stuck close to a valley side as he searched for updraughts that would assist our climb out via the head of the valley. At one point we were flying so close to a steep face that I feared the helicopter's blades would hit the bony tree branches that reached out towards us. We finally crested the valley head where abruptly, due to the near-vertical drop-off, the mountain disappeared from beneath us. Suddenly we found ourselves flying high above the many valleys that spread out below and in front of us. As far as the eye could see were snow-covered mountain peaks, narrow bush-filled valleys, and fiords. To the west we could see the coast and a series of large bays.

Needless to say I was straining my eyes to spot a deer or two as we travelled. The open tussock tops and rock faces which we flew over briefly as we left the valley were ideal deer country, but we didn't spot any. I got a bit of a surprise when the helicopter veered away from the coast and headed inland. Minutes later the pilot declared that we had arrived, as he lowered the machine through some low scrub before settling unsteadily on an uneven, rock-covered clearing. We unloaded while the pilot remained in the helicopter, making sure it didn't slide from its precarious perch. With the words, 'You should do really well here. As far as I know, no one's been in this valley for at least two years,' the pilot departed and silence took over. I couldn't help but notice that we were a bloody long way from the sea as I stood there holding my fishing rod.

At the same time as we arrived the weather took a turn for the worse and it started to rain lightly. With almost indecent haste we selected three campsites. I had taken a very large, three-roomed dome tent that could easily sleep all four of us, but the others wanted some privacy, thus the three tent sites. We all knew how heavily it could rain in Fiordland and had heard numerous horror stories of people getting caught out by rising floodwaters. In view of this we carefully examined each camp site for signs that water had ever flowed through it. As an added precaution we also checked the trees and bushes beside each site to see if any debris had been left there by receding floodwaters. None had, and all of the campsites were declared flood-free zones.

As we erected the tents the temperature dropped and it became very cold. The rain gradually got heavier and soon became torrential. We all gathered in my tent as we could stand up in it and had a good view over the small clearing – about an acre – that we were camped beside. As good luck would have it the rain turned to hail. I was worried that the force of it would puncture the tent. The other tents were safe as they had been erected within the bush and were protected from the full force of the hail.

With coffees in hand we sat and despondently watched the hail tumbling down. To entertain ourselves we practised our stag roaring – that might fire up the local stags, we thought.

'Ahoy there,' a voice shouted.

We all looked at each other with 'What the hell?' expressions.

'Ahoy there,' the voice called again.

We took a gander down the valley and saw two rifle-carrying men standing on the far side of the now voluminous and dirty river. They linked arms and slowly forded it. It was only waist deep and they crossed without difficulty.

Shivering and dripping wet, the two men arrived at our camp. After introductions they told us that they were on a four-day fly-camping hunt. Their main base was down in Poison Bay proper, where several other members of their party were also camped.

Hang on a minute, mate. Wasn't that supposed to be our destination? I was starting to have some strong reservations about the integrity of this helicopter chap. We had been sold on the idea of hunting at Poison Bay as no one had been there for several years (obviously wrong) and told we could catch fresh fish as required (wrong again). It turned out that it was a three-hour walk to get to the coast from our current location.

Despite this we made our visitors welcome and soon had steaming hot cups of coffee in their paws. As we sat there yarning one of the two, a hard-case-looking middle-aged bloke with a week's growth of whiskers and a deeply wrinkled brow, casually asked if we had scored any venison yet. When told that we hadn't, he asked if we would like some. He was undoing his pack as he asked this so I assumed he was in the process of retrieving the meat from it.

'Some venison would be really appreciated,' I replied.

'Right you are then,' he said as he casually put down his pack. He then picked up his rifle and, while still seated inside the tent, took aim and proceeded to shoot a spiker that had wandered unseen by the rest of us onto our clearing. We were indeed very grateful for the meat, but we would have preferred to shoot our own. It wouldn't be fair to brand the man a poacher on our block as he did ask for permission, even if it was in a roundabout way. So there we were happily ensconced in a heavily populated area with total strangers shooting our animals. Further, we wouldn't be having fish for tea.

After a couple of hours the two men, whose names I don't recall, departed. Fortunately this was before they cleaned up any more of our deer. Their intention was to climb out of our valley into the next and then to stalk their way back to Poison Bay. The last I saw of them they were walking up the valley into another heavy rain squall.

I guess it's about time I introduced you to the rest of the crew. There was Scott, his ex-wife Heather (yep, you got it right) and Grant.

Now Scott and Heather had one thing in common in that they both had a huge love of the outdoors and hunting, and this bond had lasted beyond their marriage break-up. They had been on numerous hunting safaris throughout the world, and between them they had collected a large array of trophies.

Heather was about 28 and, like Scott, had energy to burn. She's a tiny woman who stands about five feet tall, is modestly built, and doesn't give the impression that she was made for the mountains. Don't be deceived by this, as this blonde lady is as hardy and humorous as any male I've ever encountered, only smaller. Heather does, however, suffer from fogged-up glasses on regular occasions.

Grant was in his late twenties at that time, and was doing postgraduate studies at university. He has darkly tanned features, is fit, has a square jaw and stands over 6'0" tall. His solid build and rugged looks no doubt make him popular with the ladies.

By late afternoon the weather had cleared and we all went for a look around. Shortly after dark Grant returned to camp with a deer on his back. His story was fairly simple, in that he was quietly bush-stalking a valley face when the deer stood up from the crown fern in front of him. After a brief staring match Grant was quicker on the draw.

The next morning dawned overcast, with a constant fine, misty rain. At first light I forded the river and hunted up the valley floor. The faint downdraught dictated the direction of my hunt. In the early stages I travelled along a narrow but quite open bench above the river. The bush was quite open, with lots of noisy crown fern. Overhead were tall pongas and a thin canopy of trees.

With the drizzle and the wetness of the forest it wasn't long before I was wet through and thinking that I would be better off back in camp nursing a beer and drying my arse in front of the fire. Then a subtle shift in the breeze brought the strong and unmistakable smell of a deer to me. Suddenly all thoughts of returning to camp vanished and I was instantly in 'I'm about to bag a deer' mode. The scent was so close and strong that I could feel the warmth of the animal in it. Typically, I was in the process of climbing through some fallen trees that were hard to get through at the time I smelt the deer. My view was severely restricted, but without doubt the animal was very close. It took me an eternity to free myself from this noisy trap before I could again move forward cautiously. The wind kept making subtle shifts and I wasn't able to pinpoint exactly where the deer was.

I had been stalking for over an hour in semi-open country before finally I was onto a deer, and it just happened to be in the heaviest, thickest patch of bush I'd encountered up to that point. Bugger! I tiptoed around a large, impenetrable bush and gingerly climbed over a series of fallen logs but still failed to see the deer. At this point I became pretty certain that I was playing 'ring-a-ring a rosy' with it. The wind suddenly shifted again, pushing my scent exactly where I didn't want it to be. I decided to make a run for it and either catch the animal off guard or scare it to death. I belted through the bush, and as I broke free of it fell arse over gimlet when my foot became trapped under a broken tree stump. As I fell a very large hind leapt over a log about six feet in front of me, laughed heartily and bounded off before I could extract myself from my predicament. This was clearly another case of deer one, me nil.

Over the following two days no more deer were sighted. On day four we woke to steady rain. Then it rained some more, only a bit harder, until finally the rain came down in an almost solid wall of water. You have to experience Fiordland rain to understand what I am describing. The river came up at a fearsome rate, but it didn't cause us any great concern given the careful selection of our campsites. The rain didn't abate all day so we spent most of it reading books and playing cards. After our evening meal we continued playing cards until Grant happened to mention that he felt things were a bit squishy beneath the tent.

'You're imagining things,' I said. 'Don't worry about it.'

We carried on playing cards until Grant again raised the matter of the floating feeling he was getting. Just to appease him I unzipped the front of the tent and was greeted by a slow-moving flow of water that was about eight inches deep and surrounded the whole tent. Holy shit! The floor of my tent and about a foot up the sides was waterproof. The water was just two inches from flowing through the non-waterproof liner above this and into the tent proper.

We were out of the tent in a flash to survey the situation. The main river had not risen up to the tent, as we first feared. Given that it would have had to rise about 30 feet and spread over the width of the whole valley this didn't surprise us. An inspection upstream revealed that the river had become semi-blocked, which had led to a build-up in water pressure. This had diverted a large flow of water onto a terrace well above the tent. It was this water that was now threatening to flow through my tent.

Together we quickly lifted the front of the tent and formed a shape resembling a boat's front. This diverted the main flow of water around it. We then went about placing large logs above the tent to divert the main water flow away from it. Next we cleared some obstructions from a previously tiny side creek that was also spilling water and adding to our problems.

Our final desperate efforts went into digging large trenches to channel any pools of water away. The two tents erected further in the bush also required rescue missions, and trenches were dug around these as well. In truth our efforts were achieving very little, and as the water level continued to rise I feared the battle would soon be lost. We were thoroughly soaked, and prepared ourselves for a quick evacuation should the need arise. The water was on the verge of beating us when the rain stopped as abruptly as it had started. This didn't immediately solve our troubles, but about an hour or so later the water started to recede. When I finally went to bed after all the excitement I couldn't sleep. Every now and then a rain squall would pass over, and I lay there hoping that it wouldn't last long.

The next day dawned fine. Everything returned to normal and the sandflies returned even more vicious and hungry than before. We all hunted for the day but again failed to see any animals.

In keeping with the standard weather pattern it was raining when we woke the following day. None of us was keen on another soaking so we mooched around the camp. Heavy rain squalls came and went throughout the day but generally speaking it was pretty much just modest, steady rain. At one point we had another heavy hailstorm. Grant decided that an afternoon on the bourbon was in order and gathered up plenty of ice for the drinks. Good on you, mate.

As we were merrily consuming vast quantities of the aforementioned drink the sky cleared and a burst of sunshine hit the tent. Heather, who hadn't been drinking, declared that she was getting stir crazy. She pulled on her wet-weather gear, grabbed her rifle and wandered outside.

Grant had just poured Scott and me another round of drinks and we were about to launch into another game of cards when we heard a rifle shot. Heather had only been outside for a few seconds before the shot went off. Down went the drinks and, with visions of her lying injured, we were outside pretty damned quick. We arrived just in time to see Heather, in a crouching position, aiming her rifle downriver. She was balanced unsteadily on a pile of slime-covered rocks. She fired again and promptly fell arse over gimlet into a tangled mess. Let's not forget that she is a small lady, and if I remember correctly she had a .270 calibre rifle.

We couldn't see what she had been aiming at so had no idea if she had made a hit or not. Having untangled herself, Heather was adamant that she had hit one of two hinds that had been standing on the stony beach where our small flat met the river.

We all went searching for the animal. Clear impressions of hoof-marks were evident on the beach but there was nothing to indicate that one had been hit. For over an hour the four of us searched but couldn't find an animal. Heather remained adamant that she had made a good shot, and we only stopped looking when it again started to pour with rain.

All that evening Heather insisted that her shot was good. The only way we could get her to drop the matter was to promise that we would make a thorough grid search of the area the next day. Come morning we did just this, and sure enough we located a large hind some distance downriver, concealed in some dense foliage. Well done, Heather.

The day we were to depart dawned cloudy, with frequent rain squalls. The helicopter arrived during a break in the weather and before long we were back at Milford Sound. Nothing was said to the pilot about our isolated 'fishing block'. We'd had a great time anyway, and isn't that what heading into the scrub is really about?

We stopped in Waimate for a night on our return journey. Scott was raised there and reckoned that he could get us onto a property for a wallaby hunt. In the early evening Scott drove Grant and me through the Waimate Gorge before turning inland onto a private forestry block. We stopped often to unlock and open gates. I was the silly bugger who scored the front passenger seat, which gave me the honour of opening all the gates, a point not missed by Grant who sat smugly in the back seat.

As I opened one gate I heard the unmistakable but distant sound of a stag roaring somewhere in the pines well below the ridge we were travelling. Not knowing the area I assumed that it would be a farm stag. I mentioned the stag when I got back in the car, and after numerous taunts of 'Bullshit' both Grant and Scott got out to listen for themselves. Right on cue the stag roared again.

Scott went from wallaby hunter to stag chaser in an instant. He informed me that there were no farms nearby and that the stag was definitely fair game. A plan was devised where I remained on the ridge and gave the occasional roar to keep the stag talking. Scott and Grant slipped over the side to stalk it. The animal was clearly worked up as he replied to most of my roars. I was therefore pretty confident that there would be venison on the table that night. I was wrong. After about ten minutes the stag stopped roaring. Why? I don't know. Perhaps he got suspicious, or maybe a wind shift had carried human scent to him.

After a very steep climb two weary hunters returned to the car. A short drive later we stopped at a road-end. The country was steep and covered with near-mature pine trees. I was both pleased and surprised that there was no gorse growing beneath them. This made hunting among them very pleasant and easy.

I had never hunted wallabies before so was offered the first shot, should we find any. We had only walked several hundred metres when one came hopping through the pines towards me. At a distance of about 40 metres it saw us and stopped. This is too easy, I thought, as I took aim and fired. The shot was a clean miss and the wallaby scurried off before a second could be taken. Take it from me, I was served up some intensive and descriptive ridicule over missing that simple shot. For that matter I wasn't particularly impressed with myself either.

A chance to redeem myself came ten minutes later when a lone wallaby was sighted grazing on a grass face across a deep gut, a bloody long way distant.

'Yah can't hit the easy ones,' taunted Grant. 'Have a go at that.'

I took careful aim, crossed my fingers (as long shots have never been my speciality) and squeezed the trigger. By some strange fluke the wallaby fell over dead. When I suggested that we go and retrieve it I was told emphatically, 'No.' I then got the 'Wallabies are just a pest like rabbits' lecture before we moved on.

Before long we crested a small ridge and had a clear view of a slow-moving river below. The valley floor was open but almost bare due to the drought the area was suffering at the time. I counted 18 wallabies dotted about on the flat, grazing on what they could. Others could be seen further up the hill face opposite. It was easy to see why my companions thought of wallabies as pests.

After sneaking a bit closer we opened up and did our best to help the farmer reduce his wallaby problem. I can't recall how many we shot but it was a good number. Every bend in the river revealed more of them, and it was obvious that they were indeed out of control. As we were driving out after dark we counted 27 wallabies on the road alone. I was astonished by the sheer number of them. Altogether we would have seen well over a hundred.

After that hunt I decided that, from then on, I'd limit myself to hunting more challenging game that could grace my table and therefore give me far greater satisfaction.

West Coast Hospitality

The hospitality of the West Coast is legendary, and I was fortunate to experience it first hand when I moved to Hokitika at the age of 20. Within minutes of arriving in town I had been recruited to the local rugby, pool and darts teams. I hadn't had to put my hand in my pocket to pay for a beer until the formal proceedings of recruitment had been taken care of either. Of course, as soon as I was committed to the local teams things changed a bit, and it quickly became 'my shout' as a way of sealing the arrangements. Nevertheless, I had nothing but fond memories of my time there and was really looking forward to heading back to the Coast on an upcoming whitebait fishing trip.

My long-time mate Richard was coming down from Auckland for a few days and the fishing arrangements had been left up to me. I was pretty sure I had things sorted after a phone call to my mate Stag, who lives at Kumara Junction, a small settlement midway between Greymouth and Hokitika.

I hadn't clapped eyes on my skinny mate Richard for a good few years and was really looking forward to catching up with him. A taxi pulled up at my address and a huge mountain of a man climbed out. I hadn't been warned that Richard was bringing a mate, and I stood there like a dumb idiot waiting for Richard to get out. The big chap paid the taxi driver and turned to me.

'Gidday, yah big bastard,' Richard's voice greeted me as he grabbed my hand and pumped it furiously. His grip was strong, and I was lucky he didn't tear my arm off in the process.

Talk about the greatest transformation of any human being I have ever seen. My puny friend, who I remembered as being about 6'2" and skinny enough to give himself a haircut with a pencil sharpener, was now a muscle-bound Mr Universe lookalike. 'Those steroids must've cost you a fortune,' I greeted him.

'Nothing but hard work, mate,' countered Richard.

With the formalities taken care of, we parked up for the night to catch up on the past 20 years. There must have been a lot of catching up to do as by morning an inspection of the Jim Beam bottle that was sitting on the table revealed nothing but clear glass.

That day we drove from Christchurch to the Coast, where we picked up some scoop fishing nets for catching the whitebait. Now, for the uninitiated, I'll tell you a few things about whitebait. Firstly, they are a tiny, transparent fish that are considered a luxury. Fishing for them is only allowed for several months each year, and is usually done with set nets or scoop nets. The best time to fish for whitebait is when they are pushed upriver by the incoming tides. There are many rules and points of etiquette that must be adhered to when fishing for them, and any breaches are dealt with immediately and harshly by the other people fishing.

Richard was keen to dip his net in a river right away, so we drove to the Hokitika River mouth. The tide was on its way out and there were very few fishermen about. We spoke with a couple of friendly locals who informed us that we were too late, as the good runs of whitebait had occurred the previous week. They showed us their catch for the day, which was no more than a cupful between them.

Realising that we had missed the incoming tide and that fishing at that time would be a total waste of effort, we decided to travel to Greymouth to have a look at the mouth of the Grey River. Strangely, I had never fished there, despite its reputation as one of the best whitebait fishing rivers on the Coast. On our arrival we were directed to 'The Rock'. Now The Rock is the best whitebait fishing spot in the whole world. Everyone knows this, and the right to fish from it is a hotly contested yearly event which goes something like this.

On most rivers there are some registered stands, which are purchased and give the owner the sole right to fish there. If the owner is absent from their stand it is acceptable for others to fish from them, but they must leave immediately if the owner arrives.

The Rock is not a registered stand, so the right to fish it goes to whoever is first there. Often a group of people will camp on the rock for months before the opening of the season, just to secure the right to fish there. These people never leave the rock unattended, because if they did someone else would take it over.

When we arrived at The Rock there were two very hard-case, heavily tattooed individuals in attendance. We stopped and yarned to them for a while, and it was clear that despite everyone else having had a bad day, they had caught several bucketfuls of whitebait. Later we were to speak with some locals who reckoned the tattooed gentlemen at The Rock were in fact despised criminals who had wrested possession of it from a group of timid teenagers who had been camped on it for months before opening day. We were informed that the police had been involved and that a lot of nastiness had occurred. I don't know what the final outcome was but I did read a newspaper article about a month later that confirmed this story.

A bit later we went over to Stag's place, arriving about early evening. He was beaming like a Cheshire cat as we pulled up.

'It's about time you lot arrived. I have a job for you before it gets dark.'

Now work wasn't exactly what we had in mind, but we followed him into his garage anyway. There, lying on the floor, was the carcass of a very large spiker stag.

'I shot it this morning on my land as I was heading to work,' Stag informed us. 'I didn't get a chance to take a shot at the other one that was with it. Still, it's good to know they are about.'

The animal was duly butchered before we took off for a quick look around Stag's property and a bush block that he was breaking in. That night we went spotlighting for deer along a few back roads. We sighted a couple but they were too quick for us. It was probably a good thing, as the farmer's house was close by and we might have woken him with our shots.

The next morning Richard and I set off for the nearby Taramakau River mouth. We were only going to be on the Coast for three days so we wanted to spend as much time as possible on the river. When we arrived there were about 15 fishermen gathered in a group near the rivermouth. Clearly these people were locals who knew the best spots to fish. Richard and I decided we couldn't be bothered queuing up behind them, so we sorted out a spot for ourselves further upriver.

At this time the tide was slack. This is the calm point when the tide has stopped going out but hasn't yet started to come in again. Ever-hopeful Richard, who was wearing chest waders, headed out into the river, dipped his scoop net and dragged it about a hundred metres towards the rivermouth. When he lifted the net from the water he was rewarded by the sight of a single whitebait wriggling in the bottom. He didn't catch any more with his next four or five efforts.

It was obvious when the tide turned. Waves started to push back up the river and the locals stopped yakking and also started to fish the river. Richard, who had been fishing the slack water up to this point, had become very confident in the water and was regularly standing chest deep in the river as he fished. As the tide started its full inward assault the waves increased in size and regularity, something Richard failed to notice. I was just starting to think that perhaps he should come a bit closer to the shore when a large wave totally swamped him. By the time I yelled my warning the wave had washed clean over the top of him. I was worried that his waders might fill with water and drag him under, but he soon reappeared coughing and spluttering on the surface. He was absolutely drenched, and sent forth a few choice words to describe his feelings about the situation. I don't think my laughter helped matters any.

Over the next three hours we caught less than a cupful of 'bait', which wasn't very encouraging. The river is about a hundred metres wide near the mouth, so we figured that most of the whitebait would have passed us by then, so we packed up our things and walked to a likely looking spot well up the river. As we arrived I heard an old jeep grinding its way along the beach behind us.

As it passed us I noticed that the driver's side of the jeep was hanging a lot lower than the other, and I decided the suspension on that side must have given out. I didn't think much more of it until the jeep turned around and came to a halt beside me. Richard had started fishing and I was about to put my net in the river when the driver's door of the jeep flew open. In her haste to get out of the vehicle an incredibly large woman literally fell out the door. In contrast, an incredibly skinny man raced from the passenger's side and came to her rescue, helping her to her feet. To my mind it was a good thing that he did, or else she might have kept rolling into the river and required serious rescuing.

'What do you think you're doing?' the woman snapped. Obviously she was blind and couldn't see our whitebait nets, so sensing that a bit of tact might be called for I replied, 'We're trawling for elephants. What did you think?'

'Well you might as well piss off then,' she hissed. 'There aren't any here.'

'Maybe not, but who knows, we might get a few whitebait if our luck holds.'

'Who told you about this spot?' she interrogated.

'What spot?' I countered.

'Are you being smart with me?' she challenged, her hands on her hips, head tilted forward in a challenging way as she peered at me through one squinting eye.

'I wouldn't be so rude,' I told her.

'Where're you from?' she demanded.

'Christchurch.'

'A bloody east coaster, eh? All you buggers do is take. You take our whitebait, you take our gold, you take our greenstone, you take our trees and you take our jobs. What's more, you leave your bloody rubbish everywhere. Why don't you ever clean up after yourselves?'

'Do you know me?' I asked.

'Too bloody right, mate. Bloody east coasters. You're all the bloody same. Why don't yah piss off, eh?'

What could I say? I decided not to waste any more breath trying to be civil and got on with the fishing. I was delighted when I caught about a cupful on my first drag. The friendly lady and her partner joined in and fished the same stretch of river as us.

I noticed Richard approach the woman. I didn't hear the start of their conversation but when I got close enough I caught the following.

'You shouldn't judge everyone by the same standard,' Richard suggested. 'For all you know we could be top people.'

'Are you being snarky?' she asked.

'My oath I am,' he replied. 'And you're being very rude.'

'I just get stuck in first, mate,' she responded. 'Can't have people thinking they're welcome, can I?'

I was pleased to see that Richard was being made as welcome as I had been, although I felt that he may have got the measure of her. After another lecture about 'you bloody east coasters' we all got on with the fishing. It was about this time that it started to rain.

'Can't have you city slickers getting wet,' said the woman. 'Why don't you piss off now?'

Here we go again, I thought.

'How long are you staying?' asked Mrs Friendly.

'We're heading south tomorrow to check out some other rivers,' I replied.

'South, eh? Why don't you go now? The further south the bloody better, I say.'

Things took a turn for the better when Richard told her that he was actually a West Coaster himself and that he had been born in Greymouth. This kicked off a major change in Mrs Friendly's attitude, and after comparing notes (just to make sure Richard wasn't conning her) she became downright friendly. After a bit Richard asked the man how best to fish that part of the river. He replied, 'You don't actually think I'd bloody well tell you, do you?'

'Well actually, yes. That's why I asked,' Richard responded.

The man just scoffed and walked away. Hey, we did our best to be friendly.

On the up side of things we actually caught a kilogram of whitebait there before we left.

It turned out that it was Richard's birthday that day, a bit of information he kept to himself until we headed out for a beer or two that night. We visited a hotel in Hokitika and met up with a good bunch of locals who went out of their way to make us welcome, in true West Coast style. It would be fair to say that I had a couple more than required and was pretty relaxed about proceedings. Richard and I ended up yarning with a bearded, hippyish-looking bloke of about 40. He told us that he was a keen hunter and that he had 'retired to the Coast'. Now this chap thought we were a couple of good bastards (in contrast to Mrs Friendly, who didn't) and invited us back to his place to sample some of the local fare. By all accounts this was to consist of home-brewed whisky, a couple of cannabis joints, then a bit of spotlighting at his favourite, sure-to-succeed deer hotspot. With our faith in the hospitality of the Coast restored, we declined his kind offer and packed it in for the night.

It was absolutely hosing down with rain the next morning, so after a great feast of whitebait we packed up and headed home.

Pin the Tail on a Honky

Clint tossed a handful of photographs across the table at me.

'Take a butchers at that lot,' he beamed.

Every photograph was of pigs. Mobs of them in open tussock country somewhere. Four or five of the photos were of a mob of about ten pigs making off around a hillside. They were in single file, just like a wagon train.

'Bloody wonderful,' I said. 'What's the story?'

'Bacon on the hoof, just waiting for us to bag them,' Clint stated with total conviction. 'Next weekend we're off to Blenheim. They're as good as in the freezer.'

Now I know stuff-all about pig hunting, but I figured it would be pretty unlikely that wild pigs would just hang about for a week or so waiting for us city slickers to wander along and nail them. Don't pigs travel about a lot seeking new food sources?

No amount of prodding could induce Clint to divulge any useful details about our upcoming hunt. The only bully I got out of him was that he'd travelled to Blenheim the previous week and had taken the photographs while he was there, unfortunately armed with a camera only. There was something about the self-satisfied smirk on his face as he talked about it that got me wondering if something was up.

By the time the weekend rolled around, Clint's photographs had been viewed by quite a number of prospective hunter types, and our party had ballooned to six. If nothing else we would have enough firepower to quell a minor revolution if required.

We left Christchurch at 6 a.m. and travelled to a farm hidden behind Blenheim. My son was with us, and it was to be his first hunt for anything bigger than rabbits and possums. Dave brought his 13-year-old son along as well.

The fifth person in our vehicle was Eeyore, an acquaintance of Clint's. Now I hadn't met Eeyore before, and I spent most of the journey listening to tales of his many great hunts throughout the highlands of New Zealand. By the time we reached Blenheim I was certain I had no chance of securing bacon for myself, as Eeyore was a master marksman, capable of pulling off incredibly accurate hip shots at great distances. The open tussock country we were to hunt would surely be to his liking, and I would therefore be assigned the menial role of bacon carrier.

On our arrival at the farm Clint's farmer mate, Percy, greeted us. Percy was a typical farmer – tall, muscular and darkly tanned – while his weathered brushed cotton shirt and denim shorts were typical farm attire. Percy wore a welcoming smile and laughed easily. I couldn't help but take an instant liking to him.

'Better come in for a brew,' he offered.

'Hell, mate,' ventured Dave; 'the day's getting on and there's bacon to be got. Hadn't we better head for the hills?'

Unfazed, Percy retorted, 'Hills never seem as steep with a cuppa in ya,' and headed for the farmhouse.

Now I was thinking along the same lines as Dave. It was after 9 o'clock and the day was already hot. The district was in the middle of a drought. A look over the bare, steep, sun-baked hills that surrounded us led me to believe that leaving much later would force us to hunt in temperatures resembling the inside of an oven.

Still, wouldn't be right to ignore country hospitality, would it?

After a bellyful of fresh scones and cream we were off, our party now numbering seven.

'Reckon we'll walk,' Percy stated as he strode off along a farm track. He took off like a sprinter, which made keeping up with him difficult. By this time the day was so hot that at times his image in front of us shimmered like an illusion. The sweat was pouring off me when Percy finally came to a halt beside a steep gut that contained a now dry creek bed.

'Better load your rifles,' he said. 'The pigs should be in this gully somewhere.'

He then went on to give us a briefing on the layout of the land.

'There are plenty of wild pigs on my property and that's the way I like it. Numbers are getting a bit out of hand, though, so you guys can take a pig or two each. There's only one rule. I've put a breeding sow in with the wild boars. Ya can't mistake her. She's the only black and white pig on the property. Shoot whatever you can but don't shoot my sow.' Everyone agreed.

About the time Percy told us to load up our rifles, Eeyore's eyes had started to glaze over and he was looking a bit excited. In view of the number of guns we had with us, we decided that Eeyore and my son, Jeremy, would lead and take the first shots, should we get onto the pigs. For safety reasons we decided to all hunt together.

Eeyore was off like a raging bull. He powered ahead and made the pleasant stroll a blistering, uphill grind. We finally caught up with him when he ran out of steam half an hour further up the gut. At this point Percy pointed out a steep spur on which he had last seen the pigs.

Jeremy, Dave, Eeyore and I set off up the spur while the others retreated up the opposite hillside to watch the hunt. Despite a plan of attack having been agreed, Eeyore took off in another direction. The country was basically steep, open tussock interspersed with patches of open manuka trees and dense, near-impenetrable matagouri scrub. I was a bit concerned when Eeyore disappeared from sight over the brow of a hill.

After a short, steep climb we entered a patch of manuka. Jeremy stopped, pointed and whispered, 'Pigs – three of them.'

Dave was safely behind us but Eeyore's whereabouts were unknown. After considering the surroundings, I gave Jeremy the nod to take the shot. Standing, he took aim and fired. The surrounding hillside exploded into action. Suddenly there were pigs going in all directions. They soon made off over a small rise above us. Almost as soon as they disappeared from sight, Eeyore, who had foolishly climbed above us, opened up. I heard shot after shot and, remembering the tales of his great marksmanship, dreaded the thought of having to carry the ten or more pigs back to the farmhouse.

When calm finally returned I asked Jeremy, 'How'd you go?'

'Shot it in the eye just like you told me to,' he quipped with a huge grin.

We made our way to the pig, and sure enough he had dropped a medium-sized boar instantly with a hit just under its eye. I was very proud of him and told him so. It looked to me like buck fever wasn't going to trouble the lad in the future.

None of us were game enough to take a look over the rise for fear of being shot by our clearly 'in full flight' hunting acquaintance. Eventually he appeared on the skyline, still in a very excited state.

'Did you see them? Did you see them?' he repeated.

'Too right, mate,' Jeremy replied. 'I got one. How many did you nail?'

'None, but I had a few shots. Let's get after them,' Eeyore urged.

Bloody hell, I thought. A few shots! He must've fired at least ten, maybe more.

If nothing else he had made sure the pigs would be a long way off by now.

Our attention was drawn to the spectators across the valley, who were waving at us furiously. After a spot of morse code deciphering and much hand-signalling we gathered that they wanted us to take a butchers further along the hill. We ran to a ridge and saw, way below us, 15 pigs making off in Indian file down the hill. Eeyore was off after them.

After helping Jeremy to field dress his pig I left him to carry it to the track below. I returned to the ridge and watched Eeyore as he trotted gaily down the spur in the general direction of the fleeing pigs. I had a marvellous vantage point, and stayed put to watch events unfold. The spur that Eeyore was following was bare but for one large, dense bush on a flattish knob near the bottom.

As Eeyore approached this bush I saw the pigs returning up the hill from below. They were still in single file, and by chance the bush was directly between them and Eeyore. As Eeyore advanced on the bush so did the pigs. It was obvious they were going to arrive at the same time, which they duly did. Given events to date I would not have been in the least surprised if Eeyore had passed the bush on one side while the pigs passed on the other, without them actually seeing each other. This didn't happen, however. At the bush both took the same path.

It was bloody funny watching Eeyore, who had his rifle slung over his shoulder, react as he literally stumbled over the leading pig. After picking himself up and regaining his composure Eeyore got stuck into the pigs, firing round after round as they scattered. None fell until finally the last pig, which was either very stupid, deaf or tame, came lumbering along without a care in the world towards Eeyore. When the distance diminished to several feet, Eeyore placed the rifle barrel against the pig's ribs and fired (I may have exaggerated this point a tad). The pig scarpered off down the side of the hill with Eeyore in hot pursuit, but strangely no longer firing a huge stream of shots after it. When he disappeared from view into some matagouri scrub, I decided to make my way back to the track.

As I neared the bottom Clint, who also had a grandstand view of proceedings, beckoned me to come up to him. When I arrived he pointed out a small mob of pigs far below that were quietly tearing up a small clearing that was surrounded by a ring of dense matagouri scrub. Now for the uninitiated, matagouri is a bastard scrub that has thousands of very sharp thorns, and travelling through it is at best painful. Clearly it was not possible to sneak up on the pigs, so we elected to travel down the spur we were on and to take long shots at them from above.

By the time we were in position only two pigs were visible. Both were asleep in the clearing. Clint lined up on one and I the other. I had a scope on my rifle but Clint was using an open-sighted 30.30 calibre rifle. The distance was about 150 metres and I had my reservations about taking the steep downhill shots.

We fired together; to my surprise my pig leapt to its feet then fell over dead. Clint also hit his pig but it made off dragging a rear leg. Clint fired again at the moving pig and it dropped instantly. An impressive shot by anyone's standards.

We had dressed out our pigs and dragged them to the track by the time Eeyore finally emerged from the scrub with a pig in tow.

His pleasure was irrepressible and he couldn't have smiled any wider without his head flopping open like a hinged gate.

'Nailed the bastard,' he gloated. 'Told ya I could shoot, didn't I?'

I refrained from mentioning the 50 to one bullet to kill ratio he had achieved. The look on Percy's face told it all. There, being dragged by Eeyore, was the largest, tamest black and white sow ever released in the valley. It was the only pig we had been told we were not allowed to shoot. Eeyore, totally oblivious to his stupidity, was too busy gloating and boasting of his great hunting powers to notice the look on Percy's face, and had no idea at all of the terrible deed he had just committed.

We took four pigs that day, and were fortunate to have enjoyed the company and hospitality of Percy, whose final gesture was to help us butcher the pigs before we headed back home.

I never gave the hunt another thought until one day, months later, I visited Clint. He tossed a pig-hunting magazine at me and told me to take a look. Inside were several photographs taken by Eeyore during our Blenheim hunt. I read the article with increasing horror. Eeyore had written to the magazine and been paid 50 bucks for his 'true' pig-hunting story. He had written of 'Blasting away', 'Bombing up', 'Sending white-hot lead at millions of feet per second', his '30.06 spitting lethal projectiles', etc., etc. He was even stupid enough to admit that he winged his pig with his final bullet, having missed with the previous half million shots. This at least explained to me why he hadn't put the wounded pig out of its misery straight after he wounded it. Instead he had chased it on foot and, like Davy Crockett, had wrestled it to the ground and 'stuck it like a man'.

If only the readers had known that the pigs we hunted were enticed into Percy's paddock by a tame, on-heat sow and were fed all the dead animals and offal from the farm to keep them there. They remained partially for the sow and partially for the easy food, but mainly because of the electric fence that surrounded the huge paddock we hunted and which prevented their escape.

A HARD SHOT IN THE HILLS

Noah's Ark

Have you ever encountered a time in your life when things are really starting to get under your skin and your tolerance has just about run out? Well, I was going through one of those times at work and was on the verge of giving the boss a smack on his chin. The final straw had leapt to the front when he had stormed into my office demanding to know where some stupid 'business return' was. The reality was that I didn't really give a stuff about his lousy return, but the boss demanded that I get off my lazy arse and submit it immediately.

The reason I was poised to smack him was that I had already worked two and a half hours of unpaid overtime solving one of his stuff-ups before he stormed into my office. Since I was on a salary there was absolutely no benefit to me or my family in my being there at all, let alone being told I was lazy and had to stay even longer to fill in his bloody return. Had I got so much as a 'Thank you' for my efforts? No bloody way, mate. All I got was the boss bitching in my ear about some bloody return that was intended to make him look great while us humble workers got told to think smarter and increase productivity.

If I was to follow through with my intention of giving him a smack on his chin I could rest assured that a new career would follow. As I clenched my fist into the required shape my telephone rang, and while I was facing the dilemma of whether to answer it or deliver the career-changing blow, my boss took the opportunity to leave.

'What?' I said rudely, picking up the phone.

'You're bloody right what!' a calm voice on the other end responded. 'What about a trip to Fiordland?'

It was my hunting mate Dave, and in the circumstances there couldn't have been a better suggestion in the world. Forgetting the formalities that normally occurred before getting down to business I inquired, 'When?'

'Next Monday?'

'That's a bit short notice, isn't it?' I asked.

'Truth is, I've had a run-in with my boss and told him to stick his job up his arse. I need some time out and a trip to Fiordland is the best place I know to get it. I've already canvassed the usual crew and most can't come. Jeff can, provided we leave Monday and get back by the following Thursday week.'

In view of my own current predicament I knew where he was coming from. Without giving any thought to the feelings of my employer, family or anyone else, I was in. I didn't ask my boss for the required leave. I told him I was having it whether he liked it or not. I think he could sense that there was no point in arguing, and quickly approved my non-negotiable verbal application, with the proviso that the previously mentioned return needed to be completed prior to my departure.

The prospect of nine days' hunting had me pretty fizzed up, and as plans were made I quickly forgot about my run-in with the boss. We were leaving in five days' time.

Some of you have already met Dave and Jeff, who featured in some of my previous adventures, but for the benefit of those who haven't I'll introduce them again.

Dave is a hard-case, portly man, who at this time was in his forties. He wears a wispy, scraggly beard that makes him look a bit like Worzel Gummidge, the old TV character. Although he has spent a lot of time in and around Fiordland Dave isn't a hunter, and he generally takes on the cooking duties for our expeditions – which is why he sometimes gets referred to as 'camp mother'.

Jeff, who is about the same age as Dave, is a great storyteller. Every small detail of his yarns gets embellished with enthusiasm and he laughs constantly as each piece of the saga unfolds. Jeff's zest for life is obvious, and in many ways he reminds me of an oversized leprechaun. He's tall and lean, with longish blond hair that is swept back from his forehead in an elf-like way and tied in a ponytail at the back. Jeff never stops smiling and has mischief written all over him. Like Dave, Jeff is not really a hunter, but he enjoys the great outdoors.

The journey to Te Anau was made in Dave's car, which was a Falcon with a jazzed-up motor. From take-off to landing took far less time than normal prudence required. When Dave is driving most of your time is taken up with holding on and trying to focus on the blurry objects that stream past your window. Clearly he'd missed his calling as a racing car driver, but he hadn't yet given up hope of achieving this goal.

Jeff spent most of the journey telling us unlikely tales of his exploits with his now ex-girlfriends. Many of his yarns would be worth telling here, but a man's love life is best kept off these pages. Jeff's a really humorous, relaxed kind of guy and seems to have no difficulty in attracting beautiful and intriguing women. Trouble is, most seem to have a disconnected wire here and there, and thus many strange and interesting happenings eventuate.

After a brief stop in Te Anau, where we checked in at the Air Fiordland office to confirm our flight the following morning, we continued on to the Hollyford Valley and Gunn's Camp. Dave was keen to catch up with his uncle, Murray Gunn, who owned the camp. As we drove the final leg the weather gradually deteriorated, and by the time we arrived just before nightfall it was absolutely pouring down. The prospect of a flight into Martins Bay in the morning wasn't looking too promising.

We settled ourselves into an old but sturdy cabin that in years gone by was situated at Marion Camp and had been used by the workers who maintained the Milford Road. There were no keys to secure the cabins so I took it upon myself to hide my rifle underneath the rear bench seat of Dave's car. No thief would think to look there for booty, I thought.

We spent the night in Murray's company. I had met him many times before, and as always I was impressed by how fit he was for a man in his late seventies. A whisky or two was consumed, and it was very late before we retired to bed. As always I found the sound of rain pounding down on the tin roof comforting as I lay snugly in my warm sleeping bag.

Nothing had changed by morning and the rain continued to pour down. The Hollyford River, which ran beside the camp, was badly swollen and visibility wasn't great either. We could hardly see across the narrow valley, and we knew that in all likelihood we would be spending our day around the camp. We couldn't check the weather forecast as there are no telephones at Gunn's Camp.

By mid-afternoon the rain hadn't let up one bit so a decision was made to head to the Milford Pub to have a few quiet beers. We were about to make a run for Dave's car when we heard the distinct sound of an aircraft motor further up the valley. We looked at each other in bewilderment. Surely to God no one would be flying in these atrocious conditions? Russell, our pilot, managed to prove us wrong when seconds later he buzzed the camp and continued down the valley to the airstrip.

'Holy shit! We're not packed or anything,' Jeff said, stating the obvious.

After several minutes of mad scrambling we had gathered up our things, thrown them into Dave's car and were racing along the gravel road to the airstrip. The gravel-throwing, sliding, sideways turn off the main road onto the airstrip caused Dave to catch his breath as the wet surface failed to hold traction. For a long moment we careered sideways toward some dense-looking scrub, until after a burst of full throttle, followed by more sliding, we arrived safely under the wing of the aircraft. Russell, who was looking rather bemused at our arrival, reckoned he was sure he was going to have to tow us from the scrub with his plane. Now that would have been worth a photo or two, wouldn't it?

The weather was still pretty rough, with low hanging cloud and steady rain. By the time we had loaded everything into the plane things hadn't improved any either.

'I think we'd better take a look-see flight down the valley to make sure we can get through to the bay,' Russell announced. 'Al, you come with me. If we get through I'll come back for the others.'

I cast a searching eye through the vehicle then, certain that we had left nothing behind other than Dave and Jeff, climbed into the plane. With a hearty roar of the motor we took off along the runway. Very soon we were headed down the valley at low altitude, just below the cloud cover. Visibility was limited due to the constant rain that splattered onto the windscreen, and the ever-increasing cloud density. Below us we could see the Hollyford River, which was our guide since we couldn't see the valley sides, or much else come to that. Russell was forced to fly lower and lower until we were barely above the treetops.

I have to admit that I was getting a bit concerned by this time, especially when I noticed the intense searching look on Russell's face, and the beads of sweat that rolled down his forehead. At one point we were engulfed in cloud and experienced total white-out conditions. Russell's head shot about all over the place as he searched for anything to get a bearing on. Suddenly, there appeared ahead a distinctive section of the Hollyford River where it was joined by the Pyke. Russell's face never lost that look of intense concentration as he veered southward into the white-out, on what seemed to me a sure-fire collision path with the Darran mountain range. I clung to my seat and waited for the impact. Moments later we broke free of the cloud and found ourselves flying in beautiful clear sky above Lake McKerrow.

After a low-level swoop over Neil's hut to see which way the wind sock was blowing, we continued out to sea. A tight bank turn was made above the seal colony that lay sunbathing near the mouth of the Hollyford River before we descended sharply onto the grass airstrip.

It wouldn't have been manly of me to kiss the grass when we finally came to a stop and disembarked. Fortunately Neil was there to greet us, so I contented myself with pumping his hand enthusiastically, while calmly trying to pretend that the flight in had been totally uneventful and maybe even a bit boring. Then we quickly unloaded the plane and Russell left to pick up the others while Neil and I caught up with the past year's events.

Neil is a good mate who has lived at Martins Bay permanently for the past 15 years. He's a short, solidly built man, with a friendly, outgoing disposition. Everything about Neil is square and solid. This includes his head, chin and broad chest. His greying hair is a bit deceptive, as when he shakes your hand you need to check if it's still there when he's finished, due to his incredible strength. Over the many years I have been coming to Martins Bay I have been fortunate to enjoy Neil's hospitality and company. Many of you will have read about Neil in my earlier books so you'll know where I'm coming from here.

As we caught up on the year's events something was niggling away in the back of my mind, but at that time I couldn't quite put my finger on what it was. After an interval Russell returned with Dave and Jeff, and there was another mad flurry of activity. As the last of our gear was thrown to the ground, I was struck by the realisation that my rifle was conspicuously absent.

'Have any of you seen my rifle?' I asked worriedly. No one had.

'Bugger, shit and bugger again,' I cursed inwardly, as I realised that my rifle was still safely hidden under the seat of Dave's car which, rather inconveniently, was parked back at the Hollyford Valley. Following Russell's unexpected arrival at Gunn's Camp we had left in such a hurry that I had forgotten about my hidden weapon. Given this monumental stuff-up it didn't look like I was going to get much hunting done on this trip.

Not wishing to miss a golden opportunity, my mates launched into torrents of abuse and ridicule, just in case I wasn't kicking myself enough. My problem was solved, however, when Neil offered to lend me his spare rifle, which was an open-sighted .303. Further, Russell volunteered to pick up my rifle and deliver it to the bay when he was next in the area. Both of these generous offers were accepted with gratitude.

When we were all finally gathered in Neil's hut having a cup of coffee Russell happened to mention that, unlike the rest of us, he hadn't had any lunch. Neil insisted on cooking him a feed of prime, aged venison to fill the spot. A great length of back steak was produced and Neil proceeded to cut a large steak from it. I couldn't help but notice that he cut the steak along the grain of the meat and not across it, as normal practice would dictate. The steak was duly cooked and eaten, and Russell appeared to really enjoy his meal, despite having a little trouble cutting it into eatable portions.

The foul weather that we had escaped earlier was catching up with us as we launched an overloaded aluminium dinghy into the Hollyford River. Russell flew overhead and with a waggle of wings disappeared toward Milford Sound. Neil had wisely decided that we could find our own way to the Hokuri Hut, and as a parting act of generosity he gave us a large leg of venison. 'Just in case you don't have any luck,' he declared.

By the time we had completed our journey up the river and across Lake McKerrow the rain was pelting down. We quickly carried our gear to the hut before settling in to wait out the weather. Needless to say, we had a good supply of beer with us to cover situations such as this.

After three straight days of torrential rain I gave in to cabin fever and ventured into the big wet for a hunt. I was keen to reach the small flats above the forks of the Hokuri River for an evening shoot. Within minutes of leaving the hut I was thoroughly saturated. After walking up the muddy track to the river mouth I headed into the bush and stalked my way upriver. Every step increased my misery as cascades of water resoaked me every time I touched a branch or bush. Even the shelter of the trees seemed to offer little protection from the constant rain.

I reached the forks about an hour before dark and was surprised to find that the grass had been well cropped by the resident deer population. On my previous visit the grass had been almost knee-deep, but now it looked like a mown bowling green. Full of hope, I hugged the bush edge as I crept along, being eternally hopeful of finding a deer out in the rain and keen to fill my freezer. But luck wasn't with me, and as darkness fell I made a miserable return to the Hokuri Hut. The rain hadn't let up for my entire hunt. In a final gesture from the weather gods an electrical storm was occurring somewhere in the distance, and I was repeatedly hit by tremendous peals of thunder as I trudged homeward. I decided that hunting in the rain wasn't for me, and made up my mind to wait out the weather before venturing outside again.

On my arrival I discovered that a Japanese man (we'll call him Sake) had arrived and was to spend the night with us. He was a friendly sort of chap, and despite some language difficulties we communicated as best we could. Our new-found friend told us that in the morning he intended to tramp to the seal colony at the mouth of the Hollyford River and then return to the Hokuri Hut the same day.

As I mentioned, neither Dave nor Jeff are hunters, and while they both enjoy the outdoors they generally stick to tramping and fishing. On this trip Dave had brought a rifle with him, and he and Jeff had decided to bush-bash their way to Big Bay via the Jamestown Saddle as soon as the weather cleared.

Come morning the weather had finally sorted itself out and the sun was shining. Our Japanese friend left early, while Jeff and Dave packed for a two-day trip into Big Bay. I rose early, and after a brisk walk to a wallow I'd discovered years earlier I stalked the area around it. I saw nothing and returned to the hut around lunchtime. I decided to camp out overnight at the Hokuri Forks, but delayed my departure until I had managed to dry some of my gear.

At about three in the afternoon I set off. Being a man with a healthy thirst I packed four cans of beer to keep me company during the long night that I was to spend alone. I was about halfway up the Hokuri River when I noticed Dave and Jeff walking toward me. Clearly something had gone astray with their plans as they were heading in the wrong direction.

'Are you blokes lost?' I yelled when they got within earshot. They weren't. Dave explained that they had made it into the Jamestown Saddle and hit a small gorge that required a diversion. Somehow they had managed to get themselves a bit disoriented in the thick bush, and after a bit of fruitless wandering they had ended up back in the saddle. By then the weather had become overcast and rain was threatening again. Not fancying a wet night out, they decided to return to the Hokuri Hut.

Jeff reached into his backpack and handed me four cans of beer.

'You'd better take these with you,' he declared. 'There are plenty more in the hut that we can drink.'

It would have been rude to decline such a fine offer, wouldn't it, so I neglected to tell my friends that I already had a beer supply in my pack. After a few more minutes we parted company. I had about a 15-minute walk with two river crossings before I reached my intended campsite.

As my mates moved out of sight I eased my way into the river to make the first crossing. The slimy brown rocks that lined the riverbed made progress slow and every step was treacherous. As I neared the far side of the river I entered a deep section. The water was swift and my foot was swept onto a slippery rock. I stumbled as my foot slid from the rock and became jammed between two larger rocks. As I fell face-first into the river I felt my ankle give and was gripped by a searing pain. After a period of floundering I finally made it back to the riverbank but I clearly had a problem as the ankle had blown up immediately and putting any weight on it caused immense pain.

I was thoroughly wet and clearly couldn't go on. Nor could I take my boot off – well, actually I could have, but I deemed it a bad idea to risk it. The only course of action open to me was to try to limp back to the Hokuri Hut.

Every step was bloody painful and progress was slow. I couldn't find a suitable branch to use as a crutch, so I limped onward, resisting the temptation to take a few liquid anaesthetics before commencing the journey. The tramp out had taken about 30 minutes – the limp back to the hut took an hour and forty minutes.

As I reached the clearing where the hut was situated I could hear voices coming from within. Never one to miss a chance for a bit of mischief I hid above the track, cupped my hands over my mouth and let out a hearty roar. Now it was only March, and all serious hunters would have known that no self-respecting deer would be roaring at that time of year. Dave and Jeff don't fit into this category.

There was a short period of silence followed by the sound of feet hurrying about in the hut. I followed up with a second roar, which was again followed by more scurrying feet. After another short period of silence I heard the metal door-latch click open, followed by the door creaking. Moments later Dave's bearded face edged around the corner and peered in my direction. A third roar had him taking large cartoon-like strides across the clearing, rifle in hand and eyes bulging. Several short steps behind him was our Japanese mate, Sake.

As Dave approached the cover of the surrounding bush I burst out laughing and yelled, 'You'd better put that bloody rifle down before you hurt somebody.'

The shocked look on his face showed that he had been well and truly duped into thinking he was about to nail a real stag. I can't repeat the comments he made, but rest assured, they were colourful.

Later Dave described the events that had occurred in the hut before he came out:

Our Japanese mate, Sake, had returned to the hut and was feeling a bit glum. This was because he had walked all the way to the seal colony (a return trip of about nine hours) and hadn't seen any seals. I'd been there many times and never failed to see dozens of them, so I asked him to tell me about his trip. Sake said he had arrived at the seal colony but there were none there. I pushed him further and he then disclosed that he had in fact reached a sign that read 'Seal Colony'. Believing that he had arrived he stood beside the sign and searched for the seals but found none. Greatly disappointed, he then turned around and walked back to the hut.

All he had to do to see the seals was to walk a further two hundred metres along the track that led out onto the reef. Had he done this he'd have seen dozens of the smelly things. In fact, they smell so bad that I was surprised he hadn't smelt them from where he stood. I can only assume that the wind was blowing in the wrong direction. Anyway, Sake was telling us his story when you roared. I thought there was a stag outside and said, 'Stag!' Sake immediately copied me and repeated 'Schaag!' He seemed very excited by this turn of events.

You roared again and I said, 'It's a stag all right.' Sake repeated my words exactly in his broken English. I then grabbed my rifle and began searching in earnest for the bolt and ammunition. As I moved about the hut Sake followed and repeated every word and movement that I said or did. He was stuck to me like a well-glued shadow.

There you have it. Our friend had walked for almost ten hours to not see any seals. To round off his disappointment and finish off the day nicely he'd then stalked a non-existent deer. When told why he hadn't seen any seals Sake declared that he was going to do the walk all over again the following day to get some photographs of the seals as proof of his journey. I wish I had his energy.

Dinner that night consisted of a venison casserole that Jeff had prepared. It was a hearty feast that had every vegetable and spice known to mankind in it (I may be exaggerating a little here). We shared the meal with Sake, who ate with great enthusiasm. I was amazed at the quantity of tucker he was able to consume, given his thin body frame, and there was no doubt that deer meat was to his liking. He'd put in a big day, so he had earned it.

There was nothing I could do about my foot. As soon as my boot came off it swelled to giant proportions. I couldn't be sure whether anything was broken or not but it sure as hell hurt, and it wasn't going to get better before the trip finished.

That night while consuming a few beers we decided that a shift to Murray Gunn's hut was in order. Dave, being a nephew of Murray's, was especially keen on this move. The morning dawned fine but by midday it had become heavily overcast and rain again threatened. After lunch we loaded our gear into the dinghy and headed down the lake and into the lower Hollyford River. At a point almost opposite Neil's hut we turned into a side stream that led south into the McKenzie Lagoon. At the head of the lagoon we tied the boat to a small post that served as a mooring and unloaded our gear onto the bank.

Having failed to see Murray's hut I asked Dave where it was, and to my horror he announced that it was 15 minutes' walk away. Given the painful condition of my foot this wasn't the highlight of my day thus far. Further, I may well have argued against the shift had I been aware of the required walk, especially as we had to get our gear to the hut as well.

We decided to stash any unnecessary gear in the scrub near the boat and take with us only the supplies and equipment we required that day. Dave and Jeff took off toward the hut as drizzle started to fall. I shouldered a light pack and hobbled off after them. To my surprise a stag started roaring on the northern face of the May Hills.

Within minutes other stags had joined in until there were five of them challenging each other. I tried to pinpoint their locations on the hillside as each one bellowed its unseasonable challenge. I was treated to a quarter hour of roaring before it stopped as abruptly as it had started. This was only the second time in all my years of hunting that I had heard stags roaring during the day and I was thrilled to experience it.

As I reached for the door handle of the hut the rain started in earnest again. I had thought that the rain we had experienced over the past days had been torrential, but I soon learnt that it hadn't even been close to it by Fiordland standards. The rain literally thundered down onto the roof as if fired from a high-pressure hose, and visibility was reduced to a very short distance.

It soon became apparent that the essentials we had carried to the hut did not include beer. This was not acceptable by any of our standards so Dave was despatched back to our stash to obtain the required supplies. Although the rain was heavy it was not cold, but despite this I was surprised when Dave stripped to his underpants and boots and took off along the track carrying only an empty pack. He declared that he wasn't climbing back into his wet clothes, and he wasn't about to get his only dry ones wet either. This is one of those times when I wish I had taken a photograph to record the moment.

Much to our relief it wasn't too long before Dave returned safely, with beers, to the hut. He said that as a precaution he had pulled the boat out of the water and had tied it to some scrub well above the high water mark.

It was fortunate that the hut had a good supply of reading material as the torrential rain continued unabated for days. Dave made another wet trip to replenish supplies and again pulled the dinghy further away from the ever-rising lagoon. The boat had been almost full with rainwater, he said, and he'd had to bail it out before he was able to move it. At least the forced rest was beneficial to the recovery of my ankle.

The afternoon before our intended departure arrived and the rain had not let up for a moment. Sick of being hut-bound I volunteered to hobble to the boat to uplift the last of our beer supply. I followed Dave's proven method and made the journey in my underwear. The view that greeted me as I approached the boat was almost beyond belief. The lagoon had swelled to huge proportions and had risen so far that it melded into the surrounding bush. The jetty was no longer visible, having been submerged, and the track that led to the lagoon came to a halt at the water's edge some hundred or so metres away from the jetty proper. Our dinghy, which had twice been pulled further away from the rising waters, was almost submerged. It was tied by a short rope to the trunk of a bush and had been held down as the rising water engulfed it. Worst of all, our beers were stashed under a bush somewhere ahead of me and under a flood of water.

Some missions cannot be abandoned. Moving the dinghy to safer ground was one of those missions. The other was locating and recovering the missing beers, which Dave had also moved to higher ground.

As I waded to the dinghy a large black eel swam off ahead of me. I was chest deep in water when I reached it, and let's not forget that I'm 6'4" tall. After bailing out a lot of water I dragged the dinghy to higher ground before returning for the beer. My first two dives failed to locate the treasure, but finally I located the bush under which Dave had stashed the beer. The cardboard boxes containing them had disintegrated, so I was forced to retrieve the beers two cans at a time.

Dave and Jeff spent the afternoon rock-hopping along the coast to the mouth of the Kaipo River and back, a return journey of four hours. On the way there Dave had jumped off a rocky outcrop, intending to land on a smooth rock below. His landing was anything but gentle as the said rock came to life and bolted down the beach, barking furiously. The rock turned out to be a poor unsuspecting seal that had been enjoying a quiet nap beside the rocks.

As they neared their destination Dave and Jeff located six wet, miserable, waterlogged, hungry and dejected hunters in a small two-bed bivvy consisting of an open-ended shelter with a canvas flap for a door and a leaky tin roof. Like us, the hunters had suffered through over a week of torrential rain. They had all but run out of food and the helicopter that was to come and pick them up was three days overdue. Jeff invited them back to our hut to pick up additional food, coffee and tea but the offer was declined since the hunters didn't want to miss the helicopter if it arrived to pick them up. The poor suffering blokes didn't want to stay there a moment longer than they had to. It's amazing how other people's misery can lighten your load, and my mates returned to Gunners Hut with an extra spring in their step.

The rain continued all that night and we doubted that we would be leaving in the morning. But by breakfast time the rain had stopped and bursts of sunshine were occasionally breaking through. Our departure was assured.

When we got to the dinghy the water had retreated so far that we had to drag it some 30 metres or more to reach the water's edge. Under motor we headed for the Hollyford River. As we approached the junction where it met the mouth of the lagoon we were greeted by a huge volume of muddy brown floodwaters that were surging and swirling toward the ocean. We came to a stop and surveyed the mass of dirty water that blocked our path. Our fear was that on entering the main river we would be tipped over by the sheer volume of the crossflow. We watched several whole trees wash past as we contemplated our next move.

Dave took a decisive stand and declared that we would ease into the main river at an acute angle so as to minimise the impact of the crossflow as we entered it. Once we were in the main river we could angle safely across it and then return upriver to Neil's. Jeff seemed pretty relaxed about the whole affair, telling Dave to stop being a girl and get on with things. It was with some apprehension on my part that we entered the river. We were immediately swept downriver, but Dave displayed sound seamanship as he steered us slowly across the river, managing to avoid the many obstacles that swirled around us.

When we reached Neil he said he had watched us cross the river and had been as apprehensive as we were. My pilot mate Paddy always said that any landing that didn't kill you was a good one. By applying his principle to the river crossing I couldn't see what all the fuss was about.

Neil guessed that given the rain we wouldn't have bagged any venison, so he'd gone out that morning and shot a young stag which he gave to us. As I've said many times before, Neil is one of life's genuine good bastards.

As Russell flew us back to the Hollyford I had time to reflect on the trip. Over a period of nine days it had rained on seven, the two fine days being the day of departure and the day I sprained my ankle. Prior to this trip I thought I knew what torrential rain was. I was wrong!

Was this a good trip? Too bloody right it was. There is never a bad trip into the wilds of New Zealand, and each is etched into my memory in one way or another. On the bright side of things, I still had a job and I no longer wanted to give my boss a crack on the chin.

Neil's Story – the Bay

It was several years after Neil had left Martins Bay and returned to Te Anau to live that I finally managed to corner him and get him to tell his story more fully. Neil is a modest man so, despite our many years of friendship, getting him to talk about himself wasn't as straightforward as a man might have expected. A good bottle of tongue-loosener soon sorted matters out though. The following is Neil's story, as told by him.

I was launched in the Hokonui area in Southland in 1940. My parents were farmers, and owned a 270-acre farm where they ran sheep and cattle. Right from the start they decided that I was to follow in their footsteps and become a farmer too.

At 5'5" I'm not the tallest of men, which conversely means that I wasn't the tallest of children. Despite this I got stuck into rugby and just about every sport going. I didn't find myself getting tapped on the shoulder for representative duties, but I made plenty of friends and generally enjoyed the social aspects of the various sports.

There were plenty of rabbits around our farm, and the Hokonui area in general, and as soon as I could assemble an arsenal of self-made weapons I was after them. I found myself trying to harpoon them with sharpened sticks, shoot them with shanghais, and I even had a crack at them using a homemade bow and arrow. Unfortunately none of these methods were successful, but nonetheless I gained a lot of useful stalking skills and learnt to sneak in close to the rabbits without being detected.

When I was nine my father finally gave in to my harping and taught me how to use the family's .22-calibre rifle. I was soon hitting most things that I took a pop at, and it wasn't long before my brother and I were allowed to hunt rabbits without my father being present.

As soon as I was allowed to use the .22 on my own I went into business (well, in my mind I did, anyway). Rabbits were a pest whose numbers had reached plague proportions, and the deal was that I would be paid two pennies for every set of rabbit ears I got. I was out hunting at every opportunity and I think my father got a fright at the numbers I was getting. Still, he never reneged on our deal and willingly parted with the money when payment was due. With the huge numbers of rabbits that were about in those times I soon became a semi-wealthy lad. I found that I had a natural ability with a rifle and very quickly reached the stage where I became annoyed if I missed any shot at all. I think the 'get in close' stalking skills I had acquired as a youngster helped in this regard as I rarely had to take shots over 40 metres.

I was 11 years old when I shot my first pig. I had been out hunting rabbits on a neighbour's farm (I didn't tell Dad, as the rabbit ears were supposed to come from our farm). There was an undeveloped gut on the property that was full of pigfern and bordered some native bush. As I hunted the edge of the developed paddocks I heard pigs squealing in the gut. Dad had told me that a .22 rifle wasn't a heavy enough calibre to hunt pigs or deer with and had warned me not to shoot at either species if I encountered them.

'It would be cruel to leave wounded animals running about the area, wouldn't it?' he'd said. I crawled to the brow of the gut on my belly and looked down into it. I immediately saw four pigs working up an area of ground some 30 metres away. One was facing me with its nose churning up the soft ground. Without giving my father's words a moment's thought I took aim between the pig's eyes and fired. The pig collapsed on the ground and the others bolted off into the cover of the scrub.

I was absolutely delighted with my success and ran to the pig, a small boar that would have weighed about 55kg. Now I had a dilemma. Did I take the pig home and face the wrath of my father or keep it a secret and tell no one? Stuff that, I'm a big game hunter now, I thought. Feeling bulletproof after my success I threw the pig on my back and struggled home beneath it. Luckily, my fears of a telling-off were unfounded. My father took a look at the pig, saw that it had been shot fair between the eyes, and commented, 'Looks like you've mastered that,' as he nodded toward the rifle. I was the proudest kid alive.

When I was 14 I was invited on a hunt to Mt Albert, which is near Wanaka. Deer were very numerous at that time and during the trip we saw dozens of them. It was April and the roar was on. All night and for a large portion of each day we could hear stags bellowing their lion-like roars. We were looking for trophy stags to shoot and the people I was with were pretty fussy about what they shot. We stalked past many stags that to me were massive and needed shooting but I was told to wait as there were better heads to be found. One of the men I was with shot a huge 16-pointer and was thoroughly delighted with his trophy. Me – I was getting a bit pissed off as I hadn't been allowed to shoot anything.

On the last day, when we still hadn't found a suitable trophy for me, I was given the go-ahead to take an inferior stag of my choice. There isn't a great story to tell other than to say finding one didn't prove to be too difficult. After this trip I was well and truly hooked on hunting bigger game.

My parents were still adamant that I was to be a farmer, and to help me get established they purchased a neighbouring farm of 240 acres on my behalf. I was to repay them at five pounds a month, which in those days was a substantial sum of money, so at 17 years of age I entered the possum skin game. For three winters I trapped possums. There was a strong demand for the skins and prices were good. I recall receiving an average payment of nine shillings and tenpence per skin for my last season's efforts. I worked hard during those years and made really good money. During the summer months I worked on my farm and broke in more land.

By the time I was 20 I was working almost full time on the farm. During the summer months I had a haymaking business that I ran on the side with a mate, Lindsay Shaw. We worked really hard but again made good money. We ran the business for seven years before I got out of it and bought my parents' farm as well.

Alec, a farmhand who worked for me, was also a hunter. He was keen to hunt a neighbouring property up the Otapiri Gorge. He'd seen a mob of deer on a back paddock there when he called to pick up some bales of hay early one morning. Alec asked the owner if he could hunt the property but was turned down, the owner saying that he only allowed family members to hunt there. The prices being paid for deer at that time were good, and clearly the owner wanted to cash in on the extra income that wild deer provided.

Undeterred, Alec managed to convince me that we should do an overnight poaching trip there. He proposed that we sneak in on foot via the bush block at the back of the property. Come morning we would shoot the 'sure to be there easy deer' then disappear back into the bush where we wouldn't be discovered. 'As easy as that,' he declared confidently.

That evening we set out to put the plan into action, taking a roundabout back route on our motorbikes. We hid the bikes in dense scrub up a side road, and in failing light made the hour-long walk to our destination. It was late summer and the evening was warm so we hadn't bothered to bring sleeping bags with us. We made beds of tussock grass and slept rough. I had a good sleep and woke just before daybreak. Alec was already awake and was smoking a cigarette.

'Visibility's a bit limited,' he stated as my mind registered the light fog that had engulfed us.

After a bushman's breakfast (a breath of fresh air and a good look around) we snuck from the bush to the edge of the hay paddock. Visibility was limited to about 30 metres but the very light breeze was in our favour and gave promise that the fog would soon disappear. We edged slowly along the fenceline, observing the deer tracks in the soft soil as we went. A movement in the paddock caught my eye and I nudged Alec to get his attention. A nod in the right direction put him onto the two deer that were quietly wandering back towards the bush.

'I've got the one on the left. You take the other,' I whispered. Together we took aim, firing almost simultaneously. My deer fell instantly. Alec's was well hit but kept going in the direction of the bush, until his second shot stopped it in its tracks. At the same time as Alec fired his second shot I saw three more deer sneaking back toward the bush and, with my semi-automatic, shot all three in quick succession (hey, I had to pay for my farm somehow).

When the shooting stopped and silence reclaimed the morning we realised that we now had the mammoth job of gutting and carrying five deer back to the bikes. Fortunately the effort was made easier by our knowledge of the high price being paid for venison at the time.

Alec dragged the first two deer together and set about preparing them for carrying out, as I located and gutted the other three, which had fallen some distance away. As I was gutting the last deer I heard the sound of an approaching truck. With the fog and the crispness of the morning I wasn't sure how far off it was, but there was no doubt that it was headed in our direction. Between us we had ferried four of the deer back over the fence and into the bush. In for a pound, in for a penny, I thought as I quickly finished the job, threw the last deer onto my back and headed into the bush and out of sight.

Regrettably the bush also belonged to my neighbour, so if we were caught it was certain that neighbourly relations would take a big backward step. I was grateful that the fog hadn't lifted much, but when I heard the sound of dogs barking I started to get that 'We're caught for sure' feeling. The dogs would find the deer guts even in the fog, and in all likelihood they would then lead my neighbour to Alec and me.

'Grab the biggest deer and let's go,' I urged Alec. My plan was to head back to the bikes as fast as we could and to get the hell out of there before we were caught. Two deer were better than none, so off we galloped at back-breaking speed. As we went I heard the dogs barking frantically behind us. I was certain that the deer guts had been discovered and that our pursuer would soon be after us, which only encouraged us to move faster. As good luck would have it we got back to the bikes without being captured. Two bloodied and dishevelled men must have looked ridiculous sitting astride the deer as we wobbled off down the road on our motorbikes. We had set out to get a deer or two if we were lucky, so we didn't feel too aggrieved that we had to leave three deer lying on the hillside.

The sequel to this episode came when I spoke to the property owner several days later. He was pretty fired up about 'some bloody poachers that had been stealing my deer'. He told me he'd been out and about early on the morning in question intending to move some stock before heading into town later in the day. He'd heard our shots and decided to catch 'the poaching bastard' red-handed, and he was obviously pretty annoyed when he arrived to find three piles of guts but no poachers.

'Still,' he boasted, 'I reckon I won this time anyway.'

'How's that?' I asked.

'Well, I found three piles of deer guts and over the fence the dogs located three deer. By my reckoning that means the poacher got away with none of them. Better still, I threw the deer onto my truck and sold them for a healthy sum that afternoon on my way into town. That'll teach the bastard,' he smirked.

I agreed with his sentiments wholeheartedly. It surely wouldn't do for poachers to think they could get away with his deer now, would it? I was just glad he hadn't found the two other sets of deer guts or he might have felt somewhat less happy with the final outcome. Overall I think we all came out as winners on this one.

Throughout these years I was off hunting at every opportunity. Every weekend I wasn't working was spent chasing deer or pigs or indulging in my other passion which is fishing. Life couldn't have been better.

I worked hard on the farm and broke a lot of scrubland into pasture. At the age of 37 the sums worked out well enough for me to semi-retire. I sold the farm and moved to Te Anau. It was there, through my interest in flying, that I met Russell (later a pilot for Air Fiordland). We got on well and soon struck up a friendship. At that time Russell was gainfully employed in the wild deer recovery business.

Many rugged men with a liking for solitude and a love of the mountains were cashing in on the high price being paid for wild venison by the insatiable American and German markets. These men lived in the mountains and shot deer for a living. Many had built short, rocky and sometimes marginal airstrips to allow planes to land and carry their animals back to the buyers. Russell was one of a small group of pilots who undertook this often dangerous work.

Russell had a regular run that he made to pick up the deer carcasses. Each Wednesday he'd head into the Kaipo Valley to pick up Archie's deer, then he'd go on to Martins Bay to pick up Evan Brunton's. I was invited to go with him occasionally. Our ritual never changed. We'd land in the Kaipo Valley, where we'd have a catch-up with Archie and consume a dozen large bottles of Waitemata beer between us. After this we'd head into Martins Bay.

Living full-time in Martins Bay was Evan Brunton, his wife
Annie and their two preschool children, Jenny and Tony. I got on
really well with the family right from the start. Evan made a living
by shooting deer, while his wife tended their vegetable garden
and taught the children. There was no generator for power and
everything was cooked on a coal range that was fuelled by wood.
Lighting was by way of kerosene lamps. The simple lifestyle these
people were living appealed to me greatly, and after my first visit I
was pleased to be invited back the following Wednesday.

After this I was invited to come and stay at any time, an offer
I quickly took up. Before I knew it I was living full-time with the
Bruntons and making a living from shooting deer. We were being
paid $1 per pound for the deer and I was making tremendous
money while also getting to indulge my love of hunting.

The Bruntons lived in a small, two-roomed hut on a 50-acre block
of land. Many years previously the land had been farmed, but by
that time it was quietly reverting back to native bush and scrub.
When farmed the area had been cleared and sown in rich green
grasses, and there were still many clearings with patches of grass
that the deer found very much to their liking. Needless to say, I
shot many deer on these clearings. Evan was a very good hunter
whose rifle seemed to be a natural extension of his arms. He was
an excellent shot and had a natural instinct for finding deer.

I lived for three years with the Bruntons in their hut. I slept
in one room, which doubled as the kitchen and lounge area as
well, while all four Bruntons slept in the one bedroom. Twice a
week, Russell would fly our meat out. Most weeks Evan and I
would get 20 to 30 deer between us. Deer numbers were so high
that despite our constant pressure the number didn't seem to
decline any. In those days meat hygiene wasn't as strict as it is
today. Keeping the meat free of blowflies and maggots was often
a problem, especially in muggy weather or when Russell couldn't
fly in due to bad weather. We had a meat safe, and after putting
the carcasses in it we would saturate them with liberal doses of

flyspray. On occasion we'd have to take to the carcasses with our knives to cut out rotten meat and maggot-infected patches before Russell flew them out. These practices were common at the time, though they would be totally unacceptable now.

Evan had a boat, which opened up large areas of country for us to hunt. These included all of Martins Bay, Lake McKerrow, the Hokuri River, the Pyke River and Big Bay. We could only hunt Big Bay when the weather was settled as we travelled there by boat via the mouth of the Hollyford River. Unless sea conditions were calm this was a dangerous undertaking, and knowing that many boats had sunk at the river mouth we elected not to take any risks.

One particularly hot spot for deer was on our neighbour's property, which was owned by Jules Tapper. There was a grass airstrip on the property, beside which were a number of lush grass clearings (known as Tapper's clearings) where deer could be found all year round. Whenever Jules was away from the bay we would poach these clearings with grand results. In fact, I continued to poach these clearings until I left the bay. I'm sure I'll be forgiven this minor indiscretion, since many years have now passed.

My three years with the Bruntons passed very quickly. But Evan was keen to purchase a farm, and when Landcorp (a government department tasked with breaking in marginal land and settling fledgling farmers on it) offered him a farm he accepted. 'If you want to buy this from Annie and me it's yours,' Evan announced, waving his arm to indicate the hut and the 50 acres of land.

The bay was my home, and the thought of leaving it, or someone else taking it over, caused my gut to churn. Quicker than a woman grabs her skirt in a wind gust I accepted his offer and a deal was struck.

Living on my own doesn't trouble me, and after the Bruntons left I got busy creating a few more home comforts. One early addition was a diesel generator for lighting and to run a freezer, which made life somewhat more comfortable. The lack of communication with the outside world troubled me now that I was living on my own, so I also installed a two-way radio.

My next project was to build an airstrip, which I thought wouldn't be a problem. But when DoC found out they declared war on me and tried every backhanded trick known to mankind to stop me. They reckoned that consents and permits were needed and objected every step of the way. Further, they argued, there was already an airstrip in the bay and a second one was not only unnecessary, it would upset people walking in the neighbouring national park. Forgive my logic here, but whether a plane lands at my place or the neighbour's doesn't make any difference, does it? There is the same amount of noise and the same number of planes coming and going. It was my land and I was creating an airstrip on it whether they objected or not and with or without a consent.

Initially I worked with a wheelbarrow and shovel to fill in holes and harden up soft spots with gravel. This method wasn't very effective, though, so I brought a tractor into the bay after which progress sped up dramatically. I created a roller for compressing the gravel by filling a 44-gallon drum with concrete and towing it behind the tractor. It took me two years to complete the strip. Russell was the first to land on it, and he reckoned it was a cracker. Tongue-in-cheek he joked that it could have been finished a year earlier if I hadn't wanted to land 747s on it.

I continued to make good money by foot-hunting deer but the competition was heating up. Helicopters had now entered the meat-hunting game and they proved to be very effective at vacuuming the mountains of deer. The trouble was, the helicopters also hunted the flats and everywhere else that deer roamed, and thus my income from deer dropped dramatically.

Gradually I got to know a lot of helicopter pilots, their shooters and gutters. Sometimes I would be asked to work on a helicopter for a day or so when the usual worker was sick or injured, and I'd grab the chance, deciding, 'If you can't beat 'em, join 'em.' Usually I got the job of gutter, which meant that as deer were shot

I'd be dropped off on the hillside to gut them and make them ready for transporting back to civilisation. Every minute of flying time was expensive so the helicopter would leave me and go off to shoot more deer while I did the job. Sometimes it would be more than an hour before the helicopter returned and I'd be stuck on a remote mountain face hoping like hell that the machine hadn't crashed. If it had and the occupants had been killed it was a certainty that no one else would know where I was or even that I existed. Some of the places we hunted by helicopter were very treacherous and isolated, and walking out from them would have been all but impossible.

Now that I had an airstrip I suddenly became a popular person to visit. Planes and helicopters dropped in often, some of them forced down to wait out bad weather and others just keen to have a yarn and a brew.

Russell was busier than ever flying out deer in his fixed-wing plane. This was because the helicopters' running costs were so high, a lot more than fixed-wing aircraft. The helicopters would ferry the deer to the nearest airstrip, and Russell would pick them up from there and fly them out.

One fine day Kim Hollows, a helicopter pilot, and Evan Brunton dropped in for breakfast. Evan's love of hunting had drawn him back into the game as a shooter while his wife ran their farm. He and Kim had several loads of deer for Russell to ferry out and these were lying beside the airstrip. After a yarn and a cuppa they left at about 7.30 to get more animals. They had enough fuel onboard to fly for about an hour, and were to return to my place to refuel and unload. When they had not returned by 9 a.m. I became concerned.

Yes, it was possible that they had parked on the hill and stopped the machine, but it was very unlikely. At 9.30 I knew they were in trouble and raised the alarm by radio. A base was set up at Gunner's Camp, Murray Gunn's motor camp in the Hollyford Valley, and a search was mounted immediately. Before long the searchers located an emergency beacon signal and set about tracking it down. They struck a difficulty, however, because as they travelled so did the signal from the beacon. Every time they thought they had located the source of the signal and established a search area it moved and came from another direction. It was obvious to everyone that this wasn't right, as the helicopter would have run out of fuel long ago. Frustration levels grew and everyone's stress levels climbed through the roof. I was stuck in the bay on my own and had to stay there in case they somehow managed to get back.

A radio technician was consulted and said that in his opinion the distress signal was bouncing off the solid rock walls of the tight valleys, making it all but impossible to pinpoint a crash site.

At about mid-afternoon a tramper called in at Murray's store to buy something before returning to civilisation. When he asked what was going on and was told about the missing helicopter he said he had seen a helicopter working the area he had been in that morning. He had seen it enter the area, but couldn't recall seeing it leave. Further, he had heard three rifle shots coming from that general direction later in the morning but had thought nothing more of it.

Everything the tramper said fitted with what was known, and the area he described was in the proximity of the moving distress signal. With renewed urgency and direction the search was on again.

At about 4 p.m. I heard a radio transmission to the search base, stating that the helicopter had been found. Apparently it had crashed and was stuck up a tree. At least one person was alive, as he could be seen waving from the machine. Was the other man alive, and who was it that was waving? It was an anxious wait as plans were made to rescue the survivor or survivors.

Because the helicopter was perched precariously in a tree, recovering its crew would require careful planning. A hasty approach could prove fatal to any survivors. To everyone's relief it was quickly established that both Kim and Evan had survived, and their rescue was made without further mishap. Evan was a bit the worse for wear, with a broken arm and three broken ribs. It was initially thought that Kim had broken his back but fortunately he hadn't, and only had a few scratches and severe bruising.

It had been a very long day for me as I sat by the radio waiting for news of my mates. When I heard they were both safely back at the search base I had a large celebratory rum to toast their rescue.

It wasn't long after this that the concept of farming deer came into being, so instead of shooting the deer there was a mad scramble to capture live animals to supply the lucrative market. One fine winter's day Gary Hollows, a brother of Kim's, arrived on his own in a Robinson chopper. Now Gary is a top bloke by anyone's measure, and as tough as they come. A tanned, solidly built man who was then in his forties, he was a happy-go-lucky kind of guy who laughed easily and found no challenge too hard.

Gary had a dozen Double Brown beers stashed by his feet and suggested that we go for a joyride and a trout fish up the Pyke River while we drank the beer. 'We won't be away long,' he promised. 'They want the machine back for a hunt tonight.'

Now it was a hot day and the beer looked real cold. In view of this I chose to ignore the fact that Gary didn't have a licence to fly the chopper, and as far as I knew he had somewhere between bugger-all and not much training to fly one anyway. I felt that if a bloke had seen fit to lend him the chopper he must have been confident in his ability to fly it. Further, it would be rude to turn down such a kind offer, wouldn't it?

Gary was keen to get on with things, so as we wouldn't be away for long I jumped in clad only in my shorts and singlet and armed with my fishing rod. Shortly after take-off I discovered that I was right and the beer was cold.

After a reasonably stable flight up Lake McKerrow we followed the Hollyford River to its junction with the Pyke River, where we veered left to follow the Pyke. As we were flying over Lake

Alabaster the chopper's motor started to vibrate and shudder. The problem got worse as we neared the top of the lake and Gary's face took on an 'Oh shit' kind of look.

'We're losing power,' he said nervously. 'I'll have to put her down in the riverbed up ahead.'

Gary fought the controls as the power began to fail altogether, but he managed to get us down in one piece on an island in the middle of the river. I'll admit we touched down a bit more heavily than would otherwise have been prudent, but at least we were down in one piece.

'Bloody spark plug problem again,' Gary stated. 'I thought we'd sorted that out. Not to worry; I'll soon have us airborne again.'

He didn't seem too worried by this turn of events and soon had his tool-kit out and was busy removing and cleaning the machine's spark plugs. I decided that a bit of trout fishing was called for while he sorted out the motor.

As I fished the weather started to change and banks of dark cloud drifted in overhead. Sandflies always find overcast conditions to their liking and they set about trying to eat me alive. I had no luck in the fishing department and after half an hour or so returned to Gary.

'Jump in, my old son. We're out of here,' he declared as I joined him.

It was probably a good thing we were, as repairing the chopper must have been thirsty work and I noticed that we were out of beer. Once we were safely strapped in Gary wound the motor over. It gave a number of half-hearted splutters and coughed once, but wouldn't start. Gary spent another half hour or so fiddling with the motor before again trying to start it. Again it wouldn't go. We couldn't call for assistance on the radio as the machine didn't have a radio.

'Better tuck ourselves in for the night,' Gary finally said, rather dejectedly. 'It'll be dark in half an hour and it's unlikely anyone will come looking for us before morning.'

Sure enough, no one came looking for us before dark. We gathered up all the driftwood that was on the island and lit a hearty bonfire. There's nothing like a fire to make a person feel better, and having something to do helped pass the time. We soon ran out of wood, which probably didn't matter as it started to rain heavily at about the same time. After that we were reduced to sitting in the machine to await our rescue in the morning.

I managed to fall asleep to the sound of the heavy rain that was now pounding down on the chopper's Perspex bubble. At least we were dry and semi-comfortable. I woke at around 3 a.m. The rain was still torrential and it was pitch black outside. There were no lights in the helicopter, but I managed to roll a cigarette in the dark. As I lit the cigarette I happened to glance outside. In the glow from the lighter I saw that the river was in flood and we were surrounded by water. The chopper's landing skids were totally immersed in the swollen, muddy river and the island we were on had disappeared under water. Without question we were in deep shit. I nudged Gary awake and could tell by the horrified look on his face that his interpretation of our situation was the same as mine.

'How're you going to get us out of this one?' I asked worriedly.

'Hell, man. I got us here, you get us out,' he replied indignantly.

With sweat running down his worried brow, Gary did the only thing he could. He went through the prestart-up procedures then tried to start the helicopter. For what seemed like an eternity the motor whined, without any apparent intention of starting. Then, to our huge relief, the motor fired into life and started purring like a contented kitten. If Gary wasn't so damned ugly I'd have given the bugger a hug.

We were now able to get airborne, but this created our next dilemma. It was blacker than the inside of a coal mine outside and visibility was nil. Being able to fly was one thing, but having somewhere to fly to was another. There was only one option open to us and that was to head for a small grass bench that sat above the river about a hundred metres away. There was no room for error as the clearing was surrounded by trees and scrub. We couldn't use the cigarette lighter to navigate with as its light reflected off the helicopter's perspex bubble, making it impossible to see outside. Getting to the clearing would be by guesswork and good luck. Gary eased the machine a few metres into the air and inched sideways toward the clearing. I was standing on the skid outside the helicopter peering into the darkness, trying in vain to identify any obstacles that might be in our path. Fortunately we didn't collide with anything, and after what seemed like an eternity we reached our destination without incident.

'Now that the bloody motor's going I'm sure as hell not turning the bastard off,' Gary stated emphatically as I hauled my wet arse back into the helicopter. I couldn't disagree.

We sat in the machine with the motor idling until it was light enough to fly, then made the return trip via Big Bay and the coastline to Martins Bay. When we got back to my airstrip we found two planes on the ground and preparations being made to mount a search for us. One of the men present was Dick Deaker (aka Tricky Dick), the chopper's owner. He was relieved that his machine was undamaged, but probably felt less inclined to lend it to Gary in future after being soundly abused for supplying him with a 'crapped out machine'. Me – I decided that the next time I went for a flight in a helicopter I'd take a rain jacket with me.

One method of capturing deer alive was to net them. A three-barrelled gun had been developed that fired weights that dragged a small net behind them. The weights spread out in three directions, stretching the net out and snaring the deer. The hunter then simply had to untangle the deer, tie up its legs and place it inside the hovering helicopter. This method proved very effective and was eventually adopted by most helicopter hunters.

One morning I was sitting in my kitchen waiting for the whistling kettle to boil on the gas stove when a Hughes 500 helicopter landed at my front door. It was flown by Steve Feavor, and he had his shooter, Colin Yates, on board. They had a problem. They had netted a hind on a small slip a couple of minutes' flying time from my hut. The hind had run off into the bush with their net still attached to it. Although they were sure the deer was well caught, they had been unable to find it. They asked if I would take my dog Penny and go with them to locate the hind. Penny has a great nose and was well used to finding deer that I had shot but struggled to locate. Given that a live hind was worth about $3000 at that time I fully understood their desire to recover both the hind and the net, and agreed to help.

After throwing Penny in the back of the chopper I climbed aboard and was soon dropped off at the slip. Steve had given me a walkie-talkie radio so that I could give them a call when the hind was located. Penny quickly found the scent and made off after the deer. They had been wrong when they said the hind was well caught – it wasn't! Fifteen minutes later I caught a glimpse of it as it sidled across the steep hillside, dragging the net behind it. I had no intention of chasing the animal all around the mountain, so I sent Penny off to head it back toward me.

About ten minutes later the hind came careering past me as it tried to escape the dog. I was able to jump on the net as it went past, which caused the hind to tumble and become firmly trapped in the net. After an intense struggle, during which I received a glancing kick to the side of my head, I managed to secure the deer and place a hood over its head to calm it. I called up the helicopter, which soon arrived on the scene, and a chain was lowered through the trees so that I could attach the deer to it. Within minutes it was whisked away, and Penny and I made our way back to the slip to be picked up.

It was at this point that I realised I was bleeding heavily from the blow I had received to my head. In fact, one shoulder of my shirt was thoroughly soaked in blood. A quick feel around the wound reassured me that I wasn't about to die, so I carried on to the pick-up point. It seemed that everything was to end well.

The chopper arrived back at the slip at the same time as we did, and after I had received some stick about being an intelligent bastard for using my head to get the deer we were off back to my place. As we got nearer I started to get that 'something's not right' feeling, and it dawned on me that I had left the kettle on and that we'd been away not for a few minutes as intended but for over half an hour. As we reached the hut I could see dense black smoke billowing from my kitchen window and I was filled with panic.

Before the helicopter had even landed Colin and I were out the door and running toward the hut. Colin grabbed a bucket and raced off to the river to fill it with water as I tore open the door. I was greeted by dense, choking smoke. Strangely, I was not engulfed by the flames that I was sure were consuming my home. As the smoke cleared I could see that the kettle had boiled dry and was in the process of melting. The smoke was billowing from the frying pan beside it – it was the fat in the frying pan that was smoking furiously, and by a stroke of good fortune it had not yet burst into flames. Much to my relief, our timely return had prevented my home from being destroyed by fire.

The Silly Season

Once Neil starts recalling events from his past, the volume of noteworthy yarns just keeps growing. It would be grossly unfair for me to limit Neil's exploits to one small chapter, so I've left the telling of this one to him as well. Over to you Neil . . .

I wasn't totally alone while living in Martins Bay. As you have read, many visitors called in, and on top of this there were other people who owned blocks of land there and came in occasionally. During the silly season the population of the bay exploded to around 15 to 20 people. These extra people came to catch the elusive whitebait.

As many of you will know, whitebait are tiny, almost transparent fish that are caught during a short season that runs from 14 September to 14 November. There are strict rules on how and when the fish can be caught. Strangely, whitebait are considered to be a delicacy, and city folk pay high prices for them. Martins Bay is a long way from civilisation and has no roads or power. To get into or out of the bay you have to fly or make a long sea voyage from Milford Sound. These obstacles make getting in and out of the bay expensive. In addition, to preserve any whitebait that get caught you need a diesel-driven generator to run a freezer. There is no point in catching whitebait if you can't freeze it or fly it out the same day it's caught. For these reasons, most of those who came to Martins Bay to catch whitebait did so for commercial gain, or at the very least to recover their costs.

In my early years in Martins Bay I wasn't interested in fishing for whitebait, but I assisted those who were as best I could. Over the years a great many tonnes of whitebait have been flown out of the bay from my airstrip.

Percy and Edna were a couple of keen whitebaiters who owned a bach that was perched beside the river about a hundred metres from my hut. They came into the bay every year and were real characters. When I first met them they were in their sixties, and I enjoyed their company immensely. Each had a sharp wit, a grand sense of humour and a liking for giving the other a stir-up at every opportunity. Percy was pencil thin and had an unruly mop of grey hair on top of his long, narrow face. He was a hard, uncompromising union man, with firm opinions on most things and a liking for a debate. Edna was the perfect partner for Percy and had the measure of him when it came to debating. She was a very likable woman with a motherly nature.

Both Edna and Percy were dedicated smokers. They smoked about a hundred cigarettes a day each, and I can't recall a time when either of them didn't have a lit cigarette in their hands. Both worked as hard as they smoked, and no task was too difficult or complex for them to tackle. When the fishing and work stopped the whisky-drinking started, and they took to that with the same enthusiasm as they did everything else. I doubt there is a couple alive who drink as much whisky as they did. From time to time when a few too many may have been consumed, a raised voice could be heard coming from the direction of their hut, but all in all they were terrific and friendly people.

Often Percy and Edna would come to my hut in the evening for a drink and a yarn. It wasn't unusual for us to have a dram or two more than was necessary and my friends would stagger the short distance back to their home in the dark. Between their hut and mine there was a deep creek that had a narrow footbridge across it. Over time I took to calling the bridge 'Arse up bridge', due to the fact that Percy frequently fell off it as he tried to navigate his way home. It wasn't uncommon to find an item of Percy's clothing or a whisky bottle lying in the creek the morning after he'd visited.

Percy and Edna both had 'registered' whitebait stands. These were fixed stands that belonged to them, and they had the sole rights to fish from them. To help those of you who are unfamiliar with whitebait rules and regulations, I'll explain how things work.

As you already know, the Hollyford River is huge. It's about eight kilometres from the mouth of the river to Lake McKerrow, and it averages about a hundred metres in width. Obviously a great many people could comfortably fish the area without getting in each other's way. However, huge numbers of people fishing for whitebait year after year would be unacceptable as the stocks would become depleted over time.

To prevent this happening, both here and in other whitebaiting areas, a rule was made to allow only a limited number of registered (permanent) fishing stands on any given river. There are six registered stands allowed on the Hollyford River. Having a registered stand means that the owners can build a structure during the whitebait season that they can fish from each day. At the end of the season the structure has to be removed. Rest assured that the registered stands are erected in the best spots for catching the bait, and that they are keenly sought when one becomes available. In effect, the stands are the legal property of the owners, and they have the right to sell or trade them as they see fit.

Needless to say, if people were selling their whitebait for profit the taxman wanted his share. No one likes to pay tax, therefore most whitebaiters had arrangements to sell their bait to purchasers who were prepared to pay that most tax-invisible substance called 'cash'. The bigger commercial fishers ran things properly and the taxman got his share, but the smaller players treated it as a big game, continually finding ways of avoiding the taxman. I have no idea what Percy and Edna did with their bait, and frankly it's none of my business. What I do know is that we had many enjoyable nights together having a drink and laughing a lot. Often they would supply me with whitebait and I would give them venison. It was an arrangement that suited us all.

One night there was a frantic hammering on my door at about 3 a.m. It was Percy. He was distraught as Edna was having a heart attack. I raced to Edna and she didn't look good. She was sure she was at death's door, and was insistent that she didn't want to die in Martins Bay. She wanted out of the bay right there and then. Fortunately there was a plane at Tapper's airstrip and after some frantic efforts we managed to get Edna into it. I had made contact by radio with Te Anau, and they were going to light up Te Anau airstrip with car headlights so we could land there safely. Although it was night the sky was clear of any clouds, and visibility was reasonable as a three-quarter moon illuminated the sky.

Jules Tapper gunned the plane along the runway and we were quickly airborne and heading for Te Anau, with Percy, Edna and me on board. As we flew past Hokuri Hut Edna was gripped by another heart attack and her heart stopped. I frantically tried to revive her but unfortunately she died. It was discovered later that I had cracked several of her ribs during my efforts. Her death was the saddest event that happened during my time in the bay.

Soon after Edna's death I decided to take a break and head to Europe for an extended holiday. Knowing that people who travel into the mountains and wilds of New Zealand are, generally speaking, decent people, when I departed I left my home unlocked. I was sure that anyone who needed to use it would respect it and keep things tidy.

It wasn't until I had been away for several months and was in England that I rang home for the first time. I was told that

Percy had also died. This news had a profound effect on me and I decided I didn't feel like holidaying any more. I headed for home.

On my return to Martins Bay I was shocked at what greeted me. My home was all but wrecked. Things were lying on the floor, dishes sat in the sink unwashed and with mould growing on them, and several windows had been broken. The place looked as if it had been struck by a tornado. Several of my boat motors had been damaged and one dinghy was missing altogether. On top of this my radio had been damaged beyond use. This of all things was unforgivable, as the radio was my sole lifeline in times of trouble. It took me several days to get things back into order and to locate the missing dinghy. I never found out who did this, and it is very fortunate for them that I didn't, as I would probably have bypassed the local police and taken some remedial action of my own.

Following Edna's death her whitebait stand was given to my sister-in-law, Curls. Percy had also had enough, and he sold the bach to Curls and Charlie, my brother, while Evan Brunton took over Percy's whitebait stand. I entered the whitebait game in 1982 after I became aware that Ray Rolton of Christchurch was no longer using his stand. We negotiated a deal in which I would take over his stand and pay him the princely sum of one kilo of whitebait per year.

From 1982 until 1985 I fished commercially. The best year I had I caught two and a half tonne of whitebait. Charlie, Curls and I worked as a team, together processing and bagging the bait. It was great having them as temporary neighbours each whitebait season, and they made living in the bay much more enjoyable.

At the start of each season the air would come alive with planes and boats as people set up their stands and settled into the routine of fishing. The ritual was to fish every daylight incoming tide. It is illegal to fish after dark. Some days we would fish only the one tide and others two, depending on where the tides were at. There is a rule that a person has to be within ten metres of their net at all times. In obeyance of this I spent many thousands of hours standing on the riverbank looking for and netting whitebait. I must have squashed millions of sandflies during this time, as the little biting buggers mounted never-ending attacks on me.

Between tides the whitebait had to be cleaned. This process involved getting rid of any small sticks and debris that got caught up in the net with the bait. Good whitebait should be almost transparent, so the 'bellies' had to be removed too – belly was the name we gave to whitebait that had formed a dark gut bag and were not suitable for selling. The process of cleaning the bait was time-consuming and tedious.

Whitebaiting in the bay was a very social affair and most nights we had visitors who would drop in for a drink and a yarn. Our popularity was greatly increased by the presence of a highly skilled master brewer who came into the bay with us each year, and excelled at distilling alcohol and turning it into our favourite drink – 'rum'. This brewer's skills were legendary, and inspired many a visit from the locals. Some visitors even travelled great distances by boat and plane to taste the product and enjoy our company. It was fortunate that we had so many visitors as production was prolific and we had to drink hard just to keep up. Fortunately the end of the fishing season signalled the end of the brewing and a rest for our livers.

A word to the brewer – if you are reading this, Curls, thanks heaps.

While I have shot many hundreds of deer over the years, one particular hind sticks in my mind. The whitebaiting season had ended, the bay had returned to normal, and I was back in my routine of hunting at daybreak and again in the evening. On my return from my evening hunts I would start the generator, cook tea and have a shower. Before I went to bed I would go outside to the generator shed and turn the generator off. Without fail, as soon as I turned off the generator a hind would bark at me from the darkness of the nearby bush. She was always just inside the bush edge, off the track that leads from my hut to the airstrip. I determined that she was mine and set out to get her.

My first plan of attack was to take a spotlight with me to the generator shed, and when she barked I'd light her up and shoot her. In my mind it was going to be that easy. I tried this method many times without success. The hind was always in the same area, but far enough inside the bush edge that I couldn't locate her. I began to feel that she was mocking me and took to calling her 'the bitch hind'. The bitch hind had clearly worked out my routine and therefore wasn't afraid to stick around the general area.

My second plan was to go to bed as usual and to allow the bitch hind time to come out from the bush edge and relax before I snuck out in my socks and caught her in the open with the spotlight. I tried this method numerous times without success. It was almost like she had a sixth sense that was tuned into me and warned her about what I was up to. No matter what time of night I tried this method she would always give me a jeering bark from the protection of the bush just to let me know that she had won again. Her unwanted bark also gave warning to any other deer that were out in the open feeding on the lush grass around my airstrip. Her taunting continued throughout the summer, and I spent hours thinking up cunning plans to get the old girl, but she outsmarted them all. By this time the bitch hind had well and truly got me worked out. As time passed the contest became personal and I became even more determined to get her.

One overcast night I turned off the generator, then, instead of heading to my hut, I went to Charlie's and slept the night there. In the pitch black of night and well before dawn I snuck from the hut and quietly walked down the riverbank toward Jerusalem Creek. The wind was behind me, carrying my scent and sound away. I then took a circuitous route through the bush toward the airstrip and back toward the junction where the track leads to my hut. Over the preceding weeks I had cut a track through the bush so that I could travel there quietly. I was hoping my foe would be in her usual position, where she could see me leaving my hut and bark her warning.

I sat just inside the bush edge and waited for first light. My eyes strained into the darkness and several times I thought I saw movement at the bush edge, but it proved to be my fertile mind creating a deer that wasn't. Then suddenly a hind barked from the darkness somewhere ahead. Up to that point I hadn't noticed that the wind had changed and was now swirling about. Had my scent carried to the animal? In view of her bark, it seemed highly likely that it had. A faint shadow emerged from the darkness of the airstrip and made its way with a steady gait back to the cover of the bush. In an instant I had my rifle to my shoulder and fired. The deer was down. I was delighted and ran to inspect it. It was a very old, almost black hind, and in fact it turned out to be by far the biggest hind I shot in the bay. Was she the 'bitch hind' that I had been after for so long?

That night when I turned the generator off I fully expected to hear a bark coming from the darkness, as it had for most of the summer. But no bark came.

One of my great loves is fishing, and I was always keen to have a crack at whatever was there to be caught. In Martins Bay I caught trout, and I sometimes went up to Lakes Alabaster and Wilmot to fish for quinnat salmon. When I first moved to Martins Bay the trout fishing was absolutely marvellous and I was almost guaranteed to catch one or two every time I went fishing. By the time I left the bay 15 years later trout were all but non-existent. The reason was the population boom of the seals, which was out of control. The seals had taken to travelling up the Hollyford River and into Lake McKerrow, vacuuming off all the eatable fish. I think I can be forgiven for thinking that seals are a pest. Anyway, I'm heading in another direction here so I'll get back to my story.

Each year tuna migrate from the warmer waters of the Pacific to the cooler southern waters off the Fiordland coast. Generally speaking, they are found well out to sea but on occasions they come in close to land. Commercial fishermen have quotas for catching these prized fish and each year they pursue them with vigour. From time to time some of the fishing boats would take shelter in the Hollyford River. I enjoyed the company of these fishermen, and on occasion I would head out to sea with them as a deckhand for a day or two. Catching tuna was a thrilling experience that I could easily have become addicted to.

It wasn't long after a trip to sea on a commercial boat that I got the idea of having a crack at the tuna on my own. After all, I had a boat, and on a calm day when the tide was right I'd have no difficulty in crossing the bar at the river mouth and heading out to sea.

One clear, fine day I listened to the sea and weather forecasts on the radio and decided that, as they were good, I should go tuna fishing. With a full fuel tank and several spare containers of petrol I fired up the outboard motor of my 14'6" aluminium boat and headed out to sea. I had been speaking to my fishermen mates by radio and they had told me that the tuna were in close at that time and where I was likely to find them. The sea was as calm as I had ever seen it, with only a gentle swell, and there was no wind. Since I had no navigation equipment on board I headed out to sea with the intention of staying within sight of land.

After an hour or so of motoring along I spotted a flock of birds that were frantically diving into the water, which seemed to be seething beneath them. Knowing that when tuna feed they often drive schools of fish to the surface, which in turn attracts birds, I headed toward them. As I neared the birds I knew I was onto tuna – the sea was boiling as they chased a school of fish to the surface. After idling alongside the churning waters I turned off the motor and cast a line into the melee. Immediately the lure was taken and the fight was on. The powerful fish swam about wildly, pulling the boat this way and that as it went. After ten minutes I had a 10-kg tuna landed on the boat and nothing could wipe the smile off my face. I was rapt, and after removing the hook from the tuna I soon had my lure back in the water. I caught another tuna before the feeding frenzy stopped and I decided it was time to return to shore.

At that point I looked around for land and to my dismay there wasn't any. Given that land is visible for at least 12 kilometres, I knew that I had drifted and fished my way well out to sea. Using common sense I reasoned that since the sun sets in the west, and that the land was in the opposite direction to this, it wasn't hard to sort out a direction for travel. This was all well and good until I tried to start the motor and it wouldn't go. I hadn't had any trouble with it in the past and felt that it could have picked a better time than then to play up. Each time I turned the ignition key nothing at all happened. I'm reasonably handy with motors and electrical things and I was sure I could sort the matter out soon enough. I determined that I had an electrical problem, as the motor didn't do anything when the key was turned.

For the next two hours I tried everything I could to fix the problem, without success. There I was, bobbing about in the middle of the Tasman Sea with no food, no radio and no one knowing where I was. The day was moving along and it would be dark in another four hours. The weather was still great and I had a set of oars onboard, but the prospect of rowing 12 kilometres or more back to land didn't thrill me a lot. Reaching land was only step one – where to go after that would be my next problem. I had headed south after leaving the mouth of the Hollyford River, so I knew I was at least 15 kilometres from there. Having taken this into account I knew that the nearest civilised outpost to head to was probably Milford Sound – or was it?

Getting safely to land was my first priority. I hadn't brought any warm clothing or food with me, which didn't place me in the greatest of predicaments. It was one of those 'get rowing, you idiot' kind of situations, so I put the oars in the rowlocks, faced the sun, leaned into the task and headed for land. I had been rowing for about 20 minutes with my head down and my mind churning when I happened to look up. About a kilometre away, and heading directly toward me, was a fishing boat. As quick as a flash I was on my feet and waving furiously. I had a safety flare on board and decided that I'd use it to attract the boat's attention if I needed to. It turned out that all my attention-seeking activity wasn't necessary as the boat was headed straight for me and would probably have collided with me anyway. The skipper, Dale Hunter, pulled up beside me and asked if it was a good day for rowing about in the Tasman Sea. I didn't mind the ribbing and could have kissed him.

After hearing my explanation of how I had got into this situation Dale took my boat into tow and kindly returned me unscathed to Martins Bay. I was very fortunate, as things could have turned out far worse than they did. I decided that I would take an auxiliary motor with me the next time I went tuna fishing.

Not long after this, two interesting guests arrived in the bay and stayed for the next ten months. They were Cindy Buxton and Frances Ferlon, who were in Fiordland to make a documentary about the place. The only real way to experience Fiordland is by living there, and that's just what they did. They employed me as their full-time guide, and I ferried them to wherever they wanted to go during the filming. They were terrific women whose company I enjoyed immensely. The documentary they made was turned into a promotional movie called *Mountains of Water* and it is shown many times daily at the theatre in the DoC building in Te Anau.

My constant companion in the bay was my dog Penny. She was great company, and while out hunting she pointed out many deer that I would otherwise have walked past without even knowing they were there. On other occasions when I had shot a deer and was having trouble locating it Penny would find the animal for me every time. Needless to say, I was very upset when Penny died. My brother had a similar dog at the time and he gave it to me for company. It was a Weimaraner called Trigger, which initially had no idea at all about hunting for deer. When I first took Trigger hunting she would bark at animals and chase them off before I could take a shot at them. Over time she learnt the ropes, though, and after about a year she was almost as good at locating deer for me as Penny had been.

One morning I was hunting for velvet high on the Sara Hills. Deer velvet is considered by Asians to be a powerful aphrodisiac, and the price being paid for it at that time was high. I could make more money from shooting stags and taking just the velvet than by bringing back the meat. One day Trigger and I were quietly stalking a bush ridge that I knew stags favoured when a strange animal came bounding through the crown fern toward me. The animal showed no fear initially and came to within ten feet of me before it stopped and eyed me curiously. I quickly realised that the animal was in fact a chamois.

I had lived in the bay for a good many years at the time and had never previously encountered a chamois. I felt no inclination to shoot the animal but instead decided to capture it and take it back to my hut as a pet. My furtive leap was easily avoided by the chamois as it took evasive action and bounded down the hill-face away from me. Trigger took off after it and about ten minutes later started barking furiously. I made my way to her and discovered that she had cornered the chamois under a large, rotting log. When I reached under the log and took hold of one of the chamois' legs it came out fighting, repeatedly trying to hook me with the short, curved antlers that grew from the top of its head. Chamois antlers are about ten inches in length and are curved at the ends, giving them a similar appearance to wool bale hooks.

After hog-tying the chamois' legs together I tied it to the metal frame of my pack. The animal was quite small and only weighed about 40kg, so it was easy enough to carry except that it continually tried to hook me with its horns. To avoid getting injured I was forced to tie the horns to the top of my pack. The walk back to my hut took four hours and I was about shot when we finally got there. Although the chamois never became friendly as such, over time it took to greeting me by giving me gentle nudges with its horns. In return I would scratch the back of its neck, which it seemed to enjoy greatly. I took to calling it Buttercup, after its favourite food. After about three months of living outside of my hut Buttercup left the bay and was taken to a zoo.

DoC was most upset when some trampers accidentally set fire to the Martins Bay Hut and it burnt to the ground. Until arrangements could be made to rebuild the hut, trampers had nowhere to stay unless they carried a tent all the way into the bay with them. DoC was still a bit testy with me for building my airstrip, but they had defrosted a bit and had even taken to landing on it themselves occasionally. Soon after the Martins Bay Hut burnt down they approached me and asked if I would allow trampers to stay in one of my huts.

'You can charge them the standard $6 per night fee and keep it for yourself,' I was told.

There's no point in harbouring hard feelings, so without hesitation I agreed to their suggestion. The arrangement suited me as I would enjoy the company of the trampers, and it suited Air Fiordland, who often flew them from the bay out to the Hollyford airstrip. The Hollyford Track is a one-way affair that leads into the bay and to the seal colony. Trampers who didn't want to return by the same track could elect to fly out of the bay with Russell. Years earlier the track had continued past the seal colony, north into Big Bay, inland to the Pyke River and then downriver to its junction with the upper Hollyford River. Sadly DoC no longer maintains this track and it is now rarely used.

For almost two years this accommodation arrangement worked fabulously. I had regular paying guests of all nationalities and from all walks of life. Since I was on my own most of the time I made it my habit to invite guests to my hut for a meal of venison or whitebait, depending on the season at the time of their visit. Most would accept my invitation and I enjoyed many interesting evenings in their company.

Toward the end of March one year I answered a knock at my door. On opening it I discovered a petite, tanned woman of about 25. She had mousey brown hair, was slim, tanned, scantily dressed and drop-dead gorgeous. Her feminine features were very evident, and were highlighted by her mode of dress – a pair of tight denim shorts and an almost non-existent short cropped t-shirt. The girl was a bit stand-offish and didn't seem keen on entering into conversation of any sort. In a very brief exchange, from which I guessed that she was Irish, she arranged to stay for a week and I moved her into the small 'mouse hut' that is situated in the bush behind Charlie and Curls' hut. As was my usual custom I invited her to have tea with me that night, but was flatly declined.

The woman (for the sake of this yarn let's call her 'Irish') kept to herself and didn't seem keen on anyone's company but her own. I respected that and left her alone. Each day we would see each other in passing as Irish went for a walk or I went on my way to the river to go fishing or hunting. From time to time I would invite her to tea again and she would curtly decline my offer. On several occasions Irish saw me returning in my boat with a deer or two onboard. She would watch as I struggled to get them to shore and then carry them to my meat safe. Despite her obvious interest she never approached me or offered any assistance.

Attached to Tapper's Clearing and airstrip is flash accommodation that is owned and run by an outfit called Hollyford Walks and Tours. The company offers guided walks and jetboat trips in the Hollyford Valley and on Lake McKerrow. I was friendly with one of their guides, Julia, who took regular guided walks along the beach from Martins Bay to the mouth of the Kaipo Valley. To get there she took the trampers across the Hollyford River and into McKenzie Lagoon, where the boat was tied up, then they walked through a patch of bush and across Jericho Creek before reaching the coast and walking along the beach to the mouth of the Kaipo River. One evening Julia called at my hut for a drink and a yarn, and while there she told me that every time she made the walk to the Kaipo she saw a big stag in Jericho Stream that just stood and watched them walk past. This had happened three times in a row and her paying guests thought it was a marvellous sight. They passed Jericho Creek at about 3.30 each afternoon. I didn't mention to Julia that the stag was worth about $140 on the meat hook and that in the back of my mind a plan was formulating to turn meat into money.

At about 2.30 the following afternoon I had my rifle slung over my shoulder and was making my way toward my boat when Irish approached from her hut.

'Where are you going?' she asked.

Now this was a large step forward in the communication area, as up until that point I had initiated all conversation between us. When I told her the story and that I hoped to shoot an easy stag that wasn't going to require much walking or effort she asked if she could come with me. Now how in the hell could I concentrate on hunting when Irish was clad in the skimpiest white bikini top and the briefest shorts I'd ever seen a woman squeezed into. Generally speaking I prefer to hunt on my own, with just my dog (I still had Penny at this stage), but given that Irish was normally such an introvert I thought this was a major breakthrough and agreed to take her along.

'You can't come dressed like that,' I told her bluntly. 'You'll have to change into some dark clothing so you won't look like a beacon in the bush and you'll need some shoes as well.'

Suitably dressed, we crossed the river in my boat and headed for McKenzie Lagoon. For reasons that only a woman could understand, Irish changed from a 'wouldn't say a word' kind of woman to one who wouldn't shut up. We tied up the boat and after several minutes' walking I had to tell Irish to stop wobbling her tongue or else we wouldn't stand a show of seeing the stag. She was a bit miffed by my rebuke but managed the rest of the walk in silence.

As we entered the bush by Gunners Hut, near Jericho Stream, I told Irish that we were close to our destination, that she should stay close to me and must remain quiet. I slowed to a crawl as we neared Jericho's open creek bed and made our approach cautiously. We stood motionless just inside the bush edge and peered for some time upstream without seeing anything. We were about half an hour earlier than the time Julia had said she had seen the stag, and it was possible we were too early.

After a while I eased out onto the grass and fern at the edge of the creek so that I could get a better view upstream. Irish was only a half step behind me. Trigger was ahead of me and knew the game well. Suddenly she stiffened and her head froze, pointing steadily upstream. I followed her gaze and saw a stag that was quickly making its way toward the bush edge on my side of the creek. Irish in the meantime had moved up beside and above me, wanting to get a better look at proceedings. Immediate action was required as the stag would be safely in the cover of the bush in seconds. Reactions built into me by many years of hunting took over. Instinctively I grabbed Irish and shoved her aside as I raised the rifle and in an instant fired. Trigger took off after the stag, immediately followed by me. Within minutes Trigger had given a loud bark and I knew that my shot was good and that she had found the stag. I continued onward and soon reached my prey. I gave Trigger a big pat on the head and praised her up. The shine in her eyes and the happy look on her face told me that that was all the reward she sought.

As Julia had said, the stag was a big-bodied one, but the antlers were nothing special, being only eight points. As I bent to commence the job of gutting and preparing the carcass for carrying back to the boat it occurred to me that Irish was missing. I had a quick look around and couldn't see her anywhere, which was strange given that minutes earlier she had been standing beside me. Knowing that she couldn't have come to any harm I carried on and finished preparing the deer before setting out to see where she was. After a reasonably good look around I hadn't found her so I yelled out to see if I could get a response.

Moments later Trigger gave one loud bark. What was she on about, I wondered? Since I had only fired one shot she couldn't have found another dead deer, could she? I went to Penny and found her with her nose buried in some dense scrub. There, curled up under the scrub, shaking like a leaf and crying her heart out, was Irish.

'What's wrong, girl?' I asked.

Initially she pretended that she hadn't been found, but finally, while trying to creep backwards away from me, Irish said, 'You're going to kill me.'

'Ya what?' I blurted.

'Are you going to kill me?' Irish sobbed.

'Don't be stupid, girl. Why would I do that?' I asked her.

'You threw me to the ground and shot at me,' came her fearful response.

Now here's a girl who jumps to conclusions quicker than fleas jump onto dogs, I thought.

'Don't be silly, girl,' I responded. 'You were in the road. I pushed you out of the way so I could shoot the stag and not you. I got it too. Come and take a look.'

Obviously still a bit unsure of things, Irish crept out from under the bush and nervously followed me to the stag. When she saw it and realised that there hadn't been a murder attempt, her disposition lightened up instantly. I think she took several thousand photographs of that deer and me as I laboured underneath it on our way back to the lagoon. Let's not forget here that I'm not very big, but the stag was. Getting the bugger onto my back had taken a monumental effort on my part and when I finally got it there my legs wobbled constantly under its weight. I must have looked pretty silly with it draped over my shoulders and dragging its rear along the ground behind me as I went.

Before we arrived at the boat Irish commented, 'I thought you said this was going to be an easy deer. That doesn't look easy to me.'

'Take it from me, girl, it doesn't feel that bloody easy from under here either,' I puffed in reply.

That night Irish had her evening meal with me. I cooked a venison casserole and she was very pleased to have a proper meal after a week of bland dehydrated tucker. Irish turned out to be a lovely girl who just took a bit more time than most to come to grips with good old-fashioned backcountry Kiwi hospitality.

When I first came to Martins Bay to live a lot of hunters visited. Many had their sons or daughters with them and were giving them a chance to experience the outdoors. It was always good to see keen youngsters in the hills and I did everything I could to assist them and their parents to get a trout or deer or by giving them a ride up Lake McKerrow to save them having to walk the demon trail on their way out. Sadly, over time fewer kids came to the bay. I can only speculate that they have become addicts of inactivity, television and PlayStations. This saddens me greatly as there is so much on offer in the New Zealand outdoors.

My 15-year adventure in Martins Bay came to an end when I got emphysema and the going got a bit tricky. I wasn't keen on hanging up my hat and throwing in the towel, but eventually succumbed to common sense. I'm a long way from dead yet and can still wander a riverbed or two, so the salmon and trout had better look out. Who knows, I may even head out after another tuna or two?

Footnote: Sadly, Neil died in 2006. He was a marvellous and generous man, and we are fortunate he shared his stories with us.

Beating the Baldy

Crummy, Kevin and I were off to the Kaipo Valley in Fiordland for a hunt. My mates were from the North Island and this was to be their first venture into the wilds of the South Island.

Crummy is a good bastard. He's a fraction shorter than average and, like me, carries an oversized beer gut, it's true, but he's a good bastard nonetheless. Some of you will have met Crummy in my previous books and will have a fair idea of the hard-case character that he is. For those of you who don't know him – you'll just have to take my word for it.

Crummy has tried his hand at all sorts of things throughout his life but he reckons that the most exciting and fun job he ever had was being a helicopter shooter in the days of deer-meat recovery. Needless to say a man becomes pretty handy with a rifle when he's shooting day after day at running deer from a fast moving helicopter, and Crummy was no exception. I don't go hunting with Crummy much these days because every time we see a deer he's shot the bloody thing before I can even get my rifle up. He's often told me that I'm 'the best damn pack horse he's ever had' and that it would be a bit more practical if I was to leave my rifle at home to save me carrying the extra weight. I reckon that he may be on to something there.

Kevin is a few years older than Crummy and me and is a hell of a lot thinner and fitter. Crummy often joked that 'if mud got stuck in our rifle barrels we could pull Kevin through them to get it out'. Having owned and run pubs for many years Kevin has a grand sense of humour, a sharp wit and an immense liking for the amber liquid.

Kevin and I pulled into Queenstown expecting to find the third member of our party half-cut on grog, as he had got there four days earlier and was awaiting our arrival. When we didn't find him at our prearranged meeting point it only served to strengthen our belief. By now technology had caught up with us, so we were able to make a quick cellphone call which revealed his whereabouts.

'Get your arses up here,' Crummy gushed. 'It's great.'

As we all know, hunting trips are run on budgets that are usually pretty tight. We had expected to spend the night in Queenstown hidden on the floor in Crummy's motel, where the owner wouldn't see us and we could avoid paying for the privilege. Crummy was in Queenstown on business that concluded that evening, but when he told us we were to have a meal at the most expensive restaurant known to mankind we weren't overwhelmed with joy.

'I've left tickets for you at the sales office at the bottom of the gondola. They've been paid for,' Crummy went on.

So, dressed in our finest hunting gear we headed upward in the gondola that stretches above the township and comes to a halt at the Skyline restaurant at the top. Crummy was right – the view was impressive. We managed to down a good number of beers and before long didn't feel at all out of place in our Swanndris, track pants and hunting boots.

Morning arrived far too soon, leaving us only one further matter to attend to before we headed south to Te Anau and on to the Kaipo Valley. Sadly, Crummy had turned into a bit of an intellectual, and

after years of studying university papers by correspondence he was to sit his final exam that morning. Not drinking a lot would have been prudent the night before the exam but he reckoned he'd got such high marks in his previous papers that he only needed to get four per cent in the final paper to pass the course. He had taken great delight the previous night in telling anyone who would listen that all he had to do was spell his name correctly at the top of his test paper and he would pass. As he disappeared into the flash hotel complex where he was to sit the exam he didn't look quite so confident. The exam was to start at 10 a.m. but to be on the safe side we deposited him at the venue at 9.30.

Crummy had a long name and it would take him a while to write it down on the test paper, so Kevin told him to call us when he had finished. Meanwhile we departed for a coffee to reinvigorate ourselves. The moment Crummy completed the exam our hunting trip was to start.

Shortly after we left the hotel my cellphone rang. It was a very distressed Crummy. We thought he'd forgotten how to spell his name and had phoned to find out how, but we were wrong. The hotel that we had delivered him to knew nothing of the exam and certainly didn't have a venue booked by any university for the purposes of exam sitting. Crummy was in the throes of uncontrollable panic, so we did our best to console him and help him through his predicament.

'Bloody great,' said Kevin, who wasn't nearly as perturbed by this turn of events as Crummy clearly was. 'Let's pick up the old coot and get on with the hunting.'

Crummy was definitely at the right place, and had checked his exam slip about 50 times just to make sure. If there was a balls-up it had been made by the university, not by him. We agreed to wait until 10.30, when the exam should have been well and truly under way. If no one from the university had fronted up by then we'd grab Crummy and make a bolt for Te Anau. This way Crummy could argue that he'd done his bit and that the university must give him an aegrotat pass just for fronting up.

At 10.31 we headed off toward Te Anau with a very pissed-off Crummy seated behind us. I had never seen a man so pissed off or so stressed. Crummy was worried that his whole year's effort would be wasted due to the university's stuff-up. We were about ten kilometres out of Queenstown when Crummy's cellphone rang.

It was someone from the university, apologising frantically for their stuff-up. Could he turn his little butt around and return to the hotel, where the examiner was prepared to let him start the exam as soon as he arrived?

I can't print what was said as you may blush, but Crummy was so stressed by this turn of events that he almost ruptured a boiler over the phone. He argued that he was nearly in Te Anau and that returning would be a huge cost to him. Further, he said, he was now so stressed that he couldn't even remember how to spell his name anyway.

Crummy lost the argument, we returned to Queenstown and he sat the exam like a good little boy should. Crummy was not good company when we finally set sail again. He was still stressed to the maximum and really pissed off all at the same time. He couldn't even see the funny side when I asked him to spell his name out loud just to check if he'd got it right.

About an hour into our journey Crummy's cellphone rang again. This time it was his university tutor, who was very apologetic about the blunder that had been made by his revered institution.

'We formally apologise for our error, and let me be the first to congratulate you on having achieved a very fine pass in the exam,' he announced in his most official tones.

It took some time for the significance of this statement to filter its way through the twisted and difficult journey to enable Crummy to understand what he had just been told. His tutor had given him a pass without even seeing his exam paper. Crummy went from a dejected, lonely and miserable man to a noisy pain in the arse in moments. In view of what he had been through over the past five hours we were absolutely thrilled for him and pulled in at the next pub so he could shout for his success.

We eventually made it to Te Anau, where we stayed the night with our pilot mate Russell, intending to leave for the Kaipo the following morning. Unfortunately heavy cloud cover and light rain ensured that our departure was delayed. By mid-afternoon things had taken a turn for the better and the sun started to make infrequent appearances through the clouds. Russell flew from Te Anau to see if he could get over the main mountain divide to the Hollyford airstrip, while we waited at his base. Before long he radioed back to tell us that he had landed at the Hollyford airstrip and to shake our arses along and meet him there.

In very quick time we were airborne and winging our way down the Hollyford River. The cloud cover was still low and thick and we struck frequent rain squalls as we flew. Russell was all concentration as we hit the coast and headed south along it. I had walked the coast below before but decided that I preferred our current method of travelling.

The mouth of the Kaipo Valley was clogged with low cloud and mist, but despite this Russell veered upriver. The further we travelled up the river the less mist and cloud we encountered. Below was the wide and reasonably flat valley floor that was dissected by the lazy, meandering Kaipo River. There had been little rain over the past months, which by Fiordland's standards equated to a drought. Beside the river were numerous fern- and scrub-covered flats, creeks and clearings, which were enclosed by great expanses of native trees. I had hunted the valley previously, so I paid particular attention to the creeks and flats that I had not explored before.

We flew through a final wet cloud bank before the mist parted to reveal the Kaipo airstrip. Russell soon had us and our huge quantity of gear safely deposited beside the hut then, with the parting words 'See you in eight days' ringing in our ears, he was gone.

As I walked into the hut I was greeted by that smell of past fires and mustiness that pervades these comfortable but rarely used mountain huts. Kaipo Hut consists of two parts. The entranceway is in fact a room that contains all sorts of junk and an assortment of useful stuff such as a bunk, a wheelbarrow, axe, tools, raincoats and building materials. From inside this room a door leads into the main hut.

At the far end sits an old cast-iron stove that gave promise of warm nights and the opportunity to keep the kettle constantly warm. A roof joist that runs through the middle of the hut is held aloft by the trunk of a sturdy beech tree that stands on a very rough and uneven concrete floor. Hanging from the joist are an assortment of items that all add to the hut's lived-in feeling. Books were strewn everywhere and huge quantities of unused food crowded the shelves.

The hut was built many years ago by a professional deer hunter for his own use at a time when a good living could be made from hunting deer. Given its isolated location it is now used mostly by hunters. I have stayed in many huts throughout my life but this one undoubtedly has the best feel of them all. It is old and rustic and has obviously had a lot of use over many years. If you ever want to experience the feel of a true backcountry hut then take a visit to this one as it absolutely screams with history. It felt good to be back there.

As soon as we had stashed our supplies and fought for the best beds, plans were made for an evening hunt. Kevin was keen to head downriver along the flats just to get the lie of the land, while I was keen to explore upriver as I had not ventured there before. Crummy, who was still feeling slightly euphoric after his exam success, decided to come with me 'for a look'.

The hut is situated at the top of a series of large, broken and undulating flats. Here and there creeks flow across them and into the main river. Above the hut the native bush starts, and it continues unabated to the head of the valley and all the side streams that flow into it. There is a series of small clearings beside the river and in the bush above the hut, and it was these clearings that I wanted to locate and explore. Although the wind was now blowing up the valley and sending our scent ahead of us I was keen to get a feel for the clearings with a view to returning to them from an appropriate direction when the wind was right.

Crummy and I followed the track that led from the hut and through a large area of flax before crossing a deep creek and entering the bush. Although the track was now overgrown in places it was well worn and over the years had had a great deal of use, which made following it easy.

We had only travelled ten minutes up the track when we located the clearings we sought. They were across the river from us and looked really inviting. We elected not to disturb them, given that the wind was coming from the wrong direction, and decided to carry on up our side of the river to see where we ended up. After a further ten minutes' walk we came to an open creek that flowed into the main river. Deer hoofprints were evident in any soft sand or mud we came to, but a slow stalk through the bush beside the creek failed to locate any deer. We returned to the main river and continued up it. Several hundred metres further on we encountered another branch of the creek, with cropped grass growing on its sides and thick deer sign.

Having failed to locate an easy deer that would solve our camp meat problem, Crummy and I stood at the bush edge pondering our next move. At this point the ridiculous happened and a large hind walked boldly out of the bush onto a grass bench about 50 metres upstream from us. She stood there looking directly at us but apparently unconcerned. Crummy had his back to her, but he could see from the way I reacted that something was up and turned around.

'I've got it,' I whispered as I raised my rifle and took aim.

We had already discussed who would take the shot if we encountered a deer and had agreed that whoever saw it first took the first crack. After that it was fair game for all and sundry. In view of this I felt no guilt at declaring the hind mine.

I squeezed the trigger and was confident that the shot was good. At the same time Crummy also fired. I'll spare you any bullshit and state right here that we missed. I swear that I only missed because Crummy fired out of turn, but he insists that he fired moments after I missed and that he was trying to save the day by dropping the now running target to bring home the venison. Either way, between us we stuffed up an easy deer, and after making a thorough search of the area to ensure that we hadn't hit it we headed for home feeling rather let down by our dismal efforts. To this day Crummy insists that I missed first, and he's probably right. It's kind of peculiar how I didn't hear his shot though!

Kevin saw nothing on his hunt.

The following day saw me stalking the side creek that we had discovered on our evening recce. Again the wind was against me and I couldn't stalk the clearings across the river. I saw no deer that day but enjoyed hunting the semi-open bush anyway. During my travels I located three weathered and redundant deer traps. The wire on two of the traps was still in remarkably good condition given that they had been decaying in the bush for some years. Throughout the day I was visited regularly by small bush robins that flitted about catching the insects and sandflies that I disturbed as I went. On one occasion, after I had remained motionless for many minutes, a robin landed and perched temporarily on my outstretched arm.

Crummy and Kevin went their own ways for the day, and were both back at the hut by the time I returned. Kevin was delighted to have shot two deer that were feeding on a small clearing below the hut and across the river. Given that the deer were out in the open at around 4 p.m. he had every right to be both surprised and thrilled.

At the end of the airstrip there's a very good meat safe, with a timber frame that has fine wire mesh stretched over it to keep the flies away. Kevin hung his deer in it to await their journey to our freezers.

The following day Kevin and Crummy hunted the flats below the hut together. At about 3 p.m. they saw through their binoculars a stag that was feeding inside the bush edge above one of the flats. The deer was a long way off, and it would require a lengthy, roundabout stalk to get close enough to take a shot at it. An hour later they arrived in what they thought was the right location but couldn't locate the stag. After a long wait they gave up and returned to their original lookout post. No sooner had they returned than the stag again popped out within 50 metres of where they had first seen it.

After exchanging 'Here we go again' glances they decided to be bold and try a direct approach, in full view and over open ground. Their chances of success would have to be slim by any hunter's gauge. While keeping a sharp eye on the stag Crummy and Kevin belly-crawled and crouch-ran their way across the flat. The usually soft and quiet mosses they ran over crunched underfoot due to the dry conditions Fiordland was suffering. After an eternity they arrived at a small depression that gave them minimal cover and would allow them to take a shot at the stag should it return. Yep – yet again it had disappeared from view.

As they lay in the hollow, feeling somewhat robbed by the stag's disappearance, Crummy happened to glance across the open flat to his left. He immediately saw two spikers, young male stags with their first short growth of antler, that were about a hundred metres away. Both animals had their heads lowered and were in the process of charging. By all accounts they were about to attack my mates using their short antlers as weapons. Several panicky nudges soon had Kevin tuned in to the dilemma that was unfolding far too quickly for Crummy's liking.

'Have I got time to get out my video camera?' an unconcerned Kevin asked.

'If you want to survive you'd better get out your bloody rifle,' came Crummy's terse reply as he swung his in the direction of the deer.

Moments later the leading spiker made a skidding turn and charged back toward his mate, who rather athletically dodged the attack. To the relief of my two brave hunting mates the deer abandoned their attack on them and entered into a lengthy series of play fights and tumbles. The terrifying man-hunters were simply enjoying the fine spell of weather as they played. All very entertaining, my mates concluded, but both had wives who expected a return on their hunting investments and venison on the table.

Kevin lined up one deer and Crummy the other. After taking careful aim they fired together. One fell instantly and the other bolted for cover, pursued by numerous bullets. Before long the 'Artful Dodger' had weaved its way back to the safety of the bush. Naturally both Crummy and Kevin claimed that they had taken the spiker that was down, and a lengthy debate followed as to which of them had actually shot it. In the end they compromised, declared that they both had, and shared the carrying duties as they ferried the meat back to the safe. My day was again spent bush-stalking without seeing or spooking any deer.

On the morning of day four I woke as the day was easing out of darkness into the early light of day. Bugger – I'd slept in. I had intended to be well away from the hut by then.

'Wake up, you lazy bastards,' I grumbled. 'It's nearly lunchtime.'

'There's no need to hurry – there are plenty of deer about. How about making us a cup of coffee?' Crummy replied.

'Make your own coffee – I'm out of here,' I said as I eased out the door and into the gloom.

The previous night we had sorted out who was going to hunt where. Somehow I had yet again been delegated away from the easy hunting of the flats and into the bush upriver. This didn't trouble me at all as I wanted my mates to enjoy their first-ever South Island hunting trip. I was, however, starting to think that getting a deer myself would be a good thing.

If they're too lazy to get out of bed, I may as well check out the airstrip and flats just below the hut myself, I thought.

Maybe I'd get lucky and bag an easy one right beside the hut. With these thoughts in mind I walked the several hundred metres to the meat safe, from where I'd have a good view of the airstrip.

To my annoyance there was a dense layer of mist covering

the strip and I couldn't see more than 30 metres in front of me. Realising that I was wasting my time, I turned around and headed upriver yet again. This time there was no wind so I elected to cross the river and stalk the flats that had long been beckoning me. I located a likely looking spot to cross the river and with the aid of a stick headed across. The river wasn't too deep and I was starting to think I'd get across without giving my family jewels a dunking when World War III broke out. Shot after shot was fired from somewhere downriver from me. Given that I heard a dozen or more shots I thought Kevin and Crummy must have got onto a large mob of deer. Despite this I wasn't a happy man. Not only had the lazy buggers failed to get out of bed for an early morning hunt, now they had gone and made one hell of a racket that stuffed up any chance I had of securing a deer on the flats I was only yards away from. I carried on anyway but as expected didn't see any deer on the clearings.

Two lazy, beaming hunters greeted my return to the hut.

'How many did you get?' they enquired.

'World War III kind of mucked up proceedings,' I replied. 'Have any luck yourselves?'

Sure enough, two more deer were hanging in the meat safe. After a leisurely coffee and feed of toast my mates had wandered from the hut to the airstrip. No sooner had they arrived than a spiker emerged from the mist walking directly toward them. Both fired and it fell. As they approached it two more deer emerged from the mist and that was when all hell broke loose. One deer escaped. Here we were on day four of an eight-day trip with five deer hanging in the meat safe.

That night we unfurled our brand new mountain safety radio with the intention of contacting Russell and asking him to call in for the deer should he be in the area. The plan would have worked too if the radio had actually worked. Unfortunately it didn't, and when we returned it we received a very sincere apology from the supplier.

Meanwhile we had a dilemma. Do we continue hunting or not?

Kevin was happy to try to get some footage of wild deer on his video camera. Crummy thought he'd take a look for a good stag and decide whether to shoot it or not if he found one. Me – I was sitting on a baldy and wasn't too sure that I would be able to put up with the ribbing my mates would give me if I didn't secure one. Having said that, I don't believe in shooting a deer unless it's coming out to my freezer with me. Therefore I also had a decision to make. Like Crummy, I thought I'd make it when the time arose and elected to carry on hunting.

The next morning we had a lazy start and a sleep-in. Our solitude and tranquillity was shattered when a helicopter arrived at about 11 a.m. laden with fishermen. Usually helicopters are full of rich overseas tourists but this one had three New Zealanders aboard. They were out to enjoy our great country, and fair enough too, we thought. We stood watching these gentlemen as they tried to cast their lures into the clear waters but were stunned to see that only one of them had any idea at all of how to go about it. I would have expected that anyone who could afford to spend a thousand dollars an hour to hire a helicopter to go fishing would have taken the trouble to learn how to fish beforehand.

Late that afternoon we left the hut together intending to hunt a massive slip that was about an hour's walk down the river. Sneaking along beside the river was all but impossible given the presence of large numbers of paradise ducks that continually squawked and flew around us in ever-increasing circles, letting the whole world know that we were about. I counted 16 ducks on one small flat alone. The evening wasn't wasted, though, as we watched many trout feeding in the river and at one point saw an eel sitting in the shallows above a small rapid. The eel intrigued me as it was lying in shallow, crystal-clear water far from any tree roots, logs or branches that could offer it cover. Another highlight of the evening was seeing a paradise duck and her seven ducklings floating down the river. Up till then I had no idea how many ducklings paradise ducks had.

After leaving the river we climbed up the edge of a wide shingle fan that had numerous standing but long-dead trees on it. Deer sign was prevalent and I was at full concentration. My mates had taken pity on me and declared that any deer we saw was mine. In reality they were hoping like hell I wouldn't get one at all as they were having a grand old time poking the borax at me for being a useless hunter. 'How could you miss,' they teased; 'there are deer everywhere.' 'You must be a bloody useless hunter, mate,' they told me a hundred times or more. The way things were going they were right and I may well be headed for a baldy and going home without getting a deer. Just to rub the point in a hind barked at us from the safety of the bush. As we neared the top of the slip we sat down in a great spot that offered a view over a considerable amount of country. We glassed for deer until darkness overtook us, but none were seen.

The following night Kevin and Crummy went for an evening hunt up a gully that looked promising. They returned with yet another spiker that Kevin had shot. That settled it, we decided. We'd pay for two flights out so that all the meat could come with us and none would be wasted. I was now free to carry on hunting with the knowledge that anything I shot would come out with me. I was really beginning to wonder if I was headed for a baldy on this trip. The others seemed to have no trouble locating and shooting deer but strangely I had only seen the one, which was on our first day.

We dedicated the next day to having a major clean-up. The hut had a huge amount of unwanted junk and expired food that people with good intentions had left. After many hours' work and a well-fueled bonfire, the hut was back in immaculate shape. Several trips to the river with the wheelbarrow to collect rata and red beech for firewood rounded off our efforts.

Three items that we located in the hut during the clean-up caught my attention. One was a sign that was nailed to a ceiling joist. It read: 'For the comfort of all occupants please abstain from flatulating while in this hut.' The other two items of interest were crematorium boxes with the names 'John Robert Clark of Southland' and 'George William Applegate of Dunedin' on them. I am curious to establish the story behind these, but as yet have not followed up on my intention. Both were left in pride of place where they were found but in a much tidier environment.

The following evening Crummy secured yet another deer which only served to make me feel even worse. With only one day's hunting left I was away before first light the next morning, and hunted the clearing that had taunted me for the whole trip. The wind was finally in my favour and my mates didn't start another war as I stalked the clearing. Despite my best efforts I still saw no deer.

By early evening I was very despondent, having again put in a big day hunting without success. I decided to give things one more go and headed out the door. I had been tempted to hunt a nearby small side creek but up to this point hadn't. After a steep climb up the rocky creek bed and through a narrow gorge-like area the creek opened out onto a series of small slips with herbs and grass growing on them. There had to be a deer here, I thought. Being careful not to expose myself, I quietly eased into a position where I could get a view of the first slip. There out in the open was a spiker quietly grazing. After raising my rifle and taking aim I recalled that I'd missed my earlier standing shot and thought better of it. I had all the time in the world to get this one right, so I sat down and took the shot from a very stable position. Finally, on the eve of our departure, I'd escaped from the baldy's grasp.

The Old Man's Yarn

By anyone's yardstick my old man was a hard-case, good bastard. No two ways about it, when he was younger he took no shit and told it like it was. From time to time the truth may have got in the way of a good story and on those occasions he'd grant himself licence to embellish things a touch, but never more than good taste allowed. Over the years my old man suffered the odd run in with know-it-alls who thought they knew the story better than him when in fact they didn't. Rumour has it that he'd sort things out pretty quick like and never had cause to seek repairs at the local medical centre.

It was my old man who introduced me to the joys of hunting and to the great outdoors in general. He told hunting yarns with enthusiasm, and I could always tell by the gleam in his eye when his mind was cast back to his younger days. My old man told me one yarn that stuck in my mind and involved a well-known deer-culler of yesteryear. I reckon it's a darn good story so I'm passing it on here. The story's told in my old man's words – it has to be, it's his yarn.

I was raised in Murchison. During the latter part of my education I didn't like school much, mainly due to my teacher, Mr Spiers. I was left-handed and he wasn't. Mr Spiers deemed that the whole world should be right-handed, and he spent most of his days giving me the cane for failing to be like him. I was left-handed and that was that! I wasn't about to let Mr Spiers tell me what hand the pen fitted best. On Thursdays we had spelling tests and anyone who failed the test got the cane. To save Mr Spiers the trouble of having to mark my paper before failing me, I used to line up at the front of the class straight after the test. It seemed logical to do this as spelling wasn't my strongest subject and it saved me the bother of having to learn the words.

One day at sports we were given golf clubs and told to endeavour to hit golf balls the length of the school's rugby paddock. Being a keen cricket player I knew how to thump a ball all right. I gave the club a mighty heave and the ball sailed the length of the paddock, over the netball courts at the other end and through a classroom window. It would have been helpful if the window had been open but it wasn't. Clearly annoyed, Mr Spiers came up to me and hit me just above my ear with the large ruler he was carrying. It really hurt.

Mr Spiers said he'd given me a crack on the head for being a smart arse and not telling him I was an experienced golfer. Hell – I'd never even held a golf club until that day. Well, I reckoned he'd had a fair crack at me over the years, so I decided he wasn't getting another go this time just because I showed him how stupid he was by telling us to hit golf balls toward a building. I had been caned for not doing what he told me to do, and now he was hitting me for doing what he had told me to do. Under those circumstances a man couldn't win, could he? As he lined up the ruler for a second blow I lined up his chin.

'If you do that again I'll bloody drop you,' I warned.

'You really mean that?' came his shocked reply.

'Too bloody right I do,' I answered, and I did.

After a lengthy period in which we stood nose to nose evaluating what was to happen next, Mr Spiers backed down. I believe I won the argument, as I was never hit by him again, not even when I failed spelling tests.

On leaving school I moved to Lower Hutt and landed myself a job with TNT line staff (now Telecom) who were in the process of converting the telephone system from one that was manual operator based to automatic. I was to work alongside Barry, who would show me the ropes.

Barry was a short, podgy man of about 32 who always appeared slightly scruffy. He had a round face with a ruddy complexion and a constant smile. Barry liked to yak, and he talked non-stop. For a relatively young man he had crammed a lot into his life. He must have, as he told me many yarns of how he had been employed by this employer and that but had managed to do very little work on the journey.

Barry and I were given the job of putting automated systems into large businesses that had multiple telephones. Each installation was supposed to take a set amount of time, which for an average business was around three days. Barry was a really clever man who had a great mind for electronics. He quickly devised a system that was far more advanced, easier to put in and much less expensive than the one we were expected to install. Barry wasn't about to give up using his technological advancements, and after discovering that we could do most installs in about half a day he declared that the time saved should be spent consuming beers at a convenient hotel. Further, he decreed that the savings made on parts etc. were to be donated by our employer to us to cover the cost of our beers.

Working with Barry was tremendous fun and his yarns were always entertaining. He had a liking for beer and not much inclination toward work, unless it really couldn't be avoided. The new telephone system he devised had us working about two days a week while being paid for five. Strangely, when our employer discovered that Barry and I were absent from the coal face for much of the time and conducted an inquiry into why, neither of us was sacked. Incredibly, Barry was promoted to some top position and his system was adopted, giving great savings to the government, who at that time owned the entire New Zealand telephone system.

After Barry's promotion things weren't the same and I soon got the itch to move on. I managed to secure a job as a builder's labourer in Murchison, but after a short time I received a letter informing me that I had been conscripted into the air force for a stint of compulsory military training. I was then posted to Hobsonville Airbase in Auckland. Apparently my education didn't warrant me being trained as a pilot so they had to find other ways to engage me, and I was trained as an armourer.

Each year Hobsonville had an Open Day when the public could come and see our fine air force fleet. There was always a big turnout to this event, so finding carparking space was a problem. Another conscript, Tom, and I were given the task of collecting parking money at the gate that led to the parking area. There had to be two staff on the gate, we were informed, to ensure that the sixpence parking fee was collected and given to the bosses at the end of the day. To ensure our honesty we had to hand out a ticket for each sixpence we collected. The number of tickets sold must equal the sum collected from gate sales.

The officers who devised this scheme may have passed their spelling tests but they had no idea of how to devise foolproof money-handling systems. Tom and I knew that after a car had passed us there was no one else checking car numbers. Thus, only Tom and I knew how many tickets we sold. Soon enough we devised a system where we put the money from tickets sold into one pocket and money gathered where no ticket was given out in the other. At that time a man could buy a beer for sixpence, so at the end of the day Tom and I went to a pub and were shouted a few beers by the good people of Auckland.

Compulsory military training required that conscripts do three stints of three weeks' training, spread out over three years. These were a major inconvenience. After leaving Hobsonville I returned to normal life until I received a letter asking me to volunteer to join the Air Force on a permanent basis. I wrote back saying I was not interested in spending any more of my life bowing and scraping to supposedly 'superior' officers. I received a reply telling me that I was to front up at the Ohakea air base near Palmerston North for my second stint of compulsory military training (so much for bucking authority). My final stint was done at Woodbourne air base, near Blenheim.

Murchison is right in the heart of deer country, and when I wasn't working I was in the hills shooting deer. Who wouldn't be when the price paid for venison was as ridiculously high as it was at that time. I could shoot two or three deer in a morning and be paid more money for them than I earned for a full week's carpentry work.

My employer, Laurie Robinson, was then aged about 50. He had fought in the war and was a thoughtful, quietly spoken man. He was of solid build, tanned easily and came in at a fraction under 6'0" in height. He always wore a hat, and more often than not there were troutfishing flies and lures hanging from its sides. Laurie was a very keen fisherman and took every opportunity he could to pursue his passion. The other noticeable thing about him was that he almost always had a cigarette hanging from his mouth. Laurie smoked a full packet of roll-your-own tobacco every day and sometimes more.

Most of our work involved building or renovating houses. Our team consisted of Laurie, Robert, me and three others. Robert was a few years older than me and was a hard chap to get along with. He had no interest in sport or just about anything else, which made it hard to hold any sort of conversation with him. Robert tended to just get on with the job and not speak. Laurie was a fair boss, but he expected a decent day's work out of us. Smoko breaks were the bare ten minutes, then it was back to work. Time was money, he would say.

In the late 1950s Laurie got the job of renovating the Rainbow Station homestead, which at that time was owned by Dave Oxenham. The station, a neighbour of Molesworth Station, is situated in the high country above the Wairau River, which flows from near Hanmer to Blenheim.

Arrangements were made and the required timber, nails, claddings etc. were forwarded by truck to the work site in readiness for our arrival the following Monday. At about 6.30 on a midsummer's Monday morning Laurie pulled up at my place in his 1938 Chevrolet Coupe. The Chevy had a single bench seat that was designed to seat two people comfortably, but if necessary could seat a maximum of three. Laurie had already picked up Robert, who was shoved into the centre of the seat, and I crammed in beside him for the journey to the Rainbow homestead. Travel was uncomfortable to say the least. As the vehicle had floor change gears, Robert was in charge of the gear shift while Laurie ran the clutch, brakes and steering. A lot of verbal instructions were given when a change of gear was needed, and Robert was very careful about how close he got his working parts to the gear stick.

I noted that Laurie had more fishing lures and flies attached to his hat than usual, and assumed that he intended to do some fishing in the evenings after work. The plan was for us to stay at the homestead during the week and return to Murchison only at the weekends, and I found the idea of some after-work fishing very appealing. The prospect of having fresh trout for some evening meals was mouthwatering.

As we travelled toward the station alongside the Buller River Laurie kept looking searchingly at the river. Even I noticed a good few trout rising in the river to take morsels of food from its surface. Eventually Laurie couldn't resist temptation any longer and pulled the car to the side of the gravel road. 'I'll just give this stretch of river a wee tickle-up,' he said casually as he removed his fishing rod from the boot of the car. I noted that he also had his rifle in there.

Since the end of the war good rifles had been very hard to obtain. Most of the standard Lee Enfield .303s that were issued during the war had been retained by the military, and those that hadn't been were often very old, worn and inaccurate. Laurie had somehow managed to obtain a brand new .303. Further, it was the latest model, which had extra rifling in the barrel for increased accuracy. I and many others had eyed that rifle longingly, with a strong desire to own it or one as good.

After about an hour Laurie had finished tickling the first pond and had progressed by foot up to the next one. He had caught and released two trout in the first pool. Although Robert and I enjoyed observing this escapade, Laurie seemed to have forgotten that we were on full pay all this time. It was almost two hours later that we finally got on the road again.

Eventually we turned off the main road and travelled inland up the Wairau River toward the homestead. At that time the gravel road was very rough, and in many places there wasn't a road at all. We made frequent stops for Laurie to 'tickle the water'. In one particularly deep pool not far from the current turn-off to the Rainbow Skifield, Laurie located a massive trout that he was determined to catch. The trout was resting passively in deep water near the top of the pool. There were branches hanging directly above it, so fishing to it had to be done from the opposite side of the river and from below. Even this proved difficult as the close proximity of more beech trees meant that only a short line could be cast to the trout. Despite his best efforts with flies and nymphs Laurie couldn't get the fish to show any interest at all. The clock kept ticking, so Robert and I weren't too unhappy about the situation.

After some time Laurie declared that he was far from being beaten by this 'monster of the deep', and instructed us to find a decaying beech tree whose bark was starting to fall away. I managed to find one reasonably quickly, and at my shout Laurie came running. He declared that we were onto something, and started peeling the bark away from the tree. As he did so he told me that we should find a native weta sheltering inside the dry bark on the side of the tree that was not exposed to the rain and weather. Sure enough, as the bark fell away a large, bony weta scrambled to escape. Laurie quickly captured the insect and secured it to his line, to which he had also added some lead weights to ensure the new bait would sink deep into the river.

Laurie floundered his way back across the river well downstream from 'his' fish, then he stalked through the bush and exited almost parallel with the trout. As he flicked his line into the rapid immediately above the fish I watched the line sink, taking the weta down with it. The cast was a good one. The insect drifted downstream and would pass within a foot of the trout.

The trout showed no interest in the weta until it was almost past, then it lunged sideways and took it fully in its mouth. As Laurie emerged fully from the bush he eased his rod upward and tightened the line. The hook set firmly in the trout's mouth and I watched with interest as it raced up- and downstream while Laurie struggled after it, almost falling in on several occasions. After about ten minutes Laurie eased the trout toward the riverbank where it made one final effort to escape before Laurie edged it into his small landing net.

Laurie was absolutely delighted and set about weighing the trout immediately. It was a hen, or female, fish and weighed in at 11¾ pound. Using Laurie's camera I took a photograph of him holding the fish before he released it back into the river. 'A man can't go taking away the breeding stock, can he?' Laurie commented as the fish swam off.

A bit further up the road Laurie spotted a shag in a pool up ahead. He stopped the car, got out the rifle and loaded it, but before he could fire the shag had taken off and was flying away from us. Laurie raised the rifle and almost casually took a shot at it. The bird disappeared in a shower of feathers before our eyes. I was certain the shot had been a fluke, until Laurie repeated the feat twice more during the following weeks. He reckoned shags ate far too many trout and that shooting them was doing the fishery more good than harm.

The last leg of the journey was very slow, as there was no graded road there at that time and we travelled up the riverbed. We finally arrived at the homestead at about 3 p.m., some five hours later than we should have. The homestead was situated some 600 yards above the river on a long, gently sloping tussock-covered face, where the native bush starts to give way to large expanses of open tussock country. The homestead had a limited supply of running water from a tank that captured rainwater, so to ensure a constant supply for mixing concrete, bathing and cooking we had had a long black polythene pipe delivered. We ran this pipe above the homestead to a creek some 600 yards or so away. One of the bonuses of this was that when the water flow was turned off, the pipe heated up in the sun, enabling each of us to have a hot shower at the end of every working day. Mind you, we had to make them quick showers or the hot water would run out and the bloke who got caught in the sudden flow of freezing cold water would become most upset.

Our job was to enlarge the homestead, which was unoccupied throughout our renovations. The building was made of adobe, and so that it could be extended I was given the task of chopping away the end wall with an axe. When this was completed I had to take up part of the floor to expose the floor joists. While I was lifting the floorboards I happened to notice a small, rusty item that turned out to be a tin flint box. When I eased the lid open I discovered two 1935 threepenny coins inside. Threepenny coins were still in use at that time but I knew the 1935 ones were considered special as there were only a small number of them struck that year. I slipped the coins into my wallet and carried on working.

At the end of each day's work we took turns at cooking the evening meal. When I wasn't cooking I would borrow Laurie's rifle and spend the evening deer hunting. There were a lot of deer about at that time and getting an animal or two wasn't difficult. In fact, there were deer-cullers working on the property and on the neighbouring Molesworth Station. Dave Oxenham had instructed us to make the cullers welcome and offer them a bed and hospitality should they call at the homestead. Dave was apparently very happy to have the cullers on his property lowering the deer numbers as they had reached near plague proportions.

Laurie spent his evenings fishing the nearby river, so trout and venison featured on our menu daily.

As would be expected of all true men of my era we had a large supply of beer in camp to see us through the week. We would always have a beer with our evening meal which we'd eat when we returned from our hunting and fishing. For entertainment we had a daily shoot-out with Laurie's rifle. We sat an old sheep's skull on top of a fencepost below the homestead, at a distance of about 350 yards. Every night we had two shots each at the skull, but for the first few days none of us was able to hit the very small target.

One evening two deer-cullers walked into camp. One was Arthur Curtis, brother of the hunting author Max Curtis, and the other was a young Dutchman whose name I do not remember. We made these rugged gentlemen very welcome. Laurie caught several trout which we cooked for our evening meal, and beers were provided all round.

Our new friends were extremely pleased with this turn of events.

Before our meal we had our usual shoot-out but again Laurie, Robert and I all failed to hit the sheep's skull. During the competition I noticed that the deer-cullers were very interested in the rifle we were using, and they both questioned Laurie about how he had obtained it. That night both men approached Laurie independently and asked if they could purchase the rifle from him. Both declared that their rifles were very old and worn, and because of this their accuracy was poor. They felt that Laurie's rifle would be better employed in the service of a government culler removing the deer menace from the high country.

Laurie told them both that he would consider their proposal overnight, as he had not intended to sell the weapon. Come morning he declared that he would sell the rifle, but he said he did not wish to run an auction for it. He asked each culler to write down his best offer on a piece of paper, and to hand them to him at the same time. Each man wrote down a figure on a slip of paper and handed it to Laurie. When he looked at them he found that both men had written down exactly the same figure – 20 pounds and 5 shillings. True to his word, Laurie refused to accept any higher bids and declared that he would accept the offered price. To decide who would get the rifle he announced that the two men would have to compete in a shoot-out. Laurie promptly walked outside onto the porch, pointed to the sheep's skull on the post below and declared that the first to hit the skull got the rifle. There was one catch, he said, and that was that the shoot-out was to be done using his rifle and not their own, which they would clearly be very familiar with.

The toss of a coin sorted out the shooting order, with the Dutchman winning the right of first shot. I should state here that I believe the contest was quite fair. There can be no doubt that both were excellent shots with their own rifles, but as neither of them had used Laurie's rifle before and each rifle has its own subtle differences, they were on even terms. In reality I felt that it was unrealistic to expect either to have any success with an unfamiliar weapon.

After an eternity the Dutchman fired and missed. Arthur took a very long time over his first attempt before squeezing off a steady shot that also missed. Given that there was nothing behind the skull to allow the shooters to see where their first shots fell, it was impossible for them to know what variance to their aim was needed for their next shot. I watched as each took another two unsuccessful shots, with increasingly anxious looks on their faces. The Dutchman missed for a fourth time and Arthur took his next turn. This time he took aim with an almost casual ease and fired almost at once. The skull disappeared and the rifle was his.

'How the hell did you work out where to aim?' his mate asked. With a broad grin Arthur declared that he had seen his previous shot splash in the river far below. He saw that it was to the left of the target, which enabled him to work out what allowance he needed to make. Sure enough, he was right.

After this the two hunters left on foot, heading for a break with their families. We offered to take them back with us several days later but they declined, stating that walking was what came naturally to them and that it was no burden. When they returned Arthur would bring the money for the rifle and it would be his.

Across the river from the homestead there was a steep mountain range. Running from the top to the bottom, almost adjacent to the homestead, was a long narrow slip. Most evenings a large stag would come out of the bush near the top of the slip to feed. It was a long way off and would require a good half-hour of hard climbing to get anywhere near to it. One evening Laurie told us that he was going to give the stag a hurry up. Naturally enough we assumed that he was going to stalk the animal, and that he would be gone for some time. Further, we would have a good view of the whole stalk, which would provide us with some much-needed entertainment.

Laurie proved us wrong. After loading his rifle he raised the open sights to the maximum elevation (a mile, or 1600 metres) and propped himself over the bonnet of his truck. I was certain that he had no show of getting his shot anywhere near the stag. After a long time he fired. For about three seconds nothing happened, then the stag suddenly wheeled around in fright and bolted to the cover of the nearby trees. Although the shot had clearly missed, it was a fantastic effort.

Several weeks later the deer-cullers returned on their way back to their hunting areas. Arthur paid Laurie for the rifle and it was his. Almost a year later he wrote to Laurie and told him he had shot over a thousand deer with the rifle in that season alone.

Some months after we completed the Rainbow Station job I was back in Murchison. After having a few beers one night I decided to head across the road to the Murchison tearooms for a meal. Cyril McCallum was the owner at the time, and he was sitting at one of the tables with a large quantity of threepenny pieces spread out before him. When I asked him what he was doing he replied that he was looking for 1935 threepenny coins. 'They're worth quite a lot of money,' he said. Cyril scoffed in disbelief when I told him I had two of the coins in my pocket. I opened my wallet to show him and was disappointed to find only one coin. The second must have fallen out and was lost.

For our work Christmas party that year we had a big night out with our partners and after a meal headed to a local dance. While there Laurie rolled a cigarette and to his horror found that he had just used the last of his tobacco, his last cigarette paper and his last match. I hadn't seen him without a cigarette in his mouth since I had met the man and I guessed that to him this would be a major disaster. Laurie stood there looking into the empty tobacco packet with an expression of disgust on his face, then he suddenly looked up and declared with conviction, 'I'm sick of these bloody things anyway. I'm giving up.' Of course no one believed him, and he was the subject of a fair amount of light-hearted ribbing for the rest of the night.

I left Murchison soon after this, but returned several years later. I happened to go into the tearooms and there was Cyril again sifting through a tableful of threepenny coins. 'Crikey, mate,' I said, 'if you're that desperate you might as well have this one.' I opened my wallet to extract my 1935 threepenny coin, only to find that I had lost the second one as well.

As I sat there talking with Cyril I noticed Laurie walking across the road toward the tearooms. 'That'll be Laurie coming for his tobacco,' I speculated.

'Not a chance,' replied Cyril. 'He gave up smoking at his Christmas party several years ago.'

As far as I know Laurie never put a cigarette to his lips again.

A Hunter's Demise

Bob is a good bastard. There's no better description for him than that. He's one of those types who's always laughing and who lifts your spirit when you're down without even knowing that he's doing it. Now Bob's a razor-thin sort of a chap, with a long, narrow face that always seems ready for a shave. A dense moustache sits prominently on top of his lip, and the whole lot is topped off by a thick thatch of closely cropped sandy hair.

Whereas I don't find him overly attractive myself (due to my preference for women) there was one particular woman who did. Now we all know the effect a woman can have on a bloke when his hormones are running rampant and his brain's out of gear. All of a sudden they look real good, start tampering with the wires in your brain and start to reorganise your life. This is exactly what was happening to my mate Bob. The poor bugger suddenly found he no longer had time to come fishing and hunting, and his longtime passion for skiing was dismissed as of no importance. I could see it as clear as day, but his wiring had been altered and he couldn't.

One day I was sitting quietly at my local pub with a beer in my hand, wondering how I was going to save Bob, when he arrived unexpectedly. As he gave me a hearty slap on my back in greeting, he told me he had some news.

'I'm getting married,' he declared.

Holy heck! How am I going to get him out of this one? I thought.

'And you, my old son, are going to be my best man,' Bob then announced.

Bloody hell – he had just announced his death sentence and now I was to be the assistant executioner.

'Slow up a bit, mate,' I cautioned. 'Marriage is a pretty serious business, you know. There's no need to rush into it, is there?' Apparently there was. Everything had been planned for him and my counselling toward caution was ignored. While feigning my joy at his pending demise I was struck by the feeling that I was having a drink with a mate who was about to have his hunting, fishing, skiing and golf wings clipped even more severely.

No man should be sent down the aisle without being reminded of what he's giving up, so with this in mind arrangements were made to give Bob a huge stag do. Needless to say, I spoke with his bride-to-be and told her to steer clear of us for the night. At this point I was lined up and given a long list of things we could and couldn't do with or to Bob. Her man was to be returned to her unscathed or else I would be held personally responsible and suffer the consequences, about which she wouldn't go into any detail. By the look on her face, though, I could rest assured that they would be dire. As soon as she rounded the corner and disappeared from view the list was torn up and her instructions forgotten.

So the arrangements were made, and before long Bob's stag night arrived. A large group of us met at my place, where we consumed a few proverbials before proceeding to our local pub. Bob was doing his best to restrict his alcoholic intake but his best wasn't quite good enough and a good many beers found their way past his lips without finding too much resistance blocking their path. One of our mates, Tom, owned a hippie-type bus that was used to transport everyone to the pub. Before we all piled out of it Bob was mugged and his clothes were forcibly removed. The groom was none too happy when he was marched naked into the bar with a large clear plastic bag of 'stag doos' strung around his neck and his willy on show for all to admire.

The publican was a decent sort of a chap, and after throwing a small wobbly about Bob's lack of modesty decided to let us stay as none of his other patrons seemed at all upset by our antics. We remained in the bar for several hours, and as time progressed Bob forgot he wasn't wearing any clothes and got on with overindulging in the brown brew. Every time anyone asked what it was that was hanging around his neck we'd all yell out in unison, 'Stag doos.' We drew the line when Bob decided he was going to challenge all-comers at eight-ball pool. The thought of his white butt, meat and two veggies on display as he leaned over the table for difficult shots was more than we could collectively handle and the idea was quickly mothballed.

After a while a group of four attractive young women arrived and parked themselves at the table next to ours. They found Bob's antics, nudity and bag of 'stag doos' very amusing indeed. In turn, Bob found them to be to his liking also, and to everyone's amusement his physical attraction to them was starting to show (you'll know where I'm coming from here). At that point Bob was dragged away from the objects of his desire and thrown kicking and screaming back into the bus.

Back home we carried on drinking the keg of beer we'd cracked open earlier. For the sake of modesty Bob was allowed to put his clothes back on. It was, after all, midwinter, and a good overnight frost was a certainty.

Given the threats to my life that had been made by Bob's intended wife I took the liberty of hiding all scissors, razors and shaving gear just in case his mates decided to modify his hairstyle either above or below his waistline. I also quietly fended off a number of unoriginal suggestions throughout the night, with the intention of saving Bob's good looks for the pending wedding photographs.

What some of his mates would have liked to do with a tube of Super-Glue can't be repeated on these pages.

As the night progressed I noticed that, despite consuming huge quantities of beer, Bob appeared to be getting less rowdy and more sober by the minute. Fortunately two strippers arrived in time to revitalise him, and he was put on a chair in pride of place to watch the show. By the time it was over he had been left in no doubt at all that the strippers were female.

Despite the improvement in his state of mind Bob didn't look that overjoyed for a man who was about to marry the woman of his dreams. He asked me at one time during the show if he was doing the right thing.

'You mean with that stripper?' I asked as I observed him handling things that, it could be suggested, he shouldn't be handling.

'No, you dumb bugger. By getting married,' Bob replied.

'I wouldn't marry her myself,' I said, 'but then again, I'm not going to.' For some reason my answer didn't seem to resolve his dilemma any.

As the evening progressed I got wind of a plan that had been hatched to throw the poor groom into the creek that flows at the rear of my place. I quietly took Bob aside and told him of it.

'Don't bother trying to resist,' I told him. 'You're going in the creek whether you like it or not. Our best plan is for you to let them do it without putting up a struggle where you might injure yourself or even break a bone or two. Give me your valuables now so they don't get lost or damaged.'

Bob duly complied with my request and handed over his valuables.

'Anything else?' I asked.

After frisking himself again Bob located his cellphone, then he volunteered his new shoes as well. No one would notice that he was wandering about in his socks, or care for that matter.

'Now, are you sure that's everything?' I continued. 'Your missus will have my left one on a block if I don't get you back in one piece.'

'That's everything, mate. Let them at me.'

Before I continue I'll bring you into the picture as to the lie of the land. The creek out back crosses the section at the rear. The lawn runs to its edge, where there is a drop-off of about half a metre to the slow-flowing water below. The creek is about two metres wide and has about 600mm of crystal-clear water running through it. This is fine and dandy, but beneath the clear water is a deep layer of soft, clingy mud.

Time passed and people started drifting off home. I was beginning to think that Bob's dunking had been cancelled, but I was wrong. At some point the remaining crowd started drifting casually toward Bob, who still had his bag of 'stag doos' hanging around his neck. At a prearranged signal the mob of about ten struck and was soon carrying Bob across the lawn toward the creek. Bob proved to be a very good actor as he feigned surprise when he was captured, then pleaded not to be thrown into the water.

A car was driven onto the lawn and parked so that its headlights illuminated the creek. The night was cold and frost was already starting to form on the grass. As the mob struggled under Bob's weight their exhaled breaths formed into small cloud plumes in front of them. When they reached the creek the mob came to a halt and Bob was held aloft by his ankles and arms as the formal charges against him were read out:

'You, Bob, having committed the greatest sin of all, in that you have willingly chosen to abandon your freedom, have willingly chosen to leave the ranks of the unmarried and have willingly given signing rights to your cheque book to a woman without her being pregnant, are hereby sentenced to a public dunking.'

A nod of the head finished proceedings and without further ado Bob was swung backward and forward a half dozen times before being let go at the top of the upward swing and launched toward the creek. I watched as his arms and legs flailed about and he contorted himself as he tried to turn to face the fast-approaching water. Then, with an undignified splash, he landed in the instantly muddy water, where he thrashed about before disappearing from view. As he surfaced he was spluttering and coughing like an old steam engine. I had tears of laughter running down my cheeks as I watched him trying to catch his breath after it had been knocked out of him by the impact with the cold water. The whole affair was hilarious, especially from the creek side where I was warm and dry.

Bob didn't jump quickly out of the creek as we expected him to, but seemed to be busy practising his breaststroke while bent over with his arms outstretched in the mud beneath.

'What the b'jeepers are you doing?' I asked. 'You'll catch your death of cold if you don't get out of there soon.'

Bob turned toward me then, and with a sullen look on his face lifted up his top lip to reveal an obvious facial deformity that sent shards of horror through me. His two top front teeth were gone.

'What the hell . . . ?' I blurted out.

'I forgot to take my top plate out before getting thrown in. I'd forgotten all about it, and when I hit the cold water it knocked the breath out of me and I accidentally spat the teeth out,' Bob responded, clearly rather unhappy.

Up until that point I didn't even know he had a dental plate to take out, so I think I can be forgiven for failing to remind him to remove it before his swim.

'I take it you have a spare one?' I enquired. Bob's shake of his head said it all. Here we were three days out from his wedding and he had just lost his two front teeth.

Bob continued groping about in the thick mud but he wasn't having any luck. Before long we were all in the creek with him trying to help. Bob was right about the water – it was bloody cold – and my family jewels were suffering the effects of being immersed in it. After a long, long time we were forced to admit defeat and give up. The joyous atmosphere of the night had taken a major turn for the worse. Solemnly we collectively agreed to return in the daylight to mount a further search.

A small number of our mates turned up in the morning to continue the search, though more than one stayed away, suffering the after-effects of their excesses of the previous night. The creek had cleared a little but it was obvious that our chances of success were at best remote. Within minutes of restarting the search the water was filthy again and we had to concede that the task was impossible. Bob's missus was going to kill me, but only after she had committed numerous other acts of torture and I was nearing death anyway.

'We'd better get a new plate made pronto,' I counselled Bob. This was great advice, but it suffered a setback when I was informed that Bob's dentist was in Dunedin, which we weren't. After making a few hasty telephone calls we managed to get a new plate organised, but our troubles really started when Bob was informed that he had to be there to pick it up and get it fitted. With wedding arrangements to be finalised and a bride-to-be who wasn't yet aware of the situation, we had numerous problems to sort out. But we soon had them all solved or delegated, and on Friday morning had Bob on a plane to Dunedin. The airfare was paid for by donations from his mates, who were all fully aware of the importance of the cause. See how easily things can get resolved with a bit of teamwork?

We had managed to keep Bob away from his intended until the morning of his departure, so my torture hadn't started as yet. It would inevitably start at some point, as clearly this whole fiasco would be blamed on yours truly for failing to keep Bob safe. In an effort to avoid capture I employed native cunning and rang Bob's intended. I told her he needed a lift and that he'd lent his car to someone else. She agreed to pick him up and deliver him to his undisclosed destination – the airport – while I hid.

Come Saturday morning all our problems had been resolved and we were greeted by a magnificent fine day. Fine days are good for two things – weddings and executions. The tradition of not seeing the bride on the day until she staggered up the aisle kept me safe until late that afternoon at least.

About an hour before the ceremony the weather packed it in and light rain started to fall. Before the official kick-off it had become almost dark outside and the rain had become heavy. I took this as a sign that Bob should take to his scrapers and make a run for it while he still could, but he was petrified and couldn't get his legs to work.

As we stood in front of the altar Bob continued to ask me if he was doing the right thing. Given our current situation, with about a hundred guests present who were all dollied up and expecting a wedding, and the priest eyeing him suspiciously, he wasn't in a position to change his mind at that point anyway. Still, I couldn't lie to a mate, so I merely stated, 'You can't make a run for it, mate. They've posted a guard on the exit.'

Bob glanced in the direction I had indicated and saw his soon-to-be father-in-law standing at the exit. It wasn't hard to imagine him having a shotgun strapped to the side of his leg either. There I was standing beside my mate wanting to rescue him but feeling unable to do so. Suddenly the church fell silent and all turned toward the rear as the organist started playing 'Here comes the bride'.

I don't have a religious bone in my body, but I respect the beliefs of those who do. In view of this I was impressed by the welcome the priest gave the gathered crowd: 'I would like to welcome you all to the Church of the Holy Shepherd (not its real name). I acknowledge that there will be people here today from all walks of life and with differing religious beliefs. I wish to say that you are all most welcome here in this church. I wish to extend a special welcome to Bob and his intended on their special day. Both are well known to me as "Seven Day Absentists".'

Escape was impossible, so in less than an hour I had witnessed the demise of a good hunting mate. The damage had been done and there was no point in moping about it, so while photographs were taken I took solace in a beer or two. As the best man I was to be called upon to say a few words at the after-match function, and I was aware that the words that came readily to mind wouldn't actually go down too well. I was fast approaching the time when I wished I had put a bit more thought into the topic.

Occasionally I'll have a cigar, and I felt that now would be a good time for one. I stopped in at a tobacconist on my way to the reception, and there I found the answer to my speech problem.

After everyone else had had their say it came to my turn. I wobbled to my feet and after the usual 'How do you do's' launched into the story of how difficult and complex getting Bob to the altar had been. I told them the full story of the stag night (excluding the bits that only you and I know about), the creek, the loss of his teeth and his emergency flight to Dunedin to get another set. I concluded by stating that I wasn't about to take any further chances with Bob losing his teeth again before the wedding, so I had taken the precaution of ensuring we had a spare set. With that I pulled a set of false teeth styled ice tongs from my jacket pocket, handed them to Bob and told him that they were his responsibility from now on.

You know what? I haven't been hunting or fishing with Bob since he uttered those life-changing words 'I do'.

A Head-on Collision

It took the man who was running the show a long time to get everyone to be quiet. When 90 like-minded hunter types are assembled in a bar with beers in hand they tend to be a bit rowdy. It was proving pretty difficult to get them to keep quiet so the briefing for the hunting competition that commenced the next day could get under way.

'The rules are the same this year as they have been for every other year,' the speaker stated, finally able to out-yell the remaining murmurs from the crowd. 'We assemble here at 6.30 tomorrow morning, after which everyone will be transported to their hunting blocks. Those who are travelling by helicopter need to ensure they restrict the weight of their gear to the previously advised maximums, as weight limits will be strictly enforced. In five days' time we return here and a prize-giving function will be held.'

The speaker then went on to give more competition details as well as a safety briefing to ensure that if any of us got into difficulties we would know how to get help on its way. I happened to glance at my lad, Jeremy, who was seated nearby. This was his first week-long deer-hunting trip and he was pretty keen to get going. Nothing could have knocked the smile from his face.

There were numerous prizes on offer, including best stag's head, largest hindquarters, largest trout, heaviest pig, best chamois, most unusual trophy and best hunting yarn. There were 30 teams of three, and we had all paid a set entry fee that covered the cost of travel from the venue in Greymouth to our hunting blocks and back, followed by a function at the end.

The hunting blocks were all on public land administered by DoC, who have a policy of wanting to eradicate all wild animals that are not native to New Zealand. Unfortunately this includes deer (all seven species found in New Zealand), chamois, tahr, pigs, goats, wallabies, rabbits, hares and probably others too, all of which are highly prized by hunters. DoC had a representative at the meeting who was rubbing his hands together with glee at the prospect of us hunter types removing vast quantities of these grass-eating, tree-munching menaces from his mountains and forests.

My hunting party consisted of my son Jeremy, Russell (introduced in the chapter 'Pukataraki') and me. We had drawn a hunting block on the Trent River and were to walk to the hut, which would take us several hours. This didn't bother us, as the competition organisers had arranged to fly in our gear (and that of the other four parties who had to walk to their blocks) by helicopter. This was cheaper than flying everyone in, as one helicopter flight would get all the gear for those five hunting parties to their campsites, rather than the five flights that would be needed to fly everyone in. The lucky parties that had drawn the more remote blocks were spared the walk and were delivered there by helicopter, four-wheel-drive or jetboat.

The following morning a subdued group assembled at the pick-up point, and it was very evident that many had overindulged the previous night. Eight hunting parties boarded the bus that would take us part of the way to our blocks. After about half an hour's drive up the Grey River valley we turned off the main highway and headed inland. The first four hunting parties were dropped off at various rivers and farms as we went, and before long we reached our destination, which was Bill Perry's farm, Waikiti Downs. The four hunting parties that were still on the bus were all to be dropped off here.

Waikiti Downs is a stud deer farm that's situated just below the junction of the Tutaekuri and Waiheke rivers. I was struck by the marvellous condition the farm was in – the fences were in top shape, the roads well gravelled and the paddocks rich with lush green grass. Bill and his lovely wife were there to greet us. Both were true characters of the land and friendlier, more helpful people could not to be found anywhere. No one was going anywhere until we'd had a yarn, a cuppa and a feed of freshly baked scones.

Bill volunteered to take us as far upriver as he could in his four-wheel-drive truck. He reckoned this gave us some time to spare, and after a good yarn he took us to see his prized stag, which he had named 'Big Boy'. It was early April and the roar was on the verge of starting. This is the time of year when the brains of stags are located under their belt-line and they become very unpredictable and often dangerous. As we drove, Bill told us that he used to have three top-quality stags for breeding purposes but that two had died mysteriously several months earlier. He had found both lying dead in a paddock with no visible sign of injury or cause of death. Because of this, Bill was forced to put all his hinds in with Big Boy for servicing. It was Big Boy's job to get them all pregnant as that year's farm profits rested squarely on his (hopefully) fertile shoulders. Given that Bill had over three hundred hinds in the paddock with Big Boy I was more inclined toward feeling sorry for him than overjoyed.

As we drove into Big Boy's paddock, Bill instructed us to stay on the back of the truck. Bill got out of the truck and called Big Boy's name several times. Big Boy, who was in the middle of his hinds, came trotting up and nudged Bill to encourage him to give him some deer nuts and a scratch on his head. This was remarkable behaviour for a stag at that time of year. Bill explained that the stag had been hand-reared and was from English stock that was known for its mellow nature (sorry, but I can't remember the details). Big Boy carried a massive rack of antlers that had 27 points.

I enjoyed Bill's company immensely. Noticing that he had a pronounced limp, I asked how that had come about, and he told me he had been injured in the war. On his return from the war he had applied to the government for a farm under the land resettlement programme that was in place for returning soldiers at that time. Bill had been told that he wasn't capable of running a farm with his injury and his application was declined. He was a determined man and had worked hard for many years at various jobs as he saved to purchase a farm despite the government's ignorant view. The marvellous condition of Bill's place gave testament to the fact that he was not only capable but bloody good at farming.

Soon enough we were delivered upriver and the walking began. The valley was walled by steep sides covered in native bush.

The valley floor was about half a kilometre wide in most places, with bush running across the flats to the edge of the open, stony riverbed. Occasionally we encountered a small flat where the valley widened, and dry riverbeds where the river had once flowed.

In less than two hours we reached our home for the week, a derelict hut situated at the junction of the Trent and Tutaekuri rivers. We had been told that the hut was in a state of disrepair and might be uninhabitable, so we were prepared for the worst and had brought a tent with us. We would have been happy if the hut had just provided us with some shelter to cook in, and we were delighted when we arrived and found it in reasonably good shape.

Russell unlatched the number eight wire hasp that held the door closed and pulled it open. Immediately there was a muffled explosion inside and a great wad of orange smoke came billowing out the door. Russell got one hell of a fright, careered backwards and fell to the ground.

'Shit – I thought I was going to die,' he said, very relieved to be alive. 'What the hell was that?'

'That' turned out to be an emergency flare that some comedian had booby-trapped the door with. Since it was Russell who had opened the door and not us, Jeremy and I initially found the whole incident extremely funny. The orange powder that now coated the hut, on the other hand, was extremely annoying. At least now whoever set the booby trap will know the result of their efforts.

The hut was small and only had two beds in it, so Jeremy was relegated to a tent which we erected outside. He reckoned he'd drawn the best straw as he knew how loudly I snore.

We soon had ourselves settled in and the beds tested for comfort. Russell may have been beaten by the booby trap but he was too sharp to get beaten to the best bed. My bed had a wire base that had stretched and sagged so that it resembled a hammock. It was inside and dry, though, so I was happy enough with it. Camped across the Tutaekuri River about four hundred metres away was the hunting party who had drawn the block below ours. We were not allowed to hunt on their side of the river, or they on ours.

In the evening we all went out for a stalk above the hut, where a large, wide and open river flat started. Numerous clear streams flowed from the bush across the flats and into the main river. The area had that 'there are deer here somewhere' feel, and we were ever-hopeful as we stalked the bush edge. Nothing was seen, though, and we returned to the hut by torchlight.

After tea we wandered over to visit our neighbours and have a few beers with them. Their base was a large, comfortable-looking dome tent with an awning. They were a hard-case bunch from Invercargill who laughed easily and enjoyed a beer. One of them had already shot a deer on the bush edge about half a kilometre from their camp. Their generosity ensured that we all had fresh meat for the week.

That night our hut was filled with noisy and vicious mosquitoes that bit and buzzed, keeping me awake for most of the night. For the benefit of anyone who might visit this hut in the future, I'd advise you to take a can of flyspray with you. The following

morning, well before daylight, I gave Jeremy's tent a kick and told him to get out of bed. After a hasty breakfast we were off for another look at the flats above the camp, while Russell elected to hunt up the Tutaekuri River.

It was still too dark to see when Jeremy and I parked ourselves at the bottom of the first flat above the hut. The wind was in our faces and when it became light enough we would have a good view for several kilometres upriver. Jeremy was fizzing at the gills to shoot his first deer, and so keen to get moving that I almost had to chain him to a tree to keep him there. All going well there would be a deer or two feeding out on the flat and he could have a crack at one of them.

When it became light enough we glassed the flats for some time but there were no animals out in the open. It was time to head into the bush for a stalk. I picked a likely looking creek that led us into the bush, and headed uphill to follow it. After we had stalked quietly along its edge for about half an hour the creek narrowed into a deep gut that was choked with fallen logs. We were forced to climb a steep bank to gain access to the terrace above, which was covered with bush and ponga trees. Jeremy led the way. The going was slippery and we made a fair bit of noise as we climbed. As we neared the top a rotten log gave way as Jeremy was climbing over it, and he tumbled off the log and fell into me. That caused me to arse up as well, and we both tumbled a few metres back down the face before we managed to arrest our fall.

Jeremy thought the whole affair was hilarious and couldn't help laughing out loud. Once we had established that neither of us was injured he headed off to continue our assault on the face, with me following close behind. As he crested the top, Jeremy took several steps forward to clear the way for me. The last few metres were very steep and I had to haul myself over the top with my arms, as my legs flailed in the slippery soil beneath me. As I topped the brow I looked up and saw Jeremy standing on a narrow, well-formed deer trail. He had his rifle raised and was aiming through some tall tree ferns that were on the terrace above him. I couldn't see anything there and wondered what the heck he was doing. After regaining my feet I approached him and leaned over his shoulder, enquiring casually what he was up to.

'A stag,' he whispered in a quiet, mesmerised sort of voice.

I took another look where he was aiming and sure enough there was a big-bodied stag heading straight toward us along the deer trail we were standing on. I had a good view of it now and could see that it carried a good head of ten or more points.

'Well, you'd better shoot the bastard,' I told Jeremy.

Jeremy stood there with his rifle raised and I waited for the shot. I waited some more, and then a bit longer for good measure, but no shot came. The stag was hell bent on investigating us, and was making its way toward us at a steady pace.

'By God, that boy of mine is as calm as a cucumber,' I began to think. 'He's letting the stag get really close to ensure he can't miss it.'

A cool head with a rifle in hand is a good thing, and I was impressed with the way my lad was handling the situation, especially as it was the first stag he'd seen in the wild or had the opportunity to take a shot at. I waited . . . and waited . . . and waited. By now the stag had got to within 30 metres of us and was chest on.

'Now, lad. Take the shot now,' my mind was screaming.

At about 15 metres the stag suddenly stopped. Its eyes seemed to light up and the fear could almost be seen in them as it finally recognised the danger it was in. The animal was tightly flanked on each side by tall tree ferns and couldn't turn to make off. It reared up onto its back legs, made a twisting U-turn at the top and sprinted off along the terrace.

Still no shot came from Jeremy, who was frozen in the aiming position. My hunting instincts took over and I immediately bolted after the stag. Visibility along the terrace was reasonably good and I could easily follow its progress. My plan was to give a loud whistle as soon as the stag was in an open area, it would stop for one final look at the danger and I would shoot it. The venison was as good as in the freezer. As I was leapfrogging over logs and weaving my way though the fern trees it suddenly struck me that Jeremy was behind me with a rifle aimed in my general direction, and that he was probably feeling a need to take a shot at the fleeing deer. With this thought in mind, and suddenly filled with the same sense of terror as the fleeing stag, I launched myself face first to the moist forest floor with all thoughts of shooting the animal gone. As I landed safely I was overcome with an 'It's great to still be alive' kind of feeling. I yelled to Jeremy to come over to me, and as a precaution lay in the dirt until he arrived.

'Why didn't you shoot it?' I asked.

'Sorry, Dad,' a very dejected Jeremy replied. 'I was so rapt to actually see one that I watched it and forgot to pull the trigger.'

My mind raced back to when I was a young man of 17 and had just seen my first deer. Like Jeremy, I too had stood there with my rifle raised and hadn't pulled the trigger either. I understood how he felt, and told him not to worry about it as we would have plenty more chances over the coming week. This didn't seem to cheer him up any.

We hunted all morning before returning to camp without seeing any more deer. Our evening hunt achieved the same result. That night we invited our neighbours over for venison and hot chips. Russell refuses to go on any hunting trips without raw potatoes, oil and his chip-frying pan. Come to think of it, Russell insists on taking all sorts of luxuries no matter how extraneous they seem, and the quantities of gear we take when we go hunting together often reach ridiculous proportions.

We enjoyed the evening and more than a few beers before calling it quits at about midnight. The chips went down well too, and we had a second lot for a late-night supper. During the evening we all did our best to cheer Jeremy up, but we weren't too sure that we'd succeeded. He'd snuck off to his bed by about 10 o'clock, saying he would set the alarm on his watch and that there was no need for me to wake him.

Come morning I was up well before daylight. I knew Jeremy wouldn't be up for a while yet so I put the jug on and had a brew while Russell and I waited for him to come inside. After pouring my second mug of coffee I thought I'd better give the lad a hurry up as we needed to be away soon if we wanted to catch anything out on the flats. Barefoot I went outside and gave the top of Jeremy's tent a good shake.

'Get up, ya lazy bugger,' I urged. 'If you want to get that stag today you'd better get a wriggle on.' Without waiting for a response I returned to the hut, finished my coffee and pulled on my boots. Still no Jeremy. Rifle in hand, I returned to his tent and gave it several good kicks from various positions as I walked around it, at the same time offering my opinion on his lack of enthusiasm. Still no response. By now feeling exasperated, I pulled back the tent flap with the intention of grabbing his leg and dragging him back into the land of the awake and about to go hunting. To my surprise he wasn't there, nor were his rifle or his boots.

I smiled as I put two and two together, figuring that he was so keen to get a deer, and preferably the one he had let go the previous day, that he had taken off on his own well before I had even got up. While for safety reasons he should have told us where he was going, I still couldn't help but think, 'Good on you, lad.'

Unfortunately he didn't get his deer – in fact no more deer were seen that day or on any other for the rest of the trip. All too soon we had to pack up our gear and walk out. The helicopter was to pick up our gear again, so it was a quick and lightweight trip back to Bill's farm. The bus picked us up there, and after a farewell shake of Bill's hand we were homeward bound, stopping to collect other parties as we went.

Needless to say we were keen to see how they had all got on. The last party to be picked up had with them a massive single-cast antler that they had found. It was a strange-looking antler that was severely deformed – similar in shape to a big man's forearm, but much longer and with several uneven knobs at its end. The coronet had a circumference of 285mm, which was clearly not typical in size or shape for any of the red deer that are found in that general area. A local hunter ventured the opinion that it was from a wapiti that had escaped from a deer farm, and I reckon he's probably right.

It turned out that only five deer had been shot during the competition, which was a big disappointment to the DoC officer, who had hoped we would eradicate vast numbers of the animals. I thought the result should have pleased him greatly, since it showed how few animals were eating his precious trees and grasses, but some people will never be satisfied, will they?

Two of the deer that were shot were stags. One was a spiker and the other a poor-quality six-pointer. The prize for the best stag was a .270-calibre rifle, and Jeremy felt renewed disappointment when he realised that if he had pulled the trigger on the stag he had lined up the rifle could have been his.

The closing function was held in the saloon at the Shanty Town Historic Village, a living, working museum that replicates a turn of the century goldmining township, complete with a working gold mine. The atmosphere was terrific and many tall stories were told. When it came time for the prizegiving we were safe in the knowledge that our team would not be getting any, since we hadn't caught or shot anything. We were greatly surprised when our names were called out, and as we hurried to the front of the gathering I was wondering if a mistake had been made.

The toastmaster gave a short speech in which he outlined our achievement: 'Ladies and gentlemen, standing before you we have this competition's three most rested and relaxed competitors. These worthy hunters, having left nothing to chance, and keen to ensure that they lived in complete luxury throughout their venture into the wild New Zealand mountains, are known to have taken with them the following items:

- a chip pan, oil and bulk potatoes;
- three chairs;
- three dozen beers;
- a bottle of gin;
- two dozen cans of bourbon;
- two tilley lamps;
- four rifles between the three of them;
- six varieties of cheese, olives, dried tomatoes and other antipasto items;
- desserts for the week, including several cheesecakes;
- fillet steak;
- four pottles of marinated mussels;
- a coffee percolator;
- enough food for six weeks;
- clean clothes for every day;
- a cribbage board;
- and a sun umbrella.'

When he finally stopped I couldn't help but be grateful that no one had seen the hot-water bottles, pillows and tape deck that we had also taken with us. However, the toastmaster wasn't quite finished.

'This list,' he went on, 'merely covers those items known to have been taken by these intrepid hunters, and is probably far from complete.'

At this point the helicopter pilot stepped forward and announced that our prize was for being the team with the most gear. He went on to explain that weight is a very important issue with helicopters, and he felt that we might put our prizes to good use on our next helicopter hunt. With that he handed each of us five packets of lightweight, freeze-dried, dehydrated meals.

The mortified look on Russell's face wasn't just a reaction to the prospect of eating dehydrated food – he was also indignant at the suggestion that he had taken a sun umbrella with him. It wasn't! It was a rain umbrella.

Jeremy was given another prize, for being the youngest competitor (at 16 years of age). He had had a week off school, had seen his first stag and had developed a desire to return to the mountains to hunt with his old man again. To my way of thinking that made me a winner too.

The meal was fantastic, and consisted of roasted wild pig, wild venison, whitebait, crayfish, paua, mussels harvested from the beach that day, wild duck, groper and much more. All of the meats and fish had been hunted or caught by the local competition organisers and their efforts were greatly appreciated by all.

As I ate my meal I had cause to reflect on how lucky I am to live in this magnificent country. With the exception of the vegetables everything on the table could be harvested free by anyone with enough energy to hunt the mountains or fish the seas and rivers.

Captain Bligh

Uncle Graham isn't actually my uncle at all, but a friend of my old man's. He didn't like being called 'Mr', so we kids took to calling him Uncle Graham, a title he preferred. Uncle Graham lives on a run-down farm near the Rai Valley, less than an hour's drive from Nelson. At 71 years of age he's a confirmed bachelor and reckons he always will be.

Uncle Graham is a bit of a hermit, with a surly disposition that tends to steer people away from him, and that's the way he likes it. His old dog Ben is company enough, and Uncle Graham tells me he's the only kind of mate a man should have. 'He don't talk back, he don't mind my snoring and he appreciates my cooking,' he once told me.

As kids we visited Uncle Graham rarely, but when we did I enjoyed snooping around his property looking at all the old junk that was lying around in his paddocks and in the haybarn. Uncle Graham had forgotten to modernise and most of the things on his property were ancient – almost as ancient as the old draught horse he had lazing about in his top paddock where it had been for as long as I can remember. One of my favourite things was a

Riley vintage car that sat rusting at the back of the hayshed. Most of the farm fences were in need of repair, and stock numbers had gradually declined. Uncle Graham stated that he didn't need to work too hard, given his limited needs and the fact that he existed quite nicely on what he had.

The paddocks at the back of his farm were gradually being reclaimed by pigfern, scrub and native bush. A good few wild pigs and the occasional deer were known to come out of the bush behind his farm to graze in these paddocks. Uncle Graham said he liked to see them about and he wouldn't let anyone hunt on his property.

For a young man who liked hunting, this presented a challenge. I can tell you right now that I never got to hunt on Uncle Graham's farm, and I don't think I ever will.

Now where is this all leading to, you are probably thinking, and fair enough too. I have some mates that are right into pig hunting. They have pig dogs and have often told me tall tales and true about their hunting exploits. Uncle Graham owned a block of farmland at Wairangi Bay in the Marlborough Sounds which was infested with wild pigs, and my mates were dead keen to have a crack at them. I know I should have told them there was no way Uncle Graham would allow us to hunt on his land, but I stupidly agreed to take them there for a hunt. Normally this would only require a simple poaching trip into the bay, and Uncle Graham wouldn't even know that we had been there. Unfortunately he had had a gutsful of hunters poaching his land and had put up a large, padlocked gate at the top of the hill that leads down into the bay. If we wanted to poach his land we would have to park at the top and walk all the way down into the bay. Worse still, if we got a pig or pigs we would have to carry them all the way back up to the top again, a prospect I wasn't too keen on.

The answer lay in getting Uncle Graham's permission to hunt there and obtaining the gate key. My first phone call to Uncle Graham went badly, and I made the almost fatal mistake of asking permission to hunt on his land.

'You know I like to have a pig or two roaming my land, boy,' he said. 'What makes ya think you've got any more right than those bloody poachers to hunt there?'

My plea that I was almost family fell on deaf ears and in the end I got a flat 'No' in answer to my request.

Undeterred, my mates managed to convince me to try again, this time using another approach.

'A fishing and camping trip?' Uncle Graham questioned me suspiciously. 'There won't be any dogs or booze, will there? Booze always leads to trouble with you young fellas.'

My assurance that all we would be doing was fishing got the required result, and permission was granted, with the proviso that we call at his farm on our way there so Uncle Graham could cast an eye over my mates to see if he liked the look of them.

Early the following Saturday morning we loaded up Horse's old Valiant and headed out of Nelson. There were four of us on board, plus two dogs that were crammed into the boot. I was worried that the dogs might suffocate, but Horse reckoned the rust holes would allow enough air in to keep them ticking. He was a bit worried, though, that the tinkling of the beer bottles as they rattled in their crates might drive them mad before we reached our destination.

Horse is a mad-keen hunter who, prior to getting married, all but lived in the mountains. He's a mate, and has been since I first got into hunting as a young fellow. We still manage to connect occasionally and get into the hills to hunt up a bit of mischief. Since Horse is well over 6'0" in height and almost as solidly built as me we make a great team, crashing about the mountains scaring away nearly everything we run into. Horse is always smiling, and his round face and thick mop of hair are well recognised by many who venture out hunting around the Nelson and Murchison area. Horse and I cut our hunting teeth on deer but he soon migrated to pig hunting as he believed we walked past far too many deer without even knowing they were there.

'The dogs can do the finding,' he reasoned, 'and I'll do the carrying.'

Seated in the back of the Valiant were Smailey and Phil. I'll introduce them here as well, as they play a big part in later events. Phil is best described as a good bloke with a beaut sense of humour. At about 5'10" in height, with fiery red hair and a good-sized stomach (from too many sit-ups, he tells me), he cuts an imposing figure. Phil is a bushman in every sense, and he works in the pine forests felling, hauling and trimming pine trees. The huge muscles that bind his arms are testament to the physical work he does. It is also true that Phil has a fairly good idea of what to do with a pint or two of beer.

Smailey, on the other hand, is a happy-go-lucky mate who finds the good side of everyone. His thin frame is topped by an unruly mop of brown hair that seems to spend most of its time getting in his eyes. A handle-bar moustache that is always spread by a huge smile dominates his narrow face. Smailey would go out of his way to help anyone and doesn't have much trouble working up a laugh. Of special note is that he is always the first to arrive at a party and the last to leave. He enjoys a drink or two but never seems to fall much under the influence of it. I've always meant to ask him how he manages this, but somehow never got around to it. Smailey wasn't a hunter as such, but he came along from time to time on deer hunts to see how things were done. To my knowledge he'd never been on a pig hunt prior to this trip.

As we travelled Horse told yarns of his pig hunting exploits and of the many huge boars he'd dispatched using only his dogs and a knife. I think he got a bit carried away with things when he told us that you never back down from a pig but face it and stick it through the heart if it charges you. Smailey seemed engrossed in these tales and found it hard to believe that Horse never used his rifle to shoot the pigs.

Fifty minutes after leaving Nelson we were pulling back the moss-covered gate that sits in front of Uncle Graham's house. He was reclining on the porch on an old wooden bench seat with a pint of beer in his hand. As usual he was wearing a dark-red checked flannelette shirt and woollen pants that were held up by braces. I noticed that his big toe stuck out from a hole in one of his socks. Old Ben sat at his feet and struggled to get up as we approached.

After the usual exchange of pleasantries and introductions Uncle Graham stood on the deck above us eyeing each of us in turn.

'Don't I know you?' He nodded at Horse, squinting at him searchingly.

'No. We've never met before,' Horse replied with finality.

'Umph,' Uncle Graham grunted, as if to close the matter, but he didn't seem too certain that he'd got the right answer. At this point old Ben started barking and sniffing at the closed boot of Horse's car.

'Haven't got any dogs or grog in there, have ya?' Uncle Graham enquired as he wobbled over to the car.

My firm reply that we hadn't were ignored, as Uncle Graham made us open the boot so he could see for himself. The boot lid was lifted and all was revealed.

'There's plenty of dog hair in there. What's the story?' he asked.

'I've got a dog as a family pet,' lied Horse. 'He travels in the boot.'

At this point I was feeling very pleased that we had pulled over at the turnoff to O'Kiwi and Wairangi Bays and taken the dogs out of the boot. We had tied them to a tree above a nearby riverbank, and stashed the beers and Horse's rifle beside them. Uncle Graham had been very specific that we wouldn't get a key unless we were only going fishing, and that no dogs, beers or rifles were allowed. We were confident that our gear was safe with the dogs as they were a vicious, mangy pair that didn't take kindly to strangers.

'Where's the fishing gear?' Uncle Graham asked.

Oh lord, we're in the shit here, I thought. There wasn't any fishing gear.

Smailey reached into the boot and pulled out a potato sack. Inside it were four hand-fishing lines complete with hooks and sinkers.

He'd saved the day, and soon enough we were off, armed with a gate key.

After we had left the house I asked Horse what the exchange between him and Uncle Graham was all about. He explained that he 'may' have been poaching on Graham's property some months earlier. His dogs had chased a small pig over the hill to within sight of the homestead. Horse had seen Uncle Graham head toward him on a motorbike, with a rifle over his shoulder. Horse's dogs had baled the pig and he had been able to dispatch it and get back into the cover of the scrub before Uncle Graham got there.

'So why did he think he knew you if you weren't caught?' I asked.

'I'm wearing the same clothes as I had on that day,' came his sheepish reply.

As we neared the dogs, they were strangely quiet, and Horse sent forth an expletive when he found they'd had a fight and one had fallen over the riverbank. It was dangling by its neck from the short leash, while the second dog was quietly lying beside the tree as if nothing had happened. Fortunately, the dog that had fallen hadn't broken its neck or been strangled.

The road to the Wairangi Bay turnoff follows a very windy, single-lane, gravel road. Most of the journey follows the ridgeline high above the many bays below, and if you are prone to car sickness rest assured you will be sick here. After unlocking the gate at the top of the hill we drove down the steep road that leads to Wairangi Bay, passing through patches of native bush and large areas of manuka. At the bottom is a horseshoe-shaped bay that is flanked on each side by low, near-vertical, reddish-coloured rock and clay bluffs. The bay is shallow and tidal, with a soft, muddy, crab-ridden beach. At its head is a near-flat grassed paddock of about ten acres that slopes gently down to the beach. There were some cattle grazing in the paddock. On the steep faces surrounding the paddock were hundreds of acres of gorse. The road ran around the bay just above the high tide mark and continued on up the far face above the low bluffs.

At one end of the bay a derelict shearing shed sits on a grass strip that runs between the road and the beach. Across the road from this an equally derelict house sits in a small fenced paddock. The fencing was in desperate in need of repair and the house was literally falling down. We stopped here, and the dogs were released from the confines of the boot and allowed to run free as we set about erecting our tents. Phil reckoned it was thirsty work and knocked the top off a beer bottle to see if he could control his body temperature that way.

The bottle top had barely hit the ground when a chorus of dog barks hit our ears. Our eyes sought the source of the racket and soon picked up a large boar that was bolting down a firebreak toward us. When it reached the paddock we were in, it dropped its head and barged straight through the number eight wire as if it wasn't even there. Maintaining a straight line, the boar carried on across the open paddock toward the derelict house, which meant it was now coming toward us. The dogs were close behind.

Phil made a mad scramble toward the boot of the car to retrieve the rifle, but as he grabbed it he realised that the ammunition and bolt were safely tucked away in Horse's bag. Meanwhile the pig had seen us and reacted by veering away and heading toward the far side of the house. It disappeared from our view but we could hear the drumming of its feet as it ran along the wooden porch before leaping off and heading across the road and out onto the beach. The tide was out and as the pig made its way along the soft beach its trotters threw up sandy grit. The dogs were about 30 metres behind as the pig turned right and headed diagonally toward the far end of the bay. Leaving the rifle behind we all ran after the pig. I was sure the dogs would catch it before it reached the end of the beach and that Horse would dispatch it with the knife he had on his belt.

The boar was determined to escape and was still ahead of the dogs when it reached the end of the bay and turned left to head along the foot of the low bluffs. It very quickly realised it had made a bad choice when it couldn't find a route uphill and was forced into the sea. The dogs were close behind and entered the sea moments behind it. Four unfit males were well behind as we witnessed this turn of events. Puffing desperately we stopped to watch what unfolded. The cunning old boar made its way further out to sea before realising that there was no safe way back to shore in that direction and turning to swim back along the full length of

the bay. The dogs were no better at swimming than the pig was, and struggled to keep up with it. Clearly some affirmative action was required if we wanted to secure this mobile pork pack.

Stuck in the muddy beach about 60 metres from the high tide mark was an old wooden-hulled dinghy. It was moored to a buoy and every time the tide came in it floated free, then it resettled when the tide went out.

'Give me a hand,' Horse yelled as he reached the dinghy and started heaving it toward the open sea. It was partially full of rainwater, and being constructed of solid wood was very heavy. Inside it were two oars, and the rowlocks were still in place.

The effort required to drag and push the dinghy into the water was horrendous and I managed to fall flat on my face on the muddy beach more than once. As soon as the dinghy floated free of the sand's grasp Horse manned the oars, and with Phil and me on board set out after the pig. By this time the boar was about level with us and we would have to hurry to intercept it before it reached land again. Smailey was left onshore with instructions not to let the pig return to land.

The day was windy and because of this the sea was very choppy. Our progress was slow and we soon became drenched as we made our way after the pig. Unfortunately the pig was making better progress than either us or the dogs and it quickly became apparent that it was going to reach land before we did. To speed things up Phil and I took over rowing duties, working an oar each. Once we got our timing synchronised we started to make good progress as Captain Bligh (Horse) gave directions from the bow. We were catching up, but when it became obvious that we would lose the race by at least 50 metres we decided to give up the chase. The dogs were struggling in the choppy sea and one looked to be in trouble, so we changed direction and set out to rescue them both.

After we had pulled the second dog on board we turned to see what was happening further along the beach. The pig had been swimming for about 15 minutes or more as it approached landfall near a creek that flowed onto the beach at the foot of the hill where the road met the flat. Blocking its path, with a large hunting knife in his hand, was Smailey. He was ankle-deep in water and crouched bent-legged in a fighting stance, holding the knife out in front of him.

'You don't think Smailey believed those stories I was spinning on our way here, do you?' asked a clearly worried Horse.

'What stories?' asked Phil.

'The ones about being a real man and facing up to charging pigs and all that,' Horse answered.

We all started waving and yelling at Smailey to get the hell out of there. It was obvious he wasn't looking our way and that he couldn't hear us over the wind. It would be a stupid and very dangerous thing for anyone armed only with a knife to try to take on a clearly pissed-off big boar. Our yelling and waving intensified.

With growing horror I watched the boar touch down on solid ground. Its progress became instantly quicker as it made its way through the shallow water toward my mate, who in turn was staying directly in its line of escape. As the boar emerged from the shallow water its massive size became more obvious to Smailey. The boar seemed to grow bigger and bigger as it emerged from the water and got closer to the shore.

Suddenly Smailey lost his nerve, turned and bolted across the beach with a clearly pissed-off boar looking to take its frustrations out on the nearest target – him. Smailey headed across the road and into a manuka patch before disappearing from sight with the boar only metres behind him. We trebled our efforts as we raced to shore, hoping that Smailey was all right. We had all heard of the mess a pig can make of a hunting dog, and we feared even more what one could do to a human.

As soon as the dinghy touched ground we were all out and running. The dogs had regained their enthusiasm and shot off out of sight ahead of us. Moments later they started barking furiously from deep within the manuka. Knowing that the dogs were tired after their big swim and chase, Horse ran back to camp and got the rifle before working his way cautiously into the manuka. He was the one who claimed to know what he was doing so we bravely stayed behind out in the open.

By the time Horse reached the boar it was really fired up and was squealing in pain as one of Horse's dogs, seeing its master arrive, had latched onto one of its testicles. The second dog took the opportunity to grab one of its ears. In desperation the boar turned and twisted as it tried to dislodge its attackers. During the melee Horse put down the rifle and grabbed one of the boar's rear legs. Holding on for all he was worth he managed to flip it onto its back and stick it through the heart with his knife.

After he had killed the pig and got his breath Horse began to wonder where Smailey was and called out to him.

'I'm up here,' came the reply.

Sure enough, there was Smailey hanging from the top branches of a manuka tree, with his legs firmly wrapped around the flimsy trunk. Now as you probably know, manuka trees have a straight, slippery, smooth trunk with no lower branches at all. A large one is about seven metres high, with a trunk of no more than 250mm in diameter at the base. How Smailey got up that tree is as big a mystery to me now as it was then. Smailey doesn't recall how he got up it either, but stated that he was very pleased that he had as the boar, sick of running, had marched around the tree trunk looking up at him and waiting for him to fall. If the dogs hadn't arrived before his grip failed he may well have been converted to pork. Horse wasn't about to acknowledge that a dangerous situation had occurred and gave Smailey a serve about staying up a tree when he should have been on the ground sticking the pig.

We'd all had enough excitement for one day so we returned to camp and got stuck into the beers. Smailey decided he'd stick to fishing for the rest of the trip. We got two more pigs the next morning before returning home. Horse couldn't resist giving

Uncle Graham a wind-up and left the three pig skins draped over the fence as we left.

'When he finds them he'll think some poachers have been in stealing his pigs again,' he laughed. In truth, he was right.

Not wanting to risk having the car searched a second time I decided to post the gate key back to Uncle Graham.

Port Pegasus

The powerful diesel motors of the *Aurora* hummed effortlessly as the boat motored south toward our destination. Beside us several albatrosses soared effortlessly, perhaps in the mistaken belief that our purpose was to fish and that there might be some tasty morsels thrown their way. Colin, the skipper, was dozing in his chair and the autopilot navigation system took care of keeping us headed in the right direction.

Like many of my previous hunting adventures this one had started with a phone call. I had been caught a little bit off-guard as I didn't know the caller, although he obviously knew a bit about me.

'One of your workmates gave me your name – he reckoned you might like to come on a trip to Stewart Island with a group of us. One of my mates has had to pull out and we're looking for someone to fill the spot,' the bloke, whose name was Bob, offered.

After we had met over a beer to discuss his proposition I was in. Our destination was to be the south block of Port Pegasus, which is situated at the bottom of Stewart Island. I had been to Port Pegasus once before and was as keen as mustard to return.

Our all-male party of six was made up of a mixed bunch from all walks of life, ranging in age from 24 to 55.

The day before our boat trip we had driven in my vehicle from Christchurch to Bluff, where we spent the night at a local hotel. Travelling with me were Bob and a work colleague of his, Richard, who was a serious man aged in his late forties. Richard was solidly built and sported a big beard. We had towed his 16-foot aluminium boat behind us, and Richard had assured us we would have trouble-free boating, as the motor had just been serviced.

Bob was a quietly spoken Maori man in his mid fifties. As we drove he told us many stories of his fishing exploits, and some of the highlights of his life. I was particularly interested in his yarns about eel fishing in Lake Ellesmere, and the Maori traditions as to how many, when and where eels can be caught.

After our night in Bluff we were up early, and by 7 a.m. we had all our gear stacked aboard the *Aurora* and Colin was winching the final item, Richard's boat, on board. It was stashed beside two smaller dinghies, each with an outboard motor, that we were hiring from Colin. During the loading process Richard fussed over his boat and buzzed about constantly, making sure nothing got knocked around in the process.

Needless to say we had far too much gear with us, but we didn't feel bad about this as we didn't have to carry it anywhere other than from the shore into the South Pegasus Hut, which is only a short distance. The *Aurora* is a big boat and there was heaps of room.

The tide was coming in as we headed out of the shallow harbour and we had to fight a strong current to reach the open sea. Several months earlier a large cargo ship filled with a toxic load had grounded on rocks in the harbour and it was feared that it would break up and spill its dangerous cargo. Luckily it didn't, and it was eventually pulled from the rocks and towed out to sea. Colin pointed out where the grounding had happened and explained what had gone wrong. Put simply, the boat shouldn't have put to sea, as the channels are narrow and there was a dense fog covering the harbour at the time.

'Bloody stupid to have attempted such a manoeuvre,' Colin summed up.

After Colin woke from his catnap, and as we motored past several small islands, he pointed out where a diver had been killed by a white pointer shark the week before. The day was sunny and the sea had a gentle swell as we went past the area. It was hard to imagine such a thing happening in this picturesque spot, and it was a sobering story.

Colin was a grand host, and as we went he gave a running commentary about the area and its history. It was the season for harvesting muttonbirds (as described in 'The bullshitters' ball') and Colin pointed out several small islands where people lived temporarily during the season. He explained that he made most of his income from fishing for crayfish and blue cod. In the off seasons, or when he had caught his allowed quota of fish, he would take fishing and hunting charters to keep himself busy.

There was an array of computer screens in front of Colin – he had a fish finder for schooling fish, a Global Positioning System (GPS) on which he had plotted every good cod and cray spot he had discovered over his many years of fishing, and an autopilot system for navigation. The autopilot not only corrected the direction of travel, it also calculated the time of arrival based on the boat speed at the time of the reading.

Stewart Island has a rugged coastline of about eight hundred kilometres. There are many sandy beaches at the northern end of the island, near the only settlement, Oban, which lies in Halfmoon Bay. The further south you go the more rugged the coastline becomes, and in many places there are miles of continuous rock walls that are pounded by surging seas and offer no safe places to land. Port Pegasus is at the bottom of the island and differs from the surrounding coastline in that it is a massive natural harbour that is almost enclosed by land. At its entrance are two islands that offer further protection from the furious storms that at times ravage the area. Inside the harbour there are a number of sandy beaches and small peninsulas covered with native bush and scrub, habitat that is often favoured by our prey, the white-tailed deer. The harbour is so big it has been divided into two hunting blocks. We were headed to the southern one and the new hut that had been built there since my last visit.

After slowing to a moderate speed Colin steered the *Aurora* through the narrow canal that separates the mainland from Pearl Island at the entrance to Port Pegasus. Just past the island and snuggled in the native bush on the shore's edge is the North Pegasus Hut. As we eased past it, four or five men who were standing on the porch raised their beer cans in our direction in a mock toast to our arrival. Another member of their party was busy butchering a white-tailed deer that was hanging from a tree near the shore's edge. Moored in front of the hut were two boats that were laden with diving gear and cray pots.

It is no secret that Stewart Island is the seafood Mecca of New Zealand, with abundant supplies of crayfish, oysters, scallops, blue cod, trumpeter, paua and much, much more. Most hunting parties that travel to the island bring divers with them to harvest crayfish and gather oysters and scallops. A fishing line takes care of the fish side of things, and a rifle will in all likelihood provide some venison for the table as well. We had no divers with us, and no cray pots to catch crayfish in either. We felt sure we wouldn't starve, though.

Richard fussed twice as much as his boat was taken off the *Aurora* as he had when it was put on. He gave directions and orders left right and centre, and I gained the impression that he liked things to be well managed and orderly, in a pedantic kind of way. At the first turn of the key the motor on Richard's boat roared into life and happiness reigned. In quick time our gear was ferried to shore and Colin was gone.

The South Pegasus Hut is situated in the bush at the beginning of a small peninsula about halfway along Port Pegasus. It was a dry, comfortable-looking hut but despite this I elected to erect a tent outside and away from the hut. We had barely settled in when the sound of an approaching boat drew us back at the water's edge. By the time we arrived an orange rubber ducky-style boat had arrived and been pulled from the water. In it were three men from the North Pegasus Hut, which we'd passed earlier. They had dropped by to give us a crayfish and to have a yarn. The crayfish was huge, and would give us all a good feed. Our guests' party had been at Port Pegasus for four days and they were leaving in three days' time. As far as they were aware no one had booked their hunting block for the period following their departure, so they felt sure we would then be able to hunt their block as well. Since we had no divers in our party our new friends kindly offered to drop off more crayfish before they departed.

That afternoon we all set off to explore our block. We travelled in pairs as we had three boats and felt that they all needed testing. I went with Richard, and we headed south. After we had left the shelter of our bay the coastline returned to being a solid wall of rock that stretched unbroken for several kilometres. As we reached the next bay the rock wall ceased and native bush grew to the water's edge. At the head of this bay, which was quite large, there was a sandy beach on which we could see a number of deer prints. We carried on south, and at the head of the next bay found an impressive tidal estuary. The tide was nearly full at the time we visited, and it was no problem to travel up the estuary. There were sandy beaches on either side, and we could see deer tracks on all of these too. As we left to return to the open sea we could see scallops on the sandy sea floor beneath the boat. It was hard to guess the depth of the water as it was so clear, but I estimated it to be about four metres. The spot was carved into our memories and we decided that we would return to get some scallops when the tide was lower.

Given all the deer sign we could see on the sandy beaches it was obvious that the tried and true strategy of sitting on a beach and simply waiting for a deer to come along offered the best chance of getting one.

On our return to camp we armed ourselves with fishing lines and set out to catch some fish for tea. We picked a likely spot between a small island and the shore, and dropped our baited hooks. As soon as our lines touched the bottom the baits were taken and in a very short time two large blue cod were flapping about on the floor of the boat. We repeated this process until we had enough fish for everyone to have a taste. We caught a trumpeter fish as well, which we were pretty happy about, as trumpeter are almost as tasty as cod.

Attached to an outside wall of the hut there was a small table, so we strung a large tarpaulin above this and used the area as a kitchen and dining room. The benefit of this arrangement was that the hut remained uncluttered and free of food smells, scraps and dishes.

One small error had been made when the hut was built, and that was that an off-white semi-clear plastic water tank had been installed. The tank collected rainwater from the roof all right, but the clear light allowed green slime and algae to grow inside it. Every time we poured water from the tank the algae would get stirred up and discolour the water. Over time it would resettle, until the next time the water was used, when it would get stirred up again. Unappealing as this was, I can tell you in advance that no one died or became ill after drinking the water.

That night as we ate our evening meal we were visited by a very large, overfriendly possum that we took to calling 'Fuzzy'. Fuzzy wouldn't come close enough to get a pat on the head but he was happy to sit a couple of metres away from us to watch proceedings. I suspected that some previous occupants of the hut had been feeding him. I'll admit here that in my mind the only good possum is a dead one, but on this occasion we treated

Fuzzy like an honoured guest and even included him in our conversations.

The three members of our party that you haven't met yet – Tim, John and Richie – went out that night to shoot possums from a boat. They thought that if they got lucky they might even bag a deer. The night was calm, clear and starlit, so they would have little trouble navigating. However, when they returned several hours later they hadn't seen a single possum or deer.

The following morning Richard and I again set off to explore but this time we intended to head north. We settled ourselves in the boat and Richard gave the starter key a turn. There was a lot of spluttering and all sorts of engine noises but the motor wouldn't start. Richard was less than happy, as his well-scheduled day was suffering a setback. Painstakingly, he removed, cleaned and reinstalled every part he could, but to no avail. Several hours later everyone else had departed but Richard and I still languished on the beach, where we finally admitted defeat. The motor wouldn't start and no amount of cursing and swearing was going to change that, so we quit doing it and Richard went for a consolation hunt behind the hut.

By lunchtime a steady onshore wind was blowing. Bob and John had teamed up and after lunch they decided to go fishing. This idea appealed to me as well but there wasn't enough room for three strapping lads in a small dinghy. The problem was solved when they agreed to tow me out to sea in Richard's boat, from which I could fish as I drifted my way back to land.

The fishing was patchy. As I drifted I encountered hot spots where the fish were plentiful, but I would soon pass over these then catch nothing at all until I reached another reef or shelf where the fishing would again become hectic. The bulky life jacket I was wearing also made life awkward, as it made it difficult for me to have a drink. I simply couldn't tilt my head back far enough to pour the amber liquid into my mouth. I eventually solved this dilemma by reclining across the rear of the boat, from where I could both fish and doze as I drifted. (I know this is a bit naughty and that drinking and boating don't mix. Please take comfort from the fact that I have given myself a sound telling off for my indiscretion.) Bob and John were anchored nearby and kept a wary eye on proceedings. Each time I neared land they would come and tow me back out to sea. I had a very relaxing afternoon and stopped fishing after I had caught half a dozen large cod.

Richard returned to camp that evening full of excitement. He had followed a poorly marked track from behind the hut to a huge area of waist-high scrub, open creeks and grass about two kilometres away. During his hunt he had put up a white-tailed deer but it had leapt into cover before he had a chance to take a shot at it. He intended to return to the area the following evening, and he invited me along.

That night we enjoyed a meal of rock oysters, fish and vegetables.

Fuzzy popped in to say 'Gidday' and seemed to be even bolder than on his previous visit. Richie and Tim, who were the two youngest members of the party, had no love of possums and each night set about shooting as many as they could in the surrounding bush. They had shot about five so far, but had declared Fuzzy to be untouchable.

As arranged, Richard and I set off late the following afternoon. The plan had changed slightly and we now intended to camp out the night by the clearing. After an initial climb through high native bush we entered areas of broken scrub and manuka that eventually gave way to rolling open country. I was surprised at the sheer size of the area, which was at least three hundred acres, with the prospect of more open country that was out of view to us from where we stood.

We found a sheltered spot behind a mound and to one side of the clearing, where we erected our tents in record time. We felt we would have a good view from the mound first thing in the morning when a deer or two might be about. Richard pointed out the area where he had seen the deer the night before, and announced that he was heading in that direction. I had no objection to this so we agreed on boundaries that neither of us was to cross. I couldn't understand why Richard wanted to hunt with the wind at his back, but I didn't mention this as I liked the look of the area that had been allocated to me and which I could hunt into the wind.

It was obvious there hadn't been any rain for some time. As I walked, the moss crunched and crumbled beneath my feet and it was difficult to move quietly. The terrain ahead of me was reasonably open, rolling country. Each depression in the land was a small gully that led down toward the manuka and native bush below. I stalked up to each as quietly as I could before lying on my stomach and easing myself into a position where I could see into them. I was working my way toward the third gut from where Richard and I had parted company, with our tents still in view behind me, when a large hare bobbed and jumped its way from the gully as it headed toward the open country above and beyond me. I watched it for some time, thinking to myself that it was a really big hare. I hadn't even known there were hares on the island. Just for the hell of it I raised my rifle, put the scope to my eye and took aim.

My heart missed a beat when the hare transformed before my eyes into a small white-tailed deer. I had forgotten just how tiny they were, and I watched it through the scope for several minutes before remembering that I was there to shoot deer and not watch them. The animal was undisturbed and now browsing about two hundred metres away. I took my time and arranged a steady rest to make sure of the shot. The deer bounded onto a rock that elevated it above the surrounding low cover as the crosshairs of my rifle came to rest on its chest. For the first time in my many years of hunting I did not pull the trigger and found that I had no desire to take the animal. I reasoned that it was tiny and there would be little usable meat left after a shoulder hit from my heavy-calibre rifle. We had plenty of fresh fish to eat so we didn't really need the venison anyway. I watched the deer for another five minutes before it bounded off over the brow of a low rise. It felt good to have seen the deer and to have left it undisturbed.

I saw nothing further that evening but really enjoyed the open country that I explored. At one high point I was able to look to the south and see the full length of the harbour with its many sandy beaches and estuaries. To the north of the peninsula I was on I discovered another estuary that was all but hidden by a narrow bush-choked cutting at its entrance. I decided that that area needed further exploration.

It was approaching darkness as I crossed an open, spongy moss-covered area about ten minutes' walk from camp. A movement several hundred metres away caught my eye. I lay down to lower my visible profile and waited as a dark shadow made its way toward me. As I raised my rifle and looked through the scope I discovered that it was Richard, who was also making his way back to camp. He was travelling beside the creek that was the boundary of our respective hunting areas. By the time we arrived back in camp it was dark.

The night started out as one of those magical ones where many thousands of stars illuminate the sky and satellites can be seen every few minutes as they circle the planet. Soon all that changed, though, and at about 10 p.m. waves of dark cloud rolled overhead and blacked out the sky. Within a very short time a heavy, wetting drizzle had set in and hurried us to the shelter of our tents. Full of hope that the rain would be gone by morning I snuggled into my warm sleeping bag. I was very pleased that I had taken the trouble of carrying a lightweight camp stretcher in with me as the comfort it afforded well outweighed the small discomfort of its additional weight in my pack.

Come morning the rain had become heavier and swirling low cloud engulfed us. At times visibility was limited to less than a hundred metres, occasionally lifting briefly before the next wetting cloud rolled in. Encouraged by the rain on our tents, Richard and I stayed inside far longer than was prudent for two keen hunter types. We had just climbed into our temporarily dry clothing and were discussing heading off for a stalk when a heavy rain squall worked its way past our camp. That settled it – we were heading for home. In quick time we had our gear packed and were making our way back to the base. Rain was still falling steadily when two drenched hunters opened the door of the hut to find the rest of our crew warm and dry, playing cards and waiting out the rain.

By late afternoon the rain had let up and it was decided that fresh fish was required for tea. Bob and John volunteered for the job while Tim and Richie were content to stay in camp reading. As there was now a spare boat Richard and I took the opportunity to explore the estuary just north of our camp. As we headed out of our bay and around the point I noticed a 30 KPH sign in the bush above the rocks. Someone had obviously gone to quite a lot of trouble to purloin the sign and place it there, and I wondered who was going to police the speed limit.

The entrance to the estuary was narrow and not obvious from the open sea. As we motored through it we had to fight the outgoing tide, which was flowing rapidly. The water was crystal clear and the sea floor was clearly visible beneath us. Schools of small fish darted past us at regular intervals and the seabed was littered with cockle shells, scallop shells and other marine life. We travelled inland for almost a kilometre before the water became too shallow for the boat and we were forced to turn back. There was thick bush growing all along the sandy shores, and it struck me as being similar to what I would expect to find in the Amazon jungle. The birdlife was terrific, with numerous birds competing to be heard. The whole place had a strong spiritual feel to it.

That evening Richard left to have yet another crack at getting his motor going. He had only been gone for a minute or so before he returned and urged us all to follow him. 'You're not going to believe this,' he raved. The six of us wandered down to the edge of the low terrace, to a spot where we could look down on the bay below. The boats were moored to a large tree trunk at the far end of the sandy bay. Nothing looked out of place and we all wondered what Richard was getting so excited about.

'There,' he said, pointing. 'See it? It's coming back.'

It was then that I noticed a large shark tail protruding from the calm, clear water. The tail was large and curved, similar in shape to half a boomerang, and it poked up a foot or more out of the water. At its tip was a barb-like protrusion, which Richard said enabled him to identify it as a thresher shark.

We watched as the shark cruised toward the shallows, and as it came closer we could see that it was at least three metres long. As we watched a most unusual thing happened. The shark kept coming toward the beach and didn't stop until it had beached itself in the shallows. It thrashed its tail wildly and rolled over several times as it seemed to try to get further out of the water and up the sandy beach. After a minute or so of this it rolled back through the shallow water and with several wild swishes of its tail headed back out to sea. Then, to our surprise, it did a circuit of the small bay, returned and repeated the whole process.

'Take a look at its right side, near the middle,' Richard said. 'It's got a large wound there and I reckon it's rolling in the sand trying to clean it.'

We watched as the shark beached itself again. Sure enough, there was a large wound on its side, and it seemed to have this side in the sand more than any other part of its body. I suspect Richard's analysis was correct. The only reasons we could think of as to how the shark could have got such a severe injury were by becoming entangled in a fishing net or being attacked by a bigger shark. Either way, we'll never know. We watched for a while until, just before it became too dark to see, the shark cruised out to sea and didn't return.

That night Richie and Tim went spotlighting for possums again. They took a boat and quietly motored along the shoreline for an hour or so before returning to camp. On their return we all went down to the boat to see how they had got on. As we clambered down the steep bank to the beach their spotlight lit us up like Christmas trees and we all put our hands up above our heads in mock surrender. The guys hadn't seen many possums but they had managed to bag two or three. After the boat had been tied to its mooring we headed back to the hut for a game of cards.

Some time later Tim went outside to attend to the call of nature. Moments later he came racing back inside, grabbed his rifle and told Richie to bring the spotlight as there was a possum up a nearby tree. We all headed out to where Tim had a smallish possum cornered up a bushy tree. Richie held the light steady as Tim lined it up from a distance of about 15 feet and fired. The hair between the possum's ears parted but nothing else. He'd missed. The possum, obviously deciding it could do a better job of styling its hair without Tim's assistance, took off like a rampant monkey. Tim fired three more shots at the fleeing creature before it finally managed to scramble to safety out of sight at the top of a high tree. You can rest assured that we gave Tim heaps about his poor marksmanship before we went back inside.

Tim and Richie stayed outside while the rest of us returned to playing cards. Over the next half hour we heard two more rifle shots, and on their return to the hut they confirmed that they had nailed two more possums. The next few days were spent hunting, fishing and relaxing. They passed far too quickly, and soon our last day arrived. 'We'd better sort out a last supper,' Bob declared.

Four keen men – Bob, Richie, Tim and John – set out in the biggest boat to harvest the required seafood. Richie and Tim both had a liking for snorkelling and a yearning for scallops, and they had decided to free-dive for them at the scallop bed Richard and I had discovered earlier in the week. As they struggled to fit themselves into their thick wetsuits both claimed that they had put on a bit of weight over recent times. With a lot of tummy tucking and strenuous wrenching on the wetsuit zippers we finally managed to squeeze them in. The tide was almost at its lowest when the scallop party set off on its mission.

Richard and I were assigned the task of catching a good supply of fish. This we achieved in very quick time, having located a number of hot fishing spots during the week, and we returned to shore with a good number of blue cod and trumpeter. The cod had been cleaned and filleted as we caught them, but the trumpeter had only been gutted as Bob wanted to bake them whole with butter, herbs, garlic and lemon juice. We also caught several barracouta, which we used as bait.

Our job completed, there was nothing more to do other than ensure that our ample supply of beer was lowered, a task we took to with great enthusiasm. The scalloping party returned almost three hours later. They had had a very successful afternoon, as was clear from the large number of scallops and oysters that were unloaded from their boat. Once we had achieved the task of getting Tim and Richie out of their wetsuits, which proved to be as difficult as getting them in had been, a happier bunch of blokes could not be found.

John and Bob opened the oysters and scallops as the frying pans warmed. The oysters barely left their shells before being grabbed and eaten raw, while the scallops, which were large and succulent, were immersed in batter and quickly shallow-fried. In between these delicacies we ate blue cod cooked in a beer batter, and toward the end of proceedings several whole trumpeter that had been wrapped in tinfoil and steamed in their own juices with Bob's seasonings. My mouth's watering just thinking about it.

We all ate heartily and washed the meal down with beers. Strangely, Fuzzy wasn't to be seen, which was a bit out of the ordinary. When his absence was remarked on Tim and Richie looked a bit sheepish but said nothing. Throughout my life I have had a great many memorable meals but this one, enjoyed in the tranquil setting of Stewart Island, in the company of good people, sits in my mind as being one of the best.

As we packed up our gear, Richard was very apologetic about his motor breaking down after day one. He needn't have been, as it had enjoyed its 1210-kilometre journey, seven-hour boat trip and week-long holiday as much as the rest of us had. That's life.

As Colin eased the *Aurora* into the bay the following morning the reality that our trip had come to an end hit. Frankly – I didn't want to go.

The Bullshitters' Ball

The sealed envelope that I held in my hand looked very official, and it was formally addressed, in large, bold print type, to 'Big Al Lester, Hunter and Master Bullshitter, Canterbury, New Zealand'.

I eased the flap open and as I pulled out the enclosed card several duck feathers and a handful of possum fur fell to the ground. The card simply read:

BIG AL
Your skills as a Master Bullshitter and Hunter are hereby
acknowledged.
You are therefore cordially invited to the
'BIG GAME HUNTERS' AND BULLSHITTERS' BALL'
To be held at [venue] on Friday the 18th of May
commencing at 7.00 p.m.

The price of admission is a plate of wild game or fish hunted or
gathered by you and prepared for immediate consumption.
Prizes will be given for the best dish, best hunting hat
and tallest story told.

Entry is restricted to guests wearing hunting, fishing
and wild-food-gathering clothing.
Dress standards will be strictly enforced.

Please advise the writer if you will be attending,
on Ph (number)
B.Y.O.
R.O.A.R.

This annual event had its origins several years earlier when my cobber Batsey arranged an informal gathering of his hunting mates at his Christchurch home. Then a single man who had just purchased the property, he wanted the event to double as a house warming and hunting get-together. Knowing full well that when drunk his boisterous mates were prone to spilling beer and wine everywhere, he decided to hold the event in his garage where spillages wouldn't be a problem. It was intended to be a low-key affair where a beer or two would be consumed and many yarns spun, and Batsey told everyone they could bring a hunting buddy or two with them if they wanted. The affair was a huge success, with about 40 people turning up to the bonfire and barbecue.

Each year following this Batsey took it upon himself to arrange another function, and over time it grew into the 'Big Game Hunters' and Bullshitters' Ball'. The price of entry was always a dish of wild food or fish that had been gathered personally. This annual event quickly became bigger than Ben Hur, and the numbers attending had climbed to over three hundred, forcing Batsey to look for larger venues. There is no doubt that this was the original 'Wild Food Festival', and it certainly predated the now-famous Hokitika Wild Food Festival by many years.

A telephone call to Batsey confirmed my attendance at the function. 'This year's event will be the biggest yet,' Batsey enthused. 'I've managed to snare the use of a paddock just up the road from my place. There are houses all around it so I hope we won't annoy them too much. I'm going to visit them all tonight to invite them along. That way they mightn't get too upset by our antics. You can come with me.'

The owner of the paddock was a local dentist who had informed Batsey that the neighbour to the south of the paddock where the Bullshitters' Ball was to be held was a gnarly old coot who he'd had several run-ins with. The old geezer had wanted to cut down several trees that he felt were shading his property, and the dentist didn't agree. They'd swapped spittle as they argued over the fence and things had got a bit heated. The old chap had made a number of veiled threats to remove the said trees, or perhaps even the dentist's teeth, with or without his consent. Strangely, the trees died for no apparent reason over the following months.

'The old coot may be gnarly but his missus is worse,' warned the dentist. 'I'm not sure where she parks her broom but it must be pretty bloomin' close, as every time the old fellow opened his mouth she was there egging him on and using triple doses of foul language to wind him up. I don't think you'll get her blessing for a night of loud music, crude jokes and coarse behaviour,' he had warned.

I got the feeling this was why Batsey had invited me along when we went to approach these fine people. I was twice his size and could probably rescue him if the couple got their dander up and took to him. By all accounts I'd have to take on broom-rider, as she sounded the more vicious of the two.

That evening I bravely stood behind Batsey as he pressed the door buzzer. Tense and geared for battle, I was a bit taken aback when the door was pulled open by a stunted, weather-hardened man in his late seventies. He was completely bald on top of his head but had a dense ring of grey hair that dangled scruffily to his collar from just above his ears. A large, purple gin-drinker's nose with masses of protruding nasal hair reached challengingly toward us. His old grey woollen farmer's pants were held up by a sturdy pair of braces that stretched over a comfortably rounded tummy. The door was barely open before we were ushered inside.

'Come in, I've been expecting you. I thought you'd be here earlier, but better late than never, eh?'

We entered, wondering if our dentist mate had told them of our pending visit, and were led to the kitchen.

'There it is,' he said, nodding toward the fridge-freezer. 'Stopped last night for no reason and hasn't gone since. When do you think we'll get it back?'

Clearly the old coot had mistaken us for fridge repair men.

'We're not here about the fridge,' Batsey said.

'You're not?' the old man responded.

'No,' replied Batsey.

'Then what are you doing in my house?' he asked.

'You invited us in,' Batsey retorted.

'No I didn't – I invited the fridge repair men in.'

'No you didn't – you invited us in,' an exasperated Batsey responded.

'I'll have you know that I fought in the war, young man. I'll have you if you try anything funny,' he said, taking up a fighting stance and beginning to shuffle about the kitchen with his fists raised.

'I don't want to fight you,' Batsey said.

'What – no balls? Haven't got the guts, eh?' the old man challenged him. 'Come on, you burglar, get 'em up.'

At this moment an elderly woman entered the room, walking very straight and looking very prim and proper. When the old bloke informed her that they had burglars she armed herself with a very large carving knife that was sitting in a knife block on the kitchen bench.

'Get out, get out,' she screamed, waving the knife menacingly from me to Batsey and back again. 'There's nothing of value here and I've called the police.'

Fearing the worst, I started to back out of the kitchen toward the still open front door. I was struggling with our transformation from 'hat in hand' visitors to burglars, and was hoping that the police would indeed arrive and save us from the pair, who were clearly stark raving mad.

Now there's one thing about Batsey that everyone who knows him agrees, and that is that he has the gift of the gab. By the time I had made it safely to the door he had convinced the oldies that he was a tree surgeon who had called to advise them that in the near future he was intending to remove the dead trees from the paddock next door. He had called out of courtesy, he said, because he just wanted to let them know.

Within moments we were transformed from scum of the earth burglars to honourable tree-felling gentlemen who were to be regarded as honoured guests. No way were we leaving until Gracey (the old girl) had cooked us a batch of scones and given us a nice refreshing cup of tea. While the scones cooked we happened to mention to Bert (the old fellow) that before we removed the said trees we intended to have a bit of a party in the paddock and that it would be attended by deer-hunting types, fishermen and other like-minded people. We hoped they wouldn't mind?

'I'll tell you what, boys,' Bert responded heartily. 'The two sounds that'd give me the most pleasure about now would be your party and the revving of your chainsaws after it as those damn trees go. I used to knock over a deer or two myself when I was younger, you know – down south around Tuatapere and Lake Poteretere way.'

I couldn't help but notice that his eyes lit up and he looked about ten years younger as he mentioned this. It was the same look my father always got when he recalled his hunting adventures.

Batsey's suave manner and glib tongue had saved the day. Before we left Bert had accepted our invitation to the party, and Gracey had decided she would spend the night at her daughter's place so as to ensure that we men had 'room to play'.

'Don't worry,' she told us; 'I'll see that Bert brings a wild food dish with him.' Our protestations that that wasn't necessary were ignored.

I wasn't sure how Batsey was going to convince his dentist mate that the old couple were actually decent folks who were just fed up with having to live in the shade of his trees, but that was Batsey's problem not mine, so I didn't give it a second thought.

Meanwhile Batsey went to great lengths to tell me that preparation was the key to running a great event. He reckoned that having run a few now he had the measure of things, and that this one was going to have a few 'extras' to liven it up.

One of Batsey's mates is a West Coaster whose nickname is 'Stag'. How he got this name I do not know, but I had met him a few times and enjoyed his company. He sure was a hard shot, and he told hunting yarns one after the other all day and night without stopping to take a breath or repeating himself. His love of the outdoors and hunting took precedence over all other things. Batsey and Stag had been out hunting for deer one weekend when they came across a sow and a mob of piglets. Having discovered them out in an open paddock they decided to try to catch one alive. Their long-redundant rugby skills were put back into use and more by good luck than by skill Stag had managed to tackle and hold onto a piglet. It squealed and performed something terrible, and my mates were worried that the mother might return to reclaim her young one. Fortunately for them she didn't and the piglet was delivered to a farm on the outskirts of Christchurch where it was put in a sty with other tame pigs.

The flow-on effect of this was that 'Ting', a local pighunter who had several young dogs that he wanted to train, soon got wind of the piglet and took to visiting the farm with his dogs 'for a bit of training'. The dogs were taken downwind of the sty where they could smell the pig and would be encouraged to go after it. Although the dogs couldn't get into the sty, they would go berserk beside it as they tried to get at the pigs. Ting reckoned it was the best in-city training his dogs had ever had.

Now I'd better tell you a bit about Ting as he gets a fair mention later on in this yarn. Ting is retired and spends huge amounts of time hunting wild pigs. Pig hunting is his passion and has been for most of his life, but retirement had given him licence to really get in among them.

Ting might be old enough to be retired but you would struggle to find a fitter or healthier man alive. A woman would have to search real hard to find a single gram of fat on him anywhere, and if he had been a dog I would have described him as all ribs and tail. Ting had his 'boys', which was the way he always referred to his prized pack of pig-hunting dogs. He had four of them but the one he valued most was Major, a battle-scarred and fearless dog whose breeding was a mixture of every fence-hopping mongrel ever to walk the planet. Major was a motley tan colour, had long legs, was lean and mean, and without question the leader of the pack. Any young dog that stepped out of line was quickly reprogrammed by Major, and many bore the scars to prove it.

Ting drove a flat-deck ute that had kennels on the back. The dogs all but lived on the back of the ute and went wherever Ting did. Batsey happened to ask Ting if he was bringing his 'boys' to the Bullshitters' Ball and got the indignant response, 'Why – aren't they invited?' That settled that – all five of them were coming.

In the paddock where the ball was to be held there was a large, empty shed. It had the power connected to it, so lighting and food heating wasn't going to be a problem. But Batsey wasn't content to leave things at that and set about 'creating some atmosphere'. The walls of the shed were decorated with stag, chamois and tahr heads, mounted trout, fishing rods, hunting regalia, photographs and the like. In large letters over the entrance a sign read 'R.O.A.R.'. This play on words wouldn't be overlooked by the deerhunters who had a second meaning for roar, one that was very dear to their hearts. Batsey had even gone to the trouble of recording the sounds of roaring stags, bugling wapiti, twittering native birds, squealing wild pigs and an assortment of farm animals. The mating noises of humans were also added for additional effect.

In truth, the squealing wild pig was the now tame one that Batsey and Stag had caught some months earlier. By the time he went to record it, it had grown into a semi-tame 80-pound boar. The pig didn't feel inclined to make any squealing noises for the tape but changed its mind when Batsey's dog Jack, a huntaway-beardy cross, latched onto its ear, and it quickly became the star of the show.

Like everyone else I too had preparations to make. I took my prized 12-point stag antlers from my garage wall, where they had pride of place, and mounted them on the front of my Mini. Though I say it myself they looked very imposing wired into place there. I have to admit I didn't put too much effort into the 'best wild dish' competition, but cooked a 'Venison Italian' casserole to take with me. Then I dressed in my finest hunting shorts, which had the crotch torn out of them, a tattered old red and black checked Swanndri, my hunting belt, including knife, and my old hunting boots, minus socks. Guests were encouraged to stay the night and to take bedding and tents for this purpose. I was too clever for that, though, and intended to sleep in the back of my Mini.

I arrived to find the gate to the paddock firmly shut. Draped across the top of it was the skin and head of a very large black boar. I later found out that Winston, a well-known Canterbury pighunter and allegedly prolific poacher, had bagged the boar that morning. As I opened the gate and drove in several other people arrived, including Ting, and the stag's head on the front of my car attracted a bit of interest as people came to view it.

Batsey strolled up to Ting, nodded toward the rear of his truck where his dogs were chained up, and commented, 'Good to see that your boys made it.'

'You know they wouldn't want to miss a party,' Ting replied.

'Did you bring your knife?' Batsey asked.

Ting slapped the knife hanging at his side in answer.

'Make sure the boys stay handy. You never know what might happen tonight,' Batsey said with a smirk as he walked off.

As the guests arrived they took their wild game dishes into the shed and stashed them behind a wall of blankets that had been hung to partition off the rear. Each was clearly labelled to ensure everyone's efforts would be given due recognition when they were judged and eaten.

I was taking a mouthwatering look at the assembled dishes when old Bert limped in. What a sight he was. He wore a gumboot on his left leg and a tennis shoe, through which his big toe was poking out the front, on the right. The left leg of his pants had been torn off clear up to his hip, which left his cluster hanging out the side, although ably supported by a pair of dirty-looking, off-white long johns. The right side of his trousers was complete apart from a large hole in the knee. On his top half he wore a fawn-coloured short-sleeved shirt that was semi-hidden beneath a black and white cowskin vest. The whole ensemble was topped by a large, floppy, wide-brimmed hat similar in style to those worn by the three musketeers. The hat had a dozen or so rooster feathers standing upright on one side and a number of fishing lures embedded in the other. I thought the longbow he had draped across his shoulder set off the outfit nicely.

'Gidday, Bert. What's the story with the limp?'

'Bloody gout, Al. As soon as I even think about having a beer or hitting the top shelf it plays up.'

'You'll still be having a beer or two, won't you mate?' I asked as I handed him one of the glass jam jars that were our drinking vessels for the night.

'Try and stop me,' Bert replied with a huge grin on his face.

Bert was carrying a large white pail that was half full of ready-to-eat muttonbirds. These are very oily birds that have the texture of soft fat. Many people consider them a delicacy, and they can only be harvested from the islands in and around Foveaux Strait by the local Maori. Bert was as white as snow and didn't look like he had any Maori in him.

'Hey, white man. How'd you get your hands on those?' I asked. Bert winked, tapped the side of his nose with his index finger several times and left it at that. Just then a huge din erupted outside, so Bert and I raced out to see what was going on (well, I raced, Bert hobbled). In the middle of the paddock Crazy Craig (a local school teacher) was straining to keep hold of a wild black pig of about 80 pounds that was squealing and struggling furiously in his arms. Crazy was holding its back against his chest in a bear-hug type hold as its legs raced wildly about in midair. Ting's dogs were going berserk on the back of his truck as they tried to break free of their chains and get after the pig.

After a prolonged struggle the pig broke free from Crazy's grasp and took off across the paddock heading toward Christchurch. Ting, who had been a bit slow in summing up the situation, ran to his dogs and frantically fought to set them free. The first to go was Major, who leapt forward like an Olympian sprinter. The pig crashed through the taut number eight wire fence moments before Major got there, and made off into the neighbouring property. Major hurdled the fence effortlessly and followed. The three remaining dogs, now free of their tethers, set off after them. It was nearly dark and all of a sudden the whole neighbourhood was roused by the sound of furiously barking dogs and a squealing pig.

'Your useless dogs were supposed to catch the pig before it got out of the paddock,' Batsey puffed as he, Ting and a bunch of us ran after the rapidly disappearing melee.

'A bit of forward notice might have helped,' chuckled a clearly delighted Ting.

We leapt the fence and crashed our way through some ornamental bushes that surrounded the neighbouring property. It is possible that one or two were damaged but we didn't have time to stop and see. The barking had reached a noisy crescendo several properties further down the street so we fence-hopped and crashed our way in that general direction. The pig had become strangely quiet.

We arrived at the rear of a clearly expensive property with well-manicured lawns and a number of many valuable-looking statues and items of outdoor furniture. Smack in the middle of the expansive yard was a large swimming pool in which one very irate pig was swimming about. The pig swam in tight circles so it could keep a wary eye on its assailants, as the dogs stalked the pool's edge, barking furiously. The din was horrendous, and as we surrounded the pool a very irate man erupted from the house. I was sure he was about to burst a boiler. He demanded to know what was going on and who the hell we were.

'You've got a pig in your pool,' a clearly worried Batsey stated the obvious. 'We're trying to get it out for you.'

'I can see that,' the man spat as he suspiciously eyed the gathering crowd of rugged-looking men clad in hunting regalia. 'How did it get there in the first place?'

As more people from the Bullshitters' Ball arrived at the pool armed with their jam jars of beer it was obvious that even Batsey was going to have trouble explaining this one away. Oblivious to his plight Ting gave one of his dogs a shove into the pool and it was soon paddling along in circles behind the pig, although not actually catching up with it. The pig was a competent swimmer and managed to keep out of the dog's way as a stalemate seemed to be reached. Undeterred, Ting threw in a second dog, which only served to increase the splashing but again didn't corner the pig. The home owner was all but tearing his hair out at the plight of his pool, and the word 'police' was mentioned more than once as the crowd continued to grow.

'How deep is it?' Ting asked the man in an authoritative voice.

'One and a half metres,' came the testy reply.

By this time the dogs had pushed the pig toward one end of the pool. Without further hesitation Ting jumped into the pool and waded over to the pig. Between the three of them they managed to trap the pig in a corner. It wasn't able to climb out, and even if it had it would have been mugged by about 20 spectators. The pig, although showing undoubted ability in the pool was clearly unaccustomed to swimming, and it was quickly running out of energy. Every so often it would slip beneath the water. Ting calmly

reached underneath the swimming pig, grabbed one of its legs and tipped it upside down. As he drew his knife to stick it through the heart Batsey screamed, 'Nooooo,' dived in beside him and grabbed hold of his knife arm to prevent him administering the coup de grâce.

'We're in enough shit without filling the pool with blood,' he said furiously.

Ting reluctantly agreed, and with that the pig was hauled from the pool. No one wanted to risk it escaping again, so it was taken behind some bushes where it was stuck before being carried off back to our paddock. Batsey was left to try to explain the situation to the still very irate home owner, who had now been joined at the poolside by his wife and two children. I don't know what Batsey said but it must have done the trick, as the police weren't called and the man was soon at our do drinking beer from a jam jar.

Before long the swimming pig was being spitroasted over an

open fire. A device had been rigged up so it could be suspended lengthways over the fire and rotated slowly as it cooked. I found out later that the pig was the one Stag and Batsey had caught months earlier. When Ting found out that his dog-training pig was gone he'd be upset for sure.

When things settled down a bit I was able to have a yarn with some of the others who had arrived. One interesting chap, Paddy, had brought with him a black powder, muzzle-loaded rifle. It was a massively long affair that weighed a ton. It was so heavy that when I held it aloft I found it almost impossible to hold it steady. Paddy was born in New Zealand but had Irish parents from whom he had managed to gain a slight Irish accent. His love of black powder weapons was clear as he set about loading the weapon and packing the powder down with a long rod. I was given a lesson on how things worked as he went. A wad of harmless toilet paper was compacted on top of the powder before a percussion cap was fitted below the flint. That completed, Paddy raised the rifle, took aim at a stag's head that was hanging in the shed and pulled the trigger. A loud click was heard as the hammer struck the flint which in turn ignited the powder, but it was several seconds later before the gun went off with a horrendous bang followed by a cloud of dense grey smoke. Many people in the shed hadn't seen what Paddy was up to and got a bit of a wake up when it went off. Paddy was a bit naughty like that and throughout the night many more harmless explosions of propelled toilet paper were fired.

Another interesting chap who I hadn't met previously was Mort, a big round-faced man of about 50 with dense, rough whiskers. He was dressed as a deepsea fisherman, and was holding a whole tuna in his arms. Whole tuna are worth thousands of dollars on the Japanese market and his mates were curious as to how he had come by it. Mort worked on the West Coast as a fisherman so in the end they just assumed he had obtained it on one of his fishing trips. Mort refused to disclose any information about the tuna, and nothing could have wiped the grin from his face that night.

By around 9 p.m. a fair crowd had gathered, and there must have been about 150 people present. They were a mixed bag from various locations and all walks of life, including fishermen, carpenters, farmers, a doctor, several school teachers, a male nurse, a drainlayer, labourers, road workers, a judge and some police constables. The judge wasn't a hunter-gatherer type so he had brought several buckets of Kentucky Fried Chicken as his contribution of tucker. When our mate with the swimming pool had said he would 'call the cops' he clearly didn't know there were four already standing poolside with a beer in their hands, watching the antics.

Batsey now rounded up the crowd at the front of the shed and announced that there was to be a duck-plucking competition and that anyone who wanted to enter could. A dozen competitors stepped forward and were soon divided into two teams, one representing the South Island and the other the North. The competitors were each given a duck and the contest was to be run as a relay. Paddy started the event by firing his muzzle loader. Feathers flew as one by one the ducks were denuded and the next person started on theirs. The whole affair was hilarious to watch as the competitors, taking the whole thing far too seriously, spilled feathers everywhere. The air was thick with lightweight down feathers by the time the last feather was finally plucked from the last bird. The North Island team won by a country mile and the nice tidy shed suddenly wasn't.

As soon as that event finished my mate Tom produced a duck-plucking machine that he had invented. It consisted of a series of soft rubber flaps that dangled from a hand-held, petrol-driven motor. As the flaps spun they grabbed the feathers and pulled them free.

'Nothing can pluck a duck faster than my machine,' Tom boasted.

'Bullshit,' came a deep voice from the back. 'I can beat that thing any day.'

It was Stag's mate Brian, who is from Southland. Everyone knows Southland is the original home of duck shooting (well, Southlanders think so anyway) so if anyone was going to beat the machine it was likely to be this hardy campaigner. The challenge was readily accepted, but suddenly Tom didn't seem so sure of himself and changed the rules so that they had to pluck four ducks each. 'One wouldn't be a fair test, would it?' he argued.

To Paddy's joy he got to fire his black powder gun again to set things going. Tom took to his first duck with great enthusiasm and feathers billowed everywhere as his machine ripped them out. Brian's hands were flying and he was making progress at about the same rate. The second ducks got done in record time before both reached for the third. Tom was fractionally ahead at this point and looked like a sure winner. At this point Bert, who was standing behind Tom with a jam jar full of beer, suddenly stumbled and the beer splashed onto Tom's machine. It spluttered and died as the wet spark plugs shorted out. Tom wasn't too amused as Brian pulled the last feathers from his fourth duck and raised his arms in victory. Tom's protestations that it wasn't fair were dismissed by Brian, who commented innocently, 'I don't come to a stop when beer gets spilt on me now, do I?'

I couldn't help but notice that Bert looked pretty pleased with himself so I asked him why he was so happy. He replied simply, 'Can't have a young buck beating a Southlander now, can we?'

It was then that I remembered Bert telling me that he was from down that way. The cunning old sod had deliberately tipped his beer on Tom's machine so the Southlander would win. Bert had really got into the spirit of the night and it looked like the old codger still had a bit of spark left in him yet.

Batsey, meanwhile, was trying to sweep some of the feathers away, but his efforts were wasted as there were so many and they just kept blowing back inside each time he tried to launch them out the door. Realising the futility of his efforts he gave up and decided to put on some entertainment before supper. As he returned from his car with the tape of wild game noises it started to rain lightly and everyone crowded into the shed and under the large tarpaulin that had been erected in front of it. Fortunately the rain wasn't falling hard enough to affect the fire over which the pig was roasting. Ting, not wanting smelly wet dogs inside the shed, returned them to their kennels on the back of his truck. A firm 'Stay' was all that was required to get them to lie down in their boxes and there was no need to chain them up.

The do wasn't intended to be a male-only affair and several keen outdoors-type women had been invited, but they had all failed to turn up. This may well have been a good thing as at the rear of the shed, beyond the food area, there was a wall-mounted TV set where some homemade hunting videos were now being played. I watched several short clips of tahr, deer, goats and some sea fishing and was about to slip away when a segment came on that clearly wasn't homemade.

Bert was standing beside me and when this clip came on his 80-year-old jaw almost fell to the floor and his eyes lit up like Christmas tree lights. Instead of wildlife the screen now showed humans partaking in mating rituals in vivid colour, leaving nothing to the imagination. Old Bert didn't seem to know where to look, or if in fact he should be looking at all. I was more worried that he might have a heart attack, and was wondering how I would explain things to Gracey if he did. After a number of furtive glances to make sure no one was watching him Bert's gaze returned to the screen. It looked to me as if old Bert hadn't seen much action in this regard for many years, and I found the boyish, guilty look on his face as he pretended he wasn't watching to be thoroughly entertaining. After a short interlude the footage returned to hunting scenes, this time showing wild pigs running everywhere with dogs in hot pursuit.

'What do you reckon?' I asked Bert, nodding at the TV set.

'Too much meat and not enough veges,' he replied with a huge grin on his face, at the same time holding out his empty jam jar.

'Thirsty work this. How about getting me another beer?'

Sitting on the floor against a wall were two large stereo speakers, and on a shelf above them was a combination tape player and radio unit. As I filled Bert's jar from the beer keg, Batsey put on his tape. Soon the shed and its environs were filled with the sounds of red deer roaring. Everyone came to a standstill and many hardy campaigners entered into the spirit of things and gave impromptu stag roars of their own. Next came twittering birds, barking dogs, farm tractors, bugling elk, mooing cows and finally the segment of squealing pigs that Batsey had gone to so much trouble to obtain. The stereo was turned up loud and the whole neighbourhood must have felt they were being attacked by wild pigs.

A furious barking erupted from the direction of Ting's truck as four very worked-up pig dogs came charging across the paddock and in through the door to get at the wild pigs that were obviously hiding inside. Major led the charge through the scattering crowd and came to a claw-raking stop when he collided with the wall beside the speakers. Undeterred he shook his head, regained his feet, and with a menacing growl launched a furious attack on one of the speakers. Another mongrel, seeing a stag head hanging on the wall, launched itself at this. Latching on to it, the dog twisted and ripped at its throat until both fell to the floor, whereupon the other two dogs jumped in to assist. Pandemonium reigned as Batsey fought to get to and turn the stereo off, Ting struggled with his dogs and Stag, whose prized trophy was being torn apart on the floor in front of him, kicked and thrashed the dogs as he too tried to get them away.

As the surrounding onlookers recovered from the shock of the event that had unfolded before their eyes they saw the humour of the situation and set about poking fun at the participants. Ting wasn't at all impressed when a voice called from the crowd, 'Don't those dogs of yours know the difference between a deer and a pig, Ting?'

'If you're not careful you might find out if they know the difference between a pig's testicles and a man's,' Ting growled in reply.

Four dogs got a restraining tap or two before being chained to their kennels. One stereo speaker got destroyed, and the stag's head would require substantial patching by a taxidermist. No one was injured and Bert hadn't had a heart attack, so all in all the results were not too disastrous, and the whole event had certainly been very entertaining.

When calm returned we discovered that the rain had increased and the pig-roasting fire had all but gone out. We were all looking forward to a feed of pork so this unsatisfactory situation was fixed when a temporary shelter was erected in a tree well above the fire. Before long the fire had been poked, prodded and stoked back up to a good cooking heat. Looking round to see where Bert had got to I noticed that he had snuck back into the video area and was stationed beside our learned friend the judge.

Around 11 p.m. the meal was served, and a grander affair I have never attended. Everyone was in their hunting clobber, eating from paper plates and drinking beer from jam jars, but the food consisted of some of the best wild game and fish to be found anywhere in the world. Among the food on offer there was paua, muttonbird, crayfish, whitebait, tuna (a whole fish), salmon, duck, Canadian goose, trout, kahawai, wild Pit Island bull, peacock, mussels, tahr, chamois, goat, eel, snapper, venison, blue cod and much more. Unfortunately the pig wasn't cooked enough by the time the meal was served, so we would have to have that later.

After we had all eaten as much as we could the prizegiving session was held. A chef from a fancy hotel in town was the judge of the 'best dish' award, and first prize went to a chap who had travelled to Pitt Island where he had shot a wild bull. His dish was wild bull casserole.

Second prize went to our mate Stag. His entry was a 'peacock stew' that was presented in an old crockery dish that looked like a chicken. The lid should have had a chicken's head on it but Stag had mounted the peacock's head in its place, with a sign hanging around its neck that read 'You Bastard'.

Now the peacock dish deserves further mention as it's a yarn worth telling. Stag had been invited to go rabbit hunting on a farm on Banks Peninsula, near Christchurch. The farmer told him there were goats on the farm as well as wild cats and other vermin that needed getting rid of. 'Fact is, you can shoot anything you find on the property, other than my sheep and my dogs,' the farmer had stated. 'Feel free to shoot anything but them.'

Stag thought the farmer might have been getting a bit carried away when he said this so he double-checked that he had heard him right and was reassured that he had. Armed with his dog to flush out the rabbits and perhaps a quail if he was lucky Stag headed out the home-block gate toward the low, barren hills behind it. He had only just gone through the first gate when a peacock pranced toward him in a challenging kind of way, making its loud peacock cry. Should he shoot it or not? Was he allowed to? Hell, yes. Only minutes earlier he had been given the green light. Without further ado Stag made a clean shot, and subsequently brought the peacock dish to the ball.

The prize for the best hat went to old Bert, who by this time had had a good skinful of beer. He wobbled to the front of the crowd to receive his prize, a T-shirt that had three lines printed on it. They read: 'Hunter', 'Gatherer', 'Bullshit Artist'. Bert was as pleased as Punch, and as he pulled the T-shirt on Paddy fired his black powder rifle in a salute to his victory.

The night had got cold by now and people were starting to drift off home. Those who were staying huddled around the fire and generally yarned away the night. At about 3 a.m. we launched into the pig, which was cooked to perfection. We stood around it slicing off huge hunks with our knives and ate it from our hands – truly marvellous.

Billy, an old mate of Batsey's, was a real hard shot who had spent most of the night showing everyone how quickly he could down a pint of beer. Billy has the remarkable ability to pour beers down his throat without having to swallow, so they disappeared quickly and often. It did occur to me that if he eased back a bit on the speed and allowed the beer to run more slowly across his tastebuds he just might get a bit more enjoyment from the whole process. Billy had arrived in his long-wheelbase Land Rover, and in anticipation of having one or two beers more than the law allowed he had prepared a comfortable bed in the rear of his vehicle in readiness for a comfortable night's sleep.

When Billy decided it was time to retire he opened the door to his accommodation and was extremely annoyed to find two unknown blokes already lying there sound asleep. (Just for the record here, I'd like to add that they were in separate sleeping bags and there was no suggestion of any funny business.) Billy exploded, and turned on some rousing language to encourage them from his bed. This had no effect whatsoever, so Billy was forced to consider other options.

'Get out, ya bastards, or I'll burn you out,' he bellowed. 'You'll not get a second warning.'

This didn't have a noticeable effect either, with one of the vehicle's occupants commenting sleepily, 'There's plenty of room for three – climb in, shut up and go to sleep,' before he rolled over and appeared to go back to sleep.

Billy, by now feeling very aggrieved, flicked his cigarette lighter, removed his synthetic hat from his head, set it alight and promptly threw it inside the Land Rover. Smoke quickly filled the vehicle, and moments later two choking, wheezing men made a hasty exit from their temporary bedroom.

'And don't come back, you bed-stealing bastards,' Billy threw after them as they trudged off through the rain toward the shed. Without waiting for the smoke to clear Billy removed the smouldering hat from the vehicle, climbed in and moments later was sound asleep.

I too headed for my bed and very quickly found that a bloke of 6'4" doesn't fit too well in the back seat of a Mini. Several hours later, after a very uncomfortable and rough night's sleep, I was up and about stoking the fire back into life. A light drizzle was still falling and the day didn't look too bright. Mind you, it was never going to be, given the number of beers I had had the previous night.

After a clean-up Batsey and I wandered over to Bert's to see how he was. Gracey answered the door, and she seemed to glow with a radiance that was definitely missing the last time we had met.

'I don't know what you lot gave Bert to drink last night but he turned up at my daughter's very happy, and I'd have to say feeling a bit mischievous. He hasn't been like that for a long, long time.'

We both grinned and said nothing.

There was a sequel to the Big Game Hunters' and Bullshitters' Ball that happened about eight months later when Batsey asked me if I remembered Mort bringing a whole tuna to the ball. I told him that I did.

It turns out that Mort doesn't fish for tuna and never has. He finally let on that while unloading some fish into the fish chillers at the Greymouth wharf he had seen some tuna stored there. He went into the cabin of his boat and returned wearing a very loose-fitting raincoat, then he told the supervisor of the chiller to turn his back so he wouldn't see something that he didn't need to see. After a lot of shoving, Mort managed to squeeze a whole tuna under his raincoat and struggle away with it. The story goes that the tuna's tail was dragging along the ground between his legs, and that more than once as he made off along the wharf he received knowing glances from other fishermen.

Now I wonder if the judge, policemen, DoC and MAF workers who attended the Bullshitters' Ball would have enjoyed this treat quite so much if they had known that it was an illegally acquired tuna.

Glossary

'arse over kite' – A slang term for an 'unexpected and uncontrollable fall'

bach – A small and often rustic holiday home usually at a beach, lake or river

billy – An empty tin can with a wire handle, in which you can boil water, etc., over a fire

bivvy (bivouac) – A small hut or temporary shelter

bush lawyer – An unforgiving native vine with many small thorns

bushman's breakfast – When a person can't be bothered having breakfast

bush-stalking – To hunt within the bush or forest

camp oven – A cast-iron cooking pot with a lid

chamois – A small antelope, originally from southern Europe

DoC – Department of Conservation

dope – Cannabis

dressing – Preparing an animal carcass for carrying

fallow deer – A small deer that ranges in colour from white to black and every combination in between

glassed – Using binoculars to search large areas for deer, tahr and other animals

GPS – Global positioning system

gut (as in walking 'along the gut') – A steep-sided, often narrow depression in the land that usually runs vertically down the side of a mountain

hind – A female red, sika, samba or rusa deer

MAF – Ministry of Agriculture and Fisheries

matagouri – A hardwood shrub that has innumerable wooden thorns

points – The sum of all the tines (branches) on a deer's antlers; the more points, the more prestige

RHA – Recreational hunting area

roar – The time of year when male red deer and wapiti stags mate – usually April; named because at this time red deer stags give a lion-like roar, while wapiti stags voice a roar similar to a braying donkey

sheila – A woman

sign (as in 'deer sign') – Evidence left by a game animal that indicates it has been there or is living in that general area; includes droppings, urine, scrape marks, hoof prints and partially eaten vegetation

sluice box – A device designed to remove gold from gravel more quickly than by panning

spiker – A young male deer with two short, single-point antlers

tahr – A beardless mountain goat originally from the Himalayan mountains; these animals often live at high altitude on rocky mountain faces and the males' horns are eagerly sought as trophies

take a butcher's – Have a look at

wapiti (called 'elk' in their native country of America) – The largest round-horned animal in the world; very similar in appearance to a red deer, only bigger and bearing larger and different-shaped antler formations

weaselling – Obtaining information or favour by scurrilous means